Half of my Heart

Islamic History and Thought

13

Series Editorial Board

Peter Adamson
Beatrice Gründler
Ahmad Khan
Jack Tannous
Isabel Toral-Niehoff
Manolis Ulbricht

Advisory Editorial Board

Binyamin Abrahamov
Asad Q. Ahmed
Mehmetcan Akpinar
Abdulhadi Alajmi
Mohammad-Ali Amir-Moezzi
Arezou Azad
Massimo Campanini
Godefroid de Callataÿ
Maria Conterno
Farhad Daftary
Wael Hallaq
Konrad Hirschler
James Howard-Johnston
Maher Jarrar
Marcus Milwright
Harry Munt
Gabriel Said Reynolds
Walid A. Saleh
Jens Scheiner
Delfina Serrano
Georges Tamer

Islamic History and Thought provides a platform for scholarly research on any geographic area within the expansive Islamic world, stretching from the Mediterranean to China, and dated to any period from the eve of Islam until the early modern era. This series contains original monographs, translations (Arabic, Persian, Syriac, Greek, and Latin) and edited volumes.

Half of my Heart

The Narratives of Zaynab, Daughter of ʿAlî

Christopher Paul Clohessy

Gorgias Press

2020

Gorgias Press LLC, 954 River Road, Piscataway, NJ, 08854, USA

www.gorgiaspress.com

2020

ISBN 978-1-4632-4236-7 **ISSN 2643-6906**

First paperback edition.
First published in 2018 (Gorgias Press).

Library of Congress Cataloging-in-Publication Data

A Cataloging-in-Publication Record is available from the Library of Congress.

Printed and bound by CPI Group (UK) Ltd, Croydon, CR0 4YY

Dedicated to the memory of
Martin Derek Clohessy
01.05.1955 – 17.02.2018

TABLE OF CONTENTS

Table of Contents v
Acknowledgments vii
Preface ix
System of Transliteration x
Primary Arabic Shî'î and Sunnî Sources xi
List of Abbreviations xix
Introduction 1
Before Karbalâ' 26
In the course of the battle 26
After Karbalâ' 27
Chapter One. In the House of Prophecy 37
Chapter Two. The Pre-Karbalâ' Narratives 103
1. A Night at al-Ḫuzaymiyya 105
2. Rumours of War 109
3. The Dirge 113
Chapter Three. On the Field of Karbalâ' 131
1. The Rising Sun 133
2. A Boy 137
3. A Challenge 143
4. To Kûfa 145
Chapter Four. In the Halls of the Kings 159
1. The First Protest 159
2. 'Ubayd Allâh b. Ziyâd 172
3. Yazîd b. Mu'âwiya 189
4. The Second Protest 208
Three Addenda 221
1. The children of Zaynab 221
2. The children of al-Ḥusayn 230
3. The consolation of Zaynab 239

ACKNOWLEDGMENTS

The seeds of this work were sown in a discussion among a group of Catholic priests, sitting around a table in the Pontifical Institute for Arabic and Islamic Studies in Rome, lamenting the fact that few Islamic scholars are writing anything substantial about the great women of Islam. We challenged each other to choose one character and write about her, and this reading of the life of Zaynab, daughter of ʿAlî and Fâṭima, is the result. While I await the books from my confereres, I thank them for the pleasure of living and working with them, forming a new generation in a solid, academic understanding of Islam and promoting an authentic and ongoing dialogue between religions. I am ever indebted to my family and to my fellow clergy in Cape Town, who bear so patiently with my long absences and my enthusiasm for all things Shîʿî. I am no less grateful to numerous, cherished Shîʿî friends, in Italy, England, South Africa and America, who have unreservedly supported this work: in a special way, Dr Mohammad Ali Shomali, whose unbounded enthusiasm for interreligious harmony gladdens the heart, and whose generosity gave me access to the most crucial Shîʿî sources; and Zameer Hussein, who daily teaches his London pupils to live respectfully and reverently before the religious experience of others, and all the while kept a critical eye on my theology. To these, and so many others, my thanks for making this work possible.

PREFACE

As Abû ʿAbd Allâh al-Ḥusayn, son of ʿAlî and Fâṭima and grandson of Muḥammad, moved inexorably towards death on the field of Karbalâʾ, his sister Zaynab was drawn ever closer to the centre of the family of Muḥammad, the 'people of the house' (*ahl al-bayt*). There she would remain for a few historic days, challenging the wickedness of the Islamic leadership, defending the actions of her brother, initiating the commemorative rituals, protecting and nurturing the new Imâm, al-Ḥusayn's son ʿAlî b. al-Ḥusayn b. Abî Ṭâlib, until he could take his rightful place. This is her story.

Unless otherwise stated, all quotations from the Qurʾân are taken from the English interpretation of Muhammad Marmaduke Pickthall.[1] At times, I have compared his translation with that of other English interpreters of the Qurʾân, and these will be named in the text when they occur.

The system of transliteration, given below, has been followed throughout the text, except in instances in which other authors have been quoted, in which case the said author's system of transliteration has been respected.

Unless otherwise stated, all translations of the Arabic texts are my own. All Arabic texts have been reproduced exactly from their sources, even when mistakes are extant in the said texts.

Except when quoting from other works, all dates are given according to the Islamic calendar (*hiǧra*), followed by a backslash and the Gregorian equivalent.

---

[1] PICKTHALL M.M., *The Meaning of the Glorious Qurʾān*, Dar al-Kitab Allubnani, Beirut and Dar al-Kitab al-Masri, Cairo (n.d.).

SYSTEM OF TRANSLITERATION

ء	-	’	ض	-	ḍ
ب	-	b	ط	-	ṭ
ت	-	t	ظ	-	ẓ
ث	-	ṯ	ع	-	‘
ج	-	ğ	غ	-	ġ
ح	-	ḥ	ف	-	f
خ	-	ḫ	ق	-	q
د	-	d	ك	-	k
ذ	-	ḏ	ل	-	l
ر	-	r	م	-	m
ز	-	z	ن	-	n
س	-	s	ه	-	h
ش	-	sh	و	-	w
ص	-	ṣ	ي	-	y

Short Vowels

أ	-	a, u
إ	-	i

Long Vowels

آ	-	â
و	-	û
ي	-	î

PRIMARY ARABIC SHÎʿÎ AND SUNNÎ SOURCES

3rd/9th century

Sunnî

Abû Muḥammad ʿAbd al-Mâlik Hishâm b. Ayyûb al-Ḥimyarî Ǧamâl al-Dîn (d. 218/834: cf. GAS I: 297) in his *Sîrat Muḥammad Rasûl Allâh* (2 vols., Maṭbaʿat Muṣṭafâ al-Bâbî al-Ḥalabî, Cairo 1955).

Muḥammad b. Saʿd Kâtib al-Wâqidî (d. 230/845: cf. GAL I: 136, GAL S. I: 208) in his *Kitâb al-ṭabaqât al-kabîr* (11 vols., Maktab al-Ḫanǧî, Cairo 2001).

Abû ʿAbd Allâh Aḥmad b. Muḥammad b. Ḥanbal al-Shaybânî al-Ḏuhlî (d. 241/855: cf. GAL S. I: 309) in his *Musnad* (12 vols., Dâr al-fikr, Cairo 1995).

Abû ʿAbd Allâh Muḥammad b. Ismâʿîl b. Ibrâhîm b. Muġîra b. Bardizbah al-Buḫârî al-Ǧuʿfî (d. 256/870: cf. GAL S. I: 260) in his *Ṣaḥîḥ* (9 vols., al-Maktaba al-salafiyya, Medina) and his *al-Adab al-mufrad* (Maktaba dâr al-salâm, Riyadh 1997).

Abû al-Ḥusayn Muslim b. al-Ḥaǧǧâǧ al-Qushayrî al-Nîsâbûrî (d. 261/875: cf. GAL S. 1: 265) in his *Ṣaḥîḥ* (5 vols., Maktaba dâr al-salâm, Riyadh 2007).

Abû ʿAbd Allâh Muḥammad b. Yazîd b. Mâǧa al-Qazwînî (d. 273/886: cf. GAL S. I: 270) in his *Sunan* (2 vols., Dâr iḥyâʾ al-kutub al-ʿarabiyya, Cairo 1952).

Abû Dâwûd Sulaymân b. al-Ashʿaṯ al-Azdî al-Siǧistânî (d. 275/889: cf. GAL S. I: 270) in his *Sunan* (5 vols., Maktaba dâr al-salâm, Riyadh 2008).

Abû ʿÎsâ Muḥammad b. ʿÎsâ b. Sahl al-Tirmiḏî (d. 279/892: cf. GAL S. I: 267) in his *Sunan* (6 vols., Maktaba dâr al-salâm, Riyadh 2007).

Abû al-ʿAbbâs Aḥmad b. Yaḥyâ b. Ǧâbir al-Balâḏurî (d. 279/892: cf. GAL S. I: 216, GAS I: 320) in his *Kitâb ansâb al-ashraf* (vol. I, Dâr al-maʿârif, Egypt 1959, vol. IVa, University Press, Jerusalem 1971, vol. V, Magnes Press, Jerusalem 1936).

Abû Ḥanîfa Aḥmad b. Dâwûd al-Dînawarî (d. 282/895: cf. GAL S. I: 187) in his *Kitâb al-aḫbâr al-ṭiwâl* (E.J. Brill, Leiden 1888).

Shîʿî

Abû Ğaʿfar Muḥammad b. Ğarîr b. Rustam al-Ṭabarî (c. 224/839: cf. GAL S. I: 217 and GAS I: 540) in his *Dalâʾil al-imâma* (CRCIS, Qum 2012), and his *Kitâb al-mustarshid fî imâmat ʿAlî b. Abî Tâlib*, (CRCIS, Qum 2012).

Abû al-Faḍl Aḥmad b. Abî Ṭâhir Ṭayfûr (d. 280/893: cf. GAL S. I: 210) in his *Balâġât al-nisâʾ* (CRCIS, Qum 2012)

Aḥmad b. Abî Yaʿqûb b. Ğaʿfar b. Wahb b. Wâḍih al-Kâtib al-ʿAbbâsî al-Yaʿqûbî (d. 284/897 or 292/905: cf. GAL S. I: 405) in his *Târîḫ* (2 vols., E.J. Brill, Leiden 1969).

4th/10th century

Sunnî

Abû ʿAbd al-Raḥmân Aḥmad b. ʿAbd al-Raḥmân b. Shuʿayb al-Nasâʾî (d. 303/915: cf. GAL S. I: 269) in his *Kitâb al-ḫaṣâʾiṣ fî faḍl ʿAlî b. Abî Ṭâlib* (Maktab al-âdâb, Cairo 1986).

Abû Ğaʿfar Muḥammad b. Ğarîr b. Yazîd al-Ṭabarî (d. 310/923: cf. GAS 1: 232 and GAL S. I: 217) in his *Kitâb aḫbâr al-rusul wa-l-mulûk* (39 vols., in English translation, State University of New York Press, New York 1989).

Shîʿî

Muḥammad Yaʿqûb b. Isḥâq al-Kulaynî al-Râzî (d. 328/939: cf. GAL S. I: 320) in his *al-Kâfî fî ʿilm al-dîn* (8 vols., Dâr al-kutub al-islâmiyya, Tehran 1968).

Abû al-Ḥasan ʿAlî b. al-Ḥusayn b. ʿAlî al-Masʿûdî (d. 345/956: cf. GAS I: 333) in his *Murûğ al-ḏahab* (4 vols., Publications de l'Université Libanaise, Beirut 1965).

Abû al-Farağ ʿAlî b. al-Ḥusayn b. Muḥammad b. Aḥmad b. al-Qurashî al-Iṣfahânî (d. 356/967: cf. GAL S.I: 225 and GAS I: 378)[1]

[1] Modarressi notes that he was a Zaydî (cf. MODARRESSI H., *Tradition and Survival. A Bibliographical Survey of Early Shîʿite Literature*, vol. 1, Oneworld, Oxford 2003: 276).

in his *Maqâtil al-ṭâlibîyyîn*, (Maṭbaʿ dâr iḥyâr al-kutub al-ʿarabiyya, Cairo 1949).

Abû al-Qâsim Ǧaʿfar b. Muḥammad b. Ǧaʿfar b. Mûsâ b. Qûlûya al-Qummî (d. 369/979: cf. GAL S. I: 953) in his *Kâmil al-ziyârât* (Muʾassasat al-nashr al-islâmî, Qum n.d.).

ʿAlî b. Muḥammad b. ʿAlî al-Ḫazzâz al-Râzî al-Qummî (d. 381/991: cf. GAL S. I: 322 and GAS I: 543) in *Kifâyat al-aṯar fî-l-nuṣûs ʿalâ al-aʾimma al-iṯnâ ʿasharî* (CRCIS, Qum 2012).

Abû Ǧaʿfar Muḥammad b. ʿAlî b. al-Ḥusayn b. Mûsâ b. Bâbûya al-Qummî al-Ṣadûq (d. 381/991: cf. GAL S. I: 321 and GAS I: 544) in his *Kitâb al-amâlî fî-l-aḥâdîṯ wa-l-aḫbâr* (CRCIS, Qum 2012).

Abû ʿAbd Allâh al-Ḥusayn b. ʿAlî b. al-Ḥusayn b. Ḥamdân al-Ḫaṣîbî Zayn al-Dîn (d. 346/957 or 365/968: cf. GAS I. 584) in his *al-Hidâya (al-Kubrâ)*, (CRCIS, Qum 2012).

5th/11th century

Sunnî

Muḥammad b. ʿAbd Allâh b. Muḥammad al-Ḥâkim al-Nîsâbûrî b. al-Bayyiʿ (d. 404/1014: cf. GAL S. I: 276)[2] in his *Kitâb (Talḫîs) al-mustadrak ʿalâ al-ṣaḥîḥayn* (5 vols., Dâr al-ḥarmîn, Cairo 1997).

Abû Isḥâq Aḥmad b. Muḥammad b. Ibrâhîm al-Ṯaʿlabî al-Nîsâbûrî al-Shâfiʿî (d. 427/1035: cf. GAL S. I: 592) in his *Kitâb ʿarâʾis al-maǧâlis fî qiṣaṣ al-anbiyâʾ* (al-Maṭbaʿa al-ʿâmira al-sharafiyya, Cairo 1954).

Abû Nuʿaym Aḥmad b. ʿAbd Allâh b. Aḥmad b. Isḥâq al-Iṣbahânî (or al-Iṣfahânî) al-Shâfiʿî (d. 430/1038: cf. GAL S. I: 616) in his *Ḥilyat al-awliyâʾ wa-ṭabaqât al-aṣfiyâʾ* (11 vols., Dâr al-kutub al-ʿilmiyya, Beirut 1967).

Abû Bakr Aḥmad b. ʿAlî b. Ṯâbit al-Ḫaṭîb al-Baġdâdî (d. 463/1071: cf. GAL I: 329) in his *Târîḫ Baġdâd* (14 vols., Dâr al-kitâb al-ʿarabî, Beirut n.d.).

---

[2] Brockelmann incorrectly reports his death at 404/914 and names him al-Nîsâbûrî as opposed to al-Naysâbûrî, found in other texts.

Abû ʿUmar Yûsuf b. ʿAbd Allâh b. Muḥammad b. ʿAbd al-Barr al-Namarî al-Qurṭubî (d. 463/1071: cf. GAL S. I: 628) in his *al-Istîʿâb fî maʿrifat al-aṣḥâb* (4 vols., Maṭbaʿat Nahḍat Miṣr, Cairo n.d.).

Shîʿî

Muḥammad b. Muḥammad b. Nuʿmân al-Baġdâdî al-Karḫî al-Mufîd (d. 413/1022. cf. GAL I: 188 and GAL S. I: 322) in his *al-Irshâd fî maʿrifat ḥuğağ Allâh ʿalâ al-ʿibâd* (CRCIS, Qum 2012) and in his *al-Amâlî li-l-Mufîd* (CRCIS, Qum 2012).

Abû Ğaʿfar Muḥammad b. al-Ḥasan b. ʿAlî al-Ṭûsî *Shayḫ* al-Ṭâʾifa (d. 458/1066: cf. GAL I: 405 and GAL S. I: 706) in his *al-Amâlî fî-l-ḥadîṯ*, (CRCIS, Qum 2012).

ʿAlî Muḥammad b. Aḥmad b. ʿAlî al-Fattâl al-Nîsâbûrî al-Farisî (c. mid-5th/11th century: cf. GAL S. I: 708) in his *Rawḍat al-wâʿiẓîn wa-tabṣirat al-muttaʿiẓîn* (CRCIS, Qum 2012).

6th/12th century

Sunnî

Abû al-Muʾayyad Muwaffaq Aḥmad b. Abî Saʿîd Isḥâq al-Ḫawârizmî (d. 568/1172. cf. GAL S. I: 623) in his *Maqtal al-Ḥusayn* (Dâr anwâr al-hudâ, Qum n.d.).

Abû al-Qâsim ʿAlî b. al-Ḥasan b. Hibat Allâh Ṯiqat al-Dîn b. ʿAsâkir al-Shâfiʿî (d. 571/1176: cf. GAL S. I: 566) in his *Târîḫ madînat Dimashq* (80 vols., Dâr al-fikr, Beirut 1995).

Shîʿî

Raḍî al-Dîn Abû ʿAlî al-Faḍl b. al-Ḥasan Amîn al-Dîn al-Ṭabarsî (d. 548/1153: cf. GAL S. I: 708) in his *Kitâb al-iḥtiğâğ ʿalâ ahl al-liğâğ* (CRCIS, Qum 2012), in his *Tâğ al-mawâlîd* (CRCIS, Qum 2012) and in his *Iʿlâm al-warâ bi-aʿlâm al-hudâ* (CRCIS, Qum 2012).

Quṭb al-Dîn Abû al-Ḥusayn Saʿîd b. Hibat Allâh b. Abî al-Ḥasan al-Râwandî (d. 573/1177: cf. GAL S. I: 624) in his *al-Ḫarâʾiğ wa-l-ğarâʾiḥ fî-l-muʿğizât* (CRCIS, Qum 2012).

Abû Ğaʿfar Muḥammad b. ʿAlî b. Shahrâshûb al-Mâzandarânî al-Surrî Rashîd al-Dîn (d. 588/1192: cf. GAL S. I: 710) in his *Manâqib âl Abî Ṭâlib* (5 vols., Manshûrât ḏawî al-qurbâ, Tehran 2012, CRCIS, Qum 2012).

7th/13th century

Sunnî

Abû al-Faḍâ'il Ǧamâl al-Dîn Abû al-Farağ ʿAbd al-Raḥmân b. al-Ḥasan ʿAlî b. Muḥammad b. ʿUmar b. al-Ǧawzî (d. 597/1200: cf. GAL S. I: 914, GAL I: 500) in his *Ṣifat al-ṣafwa* (Dai'ratu'l-ma'rif'il-Osmania, Hyderabad 1968).

Abû al-Ḥasan ʿAlî b. Abî al-Karam Aṯîr al-Dîn Muḥammad b. Muḥammad b. ʿAbd al-Karîm ʿIzz al-Dîn Muḥammad b. al-Aṯîr al-Shaybânî (d. 630/1233: cf. GAL I: 345) in his *al-Kâmil fî-l-târîḫ* (9 vols., al-Ṭabâʿa al-munîriyya, Cairo 1934) and in his *Usd al-ġâba fî maʿrifat al-ṣaḥâba* (5 vols., al-Maṭbaʿat al-islâmiyya, Tehran n.d.).

Shams al-Dîn Aḥmad al-Muẓaffar Yûsuf b. Qizoğlû b. ʿAlî Sibṭ al-Ǧawzî (d. 654/1257: cf. GAL S. I: 589) in his *Taḏkirat al-ḫawâṣṣ al-umma bi-ḏikr ḫaṣâ'iṣ al-a'imma*, (Amir, Qum 1998)

Muḥib al-Dîn Abû al-ʿAbbâs (Abû Muḥammad Abû Ǧaʿfar) Aḥmad b. ʿAbd al-Raḥmân al-Ṭabarî al-Makkî al-Shâfiʿî (d. 684/1295: cf. GAL 1: 361) in his *Ḏaḫâ'ir al-ʿuqbâ* (Dâr al-maʿrifa, Beirut 1974).

Shîʿî

ʿIzz al-Dîn ʿAbd al-Ḥamîd b. Hibat Allâh al-Madâ'inî b. al-Ḥadîd (d. 655/1257: cf. GAL S. I: 497) in his *Sharḥ nahğ al-balâġa* (20 vols., Dâr iḥyâ' al-kutub al-ʿarabiyya, Cairo 1959–1964).[3]

---

[3] While some hold him to have been a Shîʿa, it is not utterly certain that Ibn al-Ḥadîd was. Modarressi mentions him tentatively in a passage concentrating on his brother, noting in passing that he transmitted from his uncle Abû Muḥammad Murâzim b. Ḥakîm al-Madâ'inî, who in turn transmitted from the fifth and sixth Imâms, but does not name the nephew's work (MODARRESSI H., *Tradition and Survival. A Bibliographical Survey of Early Shî'ite Literature*, vol. 1, 2003: 308, 319, 353). Brockelmann is no less imprecise. Others believe that Ibn al-Ḥadîd was a Muʿtazila. Notwithstanding the dearth of evidence, I have chosen to retain him among the Shîʿa, even though on a number of occasions, he carries *aḥâdîṯ* that are out of line with the Shîʿî stance.

Raḍî al-Dîn Abû Mûsâ Abû al-ʿAbbâs ʿAlî b. Mûsâ b. Ǧaʿfar b. Muḥammad b. Muḥammad b. Ṭâʾûs al-Ṭâʾûsî al-ʿAlawî al-Fâṭimî (d. 664/1266: cf. GAL S. I: 911) in his *Kitâb al-iqbâl bi-l-aʿmâl al-ḥasana* (CRCIS, Qum 2012) and in his *Kitâb al-luhûf fî qutlâ al-ṭufûf* (Dâr anwâr al-hudâ, Qum 2002).

Naǧm al-Dîn Ǧaʿfar b. Muḥammad b. Ǧaʿfar b. Hibat Allâh b. Namâ al-Ḥillî (d. 680/1281) in his *Muṯîr al-aḥzân wa munîr subul al-ashǧân* (CRCIS, Qum 2012).

Bahâʾ al-Dîn Abû al-Ḥasan ʿAlî b. ʿÎsâ al-Irbilî b. al-Faḫr (692/1293: cf. GAL S. I: 713) in his *Kashf al-ġumma fî maʿrifat al-aʾimma* (CRCIS, Qum 2012).

8th/14th century

Sunnî

Abû ʿAbd Allâh Muḥammad b. Aḥmad b. ʿUṯmân b. Qaymâz Shams al-Dîn al-Ḏahabî (d. 748/1348: cf. GAL S. II: 45) in his *Siyar aʿlâm al-nubalâʾ*,[4] (Muʾassat al-risâla, Beirut 1996).

Abû al-Fidâʾ Ismâʿîl b. ʿUmar b. Kaṯîr ʿImâd al-Dîn b. al-Ḫaṭîb al-Qurayshî al-Buṣrawî al-Shâfiʿî (d. 774/1373: cf. GAL S. II: 48) in his *al-Bidâya wa-l-nihâya* (14 vols., Cairo 1930).

Shîʿî

Ǧamâl al-Dîn Ḥasan b. Yûsuf b. ʿAlî b. Muṭahhar al-Ḥillî al-ʿAllâma (d. 726/1325: cf. GAL S. II: 206) in his *Kashf al-yaqîn fî faḍâʾil amîr al-muʾminîn* (CRCIS, Qum 2012).

9th/15th century

Sunnî

Nûr al-Dîn Abû al-Ḥasan ʿAlî b. Abî Bakr b. Sulaymân b. Ḥaǧar al-Hayṯamî (d. 807/1405: cf. GAL II: 91, GAL S. II: 82) in his *Maǧmaʿ al-zawâʾid wa-manbaʿ al-fawâʾid* (10 vols., Maktab al-qudsî, Cairo n.d.).

---

[4] Brockelmann does not record this work.

Abû al-Faḍl Aḥmad b. ʿAlî b. Muḥammad b. Ḥağar Shihâb al-Dîn al-ʿAsqalânî al-Kinânî al-Shâfiʿî (d. 852/1449: cf. GAL S. II: 72) in his *al-Iṣâba fî tamyîz al-ṣaḥâba* (4 vols., al-Maktaba al-ğâriyya al-kubrâ, Egypt 1939) and in his *Tahḏîb al-tahḏîb* (12 vols., Dâr Ṣâdir, Beirut 1968).

Shîʿî

Zayn al-ʿÂbidîn ʿAlî b. Yûnus al-Bayyâḍî al-Nabâṭî al-ʿÂmilî (d. 877/1472: cf. GAL S. II: 133) in his *al-Ṣirâṭ al-mustaqîm ilâ mustaḥaqq al-taqdîm fî al-imâma* (CRCIS, Qum 2012).

Ḥasan b. Abî al-Ḥasan al-Daylamî (d. 840/1437: cf. GAL S. I: 261, although Brockelmann provides no dates) in his *Irshâd al-qulûb* (CRCIS, Qum 2012).

11th/17th century

Sunnî

ʿAbd al-Malik b. al-Ḥusayn b. ʿAbd al-Malik al-ʿIṣâmî (d. 1111/1699: cf. GAL S. II: 516) in his *Simṭ al-nuğûm al-ʿawâlî* (4 vols., al-Maṭbaʿa al-salafiyya, Cairo 1961).

Shîʿî

Muḥammad b. al-Ḥasan al-Ḥasanî b. ʿAlî b. Ḥusayn al-Ḥurr al-ʿÂmilî al-Mashġarî (d. 1099/1688: cf. GAL S. II: 578) in his *Tafṣîl wasâʾil al-shîʿa ilâ taḥṣîl masâʾil al-sharîʿa* (CRCIS, Qum 2012), in his *al-Ğawâhir al-saniyya al-aḥâdîṯ al-qudsiyya* (CRCIS, Qum 2012) and in *Iṯbât al-hudât bi-l-nuṣûṣ wa-l-muʿğizât*, (CRCIS, Qum 2012).

Hâshim b. Sulaymân b. Ismâʿîl b. ʿAbd al-Ğawâd b. ʿAbd al-Raḥmân al-Ḥusaynî al-Baḥrânî (d. 1107/1695: cf. GAL S. II: 506) in his *al-Burhân fî tafsîr al-qurʾân* (4 vols., Muʾassasat al-wafâʾ, Beirut 1983).

12th/18th century

Sunnî

ʿAbd al-ʿIrfân Muḥammad b. ʿAlî al-Ṣabbân (d. 1206/1792: cf. GAL S. II: 399) in his *Isʿâf al-râġibîn* in the margins of *Nûr al-abṣâr fî manâqib âl bayt al-nabî al-muḫtâr* (al-Maṭbaʿa al-ʿâmira al-sharafiyya, Cairo 1898).

Shîʿa

ʿAbd Allâh b. Nûr Allâh al-Baḥrânî al-Iṣfahânî (d. 1110/1698: cf. GAL S. II: 504) in his *ʿAwâlim al-ʿulûm wa-l-maʿârif al-aḥwâl min al-âyât wa-l-aḫbâr wal-aqwâl* (CRCIS, Qum 2012).

Muḥammad Bâqir b. Muḥammad Taqî b. Maqṣûd ʿAlî Akmal al-Mağlisî al-Iṣfahânî (d. 1110/1700: cf. GAL S. II: 572) in his *Biḥâr al-anwâr* (110 vols., Dâr al-kutub al-islâmiyya, Tehran 1924–1935).

13th/19th century

Sunnî

Muʾmin b. Ḥasan Muʾmin al-Shablanğî (d. c. 1301/1883: cf. GAL S. II: 737) in his *Nûr al-abṣâr fî manâqib âl bayt al-nabî al-muḫtâr* (al-Maṭbaʿa al-ʿâmira al-sharafiyya, Cairo 1898).

14th/20th century

Shîʿî

al-Ḥâğğ Mîrzâ Ḥusayn b. Muḥammad Taqî al-Nûrî al-Ṭabarsî (d. 1320/1902: cf. GAL S. II: 832) in his *Ḫâtimat mustadrak al-wasâʾil* (CRCIS, Qum 2012).

Muḥsin b. ʿAbd al-Karîm al-Amîn al-ʿÂmilî (d. 1371/1952: cf. GAL S. II: 808) in his *Aʿyân al-Shîʿa*, (CRCIS, Qum 2012)

LIST OF ABBREVIATIONS

A.D.	*Anno Domini*
b.	*bin* (son)
bb.	*bâb* (chapter)
B.C.	before Christ
bt.	*bint* (daughter)
c.	*circa*
CE.	common era
cf.	confer
ch.	chapter
CRCIS	Computer Research Centre of Islamic Sciences
d.	died
ed.	editor
edn.	edition
edns.	editions
eds.	editors
eg.	for example
EI^2	Encyclopaedia of Islam, 2nd Edition
et al.	and others
etc.	*etcetera*
ff.	following
GAL	*Geschichte der arabischen Literatur*
GAS	*Geschichte der arabischen Schrifttums*
ibid.	*ibidem*
lit.	literally
MOD.	Tradition and Survival. A Bibliographical Survey of Early Shīʾite Literature
n.	number
NCE^2	New Catholic Encyclopaedia, 2nd Edition
n.d.	no date
nn.	numbers
n.n.	no number

n.p.	no publisher
nt.	footnote
op.cit.	work cited
pl.	plural
Q.	Qur'ân
SEI	The Shorter Encyclopaedia of Islam
sic	thus
trans.	translator
v.	verse
vol.	volume
vols.	volumes
vv.	verses

Introduction

> And so we must begin to live again,
> We of the damaged bodies and assaulted minds
> Starting from scratch, with the rubble of our lives
> and picking up the dust
> of dreams once dreamt[1]

The Karbalâʾ event, as evocative and emblematic now as it ever was, has left an ineffaceable mark on the Islamic world; on the way that world prays, the way it narrates its past, the way it does its politics, deeply enmeshed even within the waxing and waning of the various reform movements to which, intermittently, it gives birth. As an historical event, Karbalâʾ is perpetually engraved upon the memories of those who are devoted to al-Ḥusayn; for devout Shîʿî Muslims, and in particular the *iṯnâ ʿasharî* or 'Twelver' Shîʿa,[2] it is the bedrock of their worship and their sorrow, an inextinguishable echo that resonates through their history, their theology and their religious identity as the very blood that through their veins. For the the *iṯnâ ʿasharî* Shîʿa, Karbalâʾ is a central moment in their foundational story and the catalyst of all their subsequent history. Even if al-Ḥusayn is not the most important figure in the Shîʿî faith, it is patently clear that the memorialization of his life and death, conveyed by so many diverse rituals, is deeply enfolded into the spirit of the community, revitalising and impelling it, urging it to fashion

---

[1] From the poem 'Pockets Shaken' by Anna Mckenzie in CASSIDY S., *Good Friday People*, Orbis Books, Maryknoll NY 1991.

[2] As distinct from the Zaydî (sometimes referred to as 'Fiver') and Ismâʿîlî (sometimes referred to as 'Sevener'), the *iṯnâ ʿasharî* or 'Twelver' are those Shîʿa who follow the twelve Imâms.

a world devoid of all that Yazîd[3] and the model of Islamic leadership he represents. Karbalâʾ becomes the prototype around which faithful devotees are invited to shape lives for themselves, the whetstone against which they could test the mettle of everything – thoughts, philosophies, belief systems, morals and ethics and basic common sense. Al-Ḥusayn's martyrdom begins to form them into a new kind of people, and that new identity is solidified by every remembrance of Karbalâʾ.

Al-Ḥusayn dies on the field of battle and the day of Karbalâʾ passes into Islamic history forever, because Karbalâʾ has barely ever been understood as a once and for all event, but on the contrary, as an occurrence that people inhabit and constantly renew; in this way, the killing of the third Imâm endures as an extant and immediate calamity for Shîʿî Islam. As one author notes, the martyrdom of al-Ḥusayn, who on the Karbalâʾ field stands before God on humanity's behalf, has become the prototype of every struggle for justice, of every strain of suffering. This is where the Shîʿî heart lies; in that agony which is at one and the same time a devastating loss and a sign of hope.[4] To be a Shîʿî Muslim is to be found standing wherever al-Ḥusayn stood; building justice with him, waging peace with him.

The Karbalâʾ incident is conceptualized in numerous ways by Shîʿî devotees; for some, it roughs out a space in which believers can live prolific, constructive, meaningful lives before God and with each other. For others, God has, in a sense, written Karbalâʾ onto the hearts of the faithful, written it into their lives, into their consciousness, has used Karbalâʾ as the pen by which He has inscribed into humanity the capacity for justice and courage. Seen through the through the prism of Karbalâʾ, it becomes possible for people to step back and assess their lives, even in the worst moments, not as futile and desultory, but as decisive and potentially fruitful. What is ostensibly a resounding defeat possesses numerous glimpses of a final victory, so that to treat Karbalâʾ as no different from any other battle people learn about in their schoolbooks

---

[3] Yazîd b. Muʿâwiya (d. 63/683), the second caliph of the Umayyad dynasty and a chief antagonist in the Zaynab story.

[4] NEVILL A., (trans.), *Shiʾite Islam*, Blackwell, Oxford 1995: 29.

would be to ignore the way it has stitched itself through the fabric of Shî'î life and devotion, and to discount the quality of life that it has birthed in a faith community over fourteen hundred years. Karbalâ' pulls and shapes Shî'î believers as the moon pulls and shapes the tides.

Shî'î faith is a lived conviction, so that the faith of the Shî'î Muslim ought to pulse with change and growth and movement as those devoted to al-Ḥusayn constantly rethink loyalty, rethink justice, rethink hope, rethink what life ought to look like on this side of Karbalâ'. For some Shî'î Muslims, the Imâm's death beckons them into the endless process of working out how to live as they were created to live. They envisage Karbalâ' as the place where injustice and iniquity come undone, as it invites believers to live more intensely, more deeply engaged with justice, to stand before any example of inequality or iniquity with a sadness that runs deep and goads them into action. Karbalâ' becomes for them an orientation, a way of walking through life, not merely an affair of history, but a constant bending, a curving toward righteousness and integrity and justice. Karbalâ' veers toward hope, interrupting the ordinary and counselling Shî'î Muslims to cast a glance backwards in order to move forwards.

Karbalâ' and its remembrance are, in truth, an atonement. The verb 'atone' originally meant 'to reconcile' or 'to make at one'. From this, it came to signify the action by which such reconciliation was realised; for example, some form of satisfaction made for an offense or an injury, the action of making amends for something wrong. The word was borrowed by Christian scholars to articulate the theology of reparation or expiation for sin; specifically, in Christian thinking, it became synonymous with the reconciliation of God and humankind through Jesus Christ. To call Karbalâ' and the actions by which it is remembered 'atonement' is to remove from the word its Christian accretions and return it to a more elemental sense. As such, those who grieve over Karbalâ' are 'at one' with al-Ḥusayn and attempt, by their mourning and ritual action, to make amends for his murder and for an Islam distorted by everything epitomized by the caliph Yazîd.

Karbalâ' and its remembrance are an ongoing reproach to all who, like Yazîd, have convinced themselves that without military force and coercion, without wealth and weaponry, a better world can never be shaped, a different ending to the story never forged.

Ultimately, it is not within the Yazîd paradigm that real power lies, but within the ideal offered by al-Ḥusayn. Karbalâʾ is the point where Yazîd and all he represents comes unstuck, as his version of life and history is confronted by the version lived by Muḥammad's grandson, the point where his own past – years of disobedience, years of dodging God, years of short cuts and fudging the moral and social demands of the Qurʾân – catches up with him, his life and his juvenile theology interrupted by the God whom Islam calls *al-Ḫâfiḍ* ('the Abaser') and *al-Muntaqim* ('the Avenger').

Karbalâʾ is full of voices. The only voices worth listening to are those of people who comprehend what it means to be crushed, those who have been through adversity, have endured agony, who understand what destitution and privation are, but who have found a way to draw on a certain inner strength and live through these things. They have an acumen, an estimation of life that fills them with compassion and tenderness. Voices like that are alluring and forceful. They do not arise by chance. One of those voices is Zaynab's, whose story begins as her brother al-Ḥusayn dies.

There are numerous female characters in the Karbalâʾ accounts and memorials; among those who appear most frequently are al-Ḥusayn's immediate relatives, including his mother Fâṭima and his grandmother Ḫadîǧa, both present in spirit rather than in person, since Fâṭima had died in 11/632 and Ḫadîǧa thirteen years before that. There are recurrent mentions too of his sisters Zaynab and Umm Kulṯûm,[5] Layla bt. Abî Murra (one of his wives) and his daughters Umm Kulṯûm, Sukayna, Fâṭima and Ruqayya.[6] A few women, some of them very young, actively fought at Karbalâʾ and died there, although women attempting to take the field were mostly forbidden to do so by al-Ḥusayn himself; physical fighting was envisaged as a male activity, while the women were expected to lend moral and logistical support from the sidelines. Islam generally holds it unlawful for women to fight in battle, except under excep-

[5] Held by some, as will be noted later in this work, to be one and the same person, but who are almost certainly two distinct sisters.

[6] Their names and number are, as we shall see, strongly disputed.

tional circumstances.[7] This in itself serves to highlight the nature of the struggle in which Zaynab would later engage.

---

[7] In principle, *ǧihâd* in the sense of military conflict is not obligatory for women except in the cases of necessity, a principle that would later come to be defined by Islamic Law. So, for example, Ibn Ḥanbal records Muḥammad as saying that *ǧihâd* for the women consists in *ḥaǧǧ* rather than fighting (Ibn Ḥanbal., *Musnad*, vol. XI, *Musnad ʿÂʾisha*, n. 25400: 223), while in *al-Muġnî* the Ḥanbalî Ibn Qudâma names being male as one of the conditions that make it obligatory, with reference to a *ḥadîṯ* from ʿÂʾisha carried by Ibn Ḥanbal and Ibn Mâǧa: "It was narrated that ʿÂʾisha said: Messenger of God, is *ǧihâd* obligatory for women? He replied: Yes, upon them is a *ǧihâd* in which there is no fighting: *al-ḥaǧǧ* and *al-ʿumra* (Ibn Mâǧa, *Sunan*, vol. IV, bk. 25 (*Kitâb al-ǧihâd*), n. 2901: 126). The possible role of women in battle is recorded in another transmission from Ibn Mâǧa: "It was narrated that Umm ʿAṭiyya al-Anṣâriyya said: I fought alongside the Messenger of God in seven campaigns, looking after their goods, making food for them, tending the wounded and looking after the sick (Ibn Mâǧa, *Sunan*, vol. IV, bk. 25 (*Kitâb al-ǧihâd*), n. 2856: 97–98). In al-Buḫârî, al-Rubayyiʿ bt. Muʿawwiḏ narrates a similar *ḥadîṯ* of women assisting practically on the battlefield (al-Buḫârî, *Ṣaḥîḥ*, vol. IV, bk. 56 (*Kitâb al-ǧihâd*), bb. 67, n. 2882: 92). The Ḥanafî Muḥammad al-Saraḫsî (d. 483/1101) reiterates these points, listing the reasons why women ought not to fight (such as physical weakness, or mockery by the enemy), but concludes that it would be obligatory upon them in case of extreme necessity (al-Saraḫsî., *Sharḥ kitâb al-siyâr al-kabîr li-Muḥammad b. al-Ḥasan al-Shaybânî*, vol. I, bb. 35: 129–30). Certainly, al-Ḥusayn makes sure that the women and children on the field of Karbalâʾ remain as far from the conflict as possible; at least one of the reasons for this, as will be noted later, is his need to protect his progeny, specifically in his son who will become the fourth Imâm. In one instance, when Umm Wahb seizes a tent pole and advances on those killing her husband, al-Ḥusayn orders her back to the women's tent, insisting, in spite of her pleas, that fighting is not obligatory for women (HOWARD I.K.A., (trans.), *The History of al-Ṭabarî*, vol. IX, 1990: 131). However, the issue of women actively involved in combat remains a moot point, not only because there have been well-known female warriors in the history of Islam, such as Ḫawla bt. Azwar, but also by reason of the presence of women in the armed forces in a number of Islamic countries (including Saudi Arabia).

For our purposes, the chief of these women is the Pietà-like Zaynab, co-heroine of Karbalâʾ with her brother al-Ḥusayn, and who plays a significant role on the night of the tenth day of the month of Muḥarram, the day of ʿÂshûrâ. Within hours of the killing of al-Ḥusayn and his companions, the women of the now vulnerable and inconsolable household find themselves led by the venerable and attentive Zaynab, who stands over the survivors with an unwavering vigilance and a courage that eclipses any natural fear and timidity; among them, as they are taken as captives first to the court of the governor ʿUbayd Allâh b. Ziyâd in Kûfa and then to the palace of the caliph Yazîd b. Muʿâwiya in Damascus, is al-Ḥusayn's only surviving son and the fourth Imâm, ʿAlî b. al-Ḥusayn b. Abî Ṭâlib. As it turns out, before this youthful Imâm assumes his rightful position, Zaynab will become her brother's chief apologist, the defender of his actions before the governor and the caliph, and a theologian, wary matriarch and protector of the children of that 'tendency' (*tashayyuʿ*) that, fusing itself to the Karbalâʾ event would evolve into the *iṯnâ ʿasharî* Shîʿî expression of Islamic faith.

Between Karbalâʾ, Kûfa and Damascus, in spite of hugely traumatic physical and psychological suffering, Zaynab delivers some discomforting and impassioned words in support of the dead they have left behind, hurriedly buried in the sand. These appeals and protests form, in a very rudimentary sense, the beginnings of what would later develop into the *taʿziya-mağlis* genre.[8] In reality,

---

[8] The verbal noun from the Arabic verb *ʿazzâ-yuʿazzî*, which means, amongst other things, 'to comfort', 'to console', 'to offer one's condolences, 'to express one's sympathy. Many English translators render *taʿziya* as 'passion play' or 'mystery play' and even 'miracle play': but chiefly, it is, as Dabashi notes, "a performance of mourning…that has historically spread over a whole constellation of dramatic and ritual performances" (DABASHI H., "Ta'ziyeh as Theatre of Protest" in P Chelkowski (ed.), *Taʾziyeh: Ritual and Drama in Iran*, New York University Press, New York 1979: 179). These are theatrical performances or dramas, which, making use of stark and powerful imagery, such as a riderless, bloodstained horse, re-enact, recount, and recollect the lives of the family of Muḥammad specifically during the month of Muḥarram. The *taʿziya*, called by Negar

these rites of anamnesis and mourning developed over an extended period of time, into what today are politico-religious phenomena, profusely ritualistic and prized by their ardent participants. For the Imâms and their devotees who came after al-Ḥusayn and who lived in secrecy because of persecution, there was little chance of insurrection. Weeping and other ways of remembrance soon developed into 'commemorations' (*mağâlis*), which were given a powerful impetus by the fourth Imâm who had survived Karbalâ'. These active memorials were often held in the home of the Imâm, until (especially after the ʿAbbâsids) their manifestation became more public. Even then, some leaders felt threatened by the display of popular piety and attempted to suppress such commemorations. As the month of Muḥarram ends and that of Ṣafar begins,[9] Zaynab finds herself standing before Yazîd in his Damascus palace, where she becomes his most vociferous critic. As one of the popular elegies in her honour reads:

> Do not call her a woman, she is above a man, she is more faithful than a man. Do not call her a woman, there is no one

---

Mottahedeh "a twist of history in everyday life" (cf. AGHAIE K.S., (ed.), *The Women of Karbala*, University of Texas Press, Austin 2005: 25), provides a sacred space for the spectator-participants to reaffirm through the ritual their engagement with the religious and moral stance taken by al-Ḥusayn, and with which they, as members of the Shîʿa, are an integral part. The word *mağlis*, with its plural *mağâlis*, and which in its origins meant a place of meeting or social gathering, comes from the Arabic root meaning 'to sit'. It refers to the commemorative accounts of the Karbalâ' event, replete with narrative and lamentation poetry, and told in such a way as to evoke a grief and weeping that is often frenzied. Weeping is a reminder, and remembrance is more important than the actual weeping. Cf. CLOHESSY C., "Some Notes on mağlis and taʿziya" in *Encounter*, vol. 41/1 (2016), Pontificio Istituto di Studi Arabi e d'Islamistica, Rome.

[9] For this reason, the cycle of mourning continues throughout Muḥarram and the following month, Ṣafar, to commemorate the fate of the women and children, brought as hostages to Damascus.

> more courageous than Zaynab. Do not call her a woman, there is no one more knowledgeable than Zaynab.[10]

If, because of al-Ḥusayn's sacrifice, Karbalâ᾽ is inexpungible, durably ingrained upon the Shîʿî psyche, it is Zaynab's compelling voice in the halls of despots and bullies, in the streets and gathering places of Kûfa and Medina, that has secured that imperishability. "There was no other more eloquent woman than Zaynab," reads one elegy, "when she spoke, men held their breath...the fiery tongue of Ali could be heard in her speech."[11] It is not hard to understand how she has become inextricably woven into the imagery and language of Karbalâ᾽.

In her decisive role as spokesperson for her brother's cause, she became the first to drive the adversity of Karbalâ᾽ into perpetuity by moving her brother's creed and conviction off the battlefield and into the palaces of Kûfa and Damascus, not only completing al-Ḥusayn's *ǧihâd*, but becoming the agent through whom Karbalâ᾽ would become undying. Zaynab's last protest, reproaching Yazîd in his own residence by delineating the ethical and political issues that led to her brother's death, continues to buoy and buttress the Shîʿa, as she assures him:

> By God, who honoured us with Revelation and the Book and the Prophethood and the election, you will not overtake our span of time or reach our objective or efface our memory.[12]

Zaynab's crucial legacy is her role as the catalyst for the *taʿziya-maǧlis* tradition, by which, in lament and bereavement, the foundational story of Shîʿî Islam is vocalized. This is perhaps seen best of

---

[10] AGHAIE K.S., (ed.), *The Women of Karbala*, 2005: 109. In spite of the honour it gives to Zaynab, the elegy is disappointingly censorious in its view of women generally.

[11] Op. cit.: 127.

[12] Cf. al-Ṭabarsî., *Kitâb al-iḥtiǧâǧ ʿalâ ahl al-liǧâǧ*, vol. II: 308–309, Ibn Ṭâ᾽ûs., *Kitâb al-luhûf fî qatlâ al-ṭufûf*: 105–108, Ibn Namâ al-Ḥillî., *Muṭîr al-aḥzân wa munîr subul al-ashǧân*, Part 3: 101–102, al-Maǧlisî, *Biḥâr al-anwâr*, vol. XLV, bb. 39: 133–135, vol. XLV, bb. 39: 157–160. Among the Sunnî, cf. al-Ḫawârizmî., *Maqtal al-Ḥusayn*, bk. 2, bb. *fî maqtal al-Ḥusayn*: 71–4.

all by her unwavering demand in Damascus that the traditional mourning rites, neglected in Karbalâʾ, now be permitted. It was Zaynab who carried the message of rebellion to others and who made ʿÂshûrâ possible. One poet says of her:

> Touched by the shadow of purification, she is the reflection of sanctification, the aim of Muḥammad, the voice and embellishment of her father, the prayer and cloak of her mother, the anguished heart's cry, the Imâm's guidance.[13]

For a few brief historical days, she took centre stage as leader of the 'people of the house' (*ahl al-bayt*), protector and guarantor of the next Imâm and preeminent champion and advocate for Karbalâʾ. She is clearly important in the Sunnî texts, in the articulation of the chief Karbalâʾ moments; but these instances are powerfully elaborated and embellished in the Shîʿî texts precisely because she is a member of the *ahl al-bayt* and, if not one of those counted as immaculate and impeccable (*maʿṣûma*), then raised and trained by those who are.

Zaynab offers a womanly courage to a society that hides behind the force of military power, her integrity unbowed by convenience, her humility undeterred by power, her truth untainted by lies. She represents an authentic, vibrant, courageous human being breaking through all the opposition, refusing to be content with a life that is less than real, less than honest, less than true, a woman of uncommon character and substance, resolute in her quest for a valid Islam against those who claim to know the mind of God and who are prepared to use coercion, if necessary, to make others conform; those who cannot tell God's will from their own, those who wear their certainty and assurance like a cloak. For her adherents, the Zaynab of the Karbalâʾ narratives leaves her fingerprints on every struggle for justice and for an authentic expression of Islam, on all the places where people refuse to collude with corruption, or show a willingness to sacrifice for a great cause, or are persistent in the quest for righteousness despite the odds. Zaynab meets the

---

[13] D'SOUZA D., "The Figure of Zaynab in Shîʿî Devotional Life" in *The Bulletin of The Henry Martyn Institute*, Volume 17/1, January-June 1998: 47.

needs of the hour, advancing her brother's principles and so altering the course of history, assuring devotees that they can face the future with strength, courage, and wisdom.

The chronicles we will examine, carried both by Sunnî and Shî^ʿî transmitters, record specific incidents, either directly or indirectly involving Zaynab, in the days immediately preceding Karbalâ᾿, during the course of the battle itself, and in the days of imprisonment and interrogation directly after the death of al-Ḥusayn and his companions. Quite patently, the Zaynab presented in the classical sources grows in awareness of the ultimate outcome of the hostilities; she is almost certainly not entirely convinced from the beginning that it is here, at Karbalâ᾿, that her brother will be killed and the predictions of his death fulfilled. While there is a definite change in Zaynab's character, until the moment when she takes a final stand before Yazîd, and a clearly defined growth in courage and eloquence, she remains a frail and frightened woman rather than some sort of undaunted superheroine. The key to her sanctity and her excellence as a model lies precisely in that weakness, so prized particularly by those Shîʿî adherents who contruct their lives and spirituality around Karbalâ᾿, rather than in what seems to be a false construct to suit a particular ideological narrative; that of the unflinching revolutionary.

This concept of 'weakness' needs prudent definition. Quite patently Zaynab, as one brought up by those deemed to be 'infallible' (*maʿṣûm*) and therefore as one who shares a secondary or minor infallibility, is not, in the eyes of her Shîʿî devotees, any ordinary woman. Nevertheless, nor is she *de facto* shielded from a substantial amount of suffering, both physical and mental, anymore than her mother Fâṭima had been immune to such things. The physical weakness and suffering of Fâṭima, both in her grief and in the rigors of her daily life, are well documented. Such a phenomenon is clearly highlighted, for example, by some of the writings of *Shayḫ* al-Ṣadûq, in works such as *Ṣifât al-shîʿa* and *Faḍâ᾿il al-shîʿa*. Enfolded into the Shîʿî corpus of *aḥâdîṯ*, and in texts ranging from al-Kulaynî's *al-Kâfî* to *Shayḫ* al-Ṣadûq's *Ṣifât al-shîʿa* and Ibn Shahrâshûb's *Manâqib*, is a set of distinct traits which distinguish and individuate the *iṯnâ ʿasharî* devotees, and each of which assists in painting the portrait a life that is filled with mourning and sorrow. Prolonged night vigils have rendered their faces ashen and haggard, their stomachs ache from long fasts, unflagging prayer has desiccated their mouths. They are a people covered with the dust of the humble, emaciated, slender and wasted; their backs bent from standing in prayer and their eyes unfocused from incessant weeping. Their faces sallow from long hours of worship, long nights of prayer have exhausted them and the heat of the midday sun has taken its toll on their bodies. Their tears, like their prayers and supplications, are unceasing. They grieve, while all around them people are happy.[14]

The whole infrastructure of *iṯnâ ʿasharî* Shîʿî spirituality is held together by a grief that is fierce and harrowing and conspicuous, for "God loves every grieving heart."[15] It is a sorrow

---

[14] Cf. for example al-Kulaynî., *al-Kâfî fî ʿilm al-dîn*, vol. II, bk. 5 (*Kitâb al-îmân wa-l-kufr*), bb. *al-Muʾmin wa ʿalâmâti-hi*, n. 10: 233, n. 10/2289: 591, al-Ṣadûq., *Kitâb al-ḫiṣâl*, vol. II, n. 40: 444, *Ṣifât al-shîʿa*, nn. 18–19: 10, nn. 20, 22: 11, n. 33, 17, n. 40: 29, *Kitâb al-amâlî fî al-aḥâdîṯ wa-l-aḫbâr*, *mağlis* 83: 561, *Faḍâʾil al-shîʿa*, n. 20: 26, al-Mufîd., *al-Irshâd fî maʿrifat ḥuğağ Allâh ʿalâ al-ʿibâd*, vol. I: 237–238, al-Ṭûsî., *al-Amâlî fî al-ḥadîṯ*, *mağlis* 8: 216–216, *mağlis* 23: 576, al-Fattâl al-Nîsâbûrî., *Rawḍat al-wâʿiẓîn wa-tabṣirat al-muttaʿiẓîn*, vol. II: 293–294, Ibn Shahrâshûb., *Manâqib âl Abî Ṭâlib*, vol. II, bb. *al-Musâbaqa bi-l-yaqîn wa-l-khabr*: 120, al-Irbilî., *Kashf al-ġumma fî maʿrifat al-aʾimma*, vol. I: 100, 133, al-Daylamî., *Irshâd al-qulûb*, vol. I, bb. 29: 108, bb. 46: 145, al-Kafʿamî., *al-Balad al-amîn*: 334, al-Ḥurr al-ʿÂmilî., *Tafṣîl wasâʾil al-shîʿa ilâ taḥṣîl masâʾil al-sharîʿa*, vol. I, bb. 20, n. 8–205: 87, n. 16–213: 91, n. 21–218: 92–93, vol. VII, bb. 5, n. 13–8997: 157, vol. XV, bb. 4, n. 16–20242: 189, al-Mağlisî., *Biḥâr al-anwâr*, vol. XXVII, bb. 4, n. 155: 144, vol. XXXIII, bb. 23, n. 597: 363, vol. XLI, bb. 99, n. 4: 4, vol. LXIV, bb. 12: 247, vol. LXV, bb. 19, n. 2: 149, nn. 4–5: 150–151, n. 30: 169, nn. 32, 34: 176–177, n. 43: 188, vol. LXVI, bb. 37, n. 30: 308, vol. LXXIV, bb. 15, n. 30: 403, vol. LXXV, bb. 15, nn. 90, 91: 25–26, vol. XCII, bb. 129: 382.

[15] al-Kulaynî., *al-Kâfî fî ʿilm al-dîn*, vol. II, bk. 5 (*Kitâb al-îmân wa-l-kufr*), bb. *al-Shukr*, n. 30: 99, Ibn al-Ḥadîd., *Sharḥ nahğ al-balâġa*, vol. II: 193, al-Daylamî *Irshâd al-qulûb*, vol. I: 154, al-Ḥurr al-ʿÂmilî., *Tafṣîl wasâʾil al-shîʿa ilâ taḥṣîl masâʾil al-sharîʿa*, vol. VII, bb. 29, n. 8771: 76, vol. XVI, bb. 8, n. 21626: 310; al-Mağlisî., *Biḥâr al-anwâr*, vol. LXVIII, bb. 61, n. 25: 38, vol. LXX, bb. 125, n. 3: 157.

> compounded by a number of factors: the usurpation of their power at the very beginning, the unwavering refusal to accord ʿAlî and his descendants their rightful place, the ill-treatment of Fâṭima and the members of her family, and the persecution of those faithful to the 'people of the house' as a constant through Islamic history. Notwithstanding all of these factors, Shîʿî grief finds its culmination and summit in the death of al-Ḥusayn on the field of Karbalâʾ – the very name means 'land of sorrow and calamity' – and it is the Karbalâʾ event by which the grief is articulated and finds physical interpretation. All the suffering and grief of the 'people of the house' converges in the solitary figure of al-Ḥusayn, and all subsequent pain and sorrow is nothing more than a way of participating in his own grief.[16]

In his work on the possibility of a suffering in Islam that could be counted as redemptive,[17] Mahmoud Ayoub goes to great length to underscore the suffering, poverty and privation of the *ahl al-bayt*, as a sign of their favour with God. To reinforce his argument, Ayoub references a number of *aḥâdîṯ* about the calamaties inflicted upon the prophets and the pious, and all who suffer with them and who are thereby construed as members of the eternal and mystical 'house of sorrows' (*bayt al-aḥẓân*). This suffering of the *ahl al-bayt* is both material and political, the latter accentuated by the arrogation of their rightful power by others and their persecution (as well as the hounding of those who adhere to them). This is underscored especially by the martyrdom of all the Imâms, except for the twelfth; in spite of being understood as one of the divinely foreordained qualities of the Imâms, their killing is almost entirely for political motives – in this way, the divine in some sense interacts with the world of human beings. Notes Ayoub: "For the people of the Prophet's household, this meant the endurance of poverty and hunger, persecution and privation, and finally the cup of martyrdom as the seal of their struggle…in the way of God." The

---

16 CLOHESSY C.P., *Fatima, Daughter of Muhammad*, 2009: 136.

17 AYOUB M., *Redemptive Suffering in Islam. A Study of the Devotional Aspects of ʿAshura in Twelver Shiʿism*, Mouton Publishers, The Hague 1978.

ma'ṣûmûn are not spared the ordinary run of human suffering – in fact, theirs is amplified, because suffering is understood as having its own merit with God, purifying the soul and testing the devotee. This is expressed by Muḥammad in a *ḥadîṯ* carried by Ibn Mâğa:

> "On the authority of Muṣ'ab b. Sa'd, on the authority of his father Sa'd b. Abî Waqqâṣ, who said: I said: Messenger of God, which people are most severely tested. He replied: The Prophets, then the next best, then the next best. A person is tested according to his religious commitment. If he is steadfast in his religious commitment, he will be tested more severely."[18]

Consequently, Muḥammad himself was not spared various types of suffering: "The Messenger of God said: I have been tortured for the sake of God as no one else has, and I have suffered fear for the sake of God as no one else has."[19]

Zaynab's comportment in the hours leading up to Karbalâ' reveals some very human traits. The classical sources, both Sunnî and Shî'î, do not shy away from portraying the human qualities of grief and fear in her as a reaction to her brother's plight. To expunge these from her, or from any member of the *ahl al-bayt*, would be at once to pluck them from the realm of being examplars and models for imitation. Herein lies the weakness so prized by the Shî'a and the weakness experienced by Zaynab, since suffering, as a form of privation (of happiness, or peace, or material well-being, or health, for example) is a form of weakness.

The narratives comprise a number of definitive interventions by Zaynab before, during and after Karbalâ'; these interventions not only form the bulk of her biography in the classical sources, but also provide the groundwork of a theology and spirituality constructed around her life. Zaynab is quite clearly a woman whose heart beats in the places where al-Ḥusayn's heart beats and breaks in the places where al-Ḥusayn's heart breaks. In this, she is a consummate model of Shî'î Islam. I propose these accounts, therefore, in order to explore the content of a 'Zaynabian' theology and spir-

---

[18] Ibn Mâğa, *Sunan*, vol. V, *Abwâb al-fitan*, bb. 23, n. 4023: 225.
[19] Op. cit., vol. 1, *Kitâb al-sunna*, bb. 11, n. 151: 176–177.

ituality that could be relevant, without the need of ideological reinterpretation, to any Shîʿî Muslim. We will examine Zaynab precisely as she is presented by the classical sources, allowing the texts to speak for themselves and so to give her a voice.

The narrations we will consider can be separated into three groups. They commence on the road to Karbalâʾ, when on the night air Zaynab hears an unidentified voice crying out in lament and warning and turns to her brother for an explanation. Days later, on the edges of the Karbalâʾ field, she is alarmed by the noise of the enemy army drawing near and approaches al-Ḥusayn, as he sits in front of his tent, legs drawn up and dreaming of his grandfather Muḥammad. She suffers an emotional collapse as he sings a dirge about those who would be dead by the next day.

The second group of narrations begins after the start of battle as Zaynab, reinvigorated and 'like the sun rising', emerges from her tent to bewail the death of her nephew ʿAlî b. al-Ḥusayn. She emerges a second time in an unsuccessful attempt to prevent a small boy, possibly another nephew, from entering the fray, a boy forever remembered for the cutting words he shouts at his killer. And she emerges a third time, in al-Ḥusayn's final moments, to challenge and shame his killers. This group of texts ends with Zaynab's tormented elegy as the survivors, herded in a dishevelled group from Karbalâʾ to Kûfa and then to Damascus, leave behind them the bodies of al-Ḥusayn and his companions.

The third group of reports starts as Zaynab's haunting lament is transformed a few days later into her first forceful protest directed at the citizens of Kûfa and continues with her verbal battles, initially with Ibn Ziyâd and then in Damascus with Yazîd. The epochal lecture she delivers before a chastened Yazîd marks her final intervention, the moment when Zaynab begins to take her leave, stepping back from the central drama of Shîʿî history while her nephew, the fourth Imâm, assumes his legitimate place.

In spite of numerous other aspects of her biography – specifically her childhood years and the last months of her life – being less well-documented and even disputed in so many of their aspects, these Karbalâʾ interventions recorded by the classical authors provide sufficient material for a 'Zaynabian' theology and praxis. The first stage in constructing such a theology and mode of spirituality is to attempt to retrieve the truest possible picture of Zaynab from the figure she has become; to liberate the genuine Zaynab, imprisoned to a lesser or greater degree by hagiography and by some of the socio-political discourses and religious narratives of the last half a century or more, which fundamentally reinterpreted as her a fearless and intrepid activist. In doing so, such readings of her life have offered something of a false construct, in that such a reading is nothing more than another strand of hagiography. For one thing, pious stories, even if inspiring, do not help us to establish a rigorously academic biography. For another, there was no need for any mechanical reinterpretation of Zaynab using a revolutionary narrative; a careful reading of the classical texts already reveals quite distinctly the transformation from a confused and frightened woman into an articulate defender of the *ahl al-bayt* and a defender of her brother's cause. Defining her holiness by turning her into a courageous preacher of justice fails to take into account that in reality it is weakness, not strength, which lies at the heart of Shîʿî spirituality and power. As Dabashi writes so vividly:

> Shi'ism, in the end, is a paradox. It thrives and is triumphant when it is combative and wages an uphill battle. It loses its moral authority and defiant voice the instant it succeeds and is in power. It is, paradoxically, only in power when it is not in power. When it is in power it lacks legitimacy, authority, audacity.[20]

A solid Zaynabian theology begins, then, with situating Zaynab as she is presented in the classical sources; a terrified, grieving woman who has lost everything, but who at a particular instant summons all the strength God has given her to clarify and defend her brother's actions before the highest power in the land and establish the history and mourning rites of Karbalâʾ.

In two ways, the recent revisionist approach to Zaynab follows a similar recalibration of her mother, Muḥammad's daughter Fâṭima. In the first instance, Rosiny[21] writes of a contemporary

---

[20] DABASHI H., *Shiʾism: A religion of protest*, Harvard University Press, Cambridge Mass., 2011: xiv.

[21] ROSINY S., "The Tragedy of Fāṭima al-Zahrāʾ in the Debate of Two Shiite Theologians in Lebanon" in R BRUNNER and W ENDE (eds.), *The Twelver Shia in Modern Times*, Brill, Leiden 2001: 207–219.

deliberation, between two distinct theological tendencies, about Fâṭima's life; the conservative 'historical school', represented by Ǧaʿfar Murtaḍâ al-ʿÂmilî, and the 'modern reformist' by Muḥammad Ḥusayn Faḍlallâh. The debate centres on the incidents that would take place shortly after the death of Muḥammad and the succession to the caliphate of Abû Bakr, including some violent scenes at the house of ʿAlî and Fâṭima. Determined to force ʿAlî's allegiance, an armed group forced its way into the home, injuring Fâṭima in the process, and ostensibly causing the miscarriage of her unborn son.[22] There are numerous disparate reports about this incident.

While Faḍlallâh does not deny some form of aggression, he insists that there are too many embellished and unsubstantiated legends, leading him to him censure many of the texts about Fâṭima, especially those which present a more mystical and esoteric image of Muḥammad's daughter. He wants, instead, an accentuation of her political, religious and social activities, so that she could become a model for the modern activist female Muslim. Fâṭima's life demonstrates that it is possible for women to enter fully into the cultural and social *milieu*, offering to all Muslim women a paradigm that can be imitated. Faḍlallâh depicts the members of the *ahl al-bayt* as human beings with explicable reasons for their actions and habits and underscores the human traits of the Shîʿî holy ones, so as to offer them as prototypes for contemporary life.

Al-ʿÂmilî defends the more arcane aspects of the Shîʿî approach to Fâṭima, insisting that the mystical aspects of her life are crucial to Shîʿî belief, so that minimizing or denying them would in consequence seriously demoralize the faith. These elements include Fâṭima's creation from a fruit of paradise, her conversing with her mother from the womb, her preservation from menstruation, and her never having shed blood when giving birth.

---

[22] This is the claim of the Shîʿa: but cf. Ibn Ḥanbal., *Musnad*, vol. I, *Musnad ʿAlî b. Abî Ṭâlib*, n. 769: 211–212, n. 953: 250–251, where his birth is recorded, and n. 1370: 335 where it is omitted.

In the second instance, best encapsulated in the book *Fatima is Fatima*,[23] its author, French-educated sociologist Ali Shariati, introduces Fâṭima as the archetypal woman, a role model for Muslim women and the woman that Islam would like every woman to be. Shariati's Fâṭima is entirely without supernatural attributes and although in some ways incomparable, she is, primarily, entirely human. By her own will and sound judgment she had chosen to be loyal, devoted, compassionate and ready to sacrifice herself for her family and her true fate. All women in Iran, posited Shariati, should adhere to her example and be, like her, an object of sacrifice. Shariati proposes his own very distinct vision of Muḥammad's daughter to every good Muslim woman, confused and disorientated, he thought, by the Iranian Pahlavî dynasty,[24] which he believed had created a class of women devoid of character or identity, a distorted genre, severed from its origins, heritage and fate.

Notwithstanding evident differences between the two – as Deeb points out, Fâṭima is perceived as more passive and docile than her daughter Zaynab, characterized as she is by stoicism, patience and maternalism[25] – an almost identical debate could be launched around the life of Zaynab; the 'ordinary' wife and mother in contrast to the woman imbued with heavenly virtues, the panic-stricken, anguished Zaynab on the field of Karbalâ' in contrast to the determined and courageous revolutionary and model for all women.

The revisionist interpretation of Zaynab, examined by a number of contemporary authors such as Hamdar, Ruffle, Pandyar and Deeb,[26] has taken place on a number of levels. The first is on the

---

23 SHARIATI A., *Fatima is Fatima*, The Shariati Foundation, Tehran (n.d.).

24 1344/1925 – 1399/1979. Cf. BOSWORTH C.E., *Islamic Surveys 5. The Islamic Dynasties*, 1967: 180.

25 DEEB L., "Emulating and/or Embodying the Ideal: The Gendering of Temporal Frameworks and Islamic Role Models in Shi'i Lebanon" in *American Ethnologist*, vol. 36, n. 2 (May, 2009): 252.

26 HAMDAR A., "Jihad of Words: Gender and Contemporary Karbala Narratives" in *The Yearbook of English Studies*, vol. 39, n. 1/2, Literature and Religion (2009), Modern Humanities Research Association,

level of gender. If in the past it was the men of the *ahl al-bayt* and their supporters who were the principle locus of the Karbalâʾ accounts, while the emotional sufferings of women, although not ignored, remained on the fringes, such a narrative has been rewritten. The women of Karbalâʾ have become heroines in the more contemporary retellings of the event, not so much in the appalling agony of seeing their men slain or even in their atrocious treatment at the hands of the authorities, but in the courage and strength they display, especially in front of a tyrannical leadership. In this, Zaynab, with her weighty verbal duels with Ibn Ziyâd and Yazîd, has become the chief protagonist.

Less and less is the struggle or *ǧihâd* of the women envisaged as something subsidiary to the undaunted actions of their male counterparts; instead, the women have come to occupy a more salient place, engaging battle, as in the case of Zaynab, with intellect and eloquence as resolutely as the men engage it with force of arms. In the writings of scholars like Shariati, Zaynab, like her mother Fâṭima, is forged into a model for the contemporary Shîʿî woman, be it in Iran, Lebanon or Bahrain. As she takes on the leonine qualities of her father, Zaynab becomes an innovative feminine marker, a paragon and inspiration who shapes new modes of behaviour. The Zaynab that Shariati presents in his *La Responsabilité de la femme*[27] takes on traditionally masculine characteristics; but, as Ruffle[28] is quick to point out, Zaynab is not transformed into a

---

Cambridge: 84–100, RUFFLE K.G., *Gender, Sainthood, and Everyday Practice in South Asian Shiʾism*, University of North Carolina Press, Chapel Hill 2011, PANDYA S., "Women's Shi'i Ma'atim in Bahrain" in Journal of Middle East Women's Studies, vol. 6, n. 2 (Spring 2010): 31–58, DEEB L., "Living Ashura in Lebanon: Mourning Transformed to Sacrifice" in *Comparative Studies of South Asia, Africa and the Middle East*, vol. 25, n. 1, Duke University Press, North Carolina 2005: 122–137, "Emulating and/or Embodying the Ideal: The Gendering of Temporal Frameworks and Islamic Role Models in Shi'i Lebanon, 2009: 242–257.

[27] SHARIATI A., *La Responsabilité de la femme*, Albouraq, Beyrouth 2011.

[28] RUFFLE K.G., *Gender, Sainthood, and Everyday Practice in South Asian Shiʾism*, 2011: 76.

woman with masculine traits. Rather, the suggestion is that certain characteristics and virtues, once the domain of the males of the species, are embodied by Zaynab and, by association, any woman who patterns her life on such an exemplar. Less out of kinship with her brother and more because of her own socio-political commitment and religious devotion, Shariati's Zaynab plunges deeply into al-Ḥusayn's revolution, and then stays with him to the end. Her subsequent battle, in which she sustains her brother's struggle, is accomplished against all odds, as by a proficient use of words she helps to defeat the oppressive powers. This, notes Shariati, is what it means to be like Zaynab; to take upon one's shoulders the enduring struggle for truth and justice and to do so with mettle and vigour. In Zaynab, qualities such as physical bravery and gallantry, which may once have been thought to be the province of the men, are seen to belong equally to women, without any loss of femininity; concomitantly, she and those who imitate her virtues can become a lesson to men who may be failing in these virtues. She is a woman of extraordinary valour, learned from her mother Fâṭima, but "whose spiritual and psychophysical capabilities are never determined in comparison with those of men",[29] and who never ceases at any instant to be quintessentially feminine.

A second level of the reshaping of Zaynab and the retelling of Karbalâʾ, already perceptible in the first, is the distinct movement of Zaynab from the fringes of the Karbalâʾ event to a central role. This is less evident in the battle itself, although her interventions on the field are clearly noted by the classical sources; instead, it concerns the post-Karbalâʾ Zaynab in her fierce and courageous engagement with the authorities, and the suggestion that she becomes, on a certain level, the saviour of Karbalâʾ and of her brother's cause. Three things become patently clear at the level of the texts; the first is that her interventions saved the life of the fourth Imâm, winning time for him and creating a critical space in which he could regain his strength before assuming his rightful place. The second is that by her protests before the people of Kûfa, Ibn Ziyâd and Yazîd, she delineated clearly the political, moral and spiritual principles that impelled the actions of her brother. The third is that

[29] Op. cit.: 81.

she was the standard-bearer in the institution of memorial services, thus ensuring that the Karbalâ' event would survive for every generation. Hamdar goes even further, suggesting that Zaynab "shook the very foundations of Yazid's rule, set the scene for its collapse."[30]

On a third level, intimately tied to the first two, there is a transfiguration of Zaynab the tearful woman into Zaynab the courageous and fearless exemplar. As Hamdar notes:

> Present-day narratives revise earlier claims regarding Zaynab's reaction to the adversaries around her. These narratives stress that, contrary to popular belief, Zaynab never broke down or lost her edge, even as she witnessed the suffering unfolding.[31]

However, this reinterpretation of her behaviour does not represent an entirely faithful reading of the classical texts which, despite showing a growing boldness and eloquence, nonetheless reveal a Zaynab who even at her strongest moments was filled with fear and grief. At her most articulate and powerful before Yazîd, she still breaks down; and while it would be incorrect, as in some earlier pieties, to make a benumbed grief the chief characteristic of Zaynab after Karbalâ', some of what Deeb[32] calls the 'authenticated' (as opposed to the more 'traditional') forms of remembering the event have so accentuated her courage and valour as to forget her human sorrow and mourning. Both sets of characteristics – the fearlessness and the sorrow – should be of equal importance, and Zaynab's life appears to be a far more imitable fusion of both. Even so, as Deeb observes, this new construal of Zaynab's comportment during and after Karbalâ' is crucial for Shî'î women.[33] She becomes the model of a woman who takes a stand before injustice and tyranny, a protector and nurturer of those in her care. She is a woman of immense compassion, clarity of thought, dedica-

---

30 HAMDAR A., "Jihad of Words: Gender and Contemporary Karbala Narratives", 2009: 91.

31 Ibid.

32 DEEB L., "Living Ashura in Lebanon: Mourning Transformed to Sacrifice", 2005: 124.

33 Op. cit.: 123.

tion to justice, articulate in her arguments, coping in situations of crisis. Women, writes Deeb,

> are utilizing the salient example of Zaynab as an outspoken, strong, and compassionate activist to push the boundaries of what is acceptable and expectable for pious Lebanese Shiʿi women...Zaynab has become an idealized standard of behaviour.[34]

Again, Hamdar goes further than this, positing that through her eloquent advocacy of her brother's cause, Zaynab

> has come to be regarded as the major catalyst in the creation of a full-fledged Shi'i movement and keeping it alive amongst the public...an educator of the public, revealing the truth about the events of Karbala and exposing the atrocities of the Umayyad rule.[35]

On a final level, Zaynab's devotees are themselves invited to a transformation, from memorial expressed in mourning and in tears to memorial expressed in action. This ties in with Shariati's activist 'Red Shi'ism' model, the call to move away from a passive remembrance to an active struggle against the forces of evil as the best way of emulating the heroes of Karbalâʾ.[36] Mourning cannot be quietist and disengaged but should encompass an activist struggle against all that Yazîd represents. The Zaynab to be emulated is the one who sacrificed herself and passed on the pattern of striving against iniquity and oppression. In these areas, she is put forward as a paragon whose embodiment of morality, spirituality and social engagement can be imitated. This imitation resonates deeply in women involving themselves in works of social welfare, in education, in political activism and in family life; in a word, Zaynab is the model of a perfectly modern yet pious Shîʿî woman. The major

---

[34] Op. cit.: 136.

[35] HAMDAR A., "Jihad of Words: Gender and Contemporary Karbala Narratives", 2009: 92.

[36] For an evaluation of this transformation, cf. AGHAIE K.S., 1994. "Reinventing Karbala: Revisionist interpretations of the Karbala Paradigm" in *Jusur: The UCLA Journal of Middle Eastern Studies* 10, 1994:1–30.

change here, observes Deeb, is that "for women, bringing Karbala into the contemporary moment requires public participation in the betterment of the community as a necessary component of being a moral person."[37]

To force a transformation on Zaynab for socio-political reasons is to ignore the natural transformation that is evident at the level of the texts. Furthermore, to turn her into a fearless revolutionary, no matter how inspirational this may prove, is to discount and deny her very human traits, breaking down, for example, in grief-stricken tears even when she was at her most powerful. Not to accept her as she is in the texts, without some later cosmetic transformation, is to diminish her power to inspire people at every level of society, and not just those who may be involved in the great socio-political movements of their time. It is my contention that the real Zaynab is an amalgam of all the elements encapsulated by the various levels of transformation. We have to understand Zaynab for who she was; a terrified and grieving woman who had lost everything, but who at a particular instant gathered all her inner strength and cemented the history and mourning rites of Karbalâʾ, as she endorsed and justified her brother's actions before the Umayyad powers.

All of the elements of the older views of Zaynab have value; she mourned deeply, with a sadness that ran through to the marrow, exercised her maternal capacity in caring for the survivors of Karbalâʾ, took a leading role in establishing the rites of mourning and ensured that both the *raison d'être* and the authentic history of her brother's struggle and martyrdom would be preserved and retold. However, as Pandya reminds us, "while in the past Zaynab was understood to be a symbol of grieving womanhood, today this would be considered an incomplete way of understanding her significance."[38] Or, perhaps, of the meaning of Karbalâʾ itself.

The Karbalâʾ story barely needs retelling. For the sake of brevity we can say that the catalyst of the affair, although not the

---

[37] DEEB L., "Emulating and/or Embodying the Ideal: The Gendering of Temporal Frameworks and Islamic Role Models in Shi'i Lebanon", 2009: 253.

[38] PANDYA S., "Women's Shiʿi Ma'atim in Bahrain", 2010: 44.

sole cause, was the caliphate of Muʿâwiya, during whose tenure al-Ḥusayn received numerous appeals to lead a revolt together with pledges of support, and the accession of Yazîd b. Muʿâwiya to the caliphate after his father's death. Al-Ḥusayn motives are simultaneously political, religious and moral; he regarded Yazîd, with his inflexible demand for allegiance, as entirely unprincipled and depraved. Both Yazîd and his father were envisaged as men who had violated the Islamic socio-political ideal, thereby threatening the foundations of the office of the caliphate and the very substructure of Islam. Tenacious, in spite of the quite obvious outcome of such a course, al-Ḥusayn was uncompromising in his rejection of allegiance to Yazîd, and for this reason he could not possibly have remained, inactive, in Medina. If, as some may think, he acted with disproportionate idealism and without the adroitness and versatility of a politician, ultimately, he appears to have had little choice. For one thing, all of this was preordained, since martyrdom is integral to the office of Imâm. For another, al-Ḥusayn felt himself to be acting in accordance with a divine command:

> "*How should ye not fight for the cause of Allah and of the feeble among men and of the women and the children who are crying: Our Lord! Bring us forth from out of this town of which the people are oppressors. Oh, give us from Thy presence some protecting friend! Oh, give us from Thy presence some defender!*"[39]

While it is difficult to determine whether he was, from the start, fully cognizant of the final outcome, al-Ḥusayn left Medina for Mecca, where he stayed about four months. Numerous *aḥâdîṯ* relate that not only al-Ḥusayn, but others too, like his grandfather, father and mother, knew that this boy, whose conception and birth is meticulously encased in accounts of heavenly intervention, would die a martyr's death. Some, but certainly not all, actually mention Karbalâʾ as the site of his martyrdom, with accounts of Muḥammad being given red soil from the place.[40] He continued to

---

[39] Q. 4: 75.

[40] These include the genre of dreams by women such as Umm Salama, Umm al-Faḍl and Umm Ayman, carried by Sunnî and Shîʿî alike, as well as similar dreams, visions and angelic visitations experienced by

Muḥammad. "Fâṭima will give birth to a boy, whom your community after you will kill," announces Ǧibra'îl to Muḥammad (al-Kulaynî., *al-Kâfî fî ʿilm al-dîn*, vol. I, *Kitâb al-ḥuǧǧa*, bb. *mawlid al-Ḥusayn b. ʿAlî*, n. 3: 464, Ibn Qûlûya al-Qummî., *Kâmil al-ziyârât*, bb. 16, n. 4: 122, Ibn Shahrâshûb., *Manâqib âl Abî Ṭâlib*, vol. IV, bb. *fî imâmat Abî ʿAbd Allâh al-Ḥusayn*: 57, al-Astarâbâḏî., *Ta'wîl al-âyât al-bâhira fî faḍl al-ʿitra al-ṭâhira*: 563, al-Maǧlisî., *Biḥâr al-anwâr*, vol. XLIII, bb. 11, n. 21: 246, n. 31: 253, vol. XLIV, bb. 30, n. 16: 231, vol. LIII, bb. 29, n. 126: 102, vol. LXVI, bb. 37: 266). In another account, Muḥammad tells Fâṭima that he has had a vision of God in 'a most beautiful form' (*fî aḥsan ṣûra*), and who declared al-Ḥusayn the first of the martyrs from first to last (Ibn Qûlûya al-Qummî., *Kâmil al-ziyârât*, bb. 21, n. 1: 140, n. 2: 70, al-Maǧlisî., *Biḥâr al-anwâr*, vol. XLIV, bb. 30, n. 29: 238). The books of *aḥâdîṯ* abound with these stories, related with an assortment of details. The Sunnî transmitter al-Ḫawârizmî, for example, dedicates a whole chapter of his *Maqtal al-Ḥusayn* to relating them from various sources, while a number of his Sunnî colleagues, including Ibn Ḥanbal in his *Musnad*, al-Nîsâbûrî in his *Kitâb al-mustadrak ʿalâ al-ṣaḥîḥayn* and al-Ṭabarî in his *Ḏaḫâ'ir al-ʿuqbâ*, relate the story in various settings, sometimes in an angelic visitation, sometimes in a vision, always containing the same strand of a tragic augury (Ibn Ḥanbal., *Musnad*, vol. I, *Musnad ʿAlî b. Abî Ṭâlib*, n. 648: 184–185; vol. IV, *Musnad Anas b. Mâlik*, n. 13539: 482, n. 13796: 527, al-Tirmiḏî., *Sunan*, vol. IX, bk. 50 (*Kitâb al-manâqib*), bb. *al-Ḥasan wa-l-Ḥusayn*, n. 3774:333, al-Nîsâbûrî., *Kitâb (Talḫîs) al-mustadrak ʿalâ al-ṣaḥîḥayn*, vol. III, bk. 31 (*Kitâb maʿrifat al-ṣaḥâba*), bb. *awwal faḍâ'il Abî ʿAbd Allâh al-Ḥusayn b. ʿAlî*, n. 4890: 213, vol. IV, bk. 31 (*Kitâb maʿrifat al-ṣaḥâba*), *Ḏikr Umm Salama*, nn. 6843, 6844: 101, vol. IV, bk. 47 (*Taʿbîr al-ru'yâ*), n. 8282: 553–554, al-Ḫawârizmî., *Maqtal al-Ḥusayn*, Part I, bb. *Faḍâ'il Fâṭima al-Zahrâ' bt. rasûl Allâh*, Ibn al-Aṯîr., *al-Kâmil fî-l-târîḫ*, vol. III: 169, al-Ṭabarî., *Ḏaḫâ'ir al-ʿuqbâ*: 147–148, al-Hayṯamî., *Maǧmaʿ al-zawâ'id wa-manbaʿ al-fawâ'id*, vol. IX, bb. *manâqib al-Ḥusayn*: 189–190, 193, al-ʿAsqalânî., *Tahḏîb al-tahḏîb*, vol. II, bb. *al-ḥâ'*: 347. Added to this is a strand of *iṯnâ ʿasharî* theology positing that each Imâm possesses a deposit of esoteric and exoteric knowledge transmitted from one Imâm to the next, although, as Momen points out, the extent of the knowledge is not agreed upon by the scholars, and the majority agree that it does not necessarily include an inherent knowledge of the future (MOMEN M., *An Introduction to Shi'i Islam. The History and Doctrines of Twelver Shi'ism*, Yale Uni-

receive letters and emissaries from Kûfa, begging him to lead an insurrection and pledging assistance. He left Mecca, finally, without having completed the Pilgrimage rites (having heard that enemies had arrived among the pilgrims and intended to shed his blood there), thus beginning the calamitous journey that would end at Karbalâʾ. This fate seemed apparent to a number of his friends and companions as al-Ḥusayn prepared to leave Mecca, but the commentators insist that it was a destiny preordained by God, aside from any political consequences that may have determined it. His journey from Mecca to Kûfa continued, despite unnerving reports of the capriciousness of the Kûfans (who had promised him their aid), the mass of military might opposing him and the desertion of a substantial number of his supporters. Aside from disheartening reports, efforts to dissuade him and attempts to intercept him, the texts give the sense that as the journey proceeded, there was increasing despair and hopelessness, not only of help but also of the possibility of negotiations. Some dispute al-Ḥusayn's resoluteness; there appears to have been a point at which he was ready to accept one of a number of possible compromises, although this is not an opinion unanimously held.

The group traveling with him diminished as many, who had been anticipating conquer, began to experience increasing doubts about his fate. With the arrival of a large group of horsemen sent to intercept him, and the warnings of its leader, al-Ḥusayn, having led both groups in prayer, insisted upon the pledges of allegiance he had received and asked for that those pledges now be honoured. He also offered to go back should the people of Kûfa give some sign that they were displeased with his coming. No such undertaking was received from Kûfa. We are also told that he used this opportunity to articulate the reasons for his risk and the jeopardy into which he was bringing his family; an oppressive ruler was violating

---

versity Press, New Haven 1985: 156). However, as noted later in this work, some sources suggest al-Ḥusayn's apparent willingness to negotiate a different outcome, as well as attempts by people close to him, including the husband of Zaynab, to dissuade him from undertaking such a venture, casting doubt on his certainty that his foreordained death would take place at Karbalâʾ.

the sanctions of God, opposing the *Sunna* of Muḥammad and ill-treating one of God's servants. To desist in fighting such a ruler would earn one a place in the Fire.

The rest of the story is both swift and grim; al-Ḥusayn and his small remnant are deprived of access to water and subsequently, on the 10th of Muḥarram, are massacred one by one by the sizable opposing force. All the elements of Karbalâʾ and the days surrounding it would be remembered and accentuated in their telling, in the traditions that grew up around them and in the remembrance services, so decisive a part of Shîʿî ritual.

In terms of the lead up to Karbalâʾ, the battle itself, and its immediate consequences, I have followed the chronology of al-Ṭabarî in his *Kitâb aḫbâr al-rusul wa-l-mulûk* ('The Annals of Messengers and Kings'), bearing in mind that he omits a number of important incidents concerning Zaynab, including the night voices that she hears at al-Ḫuzaymiyya and the challenge that she delivers to ʿUmar b. Saʿd b. Abî al-Waqqâṣ, commander of Yazîd's forces. In an attempt to trace the movements of Zaynab in the events in which she is directly or indirectly involved, I have added to al-Ṭabarî's chronology the key incidents that are missing. Accordingly, al-Ṭabarî's chronology (1–11), with additions (A–F), is:

BEFORE KARBALÂʾ

A. The al-Ḫuzaymiyya night voices (omitted by al-Ṭabarî, but also by most other transmitters)

1. The clamour of battle and al-Ḥusayn's dream (from Abû Miḫnaf)

2. The dirge of al-Ḥusayn (from Abû Miḫnaf)

IN THE COURSE OF THE BATTLE

3. The death of ʿAlî al-Akbar b. al-Ḥusayn (from Abû Miḫnaf)

4. The boy whom Zaynab cannot restrain (from Abû Miḫnaf)

B. The emergence of ʿAli b. al-Ḥusayn and Umm Kulṯûm (omitted by al-Ṭabarî and most others)

5. The killing of al-Ḥusayn's infant son, ʿAbd Allah b. al-Ḥusayn

6. The boy with pearl earrings

7. Zaynab emerges from her tent and challenges ʿUmar b. Saʿd (from Abû Miḫnaf)

8. Zaynab's lament at the departure from Karbalâ' for Kûfa (from Abû Miḫnaf)

AFTER KARBALÂ'

C. Zaynab's Kûfa protest (omitted by al-Ṭabarî)

D. Zaynab's lament upon seeing al-Ḥusayn's head (omitted by al-Ṭabarî)

9. The Zaynab-Ibn Ziyâd dialogues (from Abû Miḫnaf)

10. Zaynab before Yazîd (from Abû Miḫnaf)

E. Zaynab's lament upon seeing al-Ḥusayn's head (omitted by al-Ṭabarî)

F. Zaynab's protest before Yazîd (omitted by al-Ṭabarî)

11. The return to Medina

While many of the earlier incidents are single events, the reports depicting Zaynab after Karbalâ' encompass a collection of important encounters. The Zaynab-Ibn Ziyâd dialogues incorporate descriptions of Zaynab in disguise, hidden among her maids, the words exchanged between her and an irascible Ibn Ziyâd, the judicious intervention of Ibn Ḥurayṯ, Ibn Ziyâd's evaluation of Zaynab's character and, ultimately, Zaynab's agency in saving ʿAli b. al-Ḥusayn. Similarly, the Zaynab-Yazîd dialogues comprise the issue of Yazîd's volatile mood swings, Zaynab's lamentation upon seeing her brother's decapitated head and her protest to Yazîd, the unseemly demands of a red-headed Syrian and Zaynab's arbitration in saving her niece, the momentous bartering of Qur'ânic verses between Yazîd and the fourth Imâm, and Yazîd's cryptic accommodation of the group and dispatching of the survivors back to Medina.

Seeking a broad-spectrum perspective of Zaynab, I have attempted to use an eclectic mix of Sunnî and Shîʿî sources, a more comprehensive list of which can be found at the beginning of this work. It goes without saying that many of the classical authors did not restrict themselves to one particular genre or field of expertise, so that they are not easily classifiable; al-Dînawarî, for example, wrote with the same facility on botany and metallurgy as he did on history. Amidst the more important Sunnî historians and biographers, I have concentrated, among others, on the following texts:

1. Ibn Saʿd in his *Kitâb al-ṭabaqât al-kabîr* ('The Great Book of Lists'); as Hussein notes, none of the popular printed editions of Baṣra-born Ibn Saʿd's *Kitâb al-ṭabaqât* have included the entries for al-Ḥusayn, so that one is compelled to rely upon the later publication of a critical edition of the al-Ḥusayn entry.[41]

2. al-Balâḏurî, who in his *Kitâb ansâb al-ashrâf* ('Genealogies of the Nobles') showed himself not indifferent to al-Ḥusayn and to his cause.

3. al-Dînawarî, the polymath contemporary of al-Balâḏurî, in his *Kitâb al-aḫbâr al-ṭiwâl* ('The Lengthy Annals'); something of an Umayyad apologist, al-Dînawarî has left us a key narration about the Karbalâʾ event.

4. al-Ṭabarî in his *Kitâb aḫbâr al-rusul wa-l-mulûk* ('The Annals of Messengers and Kings'), whose detailed accounts of the Karbalâʾ events provide a crucial chronology for the battle events. He (like so many others after him, such as al-Masʿûdî, al-Mufîd, al-Shahrastânî, al-Ḫawârizmî, Ibn al-Ğawzî, Ibn al-Aṯîr) is transmitting in the main from Abû Miḫnaf, who was writing 150 years before him.[42]

5. al-Baġdâdî, writing a century after al-Ṭabarî and as famous for his preaching as he was for his scholarship, in his *Târîḫ Baġdâd* ('The History of Baghdad').

---

[41] HUSSEIN A.J., *A Developmental Analysis of Depictions of the Events of Karbalāʾ in Early Islamic History*, PhD diss., University of Chicago, 2001: 18.

[42] In al-Ṭabarî's account, notes Shoshan, "which is mainly based on Abū Mikhnaf (on occasion, in the recension of Hishām Ibn al-Kalbī) – a Ḥusayn sympathizer – one is able to observe, more than in other contemporary sources, the version that would be amplified in future Shīʿite circles." Cf. SHOSHAN B., *Poetics of Islamic Historiography: Deconstruction of Tabarī's History*, Brill, Leiden 2004: 234. Through the truncated versions found in historians such as al-Yaʿqûbî, al-Dinâwarî, al-Masʿûdî, Ibn Kaṯîr, and al-Balâḏurî, al-Ḥusayn's martyrdom has been diffused into the psyche of the entire Islamic community, and not the Shîʿa alone.

6. Ibn ʿAsâkir in his *Târîḫ madînat Dimashq* ('History of the City of Damascus'), in which he furnishes us with a substantial amount of information about al-Ḥusayn and Zaynab.

7. Turkish-born Ibn al-Aṯîr in his *al-Kâmil fî al-târîḫ* ('The Complete History') and in his intriguingly named *Usd al-ġâba fî maʿrifat al-ṣaḥâba* ('The Lions of the Forest in the Knowledge of the Companions').

8. Ibn Kaṯîr, equally proficient in *tafsîr* and *aḥâdîṯ* studies as he was in history, in his wide-ranging *al-Bidâya wa-l-nihâya* ('The Beginning and the End').

9. Damascus-born al-Ḏahabî in his *Siyar aʿlâm al-nubalâʾ* ('Biographies of the Eminent Figures among the Nobles'), with its two separate entries for al-Ḥusayn, one of them dealing expressly with his martyrdom.

10. The Meccan-based al-ʿIṣâmî in his *Simṭ al-nuǧûm al-ʿawâlî fî anbâʾ al-awâʾil wa-l-tawâlî* ('The Highest Thread of Stars in the Reports of the Ancestors and the Succession').

11. The al-Azhar scholar al-Shablanǧî in his *Nûr al-abṣâr fî manâqib âl bayt al-nabî al-muḫtâr* ('Light of Insights in the Virtues of the People of the House of the Chosen Prophet'); he wrote his work in fulfilment of a vow he had made should he be healed of an eye disease.

Among their Shîʿî counterparts I have included:

1. al-Yaʿqûbî in his *Târîḫ* ('History'); if al-Yaʿqûbî was not, in fact, a Shîʿa, and this is a moot point, he evinces a strong Shîʿî predisposition.

2. al-Masʿûdî in his *Murûǧ al-ḏahab* ('Meadows of Gold'); like al-Yaʿqûbî, he is far more economical and at times sparse in his treatment of the Karbalâʾ event.

3. Ibn Ṭâʾûs, writing 300 years after them, in his *Kitâb al-luhûf fî qatlâ al-ṭufûf* ('The Book of Sorrows over those Killed on the

Banks')[43] and his *Kitâb al-iqbâl bi-l-aʿmâl al-ḥasana* ('The Book of Turning to Good Actions').

4. al-Irbilî in his *Kashf al-ġumma fî maʿrifat al-aʾimma* ('The Unveiling of Grief in the Knowledge of the Imâms') and who, like his fellow Shîʿî historian and theologian Ibn Ṭâʾûs, offers a far more extensive account of events.[44]

Among the compilers of the indispensable *maqtal* literature, those written accounts dealing specifically with the murder of al-Ḥusayn and his companions as well as the killing of other members of the *ahl al-bayt*, I have chosen four authors:

1. Abû Miḫnaf, the Sunnî historian who died within 100 years of Karbalâʾ and whose early *maqtal*, with its sensitivity towards al-Ḥusayn, would provide much of the content of al-Ṭabarî's *Kitâb aḫbâr al-rusul wa-l-mulûk*.

2. al-Ḫawârizmî, the Sunnî Ḥanafî scholar and pupil of al-Zamaḫsharî, in his *Maqtal al-Ḥusayn* ('The Killing of al-Ḥusayn')

---

43 Sometimes *Kitâb al-luhûf ʿalâ qatlâ al-ṭufûf* or *al-Malhûf ʿalâ qatlâ al-ṭufûf*.

44 As will be noted at the end of this work, by the time Ibn Ṭâʾûs was writing his panegyrical *Kitâb al-luhûf* in the middle of the 7th/13th century, that Islamic strand or 'tendency' (*tashayyuʿ*) that would eventually come to be called 'Shîʿa', together with its distinctive vision of Karbalâʾ and of the aura surrounding the members of the *ahl al-bayt*, had undergone a considerable transformation. Ibn Ṭâʾûs' view of the battle, for example, and of Zaynab's role in those days, was significantly amplified, in comparison to, for example, the more prosaic accounts of the Sunnî historian al-Ṭabarî, writing three centuries earlier. Writing six centuries after the battle, Ibn Ṭâʾûs' work encompasses hundreds of years of theological reflection, loss of authority, persecution, spiritual embellishment and, running deeply through the Shîʿî ethos, the steady realization that they would never attain to the power they maintained was their due, and the concomitant turning increasingly to a supernatural, other-worldly potency.

imbued as it is with sympathy for al-Ḥusayn,[45] and in his *al-Manâqib* ('The Virtues of ʿAlî b. Abî Ṭâlib')

3. al-Iṣfahânî, Shîʿî poet and transmitter of *aḥâdît*, in his *Maqâtil al-ṭâlibîyyîn* ('The Killings of the Members of the Ṭâlib Line').

4. Ibn Namâ al-Ḥillî, scion of a renowned family of Shîʿî scholars, in his *Muṯîr al-aḥzân wa munîr subul al-ashğân* ('The Stimulant of Griefs and the Radiant Ways of Sorrows').

Among the plentiful Shîʿî transmitters of *aḥâdîṯ*, I have used the works of:

1. al-Ḫaṣîbî in his *al-Hidâya* (*al-Kubrâ*) ('The Guidance'), although admittedly, he was a member of the ʿAlawiyya, and his transmissions are distrusted by a sizable number Shîʿî scholars.

2. Ibn Qûlûya al-Qummî, pupil of the acclaimed al-Kulaynî and an expert in jurisprudence and *aḥâdîṯ*, sometimes referred to as Ibn Qulawayh, in his *Kâmil al-ziyârât* ('The Complete Visitations').

3. al-Ṣadûq, the prolific *shayḫ* raised in Qum, educated by his father and nicknamed 'Ibn Babawayh', chiefly in his *Kitâb al-amâlî fî al-aḥâdîṯ wa-l-aḫbâr* ('Book of Dictations in Traditions and Reports') although I have, at times, referred to a number of his other texts.

4. *Shayḫ* al-Mufîd, pupil of Ibn Qulawayh and al-Ṣadûq, in his *al-Irshâd fî maʿrifat ḥuğağ Allâh ʿalâ al-ʿibâd* ('Guidance in the Knowledge of the Proofs of God concerning Humanity') and his *al-Amâlî li-l-Mufîd* ('The Dictations of al-Mufîd').

---

[45] Al-Ḫawârizmî's work, notes Hussein, "is at times so dramatic and its depictions so emotionally charged that its effects were significant not only on Shīʿīs but Sunnī perceptions as well." He goes on to note its influence on Ibn Ṭâʾûs in his *Kitâb al-luhûf fî qatlâ al-ṭufûf*, and even years later in the works of the resolutely Sunnî scholar al-Ḏahabî (d. 748/1348). There is, in short, "a dramatic difference between the pre-Khwārazmī and post-Khwārazmī Sunnī perceptions of Husayn at Karbalāʾ." Cf. HUSSEIN A.J., *A Developmental Analysis of Depictions of the Events of Karbalāʾ in Early Islamic History*, 2001: 284–285.

5. The Persian *Shayḫ* al-Ṭûsî, himself a pupil of al-Mufîd and known as *Shayḫ al-Ṭâʾifa* ('head of the sect') in his *al-Amâlî fî al-ḥadîṯ* ('Dictations').

6. al-Fattâl al-Nîsâbûrî in his *Rawḍat al-wâʿiẓîn wa-tabṣirat al-muttaʿiẓîn* ('The Garden of the Preachers and the Enlightenment of the Exhortations'), a work detailing the history and virtues of the prophets and the members of the *ahl al-bayt* and in which he transmits from, among others, *Shayḫ* al-Ṭûsî.

7. Ibn Shahrâshûb in his highly-regarded *Manâqib âl Abî Ṭâlib* ('The Virtues of the Family of Abû Ṭâlib'), a massive work on the virtues of the family of ʿAlî, and in which he draws greatly upon al-Fattâl al-Nîsâbûrî.

8. The less well-known al-Daylamî in his *Irshâd al-qulûb* ('Guidance of the Hearts').

9. al-Ḥurr al-ʿÂmilî in his encyclopedic collection *Tafṣîl wasâʾil al-shîʿa ilâ taḥṣîl masâʾil al-sharîʿa* ('Exposition of the Means of the Shîʿa towards the Studying of the Issues of the Law'), in his *al-Ǧawâhir al-saniyya fî-l-aḥâdîṯ al-qudsiyya* ('The Shining Jewels in the Sacred Traditions'), and in his *Iṯbât al-hudât bi-l-nuṣûṣ wa-l-muʿǧizât* ('Proofs of the Guides in the Texts and the Miracles').

10. Two other encyclopaedists in the transmission of *aḥâdîṯ*, al-Maǧlisî in his mammoth *Biḥâr al-anwâr* ('Oceans of Light') and al-Baḥrânî in his *ʿAwâlim al-ʿulûm wa al-maʿârif al-aḥwâl min al-âyât wa-l-aḫbâr wa-l-aqwâl* ('The Realms of Opinions and the Knowledge of the Circumstances from the Verses, the Reports and the Testimonies').

11. al-Ǧazâʾirî, one of al-Maǧlisî's students, in his *Riyâḍ al-abrâr fî manâqib al-aʾimma al-aṭhâr* ('The Gardens of the Righteous in the Virtues of the Pure Imâms').

12. al-Ṭabarsî (called so by Brockelmann, but in other texts Ṭabrisî) in his *Mustadrak al-wasâʾil* ('Supplement of the Means'), an addendum to the work of al-Ḥurr al-ʿÂmilî.

Among their Sunnî counterparts, I have included:

1. The Persian al-Ḥâkim al-Nîsâbûrî, one of the leading scholars of his era, in his *Kitâb al-mustadrak ʿalâ al-ṣaḥîḥayn* ('Supplement to the Two *Ṣaḥîḥs*')

2. The Spanish Mâlikî judge, Ibn ʿAbd al-Barr in his *al-Istiʿâb fî maʿrifat al-aṣḥâb* ('Comprehension in the Knowledge of the Companions')

3. The erudite Ḥanbalî and renowned hunter of heresy, Ibn al-Ğawzî, in his *Ṣifat al-ṣafwa* ('The Quality of the Best'), not to be confused with his grandson, Sibṭ al-Ğawzî, author of *Tadkirat ḫawâṣṣ al-umma bi-ḏikr ḫaṣâʾiṣ al-aʾimma* ('The Memento of the Attributes of the Nation in the Remembrance of the Qualities of the Imâms').

4. al-Ṭabarî in his *Ḏaḫâʾir al-ʿuqbâ* ('The Treasures of the Final Attainment').[46]

5. al-Haytamî, not to be confused with the better known Ibn Ḥağar al-Haytamî, in his *Mağmaʿ al-zawâʾid wa-manbaʿ al-fawâʾid* ('The Collection of the Appendices and the Fountainhead of Merits').

6. al-ʿAsqalânî in his *al-Iṣâba fî tamyîz al-ṣaḥâba* ('The Wound in the Partiality of the Companions') and in his *Tahḏîb al-tahḏîb* ('Rectification of the Rectification').

In the main, I have looked at the writings of two Shîʿî exegetes:

1. al-Ṭabarsî in his *Kitâb al-iḥtiğâğ ʿalâ ahl al-liğâğ* ('Book of Remonstrance against the People of the Depths'), his *Tâğ al-mawâlîd* ('Crown of the Births'), and his *Iʿlâm al-warâ bi-aʿlâm al-hudâ* ('Notification of Mankind Concerning the Signs of Guidance').

2. al-Baḥrânî in his *al-Burhân fî tafsîr al-qurʾân* ('The Evidence in the Exegesis of the Qurʾân').

Other sources include the Shîʿî theologian al-ʿÂmilî in his *al-Ṣirâṭ al-mustaqîm ilâ mustaḥaqq al-taqdîm fî al-imâma* ('The Straight Path to

[46] There are at least three authors named al-Ṭabarî, and Sezgin warns of the danger of confusing them. There is, firstly, the Shîʿî scholar, Abû Ğaʿfar b. Rustam al-Ṭabarî (c. 224/839: cf. GAL S. I: 217, GAS I: 540). There is, secondly, the Sunnî Muḥib al-Dîn al-Ṭabarî al-Makkî al-Shâfiʿî (d. 684/1295: cf. GAL I: 361), the author of *Ḏaḫâʾir al-ʿuqbâ*. Thirdly, there is the Sunnî historian Abû Ğaʿfar Muḥammad al-Ṭabarî (d. 310/923: cf. GAS I: 232 and GAL S I: 217), author of *Kitâb aḫbâr al-rusul wa-l-mulûk*.

the Deserving of Guardianship in the Imamate'), al-Ṭabarî in his *Dalâ'il al-imâma* ('Proofs of the Imamate') and his *Kitâb al-mustarshid fî imâmat ʿAlî b. Abî Tâlib* ('The Book of Seeking Guidance in the Imamate of ʿAlî b. Abî Tâlib') and Ibn Abî Ṭâhir Ṭayfûr in his *Balâġât al-nisâ'* ('Reports of the Women').

This work has a number of diverse aims:

It offers a fresh reading of the life of the eldest daughter of ʿAlî and Fâṭima; 'fresh', because as yet, there exists no substantial biography based on the primary Arabic Shîʿî and Sunnî sources. There are certainly biographies quoted in this work; those by Bilgrami and Shahin, as well as Karbâssî's entry on Zaynab in his work on the women around al-Ḥusayn. As they stand, these are of little academic value, presenting as they do an almost entirely hagiographical portrait of Zaynab, with few or any references to the historical sources. They are referenced nonetheless, so as to offer to the reader a glimpse into what contemporary popular piety believes about Zaynab, even if the events or virtues they articulate about her are not found in the classical texts of history or *aḥâdîṯ*. This work, instead, attempts to access those classical sources, starting with the earliest ones that make reference to Zaynab (such as the histories of Abû Miḫnaf, Ibn Saʿd and al-Balâḏurî) and attentive to the development in her character as the sources get older. It is to be noted that even the earliest sources employed (except for Abû Miḫnaf) postdate Zaynab by more than 100 years; Ibn Saʿd died over a century-and-a-half after Zaynab and al-Ṭabarî, whose historical chronicle provides a useful chronology for Zaynab at Karbalâ', one hundred years after Ibn Saʿd.

Considering the centrality of the Karbalâ' event for the Shîʿa in general and the *iṯnâ ʿasharî* in particular,[47] a second aim of the

[47] There are significant differences in the approach to Karbalâ' among the divergent Shîʿî groupings. The Zaydî follow the rudimental narrative, listing the names of the extended household killed; this is congruent with Zaydî theology, believing as they do that valid politico-religious authority is found with Muḥammad's family and descendants, thus rendering crucial the death of any member of that family. Unlike the *iṯnâ ʿasharî*, the Zaydî narratives, although resonant with tragedy and heroism, do not envisage the event as part of a cosmic or eschatological strug-

work is to situate Zaynab in the days before, during and immediately after the battle, chronicling her participation and noting especially her verbal interventions in favour of her brother al-Ḥusayn and her nephew ʿAlî b. al-Ḥusayn.

A third aim is an attempt to trace the composite figure of Zaynab, as she is presented by the earliest primary sources, both Sunnî and Shîʿa, through the embellishment of her figure by later, mostly Shîʿî commentators, until the reinterpretation of her figure as a model for the contemporary Muslim woman. In this, there are three movements worth watching; firstly, the accounts of Zaynab at Karbalâʾ, revealing very human traits of fear and weakness, as described by an early historian like al-Ṭabarî. Secondly, there is the Zaynab embellished by later hagiographic accounts, which present an idealistic childhood and a Zaynab who is a model of piety, knowledge and feminine reserve. Thirdly, there is a fresh image of Zaynab as a model for contemporary women in society; a vigorous combatant of injustice and, at times, an almost fearless revolutionary. Here, we cannot fail to take into account some of the more contemporary arguments among Shîʿî scholars and commentators about what they term 'authentic' and 'inauthentic' readings of Karbalâʾ and, consequently, of Zaynab's place there. The aim is not to dismiss the more contemporary reading of Zaynab's life as much as to suggest that an early reading presents a woman who may well

gle between good and evil; it is physical historical details and lineage that holds their attention, and not the supernatural. The Ismâʿîlî have no one authoritative reading of Karbalâʾ; the majority of the Ismâʿîlî (the Nizârî) follow less emotional forms of remembrance, preferring the story stripped of any greater theological significance.The *iṯnâ ʿasharî* accounts present the most detailed amplified reports of the Karbalâʾ story, which lies at the core of their spirituality and and distintiveness. The *iṯnâ ʿasharî* Shîʿî Karbalâʾ is detailed and impassioned, permeated by cosmological and esoteric implications. However, it is a narrative, notes Haider, that has grown and developed over a period of years, from vary basic elegies for the fallen to the complex annual rituals in the modern period. Cf. HAIDER N., *Shîʾi Islam: An Introduction*, Cambridge University Press, New York 2014: 66–81.

be closer to the daily experience of numerous contemporary women.

A final, more personal aim, is a theological appreciation of Zaynab by a non-Muslim, offering the possibility of drawing potential parallels between her and the figure of Mary in Roman Catholic theology and piety. While such parallels are normal drawn between Mary and the Maryam of the Qur'ân, or between Mary and Fâṭima, mother of Zaynab, powerful female figures are sadly rare in Islam and Christianity, making Zaynab a prime candidate for such a comparative theology.

It is a glimpse at Zaynab, and at the possibilities of a 'Zaynabian' theology and spirituality, through various lenses; through the eyes of the hagiographers, those of the historians, who ostensibly relate eyewitness accounts,[48] those of pious Shî'î devotees and those of more contemporary socio-political commentators who used her as a rallying point and exemplar.

It is my hope that this brief monograph will illustrate that the contemporary reshaping of Zaynab's life should in no way detract from cultivating devotion to the Zaynab of earlier, more quietist and mournful pieties, but instead brings to the fore some of her qualities crucial to a time of crisis; that this stirring and articulate woman, deeply pious, candid in the face of tyranny, willing to speak the truth in the face of enormous personal danger, also lived with profound anguish and loss. Even more, I hope to encourage imitation of Zaynab as achievable, not only for women and men who live on what someone once called society's seismic fault lines, deeply engaged in justice struggles, but also for those whose engagement with daily life may be given over to entirely more ordinary and mundane things; I am thinking particularly of those who suffer an authentic martyrdom by pouring out their lives and energy in the conscientious endurance of everyday life. It is these especially whom, I trust, would reread Zaynab's story in the light of faith and draw fresh strength from this astonishing and gutsy woman.

---

[48] Noting, as ever, that al-Ṭabarî, who died in 310/923, postdates Zaynab and Karbalâ' by 250 years, but that the major incidents he relays concerning Zaynab in and around Karbalâ' are from eyewitness accounts transmitted by Abû Miḫnaf (d. 157/774).

Chapter One. In the House of Prophecy

Alas! Mourning has begun.
Alas! The moon of grief has shown her face.

A number of texts, each of them slightly different in the telling, chronicle for their readers an enigmatic story; in *Biḥâr al-anwâr*, al-Mağlisî's encyclopedic collection of *aḥâdîṯ*, he relates it from al-Râwandî's[1] *al-Ḫarâ'iğ wa-l-ğarâ'iḥ fî-l-muʿğizât* and from Ibn Shahrâshûb's *Manâqib âl Abî Ṭâlib.* In the days of Caliph al-Mutawakkil (d. 247/861), the story goes, a woman appeared, contending that she was in fact Zaynab, daughter of ʿAlî and Fâṭima and granddaughter of Muḥammad. Not surprisingly, al-Mutawakkil expressed vigorous doubts, since this was a young woman, while more than two hundred years had elapsed since the time of Muḥammad. The woman's response was that her grandfather had stroked her with his hand and had asked God to restore her youthfulness to her every forty (in some texts, fifty) years. Ostensibly, she had been transported to Syria, living there in anonymity, and this was the first time, and only because of necessity, that she was making an appearance.

Al-Mutawakkil then summoned the elders of the family of Abû Ṭâlib and the descendants of al-ʿAbbâs and the Quraysh, to inform them about her and ask their opinion. Since the death of Zaynab had in fact been reported in a particular year, al-Mutawakkil felt impelled to ask the woman what she thought about this. In reply, she insisted that the reports were lies and falsehoods:

---

[1] Quṭb al-Dîn Abû al-Ḥusayn Saʿîd b. Hibat Allâh b. Abî al-Ḥasan al-Râwandî (d. 573/1177: cf. GAL S. I: 624).

"My affairs were hidden from the people," she insisted, "and neither death nor life acknowledged me." Al-Mutawakkil then asked the elders if they had any evidence that the woman was lying, and they replied in the negative, suggesting that perhaps Ibn al-Riḍâ, a descendant of the Imâm who died in 202/818 – in a few texts, named as his grandson Imâm al-Hâdî (d. 254/868) – possessed some evidence that they did not. In some transmissions, this descendant denounced the woman as a liar because of the certainty that Zaynab had died in a particular year, in a particular month and on a particular day (although the texts never reveal these dates). In a more specific ending, the descendant announced that there was in fact a sign to determine the genuine offspring of ʿAlî; it was that lions would never attack them. The plan was then to put the woman among lions, and if they did not harm her in any way, it would be a sign that she had been telling the truth. At this, the woman took fright, and turning to al-Mutawakkil, cried out: "Commander of the Faithful, by God, God, he means to kill me!" She then mounted a donkey and began to exclaim: "I am, in truth, Zaynab the liar!"[2]

It is an arcane story, but not a bad one with which to begin our hunt for the authentic Zaynab, whose life, at first glance, would dishearten any would-be chroniclers; at the very most, one could cull some biographical notes from the sources and hagiography available, but little more than that, and certainly no comprehensive biography.

Zaynab was born in Medina sometime after the 622 emigration (*hiğra*), plausibly in the year 6/627, to ʿAlî b. Abî Ṭâlib and Fâṭima al-Zahrâʾ, Muḥammad's son-in-law and daughter.[3] Scholars wrangle over the precise dating of her birth, although significantly less so than over that of her mother Fâṭima. Sources suggest that

---

[2] Cf. for example al-Râwandî., *al-Ḫarâʾiğ wa-l-ğarâʾiḥ fî-l-muʿğizât*, bb. 11: 405, Ibn Shahrâshûb., *Manâqib âl Abî Ṭâlib*, vol. IV, bb. *faṣl fî âyâti-hi*: 416, al-ʿÂmilî., *al-Ṣirâṭ al-mustaqîm ilâ mustaḥaqq al-taqdîm fî al-imâma*, vol. II, n. 10: 204, al-Ḥurr al-ʿÂmilî., *Iṯbât al-hudât bi-l-nuṣûṣ wa-l-muʿğizât*, vol. IV, n. 43: 476, al-Mağlisî., *Biḥâr al-anwâr*, vol. L, bb. 3, n. 35: 149, bb. 4, n. 14: 204.

[3] al-Balâḏurî., *Kitâb ansâb al-ashrâf*, vol. III: 393.

Zaynab's birth was in the fifth year of the *hiğra*, on Wednesday 5th Ğumâdâ al-awwal (2nd October) 6/627. Karbâssî holds that it was in fact in Medina on Tuesday 5th Ğumâdâ al-awwal in the sixth year of the *hiğra*, although he notes that some say the first day of Shaʿbân of that year.[4] The debate, therefore, concerns both the day and the year; 5th Ğumâdâ al-awwal or 1st Shaʿbân, in the fifth or the sixth year of the *hiğra*. Qutbuddin resorts to the 'early' days of Shaʿbân, in the year 6/627; Bilgrami and Shahin posit the fifth year of the *hiğra* but offer no sources. Rizvi claims 5th Ğumâdâ al-awwal in the fifth year of the *hiğra*, one year after the birth of Zaynab's brother al-Ḥusayn, but he too offers no sources.[5] Al-Kâshânî suggests 5th Ğumâdâ al-awwal in either the the fifth or sixth year year of the *hiğra*, rejecting those who put it as late as the ninth year; this would be an unrealistic date considering the death of Fâṭima in 11/632 (having given birth, after Zaynab, to a second daughter, Umm Kulṯûm, and by all accounts miscarried one other child).[6]

---

[4] KARBÂSSÎ M.S., *Muʿğam anṣâr al-Ḥusayn – al-nisâʾ*, Hussaini Charitable Trust, London 2009: 334–5.

[5] QUTBUDDIN B.T., "Zaynab bint Ali" in Lindsay Jones (ed.), *Encyclopedia of Religion*, 2nd edn., Thomson Gale, New York 2005: 9937, BILGRAMI M.H., *The Victory of Truth: The Life of Zaynab bint ʾAli*, 1986: 3, SHAHIN B., *Lady Zaynab*, Ansariyan, Qum 2002: 61, RIZVI A.A., *Bibi Zainab*, al-Raza Printers, Karachi 2007: 17.

[6] As to this child, a boy named al-Muḥsin or al-Muḥassin, there is some uncertainty, many of the Sunnî omitting any mention of him, or saying that he was born, but died in childhood; the Shîʿa remain adamant that Fâṭima miscarried because of physical violence perpetrated against her after Muḥammad's death. For mention of the boy among the Sunnî, cf. for e.g. Ibn Ḥanbal., *Musnad*, vol. I, *Musnad ʿAlî b. Abî Ṭâlib*, n. 769: 211–212, n. 953: 250–251, where his birth is recorded, n. 1370: 335 where it is omitted, al-Balâḏurî., *Kitâb ansâb al-ashrâf*, vol. I, *Azwâğ rasûl Allâh*, n. 865: 402, 404, al-Ḫawârizmî., *Maqtal al-Ḥusayn*, bk. 1, bb. *faḍâʾil Fâṭima al-Zahrâʾ bt. rasûl Allâh*, n. 73: 128, al-Ğawzî., *Ṣifat al-ṣafwa*, vol. II, *Fâṭima bt. rasûl Allâh*: 2, al-Ṭabarî., *Ḏaḫâʾir al-ʿuqbâ*, 55. Cf. AL-KÂSHÂNÎ A., *250 Karâma li-l-sayyida Zaynab wa-sayyidât bayt al-nubuwwa*, Dâr al-Ğawâdayn li-l-Ṭibâʿa wa-l-Nashr wa-al-Tawzîʿ, Beirut 2008: 12.

Muḥammad had moved his daughters Umm Kulṯûm and Fâṭima to Medina after the *hiğra* and, according to the Sunnî scholars, the marriage of ʿAlî and Fâṭima took place around 1–2/623 or 3/624,[7] when, the Sunnî maintain, Fâṭima was about nineteen or twenty. The Sunnî historian al-Ṭabarî, in harmony with some other scholars, places their marriage just before the end of the month of Ṣafar in 622, before the battles of Badr (1–2/623) and Uḥud (3/624).[8] A number of sources assert that ʿAlî and Fâṭima consummated the marriage upon his return from Badr; their first child, al-Hasan,[9] was born in the second year of the *hiğra*, followed, fifty days after his birth, by the conception of their second child, al-Ḥusayn.[10] Al-ʿIṣâmî transmits more than one strand suggesting that the marriage was either in the second or third year of the *hiğra*, some saying before the battle of Uḥud, others saying before Muḥammad married ʿÂʾisha, when Fâṭima was fifteen and ʿAlî

---

[7] Cf. for e.g. Ibn al-Aṯîr., *Usd al-ğâba fî maʿrifat al-ṣaḥâba*, vol. VI, bb. 7175 (*Fâṭima bt. Rasûl Allâh*): 223.

[8] al-Ṭabarî., *Kitâb aḫbâr al-rusul wa-l-mulûk*, vol. IV, n. 1273: 410, n. 1367: 485, al-Ḥâkim al-Nîsâbûrî., *Kitâb (Talḫîs) al-mustadrak ʿalâ al-ṣaḥîḥayn*, vol. III, bk. 31 *(Kitâb maʿrifat al-ṣaḥâba), Manâqib Fâṭima bt. rasûl Allâh*, n. 4807: 185, al-Ğawzî., *Ṣifat al-ṣafwa*, vol. II, *Fâṭima bt. rasûl Allâh*: 2, al-Ḏahabî., *al-ʿIbar fî aḫbâr al-bashar muntaḫab al-taʾrîḫ al-kabîr*, vol. I: 4, Ibn Ḥağar al-ʿAsqalânî., *Tahḏîb al-tahḏîb*, vol. XII, *Kitâb al-nisâʾ*, n. 4434: 441, al-Muttaqî al-Hindî., *Muntaḫab kanz al-ʿummâl* in the margins of *Musnad Ibn Ḥanbal*, vol. V: 99, al-ʿIṣâmî., *Simṭ al-nuğûm al-ʿawâlî*, vol. I, bb. 5: 425, al-Shablanğî., *Nûr al-abṣâr fî manâqib âl bayt al-nabî al-muḫtâr*, bb. *fî ḏikr manâqib ʿAlî b. Abî Ṭâlib*: 43.

[9] Ibn Saʿd., *Kitâb al-ṭabaqât al-kabîr*, vol. XII, bb. *ḏikr banât rasûl Allâh*, n. 4927 (*Fâṭima*): 21–24, it is posited here that the marriage took place five months after the *hiğra* and was consummated when ʿAlî returned from the battle of Badr and when Fâṭima was eighteen years old.

[10] al-Balâḏurî., *Kitâb ansâb al-ashrâf*, vol. I, *Azwâğ rasûl Allâh*, n. 864: 404, al-Ṭabarî., *Kitâb aḫbâr al-rusul wa-l-mulûk*, vol. IV, n. 1431: 537, who posits that al-Ḥasan was born in the third year of the *hiğra* (thus c. 4/625), with al-Ḥusayn conceived fifty days later; but in the same volume, n. 1367: 485, he concedes that some hold al-Ḥasan to have been born in the second year of the *hiğra*.

twenty-one.[11] ʿAbd al-Barr agrees with the ages, but places the marriage after Uḥud.[12] According to the Shîʿî scholars, who place Fâṭima's birth around 615, a whole ten years later than Sunnî reckonings, she was about seven or eight years of age when she was betrothed to ʿAlî (within the first year of the *hiǧra*).[13]

Writing in his *Kashf al-ġumma*, al-Irbilî informs us that the four children of ʿAlî and Fâṭima were al-Ḥasan, al-Ḥusayn, Zaynab al-Kubrâ ('the greater') and Zaynab al-Ṣuġrâ ('the younger'), whose *kunya* (pl. *kunâ*)[14] was Umm Kulṯûm. He takes note of the death of al-Muḥassin, the younger brother of al-Ḥasan and al-Ḥusayn, using the verb *saqaṭa*, which, observes Lane, indicates that the child was born abortively, but having a developed form.[15] It was a death, notes Ibn Shahrâshûb, transmitting from al-Qutayba's *Maʿârif*, resulting from an injury done to Fâṭima when she was pushed rough-

[11] al-Nasâʾî., *Kitâb al-ḫaṣâʾiṣ fî faḍl ʿAlî b. Abî Ṭâlib*: 5, Ibn al-Aṯîr., *Usd al-ġâba fî maʿrifat al-ṣaḥâba*, vol. VI, bb. 7175 (*Fâṭima bt. Rasûl Allâh*): 223, al-ʿIṣâmî., *Simṭ al-nuǧûm al-ʿawâlî*, vol. I, bb. 5: 425.

[12] Ibn ʿAbd al-Barr., *al-Istîʿâb fî maʿrifat al-aṣḥâb*, vol. IV, *Kitâb al-nisâʾ*, n. 4057: 1893. Cf. also Ibn al-Aṯîr., *Usd al-ġâba fî maʿrifat al-ṣaḥâba*, vol. VI, bb. 7175 (*Fâṭima bt. Rasûl Allâh*): 223, Ibn Kaṯîr., *al-Bidâya wa-l-nihâya*, vol. VI: 332.

[13] al-Yaʿqûbî., *Târîḫ*, vol. II: 42, al-Masʿûdî., *Murûǧ al-ḏahab*, vol. III, bb. 72, n. 1485: 22–23, bb. 73, n. 1486: 27–28.

[14] QUTBUDDIN B.T., "Zaynab bint Ali" in Lindsay Jones (ed.), *Encyclopedia of Religion*, 2nd edn., 2005: 9937, AL-KÂSHÂNÎ A., *250 Karâma li-l-sayyida Zaynab wa-sayyidât bayt al-nubuwwa*, 2008: 11. The authors provide no references for these appellations. A *kunya* is patronymic, comprising two parts: 'Abû' or 'Umm' in connection with a second term. It comes from the root meaning 'to speak of someone or something in an allusive way'. If the name is of a person, the *kunya* indicates the relationship of parent to child. It is possible to distinguish between this, the 'real' *kunya*, and a metaphorical, figurative *kunya*, in which this bond of kinship is impossible. For a succinct explanation of the components of Arabic names, cf. PIERCE M., *Twelve Infallible Men. The Imams and the Making of Shiʿism*, Harvard University Press, Cambridge Mass., 2016: 155.

[15] LANE E.W., *An Arabic-English Lexicon*, Librairie du Liban, Beirut 1968, vol. IV: 1380.

ly during an assault on her home.[16] Al-Ḥasan, al-Ḥusayn, Zaynab al-Kubrâ and Umm Kulṯûm are the four, insists al-Irbilî, who have sprung from the purity of Fâṭima the Virgin (*al-batûl*),[17] daughter of the Messenger of God.[18]

Al-Maǧlisî transmits that the marriage of ʿAlî and Fâṭima took place in the second year of the *hiǧra* and that the couple consummated it upon ʿAlî's return from Badr; he names the four children as al-Ḥasan, al-Ḥusayn, Zaynab al-Kubrâ and Umm Kulṯûm al-Kubrâ.[19] He notes that Ibn al-Ḥadîd in his *Sharḥ nahǧ al-balâġa* names the two girls as Umm Kulṯûm al-Kubrâ and Zaynab al-Kubrâ,[20] and observes the same of Ibn Manda al-Aṣfahânî in his *Kitâb al-maʿrifa* (who places the marriage as one year after the

---

[16] Ibn Shahrâshûb., *Manâqib âl Abî Ṭâlib*, vol. III, bb. *faṣl fî ḥilyati-hâ wa-tawârîḫ-hâ*: 358.

[17] The title *al-batûl*, as well as that of *al-ʿaḏrâʾ*, both rendered as 'the Virgin', are ascribed to Fâṭima in numerous *aḥâdîṯ*. Of all the theological and spiritual titles given to her, the designation 'virgin', remains the most enigmatic. Quite clearly speaking of a virginity that is not the same as the physical virginity of Maryam in the Qurʾân, Shîʿî Islam presents Fâṭima as married with (at least) four children, and nowhere suggests that any of these were not the result of sexual intercourse or that her marriage with ʿAlî was devoid of sexual relations. It is patently clear that Fâṭima must be declared a virgin if she is not to become in some sense 'secondary' to Maryam, whose virginity is underscored both in the Qurʾânic text and in the books of *aḥâdîṯ*. Nonetheless, the explanation of Fâṭima's virginity, unlike that of Maryam, is not of something physical, but of something esoteric. At no time is there a hint that any of her children are parallel to ʿÎsâ in that they are unfathered. Hers is a singularity that is expressed in multifaceted theology. Cf. CLOHESSY C.P., *Fatima, Daughter of Muhammad*, Gorgias Press, Piscataway 2009: 107–108.

[18] al-Irbilî., *Kashf al-ġumma fî maʿrifat al-aʾimma*, vol. I: 440–441. Cf. also AL-MÛSAWÎ M., *al-Kawṯar fî aḥwâl Fâṭima bt. al-nabî al-aṭhar*, vol. VII, ch. 17, nn.1/3858, 3/3860: 99, n. 5/3862: 99–100.

[19] al-Maǧlisî., *Biḥâr al-anwâr*, vol. XXII, bb. 1, n. 25: 167.

[20] As noted too by al-Mûsawî; cf. AL-MÛSAWÎ M., *al-Kawṯar fî aḥwâl Fâṭima bt. al-nabî al-aṭhar*, vol. VII, ch. 17, n. 11/3868: 102. Cf. also al-Ṭabarî., *Ḏaḫâʾir al-ʿuqbâ*: 204.

hiğra).[21] Transmitting from Ibn Shahrâshûb's *Manâqib*,[22] al-Mağlisî names her Umm Kulṯûm al-Kubrâ and adds the miscarried al-Muḥassin to the list.[23]

Al-Kâshânî refers us to *al-Risâlat al-zaynabiyya* of the extremely prolific al-Suyûṭî; Brockelmann (almost certainly incorrectly) names this text as *al-ʿUğâla (ʿAğâğa) al-zarnabiyya fi-l-zulâla al-zaynabiyya*, while Witkam, based on an extant copy in Leiden, calls it *Risalat al-sulala wa-l-zaynabiyya*. On the manuscript itself, the text is entitled *al-ʿAğâğa al-zarnabiyya fî-l-sulâlat al-zaynabiyya* ('The Perfumed Cloud in the Zaynabian Progeny').[24] Al-Suyûṭî names the five children of ʿAlî and Fâṭima as al-Ḥasan, al-Ḥusayn, al-Muḥassin ('born abortively'), Umm Kulṯûm and Zaynab. However, as soon as he begins to detail the marriages of the latter two, it becomes apparent that he has mixed up the two girls and has the order wrong; it ought to be Zaynab, followed by Umm Kulṯûm.[25]

---

21 al-Mağlisî., *Biḥâr al-anwâr*, vol. XLII, bb. 120, n. 18: 90, vol. XLIII, bb. 7: 214.

22 Ibn Shahrâshûb., *Manâqib âl Abî Ṭâlib*, vol. III, bb. *faṣl fî azwâği-hi*: 308.

23 al-Mağlisî., *Biḥâr al-anwâr*, vol. XLII, bb. 120, n. 20: 91, vol. XLIII, bb. 7, n. 44: 214, b. 9, n. 10: 233. A recent English translation of this volume of *Biḥâr al-anwâr* reads this as 'al-Muḥsin'; cf. SARWAR M., (trans.), *Behar al-anwar*, vol. 43, The Islamic Seminary Inc., New York 2015: 302. Cf. AL-MÛSAWÎ M., *al-Kawṯar fî aḥwâl Fâṭima bt. al-nabî al-aṭhar*, vol. VII, ch. 17, n. 5/3862: 99–100. He also lists the two girls as Zaynab al-Kubrâ and Umm Kulṯûm al-Kubrâ (n. 9/3866: 101).

24 Abû al-Faḍl ʿAbd al-Raḥmân b. Abî Bakr Kamâl al-Dîn b. Muḥammad b. Abî Bakr Ğalâl al-Dîn al-Suyûṭî (d. 911/1505: cf. GAL S. II: 178 and GAL. II: 143). Cf. WITKAM J.J., *Inventory of the Oriental Manuscripts of the Library of the University of Leiden*, Ter Lugt Press, Leiden 2008: 237.

25 al-Suyûṭî., *al-ʿAğâğa al-zarnabiyya fî-l-sulâlat al-zaynabiyya*: 2. The general aim of his text is to clarify that the numerous descendants of Zaynab and her husband ʿAbd Allâh b. Ğaʿfar are indeed related in a real way to Muḥammad; in doing so, al-Suyûṭî delineates the names and numbers of the children of ʿAlî and Fâṭima as well as those of ʿAbd Allâh b. Ğaʿfar and Zaynab.

It seems almost certain, then, that there were four children born to this couple: al-Ḥasan, al-Ḥusayn, Zaynab and Umm Kulṯûm,[26] and that Zaynab is the third child born to ʿAlî and Fâṭima, after al-Ḥasan and al-Ḥusayn, with a roughly one-year interval between each child (the author of the standard biography of her life notes that al-Ḥusayn was about three-years-old when she was born).[27]

It is 'well-known', notes Karbâssî, that she was the third child born to Fâṭima, and the first girl – there are some who believe her to be the second girl or the fourth child, but these differ with what is both "well-known and preferred,"[28] and her birth was followed by that of her sister Umm Kulṯûm. A handful of scholars believe that Zaynab and Umm Kulṯûm were the same person, and that ʿAlî

---

[26] Ibn Saʿd., *Kitâb al-ṭabaqât al-kabîr*, vol. XII, bb. *ḏikr banât rasûl Allâh*, n. 4927 (*Fâṭima*): 27, al-Nasâʾî., *Kitâb al-ḫaṣâʾiṣ fî faḍl ʿAlî b. Abî Ṭâlib*: 5, Ibn ʿAbd al-Barr., *al-Istîʿâb fî maʿrifat al-aṣḥâb*, vol. IV, *Kitâb al-nisâʾ wa-kunâ-hunna*, n. 4057: 1894, Sibṭ al-Ğawzî., *Taḏkirat ḫawâṣṣ al-umma bi-ḏikr ḫaṣâʾiṣ al-aʾimma*: 270. These authors mention only four children, omitting al-Muḥsin (or al-Muḥassin), apparently miscarried in an act of violence perpetrated against Fâṭima. Cf. also al-Mağlisî., *Biḥâr al-anwâr*, vol. XLVV, bb. 120 (*Aḥwâl awlâdi-hi wa azwâği-hi*): 74. Fâṭima shaved the hair of her four newborn children and gave in charity the weight in silver ("Fâṭima, the daughter of the Messenger of God, God bless him and grant him peace, weighed the hair of Ḥasan, Ḥusayn, Zaynab and Umm Kulṯûm, and gave away in *ṣadaqa* an equivalent weight of silver"). Cf. Ibn Mâlik., *al-Mawaṭṭaʾ*, bk. 26 (*Kitâb al-ʿaqîqa*), bb. 1, nn. 2–3: 501. Cf. CLOHESSY C.P., *Fatima, Daughter of Muhammad*, 2009: 37. Cf. also Ibn al-Ğawzî., *Ṣifat al-ṣafwa*, vol. I, bb. *ḏikr awlâdi-hi*: 119, vol. II, bb. *Fâṭima bt. Rasûl Allâh*: 2, where he confirms her as ʿAlî and Fâṭima's third child after her brothers al-Ḥasan and al-Ḥusayn.

[27] BILGRAMI M.H., *The Victory of Truth: The Life of Zaynab bint ʾAli*, Zahra Publications, Pakistan 1986. This text is of little help academically, containing neither references, nor indices nor bibliography. Nonetheless, al-ʿÂmilî carefully establishes her pedigree as granddaughter of the Messenger, daughter of the one authorized for leadership (*al-waṣî*) and of the Virgin (*al-batûl*), and sister to al-Ḥasan and al-Ḥusayn, born of the same parents. Cf. al-ʿÂmilî., *Aʿyân al-Shîʿa*, vol. VII: 137.

[28] KARBÂSSÎ M.S., *Muʿğam anṣâr al-Ḥusayn – al-nisâʾ*, 2009: 334–5.

and Fâṭima had no second daughter named Umm Kulṯûm; this contention has been clearly and eloquently refuted by Jaffer Ladak, especially since it contradicts most of the classical sources.[29] The insistence upon four children, not including the miscarried al-Muḥassin, thus affirming that Zaynab al-Kubrâ and Zaynab al-Ṣuġrâ are indeed two different individuals, is found also in other writers, such as Ibn al-Biṭrîq, al-Ṭabarsî, al-Ṭabarî and al-Ḫaṣîbî. Shahin and al-Kâshânî both note that ʿAlî was referred to as 'father of Zaynab' (during the Umayyad rule, when mention of ʿAlî's name was largely taboo), a *kunya* used especially in the transmission of *aḥâdîṯ*. This is recorded by Ibn al-Ḥadîd in his *Sharḥ nahǧ al-balâġa*, and suggests strongly that Zaynab was indeed the firstborn daughter of ʿAlî and Fâṭima.[30]

Ibn al-Aṯîr in *Usd al-ġâba fî maʿrifat al-ṣaḥâba* has a short passage dedicated to Zaynab, and which is quoted by al-Kâshânî, describing her as intelligent (*ʿâqila*) and understanding (*labîba*), confirming her parents as ʿAlî and Fâṭima, noting that her birth was during the lifetime of Muḥammad, and that after Muḥammad's death Fâṭima gave birth to no more children.[31] Al-Kâshânî also quotes Ibn Ḥaǧar al-ʿAsqalânî's *al-Iṣâba* (who is himself quoting from Ibn al-Aṯîr) to establish her pedigree as daughter of ʿAlî b. Abî Ṭâlib b. ʿAbd al-Muṭṭalib al-Hâshimiyya, granddaughter of the Messenger of God and whose mother was Fâṭima al-Zahrâʾ.[32]

Both al-Kâshânî and Karbâssî relate that when Zaynab was born, her mother Fâṭima carried her to her father ʿAlî and told him to name the newborn. ʿAlî deferred to Muḥammad ("it is not for me to take precedence over the Messenger of God"), who was

---

[29] LADAK J., *The Hidden Treasure. Lady Umm Kulthum, Daughter of Imam Ali and Lady Fatima*, Sun Behind the Cloud Publications, Birmingham 2011.

[30] SHAHIN B., *Lady Zaynab*, 2002: 63, AL-KÂSHÂNÎ A., *250 Karâma li-l-sayyida Zaynab wa-sayyidât bayt al-nubuwwa*, 2008: 11.

[31] Ibn al-Aṯîr., *Usd al-ġâba fî maʿrifat al-ṣaḥâba*, vol. VI, bb. 6961 (*Zaynab bt. ʿAlî*): 136–137. Cf. AL-KÂSHÂNÎ A., *250 Karâma li-l-sayyida Zaynab wa-sayyidât bayt al-nubuwwa*, 2008: 15.

[32] Ibid. Cf. al-ʿAsqalânî., *al-Iṣâba fî tamyîz al-ṣaḥâba*, vol. IV, n. 510: 314–315, al-ʿÂmilî., *Aʿyân al-Shîʿa*, vol. VII: 137.

away on a journey. When Muḥammad returned, ʿAlî questioned him about the name of his new daughter, and Muḥammad deferred to God ("it is not for me to take precedence over my Lord, the Most High"). The angel Ǧibra'îl[33] then descended, bringing words of peace from God the Majestic (*al-Ǧalîl*), and said to Muḥammad: "Name this newborn Zaynab, for God has chosen this name for her."[34] Shahin too notes that Muḥammad named her at the prompting of Ǧibrîl, who descended from heaven to pronounce 'Zaynab' as the name chosen by God for the girl.[35]

The concept of God Himself determining the name for a newborn, as well as the themes of naming and the reluctance to take precedence in the affair, are related often in the classical sources, but not of Zaynab; instead, they generally concern her two brothers, al-Ḥasan and al-Ḥusayn.[36] In the classical accounts of the naming of her brother al-Ḥusayn, for example, there are two major strands among the transmitters; the first is that Muḥammad named

---

[33] Ǧibrîl is the principal entity in Islamic angelology and is mentioned by name three times in the Qur'ân (Q. 2: 97–98, 66: 4), which also refers to him as 'the Faithful Spirit' (al-rûḥ al-amîn, Q. 26: 193), 'the Spirit of holiness' (rûḥ al-qudus, Q. 2: 87, 16: 102, erroneously translated by some as 'the holy Spirit') and 'Our Spirit' (rûḥa-nâ, Q. 19: 17). In a number of other verses, he is implied, but given neither name nor epithet (Q. 53: 5–18, 81: 19–25). Throughout the Shîʿî and Sunnî aḥâdîṯ, his name is written in an assortment of ways; sometimes 'Ǧibrîl', at other times 'Ǧibra'îl' and occasional 'Ǧibrâ'îl'. Unless the text dictates otherwise, I have attempted to use 'Ǧibrîl' throughout.

[34] AL-KÂSHÂNÎ A., *250 Karâma li-l-sayyida Zaynab wa-sayyidât bayt al-nubuwwa*, 2008: 11, KARBÂSSÎ M.S., *Muʿǧam anṣâr al-Ḥusayn – al-nisâ'*, 2009: 335.

[35] SHAHIN B., *Lady Zaynab*, 2002: 57.

[36] Cf. al-Ṣadûq., *Kitâb al-amâlî fî-l-aḥâdîṯ wa-l-aḫbâr, maǧlis* 28: 134–135, *ʿIlal al-sharâ'iʿ wa-l-aḥkâm*, vol. I, bb. 116: 137–138, *Maʿânî al-aḫbâr*: 57, al-Ṭûsî., *al-Amâlî fî al-ḥadîṯ, maǧlis* 3: 92–93, al-Ṭabarsî., *Iʿlâm al-warâ bi-aʿlâm al-hudâ*: 210, 218, al-Ḥurr al-ʿÂmilî., *Tafṣîl wasâ'il al-shîʿa ilâ taḥṣîl masâ'il al-sharîʿa*, vol. XXI, bb. 36: 409, al-Maǧlisî., *Biḥâr al-anwâr*, vol. XLIII, bb. 11: 238, 240–241, vol. XLIV, bb. 31: 238, 250, al-Ṭabarsî., *Ḫâtimat mustadrak al-wasâ'il*, vol. XV, bb. 32: 145.

him 'al-Ḥusayn' at the command of God given through Ǧibrîl.[37] The second strand, commonly carried by the Sunnî (although almost always without reference to an angelic visitation) has Muḥammad questioning ʿAlî about the name he has given to his eldest son and, upon discovering that ʿAlî has named him 'Ḥarb', changing it to al-Ḥusayn.[38] There are also a number of *rarer aḥâdîṯ* found in the Shîʿî texts; one insists that al-Ḥusayn is given a derivative of his brother al-Ḥasan's name because he is 'better' than al-Ḥasan.[39] Another holds that al-Ḥusayn's name is 'cleft' from that of al-Ḥasan,[40] although this contradicts an *ashbâḥ ḥadîṯ* in which God claims to have cleft for al-Ḥusayn a name from the divine names.[41]

---

[37] Cf. al-Ṣadûq., *Kitâb al-amâlî fî-l-aḥâdîṯ wa-l-aḫbâr*: 134, *ʿUyûn aḫbâr al-Riḍâ*, vol. II, bb. 31, n. 5: 25, *Maʿânî al-aḫbâr*, n. 6: 57, *ʿIlal al-sharâʾiʿ wa-l-aḥkâm*, vol. I, bb. 112, n. 7: 138, al-Fattâl al-Nîsâbûrî., *Rawḍat al-wâʿiẓîn wa-tabṣirat al-muttaʿiẓîn*, vol. I: 153, al-Ṭabarsî., *Iʿlâm al-warâ bi-aʿlâm al-hudâ*: 205, 218, Ibn Shahrâshûb., *Manâqib âl Abî Ṭâlib*, vol. III, bb. *maʿâlî umûri-himâ*: 448, al-Maǧlisî., *Biḥâr al-anwâr*, vol. XLIII, bb. 11, n. 3: 238, n. 4: 238–239, n. 8: 240–241, n. 10: 241, n. 26: 250–251, vol. XLIII, bb. 22, n. 3: 134, bb. 11, nn. 3–4: 238–239, n. 8: 240–241, n. 10: 241, n. 40: 257, vol. CI, bb. 4, n. 18: 110.

[38] Among the Shîʿa, cf. al-Ṣadûq., *ʿUyûn aḫbâr al-Riḍâ*, vol. II, bb. 31, n. 5: 25, al-Fattâl al-Nîsâbûrî., *Rawḍat al-wâʿiẓîn wa-tabṣirat al-muttaʿiẓîn*, vol. I: 153, al-Ṭabarsî., *Iʿlâm al-warâ bi-aʿlâm al-hudâ*: 218, Ibn Shahrâshûb., *Manâqib âl Abî Ṭâlib*, vol. III, bb. *maʿâlî umûri-himâ*: 448, al-Maǧlisî., *Biḥâr al-anwâr*, vol. XXXIX: 62, vol. XLIII, bb. 11, n. 4: 238, n. 28: 251, n. 33: 254. Among the Sunnî, cf. for e.g. Ibn Ḥanbal., *Musnad*, vol. I, *Musnad ʿAlî b. Abî Ṭâlib*, n. 569: 211–212, n. 953: 251.

[39] Cf. al-Ṭabarî., *Dalâʾil al-imâma*: 20, al-Ṣadûq., *Maʿânî al-aḫbâr*, n. 7: 57, *ʿIlal al-sharâʾiʿ wa-l-aḥkâm*, vol. I, bb. 112, n. 10: 138, Ibn Shahrâshûb., *Manâqib âl Abî Ṭâlib*, vol. III, bb. *maʿâlî umûri-himâ*: 448, al-Maǧlisî., *Biḥâr al-anwâr*, vol. LXIII, bb. 11, n. 12: 242, n. 28: 251.

[40] Cf. al-Maǧlisî., *Biḥâr al-anwâr*, vol. LXIII, bb. 11, n. 11: 241–242.

[41] The *ashbâḥ aḥâdîṯ*, part of the Shîʿî mystical tradition, are intimately related to the Shîʿî understanding of the *ahl al-bayt* and particularly the five 'impeccable' ones (*maʿṣumûn*). The *aḥâdîṯ* differ in details, but generally tell of Âdam (and sometimes Ḥawwâ' [Eve] with him), who sees various figures of light in his own shape and form prostrating before God, and,

In a further thread, in which ʿAlî's relation to Muḥammad is compared with Hârûn's relation to Mûsâ, Ğibrîl commands that ʿAlî's two children be named after the children of Hârûn – Shabbar and Shabbîr. "My tongue is Arabic," complains Muḥammad, not understanding the names, and Ğibrîl translates them as 'al-Ḥasan' and 'al-Ḥusayn'.[42] Al-Mağlisî carries yet another strand, in which ʿAlî names his sons Ḥamza (al-Ḥasan) and Ğaʿfar (al-Ḥusayn), but changes them at Muḥammad's order.[43]

In the case of Fâṭima, mother to al-Ḥusayn and Zaynab, the name 'Fâṭima' and the appellation al-Zahrâʾ are her chief names and receive significant attention in the books of *aḥâdîṯ*; her other

---

thinking himself to be alone, asks after their identity. He is informed that these are Fâṭima, ʿAlî and their two sons al-Ḥasan and al-Ḥusayn (cf. for e.g. al-Ḫawârizmî., *Maqtal al-Ḥusayn*, bk. 1, bb. *faḍâʾil Fâṭima al-Zahrâʾ bt. rasûl Allâh*, n. 37: 106–107, Ibn Ḥağar al-ʿAsqalânî., *Lisân al-mîzân*, vol. III, n. 1409: 346–347). In one of these *aḥâdîṯ*, God relates that He has cleft names for al-Ḥasan and al-Ḥusayn from His own divine names (cf. al-Mağlisî., *Biḥâr al-anwâr*, vol. XI, bb. 2, n. 25: 150–151, vol. XXVI, bb. 7, n. 10: 326–327).

42 Cf. Ibn Qays al-Hilâlî., *Kitâb Sulaym b. Qays*: 705, al-Ṭabarî., *Bishârat al-muṣṭafâ*: 174, al-Ṣadûq., *Kitâb al-amâlî fî-l-aḥâdîṯ wa-l-aḫbâr*, n. 3: 134, 191, 439, *ʿUyûn aḫbâr al-Riḍâ*, vol. II, bb. 31, n. 5: 25, *Maʿânî al-aḫbâr*, n. 6: 57, *ʿIlal al-sharâʾiʿ wa-l-aḥkâm*, vol. I, bb. 116, n. 6: 138, al-Fattâl al-Nîsâbûrî., *Rawḍat al-wâʿiẓîn wa-tabṣirat al-muttaʿiẓîn*, vol. I: 123, 153, al-Ṭabarsî., *Iʿlâm al-warâ bi-aʿlâm al-hudâ*: 160, 218, Ibn Shahrâshûb., *Manâqib âl Abî Ṭâlib*, vol. III, bb. *maʿâlî umûri-himâ*: 448, al-Râwandî., *al-Ḫarâʾiğ wa-l-ğarâʾiḥ fî-l-muʿğizât*, vol. I: 345, Ibn Ṭâʾûs., *Kitâb al-iqbâl bi-l-aʿmâl al-ḥasana*: 382, al-Mağlisî., *Biḥâr al-anwâr*, vol. IX, bb. 2: 298, vol. XIII, bb. 11, n. 11: 331, vol. XXXVI, bb. 50, n. 4: 36, vol. XXXVII, bb. 50: 37, 92, vol. XXXVIII, bb. 63: 190, vol. XXXIX, bb. 72: 33, 62, vol. XLIII, bb. 11, n. 1: 237, nn. 3–4: 238, n. 10: 241, n. 29: 245, vol. XLIX, bb. 4: 77, vol. XCIX, bb. 8: 191, vol. CI, bb. 4, n. 18: 110, al-Ṭabarsî., *Ḫâtimat mustadrak al-wasâʾil*, vol. I, bb. 8, n. 7–1163: 461, vol. XV, bb. 32, n. 7–17805: 144.

43 al-Mağlisî., *Biḥâr al-anwâr*, vol. LXIII, bb. 11, n. 28: 251, n. 33: 254–255. For the tradition that no one had been named Ḥusayn before, cf. Ibn Qûlûya al-Qummî., *Kâmil al-ziyârât*, bb. 28, n. 10: 182–183, al-ʿAyyâshî., *Tafsîr al- ʿAyyâshî*: 295, al-Mağlisî., *Biḥâr al-anwâr*, vol. XLV, bb. 40, n. 22: 211.

titles, at least twenty-seven in al-Mağlisî's 'official' litanies,[44] are accorded less elucidation, although they are used consistently throughout the corpus of *aḥâdîṯ*. What is noteworthy is that although she has many names both on earth and in heaven, the texts do not make it abundantly clear that God Himself has chosen all these names for her and ordered them be given her. In a number of *aḥâdîṯ*, Muḥammad explains why he named his daughter 'Fâṭima', without explicit reference to God giving her the name. On the other hand, the naming of Zaynab by God Himself, much written about in hagiographical texts, finds barely an echo in the classical sources.

The naming of Fâṭima is of particular importance for Zaynab's future; transmitting from the *Tafsîr Furât b. Ibrâhîm al-Kûfî*[45] and from *Shayḫ* al-Ṣadûq's *Maʿânî al-aḫbâr*, al-Mağlisî reports that 'Fâṭima' is the earthly name of Muḥammad's daughter, and is given for good reason: "(Ğibra'îl) said: She is called Fâṭima on earth because she has separated her adherents (*shîʿa*) from the Fire, and her enemies have been separated from her love."[46] 'Fâṭima' is a wordplay on the Arabic root *f-ṭ-m*, with its primary meaning 'to wean'. The concept of Muḥammad's daughter as one whom God 'weaned' and by whom He weans others, is expressed by numerous *aḥâdîṯ*, and although most of these have diverse phraseology, the wordplay constituting the central element remains the same. Al-Mağlisî records this *ḥadîṯ* from al-Ṣadûq's *ʿUyûn aḫbâr al-Riḍâ*: "The Messenger of God said: I called my daughter Fâṭima because God, powerful and lofty, has separated her and separated those who love her from the Fire."[47] Transmitting from *ʿIlal al-sharâʾiʿ* by the same

---

[44] al-Mağlisî., *Biḥâr al-anwâr*, vol. XLIII, bb. 2, n. 1: 10–11, n. 15: 16–17.

[45] Furât b Ibrâhîm b. Furât al-Kûfî (d. 310/992: Cf. MOD: 413 and GAS I: 539).

[46] al-Mağlisî., *Biḥâr al-anwâr*, vol. XLIII, bb. 1, n. 3: 4, bb. 2, n. 17: 18. Cf. al-Ṣadûq., *Maʿânî al-aḫbâr*, n. 53: 396.

[47] al-Mağlisî., *Biḥâr al-anwâr*, vol. XLIII, bb. 2, n. 4: 12. Cf. al-Ṣadûq., *ʿUyûn aḫbâr al-Riḍâ*, vol. II, bb. 31, n. 174: 46. Among the Sunnî, cf. al-Ḥâkim al-Nîsâbûrî., *Kitâb (Talḫîs) al-mustadrak ʿalâ al-ṣaḥîḥayn*, vol. III, bk. 31 (*Kitâb maʿrifat al-ṣaḥâba*), *Manâqib Fâṭima bt. rasûl Allâh*, nn. 4788, 4789:

al-Ṣadûq, al-Mağlisî notes that the concept of being weaned means 'to be separated'.[48] In this sense, the texts delineate a four-fold separation for Fâṭima by God: she is separated from the Fire,[49] from evil[50] (suggesting that her purification, at the very least, took place in the womb), from polytheism (*shirk*)[51] and from menstruation.[52] The texts demarcate four recipients of this separation from the

---

178–179, n. 4792: 180, al-Ḫawârizmî., *Maqtal al-Ḥusayn*, bk. 1, bb. *faḍâʾil Fâṭima al-Zahrâʾ bt. rasûl Allâh*, n. 2: 90, al-Ğawzî., *Kitâb al-mawḍûʿât min al-aḥâdîṯ al-marfûʿa*, vol. I, bb. *fî ḏikr tazwîğ Fâṭima bi-ʿAlî*: 421, al-Ṭabarî., *Ḏaḫâʾir al-ʿuqbâ*: 26, al-Ṣaffûrî., *Nuzhat al-mağâlis wa-muntaḫab al-nafâʾis*, vol. II, bb. *manâqib Fâṭima al-Zahrâʾ*: 179, al-Muttaqî al-Hindî., *Muntaḫab kanz al-ʿummâl* in the margins of *Musnad Ibn Ḥanbal*, vol. V: 97, al-ʿIṣâmî., *Simṭ al-nuğûm al-ʿawâlî*, vol. I, bb. 5: 425, al-Shablanğî., *Nûr al-abṣâr fî manâqib âl bayt al-nabî al-muḫtâr*, bb. *faḍl fî ḏikr manâqib ʿAlî b. Abî Ṭâlib*: 43.

48 al-Mağlisî., *Biḥâr al-anwâr*, vol. XLIII, bb. 2, n. 7: 13. Cf. al-Ṣadûq., *ʿIlal al-sharâʾiʿ wa-l-aḥkâm*, vol. I, bb. 142, n. 2: 178.

49 al-Ṭabarî., *Dalâʾil al-imâma*: 15, al-Ṣadûq., *ʿUyûn aḫbâr al-Riḍâ*, vol. II, bb. 31, n. 336: 72, *ʿIlal al-sharâʾiʿ wa-l-aḥkâm*, vol. I, bb. 142, nn. 5–6: 179, al-Ṭûsî., *al-Amâlî fî al-ḥadîṯ*, bb. 22, n. 5–1179: 570, Ibn Shahrâshûb., *Manâqib âl Abî Ṭâlib*, vol. III, bb. *manâqib Fâṭima al-Zahrâʾ*: 377, al-Irbilî., *Kashf al-ġumma fî maʿrifat al-aʾimma*, vol. I: 463, al-Mağlisî., *Biḥâr al-anwâr*, vol. XLIII, bb. 2, nn. 3–4: 12, n. 10: 14, nn. 12, 14: 15, nn. 17–18: 18–19.

50 al-Ṣadûq., *Kitâb al-amâlî fî-l-aḥâdîṯ wa-l-aḫbâr*, n. 18: 592, *Kitâb al-ḫiṣâl*, vol. II, n. 3: 414, *ʿIlal al-sharâʾiʿ wa-l-aḥkâm*, vol. I, bb. 142, n. 3: 178, al-Fattâl al-Nîsâbûrî., *Rawḍat al-wâʿiẓîn wa-tabṣirat al-muttaʿiẓîn*, vol. I: 148, Ibn Shahrâshûb., *Manâqib âl Abî Ṭâlib*, vol. III, bb. *manâqib Fâṭima al-Zahrâʾ*: 377–378, al-Irbilî., *Kashf al-ġumma fî maʿrifat al-aʾimma*, vol. I: 463, al-Mağlisî., *Biḥâr al-anwâr*, vol. XLIII, bb. 2, n. 1: 10, n. 14: 15–16.

51 al-Ṭabarî., *Dalâʾil al-imâma*: 10.

52 al-Kulaynî., *al-Kâfî fî ʿilm al-dîn*, vol. I, bk. 4 (*Kitâb al-ḥuğğa*), bb. *mawlid al-Zahrâʾ Fâṭima*, n. 6: 460, al-Ṣadûq., *ʿIlal al-sharâʾiʿ wa-l-aḥkâm*, vol. I, bb. 142, n. 4: 179, Ibn Shahrâshûb., *Manâqib âl Abî Ṭâlib*, vol. III, bb. *manâqib Fâṭima al-Zahrâʾ*: 378, al-Irbilî., *Kashf al-ġumma fî maʿrifat al-aʾimma*, vol. I: 463, al-Mağlisî., *Biḥâr al-anwâr*, vol. XLIII, bb. 2, n. 9: 14–15, n. 14: 15–16.

Fire: her followers (*shîʿa*),[53] those who love her,[54] her offspring[55] and those who support her and her offspring.[56]

The separation of Fâṭima's offspring from the Fire is intimately connected to a *ḥadîṯ* that is more profuse both in Sunnî and Shîʿî sources. A number of texts speak of Fâṭima's dedication to chastity: "Fâṭima has guarded her chastity and God has forbidden her offspring to the Fire."[57] This concept, literally translated as 'forti-

---

[53] al-Ṭabarî., *Dalâʾil al-imâma*: 53, al-Ṣadûq., *ʿUyûn aḫbâr al-Riḍâ*, vol. II, bb. 31, n. 336: 72, *Maʿânî al-aḫbâr*, n. 53: 396, *ʿIlal al-sharâʾiʿ wa-l-aḥkâm*, vol. I, bb. 142, n. 5: 179, Ibn Shahrâshûb., *Manâqib âl Abî Ṭâlib*, vol. III, bb. *fî manzilati-hâ*: 377–378, al-Irbilî., *Kashf al-ġumma fî maʿrifat al-aʾimma*, vol. I: 463, al-Mağlisî., *Biḥâr al-anwâr*, vol. XLIII, bb. 1, n. 3: 4, bb. 2, n. 3: 12, n. 10: 14, n. 14: 15, n. 17: 18, vol. LXV, bb. 15, n. 135: 76. Cf. also al-Kûfî., *Tafsîr Furât b. Ibrâhîm*, n. 435: 321.

[54] al-Ṭabarî., *Bishârat al-muṣṭafâ*: 123, 131, 184, al-Ṣadûq., *ʿUyûn aḫbâr al-Riḍâ*, vol. II, bb. 31, n. 174: 46, *Maʿânî al-aḫbâr*, n. 14: 64, *ʿIlal al-sharâʾiʿ wa-l-aḥkâm*, vol. I, bb. 142, n. 1: 178, al-Ṭûsî., *Tahḏîb al-aḥkâm*, vol. III: 98, *al-Amâlî fî al-ḥadîṯ*, bb. 11, n. 18–571: 294, al-Ṭabarsî., *Iʿlâm al-warâ bi-aʿlâm al-hudâ*: 148, Ibn Shahrâshûb., *Manâqib âl Abî Ṭâlib*, vol. III, bb. *manâqib Fâṭima al-Zahrâʾ*: 377, Ibn Ṭâʾûs., *Kitâb al-iqbâl bi-l-aʿmâl al-ḥasana*: 182, al-Irbilî., *Kashf al-ġumma fî maʿrifat al-aʾimma*, vol. I: 463, al-Daylamî., *Irshâd al-qulûb*, vol. II: 232, al-Ḥillî al-ʿAllâma., *Kashf al-yaqîn fî faḍâʾil amîr al-muʾminîn*: 352, al-Mağlisî., *Biḥâr al-anwâr*, vol. XLIII, bb. 2, n. 4: 12, n. 8: 13, n. 12: 15, n. 14: 16, vol. LXV, bb. 18, n. 66: 133, vol. XCV, bb. 7: 139.

[55] al-Ṭabarî., *Dalâʾil al-imâma*: 53, al-Ṭûsî., *al-Amâlî fî al-ḥadîṯ*, bb. 22, n. 5–1179: 570, al-Mağlisî., *Biḥâr al-anwâr*, vol. XLIII, bb. 2, n. 18: 18–19.

[56] al-Ṣadûq., *ʿIlal al-sharâʾiʿ wa-l-aḥkâm*, vol. I, bb. 142, n. 6: 179, al-Irbilî., *Kashf al-ġumma fî maʿrifat al-aʾimma*, vol. I: 463, al-Mağlisî., *Biḥâr al-anwâr*, vol. VIII, bb. 21, n. 57: 50, vol. XLIII, bb. 2, n. 11: 14.

[57] al-Ṣadûq., *ʿUyûn aḫbâr al-Riḍâ*, vol. II, bb. 31, n. 264: 63, bb. 58, n. 1: 232, *Maʿânî al-aḫbâr*, nn. 1–6: 105–106, al-Râwandî., *al-Ḫarâʾiğ wa-l-ğarâʾiḥ fî-l-muʿğizât*, vol. I: 281, Ibn Shahrâshûb., *Manâqib âl Abî Ṭâlib*, vol. III, bb. *Manâqib Fâṭima al-Zahrâʾ*: 373, al-Irbilî., *Kashf al-ġumma fî maʿrifat al-aʾimma*, vol. I: 468, vol. II: 144, 310, 346, al-Ḥillî al-ʿAllâma., *Kashf al-yaqîn fî faḍâʾil amîr al-muʾminîn*: 351, al-Mağlisî., *Biḥâr al-anwâr*, vol. XLIII, bb. 3, n. 6: 20, bb. 9, n. 2: 230, nn. 3–6: 231, n. 7: 232, vol. XLVI, bb. 11, n. 51: 185, vol. XLVIII: 315, vol. XLIX, bb. 16, nn. 2–3: 217, vol. LXXV, bb. 16, n. 52: 78, vol. XCIII, bb. 27, nn. 14–18: 221–223. Among the Sunnî,

fied' or 'made inaccessible her private parts' (the same words used of Maryam in Q. 21: 91) certainly confirms her physical virginity, that is, prior to her marriage with ʿAlî. Thus, while her name indicates the fact of the weaning or separation, it is her chaste lifestyle that becomes the *raison d'être* for the salvation of her progeny, starting with her four children. While a number of texts do not define these offspring by using names,[58] others name al-Ḥasan and al-Ḥusayn, sometimes adding 'especially', as well as 'those born from her womb',[59] while others add the names of Zaynab and Umm

cf. al-Ḥâkim al-Nîsâbûrî., *Kitâb (Talḫîs) al-mustadrak ʿalâ al-ṣaḥîḥayn*, vol. III, bk. 31 (*Kitâb maʿrifat al-ṣaḥâba*), *Manâqib Fâṭima bt. rasûl Allâh*, n. 4789: 179, Abû Nuʿaym al-Iṣbahânî., *Ḥilyat al-awliyâʾ wa-ṭabaqât al-aṣfiyâʾ*, vol. IV, bb. 268, n. 5277: 209, al-Ḫawârizmî., *Maqtal al-Ḥusayn*, bk. 1, bb. *faḍâʾil Fâṭima al-Zahrâʾ bt. rasûl Allâh*, n. 9: 94, al-Ṭabarî., *Ḏaḫâʾir al-ʿuqbâ*: 48, al-Hayṯamî., *Maǧmaʿ al-zawâʾid wa-manbaʿ al-fawâʾid*, vol. IX, bb. *manâqib Fâṭima bt. rasûl Allâh*: 202, al-Muttaqî al-Hindî., *Muntaḫab kanz al-ʿummâl* in the margins of *Musnad Ibn Ḥanbal*, vol. V: 97.

58 al-Baḥrânî., *al-Burhân fî tafsîr al-qurʾân*, vol. V: 431, al-Maǧlisî., *Biḥâr al-anwâr*, vol. XLIII, bb. 3, n. 6: 20 (from *ʿUyûn aḫbâr al-Riḍâ*), bb. 9, n. 5: 231 (from *Maʿânî al-aḫbâr*), vol. XLVI, bb. 11, n. 51: 175 (from al-Râwandî's *al-Ḫarâʾiǧ wa-l-ǧarâʾiḥ fî-l-muʿǧizât*), vol. XLVIII: 315, vol. XCIII, bb. 27, n. 17: 223 (from *ʿUyûn aḫbâr al-Riḍâ*).

59 al-Ṣadûq., *ʿUyûn aḫbâr al-Riḍâ*, vol. II, bb. 58, n. 1: 232, *Maʿânî al-aḫbâr*, n. 1: 106, Ibn Shahrâshûb., *Manâqib âl Abî Ṭâlib*, vol. III, bb. *faṣl fî manzilati-hi*: 325, quoting Ibn Manda, al-Irbilî., *Kashf al-ġumma fî maʿrifat al-aʾimma*, vol. II: 311, 346, al-Maǧlisî., *Biḥâr al-anwâr*, vol. XLIII, bb. 9, n. 2: 230 (from *Maʿânî al-aḫbâr*), n. 6: 231 (from *Maʿânî al-aḫbâr*), n. 7: 232 (from *Manâqib âl Abî Ṭâlib*), vol. XLIX, bb. 16, n. 3: 218 (from *ʿUyûn aḫbâr al-Riḍâ*), vol. LXXV, bb. 16, n. 52: 78 (from *Kashf al-ġumma fî maʿrifat al-aʾimma*), vol. XCIII, bb. 27, n. 14: 222 (from *ʿUyûn aḫbâr al-Riḍâ*), n. 18: 223 (from *ʿUyûn aḫbâr al-Riḍâ*).

Kulṯûm.[60] Curiously, there is one text which names al-Ḥasan, al-Ḥusayn and Umm Kulṯûm, but omits Zaynab entirely.[61]

'Zaynab', the name (*ism*) given by God to the daughter of ʿAlî and Fâṭima, derives from two Arabic words, *zayn* from the verb *zâna-yazînu* ('to ornament, beautify, embellish') and the Arabic for 'father' (*âb*), and thus means the 'adornment' or 'grace' or 'beauty' of the father'.[62] She is called Zaynab al-Kubrâ, to distinguish her from her sister Umm Kulṯûm (Zaynab al-Ṣuġrâ); al-Kâshânî notes that the appellation *al-kubrâ* is to differentiate between her and her sisters, (using the plural but without naming those sisters) who also have the name Zaynab or the same *kunya*. Referring us to al-Ṣadûq's *ʿIlal al-sharâʾiʿ wa-l-aḥkâm* as transmitted by al-Maǧlisî, al-Kâshânî notes an incident when, supposedly, Fâṭima was informed that ʿAlî intended to marry a second wife.[63] According to the text,

---

[60] al-Ṣadûq., *Maʿânî al-aḫbâr*, n. 2: 106, n. 3: 107, al-Maǧlisî., *Biḥâr al-anwâr*, vol. XLIII, bb. 9, n. 3, n. 4: 231 (from *Maʿânî al-aḫbâr*), vol. XCIII, bb. 27, n. 15: 222 (from *Maʿânî al-aḫbâr*).

[61] al-Ṣadûq., *Maʿânî al-aḫbâr*, n. 3: 108, al-Irbilî., *Kashf al-ġumma fî maʿrifat al-aʾimma*, vol. I: 468, al-Maǧlisî., *Biḥâr al-anwâr*, vol. XCIII, bb. 27, n. 16: 223.

[62] Cf. LANE E.W., *An Arabic-English Lexicon*, vol. III, 1968: 1279. Lane notes the meanings carried by *zayn*, including a 'grace', a 'beauty', a 'comely quality', a physical or intellectual 'adornment', an 'honour', a 'credit' and anything that could be described as someone or something's 'pride' and 'glory'. Steingass also records 'Zaynab' as the name of a particular aromatic tree (cf. STEINGASS F., *Learner's Arabic English Dictionary*, Hippocrene Books, New York 1993: 472).

[63] A number of *aḥâdîṯ* intimate that ʿAlî was going to take the daughter of Abû Ǧahl as a second wife; according to al-Buḫârî and others, Muḥammad worried about the distress this would cause Fâṭima (cf. al-Buḫârî., *Ṣaḥîḥ*, vol. IV, bk. 53 (*Kitâb farḍ al-ḫums*), bb. 5, n. 342: 219–220, vol. V, bk. 57 (*Kitâb faḍâʾil al-aṣḥâb*), bb. 17, n. 75: 56–57, Muslim., *Ṣaḥîḥ*, vol. IV, bk. 44 (*Kitâb faḍâʾil al-ṣaḥâba*), bb. 10 (*Faḍâʾil Fâṭima bt. al-nabî*), n. 95: 1903, al-Tirmiḏî., *Sunan*, vol. IX, bk. 50 (*Kitâb al-manâqib*), *Manâqib Fâṭima bt. Muḥammad*, bb. *fî faḍl Fâṭima*, n. 3868: 387). Muḥammad, receiving complaints from Fâṭima, protested from the pulpit that the daughter of God's Prophet and the daughter of God's enemy could not live under

she was greatly distressed thinking about this, and finally, as night fell, took al-Ḥasan, al-Ḥusayn and Umm Kulṯûm and went to see her father. It seems most likely, as al-Kâshânî points out, that the Umm Kulṯûm mentioned in the text is Zaynab.[64] Al-Kâshânî also refers us to Ibn ʿInaba's *Ansâb al-Ṭâlibîyîn*,[65] in which the author confirms that Zaynab al-Kubrâ was the daughter of ʿAlî, that her *kunya* was Umm al-Ḥasan, and that she transmitted on the authority of her mother Fâṭima, daughter of the Messenger of God.

Karbâssî draws our attention to an inexplicable note in the margin of al-Sharastânî's *Nahḍa al-Ḥusayn*,[66] which reminds the reader that ʿAlî had two daughters by the name of Zaynab and with the *kunya* Umm Kulṯûm, that al-Kubrâ was the mistress of Ṭaff

---

the same roof (Muslim., *Ṣaḥîḥ*, vol. IV, bk. 44 (*Kitâb faḍâʾil al-ṣaḥâba*), bb. 10 (*Faḍâʾil Fâṭima bt. al-nabî*), n. 96: 1903–1904). The Shîʿa record the *aḥâdîṯ*, while denying the context of ʿAlî attempting a second marriage while Fâṭima was still alive (among many, cf. for e.g. Ibn Qays al-Hilâlî., *Kitâb Sulaym b. Qays*: 830, 868, al-Ṭabarî., *Dalâʾil al-imâma*, bb. *ḫabar al-wafât wa-l-dafn*: 45, *Bishârat al-muṣṭafâ*, 70, 177, al-Ṣadûq., *Kitâb al-amâlî fî-l-aḥâdîṯ wa-l-aḫbâr*, n. 3: 102, n. 18: 486, *ʿIlal al-sharâʾiʿ wa-l-aḥkâm*, vol. I, n. 2: 185, 187, al-Mufîd., *al-Amâlî li-l-Mufîd*, n. 2: 259, al-Fattâl al-Nîsâbûrî., *Rawḍat al-wâʿiẓîn wa-tabṣirat al-muttaʿiẓîn*, vol. I: 149, Ibn Shahrâshûb., *Manâqib âl Abî Ṭâlib*, vol. III, bb. *manâqib Fâṭima al-Zahrâʾ*: 378, al-Irbilî., *Kashf al-ġumma fî maʿrifat al-aʾimma*, vol. I: 363, 466, al-ʿÂmilî., *al-Ṣirâṭ al-mustaqîm ilâ mustaḥaqq al-taqdîm fî al-imâma*, vol. I: 170, vol. II: 118, 282, 289, vol. III: 12, al-Ḥurr al-ʿÂmilî., *Tafṣîl wasâʾil al-shîʿa ilâ taḥṣîl masâʾil al-sharîʿa*, vol. XX, bb. 24, n. 25054: 67, bb. 129, n. 25510: 232, al-Maǧlisî., *Biḥâr al-anwâr*, vol. XXI, bb. 32: 279, vol. XXIII, bb. 7, n. 97: 143, bb. 13: 234, vol. XXVII, bb. 1: 62, al-Ṭabarsî., *Ḫâtimat mustadrak al-wasâʾil*, vol. XIV, bb. 61, n. 16450: 182.

64 AL-KÂSHÂNÎ A., *250 Karâma li-l-sayyida Zaynab wa-sayyidât bayt al-nubuwwa*, 2008: 12. Cf. al-Ṣadûq., *ʿIlal al-sharâʾiʿ wa-l-aḥkâm*, vol. I, bb. 149: 185, al-Maǧlisî., *Biḥâr al-anwâr*, vol. XLIII, bb. 7, n. 31: 207.

65 This is the work *ʿUmdat al-ṭâlib fî nasab (ansâb) âl Abî Ṭâlib* by Ǧamâl al-Dîn Aḥmad b. ʿAlî b. al-Ḥusayn b. Muhannâ b. ʿInaba b. al-Ḥasan b. ʿAlî b. Abî Ṭâlib al-Zaydî al-Aṣġar al-Dâʾûdî al-Ḥasanî (d. 835/1432: cf. GAL S. II: 271).

66 Muḥammad ʿAlî b. Ḥusayn b. Muḥsin b. Murtaḍâ b. al-Ḥusaynî Hibba al-Dîn al-Shahrastânî (d. 1387/1967).

(Karbalâʾ), that Ibn ʿAbbâs referred to her as 'the most esteemed of the Banû Hâshim' (*ʿaqîla banî Hâshim*)[67] and that Fâṭima gave birth to her two years after her brother al-Ḥusayn. Al-Sharastânî notes further that she was married to ʿAbd Allâh, son of her uncle Ǧaʿfar after the death of her sister Umm Kulṯûm, during the caliphate of ʿUṯmân or Muʿâwiya, and that Zaynab was the leading personality in the circle of dependents in the Ḥusaynî tents.[68] Quite clearly, al-Sharastânî's thesis about her marriage is incorrect; Zaynab had one sister, Umm Kulṯûm, who was alive and present at Karbalâʾ, well after Zaynab's marriage.

Karbâssî notes that while Zaynab's *kunya* is Umm Kulṯûm, this is not the name by which she became known, in order to differentiate her from her younger sister, known by her *kunya* Umm

---

[67] Zaynab is referred to both as *ʿaqîla* (عقيلة) and as *ʿâqila* (عاقلة). The latter refers specifically to gifts of the intellect; a woman who is thus described is one who is understanding, rational, judicious and sensible – one, notes Lane who restrains herself, turning her soul away from flawed inclinations (cf. WEHR H., *A Dictionary of Modern Written Arabic*, 1980: 737, LANE E.W., *An Arabic-English Lexicon*, vol. V, 1968: 2115). The former has a different nuance, indicating what Lane terms "a woman of generous race", modest or bashful, "kept behind the curtain" or "held in high estimation" (LANE E.W., *An Arabic-English Lexicon*, vol. V, 1968: 2115). Wehr offers a more limited definition, as "the best" or the "pick", noting too that the word can refer to a wife or a spouse (WEHR H., *A Dictionary of Modern Written Arabic*, 1980: 737). If *ʿaqîla* does indeed include the connotation of 'kept behind a curtain', in Zaynab's case this must be understood metaphorically (in spite of some pious legends that suggest a literal seclusion), considering her active and public role during and after Karbalâʾ – during her protest in Kûfa, at least one bystander (Ḥaḏlam b. Satîr) notes that he has never witnessed one so modest and yet so articulate (cf. for e.g. al-Mufîd., *al-Amâlî li-l-Mufîd*, *maǧlis* 38: 321–323, al-Ṭûsî., *al-Amâlî fî al-ḥadîṯ*, *maǧlis* 3: 92–93, al-Ṭabarsî., *Kitâb al-iḥtiǧâǧ ʿalâ ahl al-liǧâǧ*, vol. II: 304, al-Ḫawârizmî., *Maqtal al-Ḥusayn*, bk. 2, bb. *fî maqtal al-Ḥusayn*: 45, Ibn Shahrâshûb., *Manâqib âl Abî Ṭâlib*, vol. IV, bb. *fî maqtali-hi*: 115, Ibn Ṭâʾûs., *Kitâb al-luhûf fî qatlâ al-ṭufûf*: 86–87, Ibn Namâ al-Ḥillî., *Muṯîr al-aḥzân wa munîr subul al-ashǧân*, Part 3: 86).

[68] KARBÂSSÎ M.S., *Muʿǧam anṣâr al-Ḥusayn – al-nisâʾ*, 2009: 340.

Kulṯûm and hardly ever by her given name, also Zaynab.[69] According to al-Mufîd, ʿAlî and Fâṭima's two daughters were Zaynab the 'elder' and Zaynab the 'younger', who was given the *kunya* Umm Kulṯûm.[70] Zaynab herself has a list of *kunâ*: Umm Kulṯûm, Umm al-Ḥasan (a reference to her brother),[71] Umm Hâshim ('mother of the clan of Hâshim'), Umm al-ʿAwâğiz ('mother of the weak'), Umm al-Masâkîn ('mother of the poor'), Umm Miṣr ('mother of Egypt', especially in that country)[72] and Umm al-Maṣâ'ib ('mother of afflictions').[73] Her *laqab* (pl. *alqâb*)[74] include *al-ʿaqîla* ('the most esteemed'),[75] *ʿaqîla banî Hâshim* ('the most esteemed of the Hâshim

---

[69] Op. cit.: 335.

[70] Cf. al-Mufîd., *al-Irshâd fî maʿrifat ḥuğağ Allâh ʿalâ al-ʿibâd*, vol. I, bb. *ḏikr awlâd amîr al-mu'minîn*: 355.

[71] AL-KÂSHÂNÎ A., *250 Karâma li-l-sayyida Zaynab wa-sayyidât bayt al-nubuwwa*, 2008: 11. The author provides no references for these appellations. Cf. also KARBÂSSÎ M.S., *Muʿğam anṣâr al-Ḥusayn – al-nisâ'*, 2009: 335.

[72] QUTBUDDIN B.T., "Zaynab bint Ali" in Lindsay Jones (ed.), *Encyclopedia of Religion*, 2nd edn., 2005: 9937. The author provides no references for these appellations.

[73] SHAHIN B., *Lady Zaynab*, 2002: 59–61. The author provides no references for this appellation, although it is used by al-ʿÂmilî, who lists the numerous afflictions she experienced in the deaths of all those close to her, including her two sons who, he notes, were killed before her eyes. Cf. al-ʿÂmilî., *Aʿyân al-Shîʿa*, vol. VII: 137.

[74] A nickname conveying a certain esteem, of which one might be the bearer of several. The *laqab* might signal some moral quality or distinct merit, might accentuate a physical peculiarity or simply underscore one's belonging to a particular sect or group.

[75] QUTBUDDIN B.T., "Zaynab bint Ali" in Lindsay Jones (ed.), *Encyclopedia of Religion*, 2nd edn., 2005: 9937, AL-KÂSHÂNÎ A., *250 Karâma li-l-sayyida Zaynab wa-sayyidât bayt al-nubuwwa*, 2008: 11. The author provides no references for this appellation but points out that *al-ʿaqîla* refers to the one who is the most noble woman of her people (*al-makrîma*), the most august (*al-ʿaẓîẓa*) in her own house, and that Zaynab was above even this. The word indicates 'the best', 'the most excellent', 'esteemed', 'modest', 'secluded', and with the connotation of a precious pearl; cf. LANE E.W., *An Arabic-English Lexicon*, vol. V, 1968: 2115.

clan'),[76] *ʿaqîla al-ṭâlibiyîn* ('the most esteemed of the Ṭâlib line'), *al-ṣaddîqa al-ṣuġrâ* ('the younger truthful one' or 'righteous one', to differentiate between her and her mother Fâṭima al-Zahrâʾ, known as *al-ṣaddîqa al-kubrâ*),[77] *al-ʿâlima* ('the knowledgeable') *ʿabîda âl ʿAlî* ('the worshipper in the family of ʿAlî'), *al-kâmila* ('the perfect') and *al-fâḍila* ('the virtuous').[78] She is also known as *ṯânî al-Zahrâʾ* ('the second Fâṭima') and, in Egypt, *al-ṭâhira* ('the pure one') or simply as *al-sayyida*. In his *Maqâtil al-ṭâlibîyyîn*, al-Iṣfahânî notes that when Ibn ʿAbbâs transmits from Zaynab the words of Fâṭima about Fadak, he refers to Zaynab as 'our most esteemed' (*ʿaqîlatu-nâ*).[79] Musa Muhammad adds *al-ʿarîfa* ('the cognizant') and *al-muwaṯṯaqa* (the trustworthy),[80] while Bilgrami adds *al-fâṣiḥa* ('the fluent') and *al-balîġa* ('the eloquent').[81]

Muḥammad was her maternal grandfather, so that she is a member of the *ahl al-bayt*, revered not only for her admirable characteristics and actions but also for her membership in and continuation of the biological line of Muḥammad. In spite of this, her name does not occur in the famous *aḥâdîṯ* in which Muḥammad defines the 'people of his house' – only ʿAlî, Fâṭima, al-Ḥasan and al-Ḥusayn are mentioned. Writing in his *Ḏaḫâʾir al-ʿuqbâ*, al-Ṭabarî refers to her presence in other works, such as Ibn Saʿd's *Ṭabaqât*, al-Ṭabarî's *Târîḫ*, Ibn ʿAsâkir's *Târîḫ*, Ibn Aṯîr's *Usd al-ġâba fî maʿrifat*

---

[76] Cf. also KARBÂSSÎ M.S., *Muʿǧam anṣâr al-Ḥusayn – al-nisâʾ*, 2009: 335, nt. 1: 340.

[77] AL-KÂSHÂNÎ A., *250 Karâma li-l-sayyida Zaynab wa-sayyidât bayt al-nubuwwa*, 2008: 11. The author provides no references for these appellations.

[78] SHAHIN B., *Lady Zaynab*, 2002: 59–61, AL-KÂSHÂNÎ A., *250 Karâma li-l-sayyida Zaynab wa-sayyidât bayt al-nubuwwa*, 2008: 11. The authors provides no references for these appellations.

[79] al-Iṣfahânî., *Maqâtil al-ṭâlibîyyîn*: 91. Cf. AL-KÂSHÂNÎ A., *250 Karâma li-l-sayyida Zaynab wa-sayyidât bayt al-nubuwwa*, 2008: 15–16, SHAHIN B., *Lady Zaynab*, 2002: 65.

[80] Musa Muhammad, in his short work entitled 'Lady Zaynab', accessible at www.alhassanain.com.

[81] BILGRAMI M.H., *The Victory of Truth: The Life of Zaynab bint ʾAli*, 1986: 5.

al-ṣaḥâba as well as his own *al-Simṭ al-ṯamîn fî manâqib ummahât al-mu'minîn*, and then notes:

> We deferred mention of her and the mention of her sister Umm Kulṯûm from the *aḥâdîṯ* of the 'people of the house'...because the above-mentioned *aḥâdîṯ* of the 'people of the house' do not include the two of them; God knows best! They were not present when the verse came down, when they were all enwrapped with the cloak and the Prophet said what he said.[82]

Nor does Zaynab find a place among the fourteen 'infallibles' or 'immaculate ones' (*maʿṣûmûn*); Muḥammad, Fâṭima and the twelve Imâms. To these belong an exalted spiritual station of inerrancy and impeccability (*ʿiṣma*), so that they are deemed as being pure (*maʿṣûm*), protected from sin and error, attributes indicated by the words of Q. 21: 73.[83] Zaynab's *ʿiṣma* is a subordinate one (*al-ʿiṣma al-ṣuġrâ*), raised and educated as she was by members of the fourteen.

However, for all her exalted position, Zaynab, like her brother al-Ḥusayn, was born in tears. The conception and birth of al-Ḥusayn is methodically enwrapped in accounts of heavenly intervention and immense grief. One example describes a visit by God to Muḥammad as he sits in Fâṭima's house with al-Ḥusayn in his lap. Inexplicably, Muḥammad begins to weep, and in response to Fâṭima's confusion and questions, says that he has, in that very hour, seen the Most High in a most beautiful form (*fî aḥsan ṣûra*). God questions Muḥammad about his love for al-Ḥusayn: "He is the delight of my eye," replies Muḥammad, using a phrase he also uses for the boy's mother, "my sweet basil, the fruit of my heart and the skin between my eyes." God then places His hand on al-Ḥusayn's head, saying that His blessings, prayers, mercy and favour are upon the boy, but announcing that he is the chief of the mar-

---

[82] al-Ṭabarî., *Ḏaḫâ'ir al-ʿuqbâ*: 285–6.

[83] "*And We made them chiefs who guide by Our command, and We inspired in them the doing of good deeds and the right establishment of worship and the giving of alms, and they were worshippers of Us (alone)*".

tyrs from first to last.[84] In some of the accounts, Muḥammad is given red soil from Karbalâ', the place of al-Ḥusayn's death; in others, it is either Ǧibrîl or God who makes the actual announcement of his martyrdom. Still others place these angelic portents before his birth, or omit any reference to Divine or angelic visitation, and articulate the announcement of death through a vision given to Muḥammad.[85]

Al-Kâshânî relates that when Ǧibrîl descended to give instructions about her naming, he also informed Muḥammad of the afflictions (*maṣâ'ib*) that Zaynab would suffer, causing her weeping grandfather to say: "Whoever weeps over the affliction of this girl is as one who weeps over her brothers, al-Ḥasan and al-Ḥusayn."[86] Karbâssî transmits an expanded version, not found in the classical texts:

> The Messenger said (to Fâṭima): "My daughter, give me your newborn daughter." When she had fetched her, he clasped her to his noble breast, laid his lofty cheek against her cheek and wept bitterly, the tears flowing over his beautiful and noble parts. Fâṭima said to him: "Why your tears? May God not cause your eye to weep, my father!" He replied: "My daughter, Fâṭima, He informed me that this girl will be afflicted with tribulations after you and after me, and diverse afflictions and

---

[84] Cf. Ibn Qûlûya al-Qummî., *Kâmil al-ziyârât*, bb. 21, n. 1: 140, n. 2: 70, al-Mağlisî., *Biḥâr al-anwâr*, vol. XLIV, bb. 30, n. 29: 238.

[85] Among the Sunnî transmitters of this genre, cf. al-Tirmiḏî., *Sunan*, vol. IX, bk. 50 (*Kitâb al-manâqib*), bb. *manâqib al-Ḥasan wa-l-Ḥusyan*, n. 3774: 333, al-Ḥâkim al-Nîsâbûrî., *Kitâb (Talḫîs) al-mustadrak ʿalâ al-ṣaḥîḥayn*, vol. III, Part 3, bk. 31 (*Kitâb maʿrifat al-ṣaḥâba*), bb. *awwal faḍâ'il Abî ʿAbd Allâh al-Ḥusayn b. ʿAlî*, n. 4884: 210, n. 4888: 211–212, nn. 4890, 4892: 213, al-Ṭabarî., *Ḏaḫâ'ir al-ʿuqbâ*: 146–147, al-Tibrîzî., *Mishkât al-maṣâbîḥ*, vol. III, bk. 30 (*Kitâb al-manâqib*), bb. 10 (*Manâqib ahl bayt al-nabî*), n. 6136: 1733, n. 6157: 1737–1738, Ibn Ḥağar al-ʿAsqalânî., *Tahḏîb al-tahḏîb*, vol. II: 347, al-Hayṯamî., *Mağmaʿ al-zawâ'id wa-manbaʿ al-fawâ'id*, vol. IX, bb. *manâqib al-Ḥusayn*: 187–189, al-Shablanğî., *Nûr al-abṣâr fî manâqib âl bayt al-nabî al-muḫtâr*: 114.

[86] AL-KÂSHÂNÎ A., *250 Karâma li-l-sayyida Zaynab wa-sayyidât bayt al-nubuwwa*, 2008: 11.

> the most calamitous and heavy losses will come to her." Fâṭima asked him: "What is the reward for one who weeps for her and for her afflictions?" He replied: "Part of me[87] and delight of my eye, whoever weeps over her and over her afflictions, is as one who weeps over her brothers, al-Ḥasan and al-Ḥusayn."[88]

In another story, also related by Karbâssî but missing in the classical sources, it is related that the Companions came to Muḥammad to congratulate him on the birth of his granddaughter; one of them, named Salmân al-Fârsî,[89] went to congratulate ʿAlî, and found him

---

[87] A reference to Muḥammad's widely transmitted declaration: "Fâṭima is part of me. Whatever troubles her troubles me, and whatever injures her injures me." Cf. for e.g. among the Sunnî, Muslim., *Ṣaḥîḥ*, vol. IV, bk. 44 (*Kitâb faḍâʾil al-ṣaḥâba*), bb. 10, n. 93: 1902, nn. 95, 96: 1903–1904, al-Tirmiḏî., *Sunan*, vol. IX, bk. 50 (*Kitâb al-manâqib*), bb. *fî faḍl Fâṭima bt. Muḥammad*, n. 3866: 386, n. 3868: 386–387, Ibn Ḥanbal., *Musnad*, vol. VI, *Ḥadîṯ al-Masûr b. Maḫrama al-Zuhrî*, n. 18929: 486–487, n. 18933: 492, n. 18935: 492–493, n. 18952: 501–502, vol. V, *Ḥadîṯ ʿAbd Allâh b. Zubayr b. al-ʿAwwâm*, n. 16123: 453, al-Buḫârî., *Ṣaḥîḥ*, vol. IV, bk. 53 (*Kitâb farḍ al-ḫums*), bb. 5, n. 342: 219–220, vol. V, bk. 57 (*Kitâb faḍâʾil al-aṣḥâb*), bb. 13, n. 61: 50, ch. 17, n. 75: 56–57, bb. 29, n. 111: 75, al-Balâḏurî., *Kitâb ansâb al-ashrâf*, vol. I, *Azwâǧ rasûl Allâh*, n. 865: 402–403, al-Nasâʾî., *Kitâb al-ḫaṣâʾiṣ fî faḍl ʿAlî b. Abî Ṭâlib*: 80–81, al-Ḥâkim al-Nîsâbûrî., *Kitâb (Talḫîs) al-mustadrak ʿalâ al-ṣaḥîḥayn*, vol. III, bk. 31 (*Kitâb maʿrifat al-ṣaḥâba*), *Manâqib Fâṭima bt. rasûl Allâh*, nn. 4813, 4814, 4815: 187–188, al-Ḫawârizmî., *Maqtal al-Ḥusayn*, bk. 1, bb. *faḍâʾil Fâṭima al-Zahrâʾ bt. rasûl Allâh*, n. 6: 91–92, Ibn al-Aṯîr., *Usd al-ġâba fî maʿrifat al-ṣaḥâba*, vol. VI, bb. 7175 (*Fâṭima bt. Rasûl Allâh*): 223, Ibn Kaṯîr., *al-Bidâya wa-l-nihâya*, vol. VI: 333. Cf. CLOHESSY C.P., *Fatima, Daughter of Muhammad*, 2009: 41.

[88] KARBÂSSÎ M.S., *Muʿǧam anṣâr al-Ḥusayn – al-nisâʾ*, 2009: 335.

[89] Modarressi notes that Salmân al-Fârsî was one of a number of the companions of Muḥammad who kept a special attachment to the 'people of the house' until the end of their lives. Abû Ḏarr al-Ġifârî, whose name will appear later in the Zaynab story, was another. The Shîʿa look upon these as comprising their first generation. Cf. MODARRESSI H., *Tradition and Survival. A Bibliographical Survey of Early Shîʾite Literature*, vol. I, Oneworld, Oxford 2003: 6.

despondent and sorrowing. ʿAlî explained to Salmân what his daughter would suffer at Karbalâʾ.[90] Karbâssî adds a note to say that in the days that she was pregnant with Zaynab, Fâṭima was overwhelmed with disquiet (*hamm*) and affliction (*ġamm*), not only because of Ğibrîl's visit to Muḥammad to inform him of the afflictions that Zaynab would suffer, but also because she carried both Zaynab and Umm Kulṯûm on the left side, completely different to al-Ḥasan and al-Ḥusayn.[91]

Aside from the trauma she would suffer around the Karbalâʾ event, tribulation shadowed Zaynab's life. Karbâssî tells us that the childhood that Zaynab left behind her was one filled with afflictions and adversities, including the loss of a number of people close to her heart; Karbâssî names among these her uncle Ğaʿfar al-Ṭayyâr. He notes that she had seen and heard numerous crucial events, some painful and some comforting, and it was these events that had burnished both the inner and the physical life with which she had been blessed. She was, he reminds us, born in the house of revelation and prophecy, and became seasoned with the wisdom usually found in one much older than her, and well-versed in general affairs, on the same level as a leader of people. The days passed her by, like the passing of the years, with their griefs and their festivities; she possessed an attentiveness that was more than the attentiveness of adults.[92]

Lamentation and grief are stitched into the fabric of her mother Fâṭima's life during the final illness and death of Muḥammad[93] and Fâṭima's own last months – Karbâssî notes that

---

[90] KARBÂSSÎ M.S., *Muʿǧam anṣâr al-Ḥusayn – al-nisâʾ*, 2009: 336.

[91] Op. cit.: 334.

[92] Op. cit.: 339.

[93] Ibn Saʿd., *Kitâb al-ṭabaqât al-kabîr*, vol. II, bb. *ḏikr al-ḥuzn ʿalâ rasûl Allâh*: 720, Ibn Ḥanbal., *Musnad*, vol. IV, *Musnad Anas b. Mâlik*, n. 13030: 392, al-Buḫârî., *Ṣaḥîḥ*, vol. V, bk. 59 (*Kitâb al-maġâzî*), n. 739: 526–527, Ibn Mâğa., *Sunan*, vol. I, bk. 6 (*Kitâb al-ğanâʾiz*), bb. 65, n. 1630: 522, al-Nasâʾî., *al-Sunan al-kubrâ*, vol. IV, *Kitâb al-ğanâʾiz*, bb. *fî al-bukâʾ ʿalâ al-mayyit*: 12–13, al-Ḥâkim al-Nîsâbûrî., *Kitâb (Talḫîs) al-mustadrak ʿalâ al-ṣaḥîḥayn*, vol. I, bk. 13 (*Kitâb al-ğanâʾiz*), n. 1409: 532–533, vol. III, bk. 30 (*Kitâb al-maġâzî*), n. 4457: 65, al-Baġdâdî., *Târîḫ Baġdâd*, vol. VI, n. 3292: 261–262.

when Muḥammad's death drew near, ʿAlî and Fâṭima, seeing all the indications of his death, were seized with weeping and sadness.[94] "Among the women believers," Ǧibrîl tells Fâṭima when her father dies, "there is no greater grief than yours",[95] while Ibn Kaṯîr, among others, reports that she never once laughed after her father's death.[96] All of this sadness could not have failed to affect Zaynab.

It was after Muḥammad's death that two momentous events, to which Zaynab was almost certainly a young and bewildered witness, thrust Fâṭima precipitously into conflict. The first was the alleged attempt to force ʿAlî's allegiance (*bayʿa*) to Abû Bakr, an incident relayed by a number of Sunnî transmitters and accentuated by the Shîʿa. Ostensibly, the intention of ʿUmar, Abû Bakr and some others, unindulgent towards ʿAlî's refusal to concede, was to take him by force to the mosque and compel him to do so. An armed group went to the house of ʿAlî and Fâṭima, threatening to burn it down. They forced their way in, wielding their swords in the house and injuring Fâṭima in the process, causing her to miscarry her unborn child. There are numerous reports of this incident, all of them fragmented and at variance in their details.[97] Al-Ṭabarî's report reads:

> "ʿUmar b. al-Khaṭṭāb came to the house of ʿAlī. Ṭalḥah and al-Zubayr and some of the Muhājirūn were [also] in the house [with ʿAlī]. ʿUmar cried out, "By God, either you come out to

---

[94] KARBÂSSÎ M.S., *Muʿǧam anṣâr al-Ḥusayn – al-nisâʾ*, 2009: 336.

[95] Ibn Ḥaǧar al-ʿAsqalânî., *Fatḥ al-bârî*, vol. VIII, bk. 6 (*Kitâb al-maġâzî*), bb. 84, n. 4434: 171.

[96] Abû Nuʿaym al-Iṣbahânî., *Ḥilyat al-awliyâʾ wa-ṭabaqât al-aṣfiyâʾ*, vol. II, bb. 133: 42–43, Ibn Kaṯîr., *al-Bidâya wa-l-nihâya*, vol. VI: 333.

[97] For Sunnî accounts, cf. al-Balâḏurî., *Kitâb ansâb al-ashrâf*, vol. I, nn. 1184, 1186: 586, HOWARD I.K.A., (trans.), *The History of al-Ṭabarî*, vol. IX, 1990: 186–187, Ibn al-Ḥadîd., *Sharḥ nahǧ al-balâġa*, vol. II: 23, vol. VI: 11, 47–49. For Shîʿî accounts, cf. al-Yaʿqûbî., *Târîḫ*, vol. II: 141.

> render the oath of allegiance [to Abū Bakr], or I will set the house on fire.'"'[98]

Al-Ṭabarî omits mention of violence against Fâṭima; the translator of the text, in a footnote, remarks that the scene grew violent and that Fâṭima was intensely angry.[99] The Sunnî transmitters are cautious in their telling of the story; for the most part, the threat by ʿUmar to burn everyone alive is the only actual violence mentioned. Ibn al-Ḥadîd includes in his account the vow by an angry Fâṭima that she will never again speak to ʿUmar.[100]

In his transmissions about the attack on the house, al-Mağlisî repeats his enumeration of the four children, and, following a number of transmitters, adds the name of Fiḍḍa,[101] Fâṭima's servant, who will play a later role in Zaynab's life and who is practically

---

[98] HOWARD I.K.A., (trans.), *The History of al-Ṭabarî*, vol. IX, 1990: 186–187.

[99] HOWARD I.K.A., (trans.), *The History of al-Ṭabarî*, vol. IX, 1990: 187, nt. 1291.

[100] Ibn al-Ḥadîd takes a view held by some Shîʿî transmitters: cf. Ibn al-Ḥadîd., *Sharḥ nahğ al-balâġa*, vol. VI: 11, 47–49.

[101] Fiḍḍa was supposedly a Nubian (Sudanese) princess named Maymûna (although others suggest that she was an Abyssinian slave) who came to work for Fâṭima and was renamed Fiḍḍa ('silver') by Muḥammad so so that she would not be ashamed of her dark colour. She seems to have been regarded as a member of the family and appears in a number of *aḥâdîṯ* about the household of Fâṭima. In terms of Zaynab, she features in a curious story about a lion, transmitted by al-Mağlisî from al-Kulaynî's *al-Kâfî*; after the death of al-Ḥusayn, when the intention of the enemy was to trample his body, Fiḍḍa, having related a strange tale to Zaynab, persuades her to allow Fiḍḍa to employ the services of a lion to prevent this terrible deed. It is a tale probably better relegated to the realms of hagiography. Cf. al-Kulaynî., *al-Kâfî fî ʿilm al-dîn*, vol. I, bb. *mawlid al-Ḥusayn*, n. 8: 465, al-Mağlisî., *Biḥâr al-anwâr*, vol. XLV, bb. 39, n. 17: 169, with a note that the *ḥadîṯ* is weak (*ḍaʿîf*) Cf. also SINDAWI K.A., "Fiḍḍa l-Nūbiyya: The Woman and her Role in Early Shiʿite History" in *al-Masāq. Journal of the Medieval Mediterranean*, v. 21. 2009: 269–287.

understood as a member of the household.[102] Al-Daylamî too, in his *Irshâd al-qulûb*, transmits that the four children were present at the incidents after Muḥammad's death.[103] A number of other writers too, including al-Mufîd and al-Ṭabarsî, insist that all four children were present when the house of ʿAlî and Fâṭima was attacked.[104]

The second event was the denial of Fâṭima's claim to Fadak,[105] a small town allocated to Muḥammad after the conquest of Ḫaybar; he dedicated its not inconsiderable revenues to the needs of the poor (travelers and members of the Banû Hâshim). After Muḥammad's death, Fâṭima asked Abû Bakr to hand over the possessions of her father he was still holding; in terms of Fadak and the shares of Ḫaybar, Abû Bakr refused, insisting that he had heard Muḥammad say that everything he left would be a public property for benevolent purposes (*ṣadaqa*).

This is strongly contentious issue, despite scholars from both sides, including al-Suyûṭî (on the authority of Abû Saʿîd al-Ḫudrî),

---

[102] al-Mağlisî., *Biḥâr al-anwâr*, vol. LIII, bb. 28, n. 4: 18. Cf. for example al-Ḫaṣîbî., *al-Hidâya* (*al-Kubrâ*), b. 14: 417. In this transmission, al-Ḫaṣîbî includes the name of Ruqayya. It is difficult to know to whom he is referring, but the number of texts which do not include a girl by that name as a fifth (already born) child suggest that it is an oversight. Al-Mûsawî names her too, transmitting from al-Ṭabarî in his *Ḏaḫâʾir al-ʿuqbâ* (on the authority of Ibn Saʿd), and noting that she died without coming of age. Cf. al-Ṭabarî., *Ḏaḫâʾir al-ʿuqbâ*: 105, AL-MÛSAWÎ M., *al-Kawṯar fî aḥwâl Fâṭima bt. al-nabî al-aṭhar*, vol. VII, ch. 17, n. 3/3860: 99.

[103] al-Daylamî., *Irshâd al-qulûb*, vol. II: 286.

[104] Cf. for example al-Ṭabarî., *Dalâʾil al-imâma*, n. 33: 104, al-Ḫaṣîbî., *al-Hidâya* (*al-Kubrâ*), bb. 2: 163, 180, bb. 14: 417, al-Ṭabarsî., *Tâğ al-mawâlîd*: 76, 80, *Iʿlâm al-warâ bi-aʿlâm al-hudâ*, bb. 5: 203, Ibn al-Biṭrîq., *al-ʿUmda fî ʿuyûn al-aḫbâr fî manâqib amîr al-muʾminîn*, *faṣl* 6: 29.

[105] Ibn Saʿd., *Kitâb al-ṭabaqât al-kabîr*, vol. XII, bb. *ḏikr banât rasûl Allâh*, n. 4927 (*Fâṭima*): 28–29, al-Buḫârî., *Ṣaḥîḥ*, vol. V, bk. 62 (*Kitâb faḍâʾil aṣḥâb al-nabî*), bb. 13, n. 60: 49–50, al-Balâḏurî., *Kitâb futûḥ al-buldân*, n. 119: 37–38, Faḫr al-Dîn al-Râzî., *al-Tafsîr al-kabîr*, vol. XV, Part 30, *Sûrat al-ḥashr*: 284, Ibn Kaṯîr., *al-Bidâya wa-l-nihâya*, vol. V: 249. Among the Shîʿa, cf. al-Yaʿqûbî., *Târîḫ*, vol. II: 142.

in their commentary on the verse, "*give the kinsman his due*" (Q. 17: 26), holding that when this verse was revealed, Muḥammad gave Fâṭima the village of Fadak.[106] There are varying accounts of Fâṭima's anger with Abû Bakr; while some maintain that she refused to see him, remaining angry with him until she died,[107] others, like Ibn Saʿd, tell us that, only for the sake of her husband ʿAlî, she saw him, but with great disinclination. While some record that she turned her face to the wall, or reduced Abû Bakr to tears with a stern lecture, Ibn Saʿd reports merely that "she was satisfied with him."[108] Zaynab was held to have been present at her mother's famous protest, prompted by these events immediately after Muḥammad's death – not only the usurpation of power, but also Abû Bakr's refusal to hand over the property of Fadak. It was delivered by Fâṭima before a gathering of believers in the mosque of her father in Medina, and in the course of which, among numerous

---

[106] al-Balâḏurî., *Kitâb futûḥ al-buldân*, n. 119: 37–38, al-Ḏahabî., *Mîzân al-iʿtidâl fî tarâğim al-riğâl*, vol. II, n. 4560: 492, Ibn Kaṯîr., *Tafsîr al-qurʾân al-ʿaẓîm*, vol. IV, *Sûrat al-isrâʾ*: 302 (he denies the possibility, insisting that the verse was revealed long before Muḥammad gave Fadak to Fâṭima), al-Suyûṭî., *al-Durr al-manṯûr fî al-tafsîr bi-l-maʾṯûr*, vol. IV, *Sûrat al-isrâʾ*: 320, al-Hayṯamî., *Mağmaʿ al-zawâʾid wa-manbaʿ al-fawâʾid*, vol. VII, *Sûrat al-isrâʾ*: 49, who declares the *ḥadîṯ* is 'weak' (*ḍaʿîf*) and 'abandoned' (*matrûk*). Among the Shîʿa, cf. al-Baḥrânî., *al-Burhân fî tafsîr al-qurʾân*, vol. II, Part 15, *Sûrat al-isrâʾ*, n. 1: 414–415 (insisting that Muḥammad was ordered by God to give Fadak to Fâṭima), al-Ṭûsî., *al-Tibyân fî tafsîr al-qurʾân*, vol. VI, *Sûrat al-isrâʾ*: 468. Cf. also al-Mağlisî, *Biḥâr al-anwâr*, vol. XXIX, bb. 11: 122.

[107] Ibn Ḥanbal., *Musnad*, vol. I, *Musnad Abî Bakr al-Ṣiddîq*, n. 25: 25, n. 60: 33, al-Buḫârî., *Ṣaḥîḥ*, vol. V, bk. 59 (*Kitâb al-mağâzî*), bb. 37, n. 545: 381–384, vol. VIII, bk. 80 (*Kitâb al-farâʾiḍ*), bb. 3, n. 718: 471–472, Muslim., *Ṣaḥîḥ*, vol. III, bk. 32 (*Kitâb al-ğihâd*), bb. 16, n. 52: 1380–1381, al-Ṭabarî., *Kitâb aḫbâr al-rusul wa-l-mulûk*, vol. V, n. 1825: 206, Ibn al-Ḥadîd., *Sharḥ nahğ al-balâğa*, vol. VI: 46, Ibn Kaṯîr., *al-Bidâya wa-l-nihâya*, vol. V: 249–250, 285.

[108] Ibn Saʿd., *Kitâb al-ṭabaqât al-kabîr*, vol. XII, bb. *ḏikr banât rasûl Allâh*, n. 4927 (*Fâṭima*): 28. Cf. also Ibn Kaṯîr., *al-Bidâya wa-l-nihâya*, vol. VI: 333, who claims that Abû Bakr came to her on her deathbed, asked forgiveness and was reconciled with her.

sentiments expressed, she asked Abû Bakr for her inheritance from her father.[109]

Suffice it to say that Zaynab, at this stage somewhere between five and seven years old, would have been inescapably enmeshed in these harrowing events, culminating in the death of her mother, but not ending there, since having lost her grandfather Muḥammad and, shortly after him, her unborn brother and her mother Fâṭima,[110] she would live to witness the murder of her father ʿAlî and her brothers al-Ḥasan and al-Ḥusayn. Transmitting from *Kitâb al-ṭirâẓ al-muḏḏahab*, Karbâssî notes that, present at the death of her mother, Zaynab there received the commission to accompany her two brothers, taking them under her wing and acting as a mother to them after Fâṭima's death.[111] Al-Kâshânî too, referring us to an historical work entitled *Nâsiḫ al-tawârîḫ*,[112] notes that Zaynab (aged six or seven) was present when Fâṭima died, and came, dragging her outer cloak, and cried out: "My father! Messenger of God! Now we come to know the deprivation of seeing you!"[113] He refers his readers to al-Maǧlisî's *Biḥâr al-anwâr*, transmitting from *Rawḍat al-wâʿiẓîn wa-tabṣirat al-muttaʿiẓîn*, which relates that upon the death of Fâṭima, Umm Kulṯûm came, dragging the train of the patched robe she was wearing and enwrapped in her preferred outer garment, and cried out: "My father! Messenger of God! In truth we are bereft of you with a bereavement never to be encountered again!" Al-Kâshânî insists that "without any doubt" this Umm

---

[109] KARBÂSSÎ M.S., *Muʿǧam anṣâr al-Ḥusayn – al-nisâʾ*, 2009: 339. Cf. al-Ṭabarsî., *Kitâb al-iḥtiǧâǧ ʿalâ ahl al-liǧâǧ*, vol. I: 99, al-Irbilî., *Kashf al-ġumma fî maʿrifat al-aʾimma*, vol. I: 482, al-Maǧlisî, *Biḥâr al-anwâr*, vol. XXIX: 221.

[110] For an overview of these events, cf. CLOHESSY C., *Fatima, Daughter of Muhammad*, 2009: 149–159.

[111] KARBÂSSÎ M.S., *Muʿǧam anṣâr al-Ḥusayn – al-nisâʾ*, 2009: 338.

[112] Authored in Persian by Muḥammad Taqî Kâshânî (d. 1296/1879), known as *Lisân al-mulk* ('mouthpiece of the nation'); this is an unfinished work, comprising two books, each containing a number of volumes.

[113] AL-KÂSHÂNÎ A., *250 Karâma li-l-sayyida Zaynab wa-sayyidât bayt al-nubuwwa*, 2008: 12–13.

Kulṯûm is in fact Zaynab, the eldest daughter of Fâṭima, and aged six or seven at her mother's death.[114]

At the death of Fâṭima, and as expressed by her final wish, ʿAlî marries his deceased wife's niece, Umâma bt. Abî al-ʿÂṣ, whose mother was Zaynab bt. Muḥammad;[115] she was, however, destined to play a far less significant role in the life of Zaynab than Fâṭima ever did.

The classical texts present two further distinct events, both ostensibly performed in haste and in secret. The first is the washing and preparation of Fâṭima's body immediately after her death. Most of the texts seem to agree that ʿAlî played the chief role in this, and that he was assisted by six others: al-Ḥasan, al-Ḥusayn, Zaynab, Umm Kulṯûm, Fiḍḍa and Asmâʾ bt. ʿUmays.[116] This is offset by one *ḥadîṯ* in al-Mağlisî in which, having washed the body of Fâṭima, ʿAlî calls Umm Kulṯûm, Zaynab, Sukayna, Fiḍḍa, al-Ḥasan and al-Ḥusayn to come and see their 'mother' for the last time. The Sukayna mentioned is the unknown quantity here, but is not of necessity a reference to another daughter, since ʿAlî uses the word 'mother' even for the relationship of Fâṭima to Fiḍḍa. Asmâʾ bt. ʿUmays is missing from the list; in that case, it could be a call addressed only intimate family members, of whom Fiḍḍa is regarded as one. Who, then, is Sukayna? It cannot be the daughter of al-Ḥusayn, who shares the name (although she is sometimes referred to as Sakîna). The English translation of *Biḥâr al-anwâr* mistakenly leaves Zaynab out of this list.[117]

---

[114] al-Fattâl al-Nîsâbûrî., *Rawḍat al-wâʿiẓîn wa-tabṣirat al-muttaʿiẓîn*, vol. I: 153, al-Mağlisî., *Biḥâr al-anwâr*, vol. XLIII, bb. 7, n. 20: 192. Cf. AL-KÂSHÂNÎ A., *250 Karâma li-l-sayyida Zaynab wa-sayyidât bayt al-nubuwwa*, 2008: 12–13.

[115] AL-KÂSHÂNÎ A., *250 Karâma li-l-sayyida Zaynab wa-sayyidât bayt al-nubuwwa*, 2008: 14, SHAHIN B., *Lady Zaynab*, 2002: 62.

[116] al-Ṭabarî., *Dalâʾil al-imâma*, n. 45: 136, al-Ḫaṣîbî., *al-Hidâya (al-Kubrâ)*, bb. 2: 178, al-Mağlisî., *Biḥâr al-anwâr*, vol. XXX, n. 164: 348, vol. XLIII, bb. 7, n. 1: 171, al-Ṭabarsî., *Ḫâtimat mustadrak al-wasâʾil*, vol. II, bb. 21, n. 1761: 186.

[117] al-Mağlisî., *Biḥâr al-anwâr*, vol. XLIII, bb. 7, n. 15: 179. Cf. SARWAR M., (trans.), *Behar al-anwar*, vol. 43, 2015: 256.

The second event is Fâṭima's burial by night in al-Baqîᶜ cemetery; Zaynab was almost certainly not present at this, and nor was her sister Umm Kulṯûm.[118] While al-Ḫaṣîbî notes that the burial and its concomitant rites were performed, at Fâṭima's request, by ᶜAlî, al-Ḥasan and al-Ḥusayn,[119] other texts add the names of al-ᶜAbbâs, al-Miqdâd and al-Zubayr.[120] With the burial of her mother, there is a thirty-year gap in what the classical texts tell us of Zaynab's life, aside from two major incidents: her marriage to ᶜAbd Allâh b. Ğaᶜfar b. Abî Ṭâlib b. ᶜAbd al-Muṭṭalib, and the 40/661 murder of her father ᶜAlî.

Karbâssî writes that when Zaynab had passed her ninth year (around 16/637), a number of high-level suitors, including Qurayshî nobles, desired to marry her, only to be turned down by ᶜAlî, who "did not find among them her equal." ᶜAlî seemed to be harking back to the words of Muḥammad, who had looked at the children of ᶜAlî and Ğaᶜfar, the two sons of Abû Ṭâlib, and said: 'Our girls for our sons and our sons for our girls'.[121] According to the classical texts, when Zaynab came of age, she was married by her father ᶜAlî b. Abî Ṭâlib to his nephew and her first cousin, ᶜAbd Allâh b. Ğaᶜfar b. Abî Ṭâlib b. ᶜAbd al-Muṭṭalib; her new husband's father was ᶜAlî's brother (Ğaᶜfar al-Ṭayyâr b. Abî Ṭâlib) and his mother, notes Qutbuddin,[122] was as that time ᶜAlî's own wife and thus Zaynab's stepmother, Asmâʾ bt. ᶜUmays. The Shîᶜî and a number of the Sunnî transmitters (including al-Ṭabarî) insist

---

[118] al-Ṭabarî., *Dalâʾil al-imâma*, n. 45: 136.

[119] al-Ḫaṣîbî., *al-Hidâya* (*al-Kubrâ*), bb. 2: 178, al-Mağlisî., *Biḥâr al-anwâr*, vol. XLIII, bb. 7, n. 1: 171.

[120] al-Mağlisî., *Biḥâr al-anwâr*, vol. XXIX: 389.

[121] KARBÂSSÎ M.S., *Muᶜğam anṣâr al-Ḥusayn – al-nisâʾ*, 2009: 340. Cf. al-Ṣadûq., *Man lâ yaḥḍuru-hu al-faqîh*, vol. III, n. 4384: 393, al-Ṭabarsî., *Makârim al-aḫlâq*: 204, Ibn Shahrâshûb., *Manâqib âl Abî Ṭâlib*, vol. III, bb. *faṣl fî azwâği-hi*: 305, al-Ḥurr al-ᶜÂmilî., *Tafṣîl wasâʾil al-shîᶜa ilâ taḥṣîl masâʾil al-sharîᶜa*, vol. XX, bb. 27: 74, al-Mağlisî., *Biḥâr al-anwâr*, vol. XLII, bb. 120: 92, vol. C, bb. 21: 373, al-Ṭabarsî., *Ḫâtimat mustadrak al-wasâʾil*, vol. XIV, bb. 23: 187.

[122] QUTBUDDIN B.T., "Zaynab bint Ali" in Lindsay Jones (ed.), *Encyclopedia of Religion*, 2nd edn., 2005: 9937.

that ʿAlî married no other woman until the death of Fâṭima.[123] By the time of Zaynab's marriage however, Fâṭima has been dead for a number of years.

About the details of the marriage, the classical sources tell us almost nothing; Karbâssî, in his hagiography, describes it in lyrical terms, remarking that the sixteen-year-old ʿAbd Allâh b. Ǧaʿfar did not hesitate in agreeing to marry Zaynab, having been captivated by her. Some of the sources do transmit that he fixed her dower, like the dower of her mother Fâṭima, at four-hundred-and-eighty dirhams.[124]

Despite the austerity of possessions, the marriage between Zaynab and ʿAbd Allâh b. Ǧaʿfar pictured by Karbâssî was fired with the warmth of faith and mutual understanding, and reigned over by a spirit of love, affection, sincere devotion and self-sacrifice in the path of God. When Zaynab was led in solemn procession to

---

[123] Amongst the Sunnî, cf. for e.g. al-Nasâʾî., *al-Sunan al-kubrâ*: 5, al-Ṭabarî., *Kitâb aḫbâr al-rusul wa-l-mulûk*, vol VII, n. 3470: 153, Ibn ʿAbd al-Barr., *al-Istîʿâb fî maʿrifat al-aṣḥâb*, vol. IV, *Kitâb al-nisâʾ*, n. 4057: 1894, Ibn Kaṯîr., *al-Bidâya wa-l-nihâya*, vol. VI: 333, Ibn Ḥaǧar al-ʿAsqalânî., *Tahḏîb al-tahḏîb*, vol. XII, *Kitâb al-nisâʾ*, n. 4434: 441. Among the Shîʿa, cf. al-Masʿûdî., *Murûǧ al-ḏahab*, vol. III, bb. 73, n. 1496: 31. The reason put forward by the Shîʿa for ʿAlî's monogamy is that Fâṭima was pure, and incomparable with other women. Even in Paradise, when other men can take the 'maidens of Paradise' as their brides, no such option will be open to ʿAlî. In Paradise, Fâṭima will be his only wife. Cf. Ibn Shahrâshûb., *Manâqib âl Abî Ṭâlib*, vol. III, bb. *manâqib Fâṭima al-Zahrâʾ*: 372.

[124] KARBÂSSÎ M.S., *Muʿǧam anṣâr al-Ḥusayn – al-nisâʾ*, 2009: 340–341. Cf. for e.g. al-Fattâl al-Nîsâbûrî., *Rawḍat al-wâʿiẓîn wa-tabṣirat al-muttaʿiẓîn*, vol. I: 146, Ibn Shahrâshûb., *Manâqib âl Abî Ṭâlib*, vol. III, bb. *faṣl fî tazwîǧi-hâ*: 351, 356, al-Maǧlisî., *Biḥâr al-anwâr*, vol. XLIII, bb. 5: 112–113. While later Shîʿî *aḥâdîṯ* take up the theme of Fâṭima's own dower being, rather than a sum of money, her prerogatives as intercessor for the sinners of her father's community, Ibn Ḥanbal records that Muḥammad gave Fâṭima a dress of velvet, a skin pillow stuffed with palm fibres, two millstones, two earthenware jars and a water skin. Cf. Ibn Ḥanbal., *Musnad*, vol. I, *Musnad ʿAlî b. Abî Ṭâlib*, n. 643: 183, n. 715: 200, n. 819: 223, n. 838: 227–228, n. 853: 231.

the house of ʿAbd Allâh al-Ṭayyâr, God blessed ʿAbd Allâh and lavishly bestowed on him the blessing of property, of children and of the acquisition of estates. His terrain, once a desert, became a lush and fruitful land, and he was a means of sustenance to the indigent and the poor.[125] Although he was a man of means, the couple is said to have lived a modest life, with much of their wealth devoted to charity, although this factor is not highlighted by any classical source.[126]

While historians like al-Balâḏurî and al-ʿAsqalânî merely note that Zaynab bore children for her husband, neither naming nor numbering them,[127] according to tradition Zaynab bore four sons and a daughter: ʿAlî, known as ʿAlî al-Zaynabî, ʿAwn al-Akbar, ostensibly killed at Karbalâʾ, ʿAbbâs, about whom there is little information, Muḥammad, also possibly a martyr at Karbalâʾ, and Umm Kulṯûm.[128] However, the names and numbers of Zaynab's children are diversely and confusingly reported by the classical texts, and the issue is dealt with briefly in an appendix to this work.

The couple remained in close contact with Zaynab's two brothers, and with ʿAlî, accompanying him when he emigrated to Kûfa in 36/657 as the fourth of the 'rightly-guided caliphs'

---

[125] KARBÂSSÎ M.S., *Muʿǧam anṣâr al-Ḥusayn – al-nisâʾ*, 2009: 340–1.

[126] He is sometimes nicknamed *baḥr al-saḫâ* or *baḥr al-ǧûd* ('the ocean of munificence'), although this is not found in the classical texts. Cf. al-Balâḏurî., *Kitâb ansâb al-ashrâf*, vol. III: 393, Ibn al-Ǧawzî., *Ṣifat al-ṣafwa*, vol. II, bb. *Fâṭima bt. Rasûl Allâh*: 2, Ibn al-Aṯîr., *Usd al-ġâba fî maʿrifat al-ṣaḥâba*, vol. VI, bb. 6961 (*Zaynab bt. ʿAlî b. Abî Ṭâlib*): 136–137, Sibṭ al-Ǧawzî., *Taḏkirat ḫawâṣṣ al-umma bi-ḏikr ḫaṣâʾiṣ al-aʾimma*: 270. Cf. also HUSAIN A.A.T., (trans.), *House of Sorrows*, Islamic Publishing House, Ontario 2010: 182, ANTHONY S.W., (trans.), *The Expeditions. An Early Biography of Muḥammad*, New York University Press, New York 2015: 316. Curiously, this text omits any mention of ʿAbd Allâh b. Ǧaʿfar's marriage to Zaynab.

[127] al-Balâḏurî., *Kitâb ansâb al-ashrâf*, vol. III: 393, al-ʿAsqalânî., *al-Iṣâba fî tamyîz al-ṣaḥâba*, vol. IV, n. 510: 314–315.

[128] QUTBUDDIN B.T., "Zaynab bint Ali" in Lindsay Jones (ed.), *Encyclopedia of Religion*, 2nd edn., 2005: 9937: cf. Ibn al-Aṯîr., *Usd al-ġâba fî maʿrifat al-ṣaḥâba*, vol. VI, bb. 6961 (*Zaynab bt. ʿAlî b. Abî Ṭâlib*): 136–137.

(*râshidûn*).[129] According to the idealistic 'The Victory of Truth',[130] Zaynab undertook the role of educating the women, holding sessions to help them study the Qur'ân and augment their knowledge of Islam, starting this practice in Medina and later continuing it when she moved with her father and family to Kûfa. The hagiographers relate that a group of the men of Kûfa asked of ʿAlî that Zaynab undertake the instruction of their womenfolk in the characteristics of religion and the exegesis of the Qur'ân; the Imâm acceded to their request. One day, ʿAlî entered his house in Kûfa and heard his daughter Zaynab speaking to the women about the disconnected letters[131] at the beginnings of the chapters of the Qur'ân. She was explaining *kâf*, *hâ'*, *yâ'*, *ʿayn*, *ṣâd*,[132] and ʿAlî said to her: "Light of my eye! Did you know that these point to what will befall your brother al-Ḥusayn in the land of Karbalâ'?"[133] While in itself, the concept of Zaynab taking a role in the education of women is an important one, none of these pious legends find any resonance in the classical texts, although Karbâssî notes that al-Baḥrânî, in his *al-Burhân fî tafsîr al-qur'ân*, in a long (although not widely diffused) *ḥadîṯ* with a chain from Imâm al-ʿAskarî,[134] explains that the *kâf* stands for Karbalâ', the *hâ'* for the perishing of the progeny (*halâk al-ʿitra*), the *yâ'* for Yazîd, whom he asks God to

---

[129] KARBÂSSÎ M.S., *Muʿǧam anṣâr al-Ḥusayn – al-nisâ'*, 2009: 341, 343.

[130] BILGRAMI M.H., *The Victory of Truth: The Life of Zaynab bint 'Ali*, 1986: 'Womanhood', n.p.

[131] A reference to the much-debated letters found at the start of twenty-nine chapters of the Qur'ân (Chapters 2, 3, 7, 10–15, 19–20, 26–32, 36, 38, 40–46, 50 and 68), just after the *bismillâh*, and variously called *fawâtiḥ al-suwar* ('the openers of the chapters'), *awâ'il al-suwar* ('the beginnings of the chapters') or *al-ḥurûf al-muqaṭṭa'* ('the disconnected letters').

[132] The five letters at the beginning of Q. 19, *sûrat Maryam*.

[133] KARBÂSSÎ M.S., *Muʿǧam anṣâr al-Ḥusayn – al-nisâ'*, 2009: 343.

[134] Abû Muḥammad al-Ḥasan b. ʿAlî al-ʿAskarî (d. 259/873 or 260/874), the eleventh Imâm.

curse, the ʿ*ayn* for al-Ḥusayn's thirst (ʿ*aṭash*) and the *ṣâd* for his patience (*ṣabr*).[135]

The next four years would be replete with military confrontations with the insurrectionary governor of Syria, Muʿâwiya b. Abî Sufyân as well as with the Ḥawâriğ rebels, one of whom, ʿAbd al-Raḥmân b. Mulğam al-Murâdî, would eventually assassinate ʿAlî in the mosque at Kûfa in January 40/661, when Zaynab was around thirty-five years old. Her husband ʿAbd Allâh b. Ğaʿfar sided with ʿAlî in the battles he fought in those years, and was one of the commanders in his army at the battles of the Camel, Ṣiffîn, and Nahrawân.[136]

Karbâssî relates an incident that almost certainly concerns ʿÂʾisha, daughter of Abû Bakr and widow of Muḥammad, and her behaviour around the battle of the Camel, although he uses no name. It was transmitted that one of the women (ostensibly Ḥafṣa, daughter of ʿUmar b. al-Ḫaṭṭâb and widow of Muḥammad) received a note from her sister (but in other texts, from ʿÂʾisha) during the Battle of the Camel, reading: "What is the news?! What is the news?! ʿAlî is like the ruddy one;[137] if he advances he will be

---

[135] KARBÂSSÎ M.S., *Muʿğam anṣâr al-Ḥusayn – al-nisâʾ*, 2009: 343, nt. 6. Cf. al-Baḥrânî., *al-Burhân fî tafsîr al-qurʾân*, vol. III, 6834/3: 697.

[136] KARBÂSSÎ M.S., *Muʿğam anṣâr al-Ḥusayn – al-nisâʾ*, 2009: 344. In the course of his Imamate, ʿAlî fought in three major battles: the 35/656 Battle of the Camel (at which ʿÂʾisha, a member of the opposing force, was taken prisoner when her side was defeated), Ṣiffîn and Nahrawân. The Battle of Ṣiffîn (37/657), fought against Muʿâwiya's army, lasted three days and was inconclusive. Negotiations, equally inconclusive, were held and Muʿâwiya, without formally giving in to ʿAlî, retained the governorship of Syria. Dismayed at the mediation and at what they deemed a compromise, a group called the Ḥawâriğ ('those who go out') abandoned ʿAlî; it was their main force whom ʿAlî would later defeat at Nahrawân in 39/659.

[137] Karbâssî omits the word 'horse', although this does not diminish the meaning. However, by *al-ashqar*, Karbâssî might well have in mind a camel, since according to Lane, the word, when can be applied to a camel, and means 'intensely red' (Cf. LANE E.W., *An Arabic-English Lexicon*, vol. IV, 1968: 1581). Furthermore, both the verbs used in the poem (ʿ*aqara*-

slaughtered, and if he delays he will be wounded." This woman gathers the women of her people, and gets them to beat tambourines and repeat the words. According to Karbâssî, Zaynab hears of what is being said and decides to go and reprove the women. Umm Salama,[138] reminding her that she is the daughter of the Commander of the Faithful and the most esteemed of the family of Abû Ṭâlib, suggests that she herself be assigned to go and reprove them. Zaynab refuses, determined to go in person. Dressed in the clothes of a serving girl, not the last time Zaynab would emply such a disguise, surrounded by other servants and accompanied by Umm Salama and Umm Ayman,[139] she approaches the woman (again, seemingly Ḥafṣa rather than ʿÂʾisha) who instigated the event and who, upon seeing her, is ashamed and dismayed and says: "They did this out of ignorance!" Zaynab responds by saying: "You two have been assisting against him just as you assisted against his brother before him."[140]

Ladak, quoting from *Biḥâr al-anwâr*, relates a very similar incident but with diverse details and wording; ʿÂʾisha writes to Ḥafṣa about ʿAlî being on the move, and says of him: "What is the news?! What is the news?! ʿAlî is on the journey, like a sorrel coloured[141]

---

yaʿqiru and *naḥara-yanḥaru*) can mean specifically 'to stab' or 'greatly wound' or 'hamstring' or 'slaughter' a camel.

138 Widow of Muḥammad and consequently one of the 'mothers of the believers', Umm Salama is held in high regard by Shîʿî Islam, not only because she helped to care for Fâṭima and later al-Ḥasan and al-Ḥusayn, but also because she transmitted some of the most crucial *aḥâdîṯ* about the *ahl al-bayt*.

139 An Abyssianian slave girl, Umm Ayman had nursed the young Muḥammad after the death of his mother Âmina and, despite his having freed her, continued to care for him throughout his adult life. She is held in great esteem in the Shîʿî sources.

140 KARBÂSSÎ M.S., *Muʿǧam anṣâr al-Ḥusayn – al-nisâʾ*, 2009: 344.

141 Ladak uses 'black'; but Lane notes that when applied to a man, the Arabic *ashqar* has a range of meanings encompassing a variety of ways of saying 'a ruddy complexion combined with fairness'. When applied to a horse, it means a horse of a clear red or sorrel colour. Although it signifies the best of horses, it is also understood as being regarded by the Arabs as

horse; if he advances he will be wounded, and if he delays he will be slaughtered." According to *Biḥâr al-anwâr*, it is Umm Kulṯûm, and not Zaynab, who hears of these words; veiling herself in her cloak (rather than a servant's dress), she approaches the celebrating women and, once unveiled, is recognised by a shocked Ḥafṣa. Umm Kulṯûm, alluding to Q. 66: 4[142] and chastising both Ḥafṣa and ʿÂʾisha, says: "You two have been assisting against him just as you assisted against his brother before him…"[143] The narration is very rare in the classical sources;[144] in both al-Mufîd and al-Maǧlisî, it is Umm Kulṯûm and not Zaynab named as the protagonist, and since al-Mufîd clearly distinguishes between the girls, there is little reason not to agree with Ladak that it is in fact the younger and not the older daughter of ʿAlî and Fâṭima involved.

Karbâssî relates an incident found in al-Mufîd's *Kitâb al-irshâd*,[145] and in which ʿAlî is in conversation with his daughter Umm Kulṯûm. He tells her that he has seen how scanty the time he will remain with them is, and when she questions this, he says: "I have seen the prophet of God in my sleep. He was wiping dust off

---

an ill omen. Cf. LANE E.W., *An Arabic-English Lexicon*, vol. IV, 1968: 1581. It was a red or roan horse (*al-ashqar*) that ʿAlî gave to his future assassin, Ibn Mulǧam (cf. al-Mufîd., *Kitâb al-irshâd*, vol. I, bb. *masîr Muʿâwiya naḥwa al-Iraq*: 11.

142 Ostensibly, as Ladak notes, a verse revealed to call ʿÂ'isha and Ḥafṣa to repentance after they had caused some trouble out of jealously of another of Muḥammad's wives, Zaynab bt. Ǧaḥsh. Cf. LADAK J., *The Hidden Treasure. Lady Umm Kulthum, Daughter of Imam Ali and Lady Fatima*, 2011: n.p.

143 al-Maǧlisî., *Biḥâr al-anwâr*, vol. XXXII, bb. *bayʿa amîr al-muʾminîn*: 90. Cf. LADAK J., *The Hidden Treasure. Lady Umm Kulthum, Daughter of Imam Ali and Lady Fatima*, 2011: n.p.

144 Cf. al-Mufîd., *al-Kâfiʾa fî ibṭâl tawba al-ḫâṭiʾa*: 16, *al-Ǧamal wa-l-nuṣra li-sayyid al-ʿitra fi ḥarb al-baṣra*: 276. Neither work is recorded by Brockelmann.

145 Also in Ibn Shahrâshûb., *Manâqib âl Abî Ṭâlib*, vol. VII, bb. *faṣl fî maqtali-hi*: 490, al-Fattâl al-Nîsâbûrî., *Rawḍat al-wâʿiẓîn wa-tabṣirat al-muttaʿiẓîn*, bb. *wafât amîr alʾmuʾminîn*, n. 7 [319]: 310, al-Ḫawârizmî., *Manâqib amîr al-muʾminîn*, n. 402: 378.

my face and saying: ʿAlî, do not worry, you have discharged all you had to do." Umm Kulṯûm notes that not even three days had passed before the fatal blow was struck. When she cried aloud at this incident, ʿAlî said to her: "Do not do that, my daughter! I see the Messenger of God beckoning with his hand: ʿAlî, come to us, for what we have[146] is better for you."[147]

Karbâssî suggests in a footnote that it is manifest from a plurality of transmissions that the intended here is Zaynab, wife of ʿAbd Allâh b. Ǧaʿfar, although it is hard to follow his logic in this. Zaynab al-Ṣuġrâ, i.e. Umm Kulṯûm would have been in her early thirties at the time of her father's assassination, so that there is no reason why this conversation could not have been with her. Certainly, Ladak transmits this story as concerning Umm Kulṯûm, and not Zaynab wife of ʿAbd Allâh b. Ǧaʿfar.[148] Karbâssî goes on to note that it is not confirmed in such a way that it is a settled matter, reminding us that al-Mufîd in his *Kitâb al-irshâd*, designates the children of Fâṭima as al-Ḥasan, al-Ḥusayn, Zaynab the elder and Zaynab the younger, nicknamed Umm Kulṯûm, thus demonstrating clearly enough that when he speaks of Umm Kulṯûm, he means the sister of Zaynab al-Kubrâ. Karbâssî finishes his note with a laconic 'God knows' and with the equivocal observation: "At any rate, there is no distinction between the two of them" (*lâ farq baynahimâ*). It is hard to know whether he means by this that they are equally important as daughters of ʿAlî and Fâṭima, or that they are one and the same person, as held by a number of other scholars.[149]

During Ramaḍân of the year 40/661, ʿAlî would break the fast one night with al-Ḥasan, one night with al-Ḥusayn and one night with ʿAbd Allâh b. Ǧaʿfar, husband of his daughter Zaynab (on

---

[146] Mistranscribed in Karbâssî as *ʿinda-hâ* instead of *ʿinda-nâ*.

[147] KARBÂSSÎ M.S., *Muʿǧam anṣâr al-Ḥusayn – al-nisâʾ*, 2009: 345. Cf. al-Mufîd., *Kitâb al-irshâd*, vol. I, bb. *masîr Muʿâwiya naḥwa al-Iraq*: 13.

[148] LADAK J., *The Hidden Treasure. Lady Umm Kulthum, Daughter of Imam Ali and Lady Fatima*, 2011: n.p.

[149] KARBÂSSÎ M.S., *Muʿǧam anṣâr al-Ḥusayn – al-nisâʾ*, 2009: 344–345, nt. 6.

account of her);[150] he never ate beyond three mouthfuls, once claiming that he would prefer that God's decision came to him while he was hungry. It was only a night or two after this declaration that he was killed. Transmitting from al-Mufîd's *Kitâb al-irshâd*, Karbâssî relates how the night before he was killed, ʿAlî remained awake and did not go to the *masğid* for the night prayer as was his custom. He was questioned about this by his daughter Umm Kulṯûm – Karbâssî adds in brackets that this is Zaynab, although this is not clarified in al-Mufîd's text – and he tells her that he did not go out, since doing so would mean his death. Then one Ibn al-Nabbâḥ[151] comes to summon him to prayer; ʿAlî goes a little way and then returns. Umm Kulṯûm (again, identified as Zaynab by Karbâssî but not by al-Mufîd) begs him to send someone else, Ğaʿda,[152] to lead the prayer, and although ʿAlî agrees at first, he later relents, saying: "The appointed time is inescapable!"[153] Again, since al-Mufîd carefully distinguishes between the two sisters, it would be surprising if the daughter in question here was in fact Zaynab and not Umm Kulṯûm. Ladak, in his book on Umm Kulṯûm, transmits the *ḥadîṯ* from *Kitâb al-irshâd* and sees no reason to doubt that the text concerns Zaynab al-Ṣuġrâ and not her elder sister.[154] Sharîf al-Raḍî, on the other hand, insists that it is Zaynab.[155]

Karbâssî transmits a number of *aḥâdîṯ* from *Biḥâr al-anwâr* surrounding the death of ʿAlî. When his death drew near, says one of

---

[150] Op. cit.: 344. The author of *Rawḍat al-wâʿiẓîn* replaces the name ʿAbd Allâh b. Ğaʿfar with that of ʿAbd Allâh b. al-ʿAbbâs: cf. al-Fattâl al-Nîsâbûrî., *Rawḍat al-wâʿiẓîn wa-tabṣirat al-muttaʿiẓîn*: bb. *wafât amîr al'mu'minîn*, n. 6 [318]: 310.

[151] ʿÂmir b. al-Nabbâḥ al-Kûfî, ʿAlî's *mu'aḏḏin*.

[152] Ibn Hubayra al-Maḫzûmî, one of ʿAlî's army leaders and supporters.

[153] al-Mufîd., *Kitâb al-irshâd*, vol. I, bb. *masîr Muʿâwiya naḥwa al-Iraq*, n. 6: 14, KARBÂSSÎ M.S., *Muʿğam anṣâr al-Ḥusayn – al-nisâ'*, 2009: 345.

[154] LADAK J., *The Hidden Treasure. Lady Umm Kulthum, Daughter of Imam Ali and Lady Fatima*, 2011: n.p.

[155] Sharîf al-Raḍî (Abû al-Ḥasan Muḥammad b. al-Ḥusayn Mûsâ al-Musawî al-Baġdâdî) in his *Ḫaṣâ'iṣ al-a'imma*: 23.

these reports, his daughters Zaynab and Umm Kulṯûm came in and sat with him on his bed. They drew close, grieving and saying: "Father, who is there for the young until he comes of age? Who is there for the old among the crowd? Our grief for you will be long and our tears will never cease!"[156] Karbâssî then transmits a second *ḥadîṯ* from al-Mağlisî in which, just prior to his death, ʿAlî's forehead is sweating and he makes as if to wipe the moisture away with his hand. Karbâssî has Zaynab question him about this, and ʿAlî replies: "My daughter, I heard your grandfather the Messenger of God saying that when the believer's death descends upon him and his demise draws near, the sweat of his forehead will be like brilliant pearls." However, as Karbâssî then notes, in the *Biḥâr al-anwâr* account, it is not Zaynab who in the interlocutor, but one of ʿAlî's sons.[157] Noting that the narrative that follows is not found in *Biḥâr al-anwâr*,[158] Karbâssî then reports:

> Immediately, Zaynab lay on the breast of her father and said: "My father, Umm Ayman recounted to me the event of Karbalâʾ, but I would love to hear it from you! ʿAlî replied: My daughter, the event is as Umm Ayman recounted it to you. It is as though I were with you and with the women, perishing as the captives of that country, those reduced to submission, "*in fear lest men should extirpate you*",[159] but patience, patience!"

When he had finished his lament, Zaynab, Umm Kulṯûm and all the other women cried out, tearing at their robes, slapping their cheeks, and "the outcry increased in the residence."[160] When they

---

[156] KARBÂSSÎ M.S., *Muʿǧam anṣâr al-Ḥusayn – al-nisâʾ*, 2009: 351–352, al-Mağlisî., *Biḥâr al-anwâr*, vol. XLII, bb. 127: 289.

[157] KARBÂSSÎ M.S., *Muʿǧam anṣâr al-Ḥusayn – al-nisâʾ*, 2009: 352, al-Mağlisî., *Biḥâr al-anwâr*, vol. XLII, bb. 127: 291.

[158] In fact, it is, but in different form: cf. al-Mağlisî., *Biḥâr al-anwâr*, vol. XXVIII, bb. 6: 60.

[159] Q. 8: 26.

[160] The report of the robe tearing and cheek beating is indeed in *Biḥâr al-anwâr*, but is reported as a result of ʿAlî's death, and not his prediction of the Karbalâʾ event and its aftermath. Cf. al-Mağlisî., *Biḥâr al-anwâr*, vol. XLII, bb. 127: 293.

began the preparation of his body, al-Ḥasan called out to his sisters Zaynab and Umm Kulṯûm: "My sisters, bring me the perfumes of my grandfather the Messenger of God!" Zaynab brought the perfumes to him in great haste, and its odour filled the house and all of Kûfa.[161] In another, similar narration, Zaynab reports:

> When Ibn Mulğam, may God curse him, struck my father, and I saw, as a result of it, the sign of death, I said to him: "My father! Umm Ayman recounted to me this and this, but I would have loved to hear it from you!" He replied: "My daughter, the *ḥadîṯ* was as Umm Ayman recounted it (to you). It was as though I were with you and the daughters of your people in that country, ignominious, reduced to submission, "*in fear lest men should extirpate you*",[162] but be patient, for by the One "*who splitteth the grain of corn*"[163] and created the soul, on that Day God will not have on the earth a *walî* better than you (pl), better than those who love you (pl) and better than your Shî'a."[164]

In a further instance, al-Mufîd's *Kitâb al-irshâd* recounts the words of Ibn Mulğam, who is brought before the dying 'Alî. "Enemy of God," Umm Kulṯûm shouts at him, "you have killed the Commander of the Faithful." Ibn Mulğam replies that he has killed no one but her father. "Enemy of God," she cries out, "I truly hope that there is no harm to him." "I see you are only crying for 'Alî,"

---

161 KARBÂSSÎ M.S., *Mu'ğam anṣâr al-Ḥusayn – al-nisâ'*, 2009: 352, where he adds words that are not in the text from which he is transmitting; al-Mağlisî., *Biḥâr al-anwâr*, vol. XLII, bb. 127: 294. Al-Ḫawârizmî in his *al-Manâqib* omits all mention of Zaynab present at the preparation of her father's body but puts 'Abd Allâh b. Ğa'far there with al-Ḥasan and al-Ḥusayn. Cf. al-Ḫawârizmî., *al-Manâqib*, bb. *fî bayân maqtali-hi*, n. 401: 386.

162 Q. 8: 26.

163 Q. 6: 95.

164 Ibn Qûlûya al-Qummî., *Kâmil al-ziyârât*, bb. 88: 265, al-Mağlisî., *Biḥâr al-anwâr*, vol. XXVIII, bb. 6: 60, vol. XLII, bb. 127: 294, vol. XLV, b. 39, n. 30: 183.

replies Ibn Mulǧam. While al-Mufîd and al-Ḫawârizmî identify the interlocutor as Umm Kulṯûm, Karbâssî insists it is Zaynab.[165]

Karbâssî reproduces another long *ḥadîṯ* from *Biḥâr al-anwâr* concerning the cosmic reaction in the instant that Ibn Mulǧam strikes the fatal blow against ʿAlî. The angels in heaven raise a great outcry in prayer, a violent wind, black and tenebrous, rages, and the angel Ǧibrîl calls out between heaven and earth, in a voice heard by all who are awake:

> By God, the pillars of guidance are torn down! By God, the stars of heaven and the guideposts of the pious are obliterated! By God, the firm hold is routed! The son of the uncle of Muḥammad the Chosen One has been killed! The elected guardian has been killed! ʿAlî the Approved (*al-Murtaḍâ*) has been killed. Killed, by God, is the master of the guardians, killed by the most wretched of villains![166]

When Umm Kulṯûm hears Ǧibrîl's death announcement, she strikes her face and cheeks, tears her robe and lets out a cry: "My father! My ʿAlî! My Muḥammad! My master!" Then she approaches her brothers, al-Ḥasan and al-Ḥusayn. Almost certainly, this is not Zaynab, as implied by Karbâssî, but her younger sister.

After the death of her father ʿAlî, Zaynab's brother al-Ḥasan, in Shîʿî eyes the rightful caliph and the second Imâm, would abdicate in favour of Muʿâwiya, who then continued as the caliph. The details of this abdication are too complex to recount here; its conditions, upon which Muʿâwiya would quite patently renege, included that after Muʿâwiya's death, the caliphate would revert to al-

---

[165] al-Mufîd., *Kitâb al-irshâd*, vol. I, bb. *shahâda al-Imâm al-Ḥasan*: 19, al-Ḫawârizmî., *al-Manâqib*, bb. *fî bayân maqtali-hi*, n. 400: 384, KARBÂSSÎ M.S., *Muʿǧam anṣâr al-Ḥusayn – al-nisâʾ*, 2009: 351. Al-Maǧlisî attributes these words to Umm Kulṯûm, who addresses Ibn Mulǧam tearfully: "Alas for you! As for my father, there is no fear for him! But God has rendered you vile in the world and the Hereafter, and your place of destiny is the Fire for all eternity!" Ibn Mulǧam replies: "Weep, since you are a mourner…" al-Maǧlisî., *Biḥâr al-anwâr*, vol. XLII, bb. 127: 289.

[166] KARBÂSSÎ M.S., *Muʿǧam anṣâr al-Ḥusayn – al-nisâʾ*, 2009: 351, al-Maǧlisî., *Biḥâr al-anwâr*, vol. XLII, bb. 127: 282.

Ḥasan, and that Muʿâwiya would not harm any of al-Ḥasan's followers. Al-Ḥasan retired to Medina, where he was to die in 48/669, poisoned, insist the Shîʿî historians and some of their Sunnî counterparts, at the instigation of Muʿâwiya. Karbâssî notes that as al-Ḥasan's body was being penetrated by poison and he began to discharge blood into a basin, whenever he heard that his sister Zaynab wanted to visit him, he would have the basin removed out of pity for her. She persisted in weeping for her brother al-Ḥasan for a whole month, and demonstrated her mourning, like all the Banû Hâshim, by dressing in black for a whole year.[167] Al-Ḥasan was

---

[167] KARBÂSSÎ M.S., *Muʿǧam anṣâr al-Ḥusayn – al-nisâʾ*, 2009: 354. Al-Maǧlisî, transmitting from al-Barqî's *al-Maḥâsin*, certainly reports that when al-Ḥusayn was killed, the women of the Banû Hâshim dressed in black to mourn him (al-Barqî., *al-Maḥâsin*, vol. II, bb. 25, n. 195: 420. Cf. also al-Ḥurr al-ʿÂmilî., *Tafṣîl wasâʾil al-shîʿa ilâ taḥṣîl masâʾil al-sharîʿa*, vol. III, bb. 67, n. 10–3508: 237, al-Baḥrânî., *ʿAwâlim al-ʿulûm wa-l-maʿârif al-aḥwâl min al-âyât wa-l-aḫbâr wal-aqwâl*, vol. XIV, n. 8: 412, al-Maǧlisî., *Biḥâr al-anwâr*, vol. XLV, bb. 39, n. 33: 177, vol. LXXIX, bb. 16, n. 24: 84, al-Ǧazâʾirî., *Riyâḍ al-abrâr fî manâqib al-aʾimma al-aṭhâr*, vol I: 259). Nevertheless, this is a report found in few classical texts, and the issue of wearing black clothing seems not entirely agreed upon in the Shîʿî sources – al-Kulaynî dedicates a chapter to the subject (al-Kulaynî., *al-Kâfî*, vol. II, bb. 6 (*Lubs al-sawâd*): 449), noting the Muḥammad did not like the colour black except for a number of items of clothing, and narrating an hadit reporting that the ʿAlî b. al-Ḥusayn was seen wearing a black outer garment. *Shayḫ* al-Ṣadûq claims that there is no sin in wearing black for the sake of piety (al-Ṣadûq., *Man lâ yaḥḍuru-hu al-faqîh*, vol. I, bb. *Ma yuṣallâ fî-hi*, n. 770: 252), while in his *al-Muqniʿ*, black is branded as the clothing of Pharoah (al-Ṣadûq., *al-Muqniʿ*, bb. *al-nawâdir*: 542). A wry *ḥadîṯ* in *ʿIlal al-sharâʾiʿ* reports that Imâm Ǧaʿfar al-Ṣâdiq instructs some Shîʿa who ask him about dressing in black that if one's heart is 'whitewashed' one can wear whatever one wants (al-Ṣadûq., *ʿIlal al-sharâʾiʿ wa-l-aḥkâm*, vol II, bb. 56, n. 5: 347. The Imâm was himself dressed in black at the time). However, in other traditions, Imâm Ǧaʿfar al-Ṣâdiq forbids praying in black, which he deems the colour of the clothing of the people of the Fire (cf. for e.g. al-Kulaynî., *al-Kâfî*, vol. III, n. 30: 403, vol. VI, n. 2: 449, al-Ṣadûq., *Man lâ yaḥḍuru-hu al-faqîh*, vol. I, bb. *Ma yuṣallâ fî-hi*, n. 766: 251, n. 771: 252, n. 774: 253, al-Ṣadûq., *ʿIlal al-sharâʾiʿ wa-l-aḥkâm*, vol II, bb. 56, n. 1:

succeeded as Imâm by his brother al-Ḥusayn. In 60/680 Muʿâwiya died, defaulting on his pledges and appointing his son Yazîd to succeed him. The Muʿâwiya caliphate, (during which al-Ḥusayn received numerous appeals and pledges of support should he lead a revolt and reclaim the caliphate) and the accession of Yazîd to leadership after his father's death would be the catalyst for the Karbalâʾ event.

After Karbalâʾ and her return to Medina, substantially little is known of Zaynab's life until her death aged around fifty-six, on 15th Rağab 62/682 or, alternatively, 11th or 21st Ğumâdâ al-ṯânî, or 24th Ṣafar, or 16th Ḏû al-Hiğğa. Although most seem to agree upon a date some six months after her return to Medina, others maintain an earlier death, sometime in 61/681. As with the details of her birth, the reports for this period are substantially conflictual, and three theses exist: according to some, she remained in Medina until her death, and was buried there. Writing in his encyclopaedic *Aʿyân al-Shîʿa*, al-ʿÂmilî asserts that al-Baqîʿ cemetery in Medina is the place of Zaynab's tomb, since "it is not established that after her return to Medina she ever left there again."[168] However, Shahin

---

346, n. 4: 347). Al-Ṣadûq reports ʿAlî b. Abî Ṭâlib declaring black to the colour of Pharoah's clothing (al-Ṣadûq., *Man lâ yaḥḍuru-hu al-faqîh*, vol. I, bb. *Ma yuṣallâ fî-hi*, n. 770: 251, al-Ṣadûq., *ʿIlal al-sharâʾiʿ wa-l-aḥkâm*, vol II, bb. 56, n. 6: 347, al-Ṣadûq., *Kitâb al-ḫiṣâl*, vol. II: 615). Considering the number of Shîʿî devotees, including those in leadership, who do where black, and especially in the month of Muḥarram, this seems not to be an issue of any import.

168 al-ʿÂmilî., *Aʿyân al-Shîʿa*, vol. VII: 140. Noting the ignorance about the dates of death and places of burial of many of the *ahl al-bayt*, especially the women, al-ʿÂmilî quotes from a letter which insists that "Zaynab al-Kubrâ, daughter of the Commander of the Faithful and whose *kunya* was Umm Kulṯûm" arrived in Damascus with her husband ʿAbd Allâh b. Ğaʿfar in the days of ʿAbd al-Malik b. Marwân in the year of the (Medina) drought, that this is where she died and that she is buried outside of Damascus, close to her husband. However, al-ʿÂmilî rejects that the authors of the letter have the correct Zaynab in mind, as he rejects the claim that her husband is buried in Syria and the story of the Medina drought.

notes that it seems unlikely that she had been buried there, for she would have had a special and unmistakeable tomb.[169] Others insist that Medinan persecution drove her to Egypt, where she would live until her death, remaining until the end as the unrivalled champion of al-Ḥusayn's struggle for justice and the Karbalâʾ event's most compelling voice. Still other reports maintain that she went to Syria with her husband, driven from Medina by a severe drought (with Bilgrami adding that her death there was the result of an accident). Again, Shahin objects that the story of this drought has no basis in history.[170]

Karbâssî writes that she returned to Medina from Karbalâʾ in the month of Rabîʿ al-awwal in the year 61/681. Here, she took the chance to address the people, rallying them against their Umayyad overlords; as a result, the citizens of Medina soon became disgruntled and began to express their disapproval of the Umayyad regime. This triggered an outraged response from the Umayyads; the Umayyad governor ʿAmr b. Saʿîd al-Ashdaq[171] wrote to Yazîd b. Muʿâwiya, urging the expulsion of Zaynab from Medina. Yazîd voiced his agreement;[172] and while Shahin notes that he suggested Zaynab be offered a choice of places of exile, Bilgrami writes that Yazîd's forces, sent to dispel a revolt in Medina, took Zaynab and other members of her family to Damascus by force.[173]

Zaynab, Karbâssî insists, rejected this move and prepared herself to oppose it. However, the women of the Banû Hâshim and perhaps also her nephew, Imâm Zayn al-ʿÂbidîn[174] intervened in the matter and counseled her to leave, to avoid the danger of staying in Medina. Zaynab yielded to their advice and left with a group of the women of the Banû Hâshim, heading towards Egypt, where preparations had been made for this eventuality. They arrived on

---

[169] SHAHIN B., *Lady Zaynab*, 2002: 225.

[170] Cf. BILGRAMI M.H., *The Victory of Truth: The Life of Zaynab bint ʾAli*, 1986: 18, SHAHIN B., *Lady Zaynab*, 2002: 226.

[171] ʿAmr b. Saʿîd b. al-ʿÂṣ al-Ashdaq (d. 70/689).

[172] KARBÂSSÎ M.S., *Muʿǧam anṣâr al-Ḥusayn – al-nisâʾ*, 2009: 369.

[173] SHAHIN B., *Lady Zaynab*, 2002: 227, BILGRAMI M.H., *The Victory of Truth: The Life of Zaynab bint ʾAli*, 1986: 18.

[174] Lit. 'the adornment of the worshippers'.

27th Rağab in in the year 61/681, received by the chiefs of the Umayyad State; present too were a number of supporters and patrons. It would be in the house of one of the patrons that the exhausted Zaynab would live out her life; she died on 15th Rağab 62/682 and was buried in the house in which she had been living, in the very shadow of the official residences.[175] Shahin suggests that it was the governor of Egypt himself, one Maslama b. Muḫallad al-Anṣârî (d. 62/682), a Companion of Muḥammad, who offered her a place in his residence.[176] Her burial in Egypt is supported by *Nûr al-absâr* (not surprisingly, since al-Shablanğî was an al-Azhar scholar).[177] Al-Shablanğî is transmitting from al-Shaʿrânî[178] in his *Laṭâʾif al-minan wa-l-aḫlâq*, who is in turn transmitting from his teacher ʿAlî al-Ḫawwâṣ, the prominent 16th century Ṣûfî poet, who insists that the Zaynab buried in Qanâṭir al-sibâʿ in Egypt is indeed the daughter of ʿAlî b. Abî Ṭâlib, and that there is absolutely no doubt that she is buried here. Al-Shaʿrânî describes how al-Ḫawwâṣ used to take off his sandals at the threshold of the path and walk barefoot until he passed by her mosque. He would stop in front of its façade and would gain access to God by means of her, who would then forgive him.[179] He also refers to al-Shaʿrânî's *Lawâqiḥ al-anwâr al-qudsiyya* to reinforce the thesis that Zaynab, 'sister of al-Ḥusayn' is entombed in Qanâṭir al-sabâʿ, and that this is further underscored in al-Shaʿrânî's *al-Ṭabaqât*, in the biography of al-Ḥusayn. The Egyptian thesis is also mentioned by scholars such as Ṣâliḥ al-Wardânî ("on the authority of ʿAbd al-Raḥmân al-Anṣârî, who said: I saw Zaynab bt. ʿAlî in Egypt just days after her arrival. I have never seen anyone like her! Her face was like a sliver of the

[175] KARBÂSSÎ M.S., *Muʿğam anṣâr al-Ḥusayn – al-nisâʾ*, 2009: 369.

[176] SHAHIN B., *Lady Zaynab*, 2002: 227.

[177] al-Shablanğî., *Nûr al-abṣâr fî manâqib âl bayt al-nabî al-muḫtâr*: 202.

[178] Abû al-Mawâhib ʿAbd al-Wahhâb b. Aḥmad b. ʿAlî al-Shaʿrânî (d. 972/1565), an Egyptian Shâfiʿî scholar and proponent of *taṣawwuf*, who would establish his own mystical school. His master was ʿAlî al-Ḫawwâṣ. (Cf. GAL S. II: 464–6).

[179] al-Shaʿrânî., *Laṭâʾif al-minan wa-l-aḫlâq*: 477.

moon").[180] Concerning the assertion that she was buried in Egypt, Karbâssî relates that when she was suffering the pain of illness and was asked whether the doctor ought to come to her, Zaynab replied: "We are not among those who look upon the world and upon remaining in it, because we are the people of the house of prophecy, and the most desirable encounter for us is the encounter with our Lord." Karbâssî notes that the doctor did not come; nor was he able to delay the moment of death.

In spite of evidence for the Egypt thesis, there are other opinions. While Sunnî Muslims with devotion to her prefer the Sayyîda Zaynab mosque in Cairo,[181] the Shîʿa favour mostly her Damascus mausoleum and most frequented shrine, the Sayyîda Zaynab mosque, so large that it has lent its name to the surrounding district of Sayyîda Zaynab.[182] "With its golden-domed mausoleum," writes Sindawi, "two tall 54-metre high minarets and decorated porticoes, her tomb covers a total area of 15,000 m^2 and can hold up to 5000

---

[180] Cf. al-WARDÂNÎ Ṣ., *al-Shîʿa fî miṣr min al-imâm ʿAlî ḥatta al-imâm Ḫumaynî*, Cairo 1993: 91.

[181] QUTBUDDIN B.T., "Zaynab bint Ali" in Lindsay Jones (ed.), *Encyclopedia of Religion*, 2nd edn., 2005: 9938.

[182] Szanto notes that the Syrian refugee camp-shrine town of Sayyida Zaynab began as a camp for refugee Palestinians in 1949 but grew incrementally by the settlement of displaced Syrians from the Golan Heights in 1967 and exiled Iraqis in the 1970s and 1980s. It became an important centre of Shîʿî education and pilgrimage when, for various reasons in the 1980s and 1990s, Karbalâ' and Najaf became inaccessible to non-Iraqi Shîʿî Muslims. Cf. SZANTO E., "Sayyida Zaynab in the State of Exception: Shii Sainthood as 'Qualified Life'" in *International Journal of Middle East Studies* 44 (2), 2012: 285. It is of note the Ibn Ǧubayr (d. 614/1217), travelling in the area of Râwiyya, some kilometres outside of Damascus, takes note of one particular shrine: "Among the religious shrines of the *ahl al-bayt* is the shrine of Umm Kulṯûm, daughter of ʿAlî b. Abî Ṭâlib." Ibn Gubayr suggests that this is Zaynab al-Ṣuġrâ, given the *kunya* Umm Kulṯûm on account of her similarity to Umm Kulṯûm, daughter of Muḥammad; but his laconic "God knows" suggests his lack of certainty. Cf. Ibn Ǧubayr., *Riḥla*, Brill, Leiden 1907: 280–281.

people."[183] A number of contemporary scholars make reference to her tomb there.[184]

For the most part, it is hagiography and popular piety that form the bulk of material on the life of Zaynab; these pious legends are numerous, and although such a genre forms a substantial part of most religious traditions, it does not greatly assist us in constructing an account that is rigorously academic. Their presence in more contemporary texts while absent in the classical sources, for example, prevents us from dating some of the traditions, as a way of establishing whether or not they are have arisen as a reaction to a particular religious, social or political question. Even in the classical sources, we see an embellishment and augmentation over the centuries, with her role in and around Karbala', for example, while fairly simple in the earlier texts like al-Ṭabarî, great enhanced in later accounts of the battle, such as those of Ibn Ṭâ'ûs, transmitting three hundred years later. Nevertheless, the hagiographic accounts that dominate the later Zaynab literature do give us a glimpse into how she is envisaged at the level of popular piety.

Zaynab is held up by her biographers as among the most abstemious and devout women of her time; Karbâssî recounts how her nephew, the fourth Imâm, transmitted: "My aunt, with all those calamities and ordeals that befell her on our journey to Syria, never relinquished her supererogatory prayers (*nawâfil*) at night."[185] In another report, he noted that during the terrible journey from Kûfa to Syria, his aunt Zaynab, who would ordinarily perform her ob-

---

183 SINDAWI K., "The Zaynabiyya Ḥawza in Damascus and its Role in Shī'ite Religious Instruction" in *Middle Eastern Studies*, vol. XLV, n. 6 (November 2009): 862–3.

184 Cf. AMORETTI B.S., "How to Place Women in History. Some Remarks on the Recent Shiite Interest in Women's Shrines" in *Oriente Moderno*, Nuova serie, Anno 89, Nr. 1 (2009): 1–12, who speaks at length about her Syrian tomb, and CALZONI I., "Shiite mausoleums in Syria with particular reference to Sayyida Zaynab's mausoleum" in *Proceedings of the Conference on La Shi'a nell'Impero Ottomano* (Roma, 15/4/1991), Roma 1993: 191–201.

185 Also recounted by Shahin, although he provides no reference to any of the classical sources. SHAHIN B., *Lady Zaynab*, 2002: 43.

ligatory (*farâʾiḍ*) and supererogatory prayers standing, prayed sitting down in some of the camp sites, and when he asked the reason for this, replied: "I pray sitting down because of the strain of the pain and the weakness the last three nights" – since she had been sharing whatever food she received with the children because of the small amounts with which they had to make do. A further story is told about her diligence in the matter of supererogatory prayers; that her brother al-Ḥusayn, in his last farewell, exhorted her: "My sister! Do not forget me in the nighttime supererogatory prayers and do not relinqish the nighttime supererogatory prayers even on the night of ʿÂshûrâ." Al-Ḥusayn's daughter Fâṭima goes on to note that her aunt Zaynab remained standing in her place of prayer all of that night, appealing to her Lord.[186] Nor do the secret prayers of the young Zaynab, whispered to her Lord at night, go unheard and unnoticed by her father ʿAlî; among those he attributes to her are: "Praise be to You, possessor of generosity and glory and exaltedness who give and hold back as You will!" Among the prayers which she used to pray during the dead of night, comes the following:

> Be praised,[187] You who have garbed and clothed yourself in
> might,

---

[186] KARBÂSSÎ M.S., *Muʿǧam anṣâr al-Ḥusayn – al-nisâʾ*, 2009: 355.

[187] The phrase *subḥâna* or *subḥâna-hu* is hard to render in English; literally, it means 'His praises', and could be used as an exclamation of surprise, such as 'Far be it from God!' or 'How far God is from every imperfection!' About the phrase *subḥâna Allâh*, Lane notes that it means: "I declare [or celebrate or extol] the remoteness, or freedom, of God [from every imperfection or impurity, or from everything derogatory from his glory, i.e.] from the imputation of there being any equal to Him, or any companion, or anything like unto Him, or anything contrary to Him; or from anything that should not be imputed to Him…[I declare, or celebrate, or extol, His absolute perfection or glory or purity: or extolled be His absolute perfection…]…I declare the remoteness of God, or His freedom from evil, or from every evil, and [especially] from the imputation of His having a female companion, and offspring: or, I declare God's being very far removed from all the foul imputations of those who assert

> Be praised, who wraps Himself in glory and is generous,
> Be praised, to whom it is not fitting to give glory to any but Him, exalted His sublimity,
> Be praised, who enumerates the number of all things in His knowledge, His noble character and His power,
> Be praised, possessor of might and blessings, possessor of power and generosity!
>
> O God, I ask You by the glories of Your throne[188] and the highest degree of the mercy of Your Book, and by Your greatest name and highest assiduity,[189] and by Your perfect words, which brought about truth and justice, that You bless Muḥammad and the noble and pure family of Muḥammad and that You arrange for me benevolence in this world and the next. God, You are the Living *(al-ḥayy)* and the Subsisting *(al-qayyûm)*; You guided me, You feed me and give me to drink, You bring me to die and endow me with life. Forgive me by Your mercy, most Merciful of the merciful.[190]

In another prayer, Zaynab offers some theological names for God:

> Bedrock, for whom there is no bedrock, Storehouse, for whom there is no storehouse, Support, for whom there is no support, Sanctuary of the weak and Treasure of the poor, Listener to the urgent request, Safety of those drowning and Saviour of the dying, Embellisher and Beautifier, Benefactor and Conferrer of benefits, You are the One to whom prostrate the blackness of night and the brightness of day, the rays of the sun, the rustling of the trees and the roar of waters. God, before whom and after whom there is nothing, Who has neither beginning

---

a plurality of gods." Cf. LANE E.W., *An Arabic-English Lexicon*, 1968, vol. IV: 1290.

[188] Lit. "by the properties wherein consists the title of thy throne to glory or by the places wherein these properties are [as it were] knit together" (cf. Op. cit., vol. V: 2107).

[189] In terms, notes Karbâssî, of assistance, good fortune, providence, but specifically favour.

[190] KARBÂSSÎ M.S., *Muʿǧam anṣâr al-Ḥusayn – al-nisâʾ*, 2009: 356.

> nor end, neither equal nor rival, and by the holiness of Your name, which has its signification in human beings, clothed in grandeur and light and majesty, Examiner of truths and Thwarter of idolatry and calamaties, and by the name, by which everlasting, eternal life endures, with which there is neither death nor annihilation, and by the holy spirit, and in the hearing of the One present and the sight of the One who penetrates, Crown of dignity, Seal of the prophethood, Attestation of the covenant, God, who has no partner.[191]

Karbâssî notes that Zaynab was similar to her grandmother, Ḫadîğa bt. Ḫuwaylid who was, he reminds us, without doubt, one of the most beautiful and intelligent of the Qurayshî women, sometimes called 'queen of the Arabs' and who was known as 'the Lady of the valley of Mecca' (*al-baṭḥâʾ*). Muḥammad himself had said that Zaynab was similar to his (maternal) aunt Umm Kulṯûm. Karbâssî tells how one day Fâṭima came to Muḥammad with Zaynab al-Kubrâ. Fâṭima sat next to her father, while Zaynab played in front of him:

> Then she fell at the door of the room, looked at her grandfather and he smiled and said to her: "Yes!" She looked at him a second time, and he said to her: "Yes!" She looked at him a third time, and he said to her: "Yes!" She looked at him a fourth time, and he said to her: "No!" Then she wept. Fâṭima said to him: "Messenger of God! By the One who sent you with the truth, what is this 'yes' and 'no' to Zaynab?" He replied: "Indeed, she asked first if she would be a leader, and I said to her: yes. She asked secondly if she would be excellent in counsel, and I said to her: yes. She asked thirdly if she would be free in the disposal of her affairs, and I said to her: yes. She asked fourthly if she would be entrusted with intercession, and I said: no, that is not permitted except to me."[192]

---

191 Cf. Q. 6: 163. KARBÂSSÎ M.S., *Muʿğam anṣâr al-Ḥusayn – al-nisâʾ*, 2009: 356.

192 KARBÂSSÎ M.S., *Muʿğam anṣâr al-Ḥusayn – al-nisâʾ*, 2009: 336–7.

Karbâssî's hagiography, firmly rooted in the pietistic tradition, uses lofty sentiments to describe how Zaynab *al-ʿaqîla* grew up in the house of revelation, in the heart (*ahḍân*) of the prophecy, and in the shelter of the infallible Imâms, ʿAlî, al-Ḥasan and al-Ḥusayn. She was educated in the school of heaven, the school of the most admirable exemplar for human perfection, the clearest criterion for the believing woman, and who desired that Zaynab be a living example for the rest of the women. She was the image of her mother Fâṭima al-Zahrâʾ and an example to be imitated. While she was not immaculate and impeccable (*maʿṣûma*) in terms of that infallibility or impeccability (*ʿiṣma*) that pertains to the fourteen (Muhammad, Fâṭima and the twelve Imâms), she was graced with the minor impeccability, and after her mother, no women was close to her in rank.[193] She was as the fourth Imâm, ʿAli b. al-Ḥusayn said of her: "You, by the praise of God, are erudite without an instructor, quick of understanding without being taught.[194]

One could understand that the Karbâssî text proposes, in a theology drawn chiefly from pious tradition and hagiography, a number of 'beautiful names' or theological titles for Zaynab, as Zaynab would herself offer a selection of theological epithets for her martyred brother in her famous Kûfa protest. Noting that she personified within herself the ideal, and that magnanimity emanated from her,[195] he lists these titles as 'newborn of the house of revelation and impeccability' (*walîdatu bayt al-waḥy wa-l-ʿiṣma*), 'suckling child of knowledge and wisdom' (*radîʿat al-ʿilm wa-l-ḥikma*), 'foster daughter of abstemiousness and piety' (*rabîbat al-zuhd wa-l-taqwâ*), 'heiress of fluency and eloquence' (*warîtat al-faṣaḥa wa-l-balâġat*), 'possessor of generosity and munificence' (*ṣâḥibat al-ġûd wa-l-karam*), 'fountainhead of contemplation and refinement' (*manbaʿ al-fikr wa-l-*

---

[193] KARBÂSSÎ M.S., *Muʿğam anṣâr al-Ḥusayn – al-nisâʾ*, 2009: 337.

[194] Words, as recorded by al-Ṭabarsî, spoken by ʿAli b. al-Ḥusayn after Zaynab's famous Kûfa protest, when he asks his aunt to be silent so that he can speak. It is one of three occasions that she is asked to be silent, and will be noted later in this work. Cf. al-Ṭabarsî., *Kitâb al-iḥtiğâğ ʿalâ ahl al-liğâğ*, vol. II: 305, al-Mağlisî, *Biḥâr al-anwâr*, vol. XLV, bb. 39: 164, SHAHIN B., *Lady Zaynab*, 2002: 200.

[195] KARBÂSSÎ M.S., *Muʿğam anṣâr al-Ḥusayn – al-nisâʾ*, 2009: 337.

adab), 'companion of martyrdom and gallantry' (*rafîqat al-shahâda wa-l-shahâma*), 'descendant of boldness and courage' (*ḏuriyyat al-ğur'a wa-l-shağâ'a*), 'branch of the tree of prophecy' (*far' shağarat al-nubuwwa*),[196] 'companion of the light of the imamate' (*qarîn nûr al-imâma*), 'cradle of honour and chastity' (*mahd al-sharaf wa-l-'iffa*) and 'possessor of praiseworthy attributes and lofty merits' (*ḏât al-ṣiffât al-ḥamîda wa-l-maḥâsin al-ğalîla*). While the titles used to address her in the *ziyâra* prayer (used specifically in pilgrimage to her tomb) almost all make reference to her status as daughter of 'Alî and granddaughter of Muḥammad, these theological titles quite noticeably pertain to her own qualities.

While many of these names have a poetic ring in Arabic (*walîda, radî'a, rabîba, warîṯa, ṣâḥiba, rafîqa, ḏuriyya*) they are not titles conferred upon Zaynab by the classical sources, even the later ones. Nor does Karbâssî refer us to any sources for them.

Both al-Kâshânî and Karbâssî record a frightening vision which Zaynab recounted to her grandfather Muḥammad:

> Zaynab went to her grandfather and said: "Grandfather, yesterday I saw a vision! A violent wind emanated, which blackened the world and everything in it, and darkened it, and shook me from side to side. I saw a great tree, and I clung to it because of the force of the wind. Then the wind uprooted it and cast it upon the ground. So I clung to one of the strong branches of that tree, but the wind severed it too. So I clung to another branch, but it broke it too. So I clung to one of two of its boughs, but it broke it too. Then I woke from my sleep." When he heard her words, Muḥammad wept bitterly, and re-

---

196 This is the only one of these titles that find an echo in the classical sources; 'branch of the tree of prophecy' is regularly used to describe the Imâms and the *ahl al-bayt*. Out of numerous examples, cf. for e.g. al-Qummî., *Tafsîr*, vol. II, bb. 37: 228, al-Saffar., *Baṣâ'ir al-darağât fî 'ulûm âl Muḥammad*, vol. I, nn. 1–3, 6–9: 56–58, al-Kulaynî., *al-Kâfî fî 'ilm al-dîn*, vol. I, bb. *anna al-a'imma ma'din al-'ilm*, nn. 1.3: 221, Furât al-Kûfî., *Tafsîr Furât b. Ibrâhîm al-Kûfî*: 395, al-Mufîd., *al-Irshâd fî ma'rifat ḥuğağ Allâh 'alâ al-'ibâd*, vol. II: 168, al-Fattâl al-Nîsâbûrî., *Rawḍat al-wâ'izîn wa-tabṣirat al-mutta'izîn*, vol. I: 206, al-Ṭabarsî., *I'lâm al-warâ bi-a'lâm al-hudâ*, vol. I: 508.

> plied: "The tree is your grandfather: the first branch is your mother Fâṭima and the second your father ʿAlî. The other two boughs are your brothers (al-Ḥasan and al-Ḥusayn). The world will be blackened by their loss, and you will put on the clothing of mourning because of their calamity."[197]

This story is not found in the classical texts: Karbâssî takes it from al-Baḥrânî.[198] In fact, the theme of the *ahl al-bayt* compared to a tree is found in other *aḥâdîṯ*, but rarely in the context of a vision attributed to Zaynab. They are, for the most part, quite similar in detail; Muḥammad claims to be the tree, naming Fâṭima as its branch (*farʿ*) or, in some texts, its fruit (*ḥaml*), ʿAlî its seed or fecundation (*laqâḥ*), al-Ḥasan and al-Ḥusayn as its fruits (*ṯamar*), and those of the *umma* who love them (or sometimes, 'our Shîʿa') the leaves (*awrâq*) of the tree.[199]

Karbâssî relates that she was present at her mother's death, accepting Fâṭima's charge that she should care for her two brothers, and relates the popular story concerning her early childhood (*ṭufûla*), when sitting on the lap of her father ʿAlî, who is petting her. ʿAlî said to her: "Say 'one'!" Zaynab replied 'one'. Then he said: "Say 'two'!" But she remained silent, so ʿAlî spoke again: "Speak to me, delight of my eye!" She answered: "My father, I am not able to say 'two' with my tongue, treating it in the same manner

---

[197] AL-KÂSHÂNÎ A., *250 Karâma li-l-sayyida Zaynab wa-sayyidât bayt al-nubuwwa*, 2008: 13, KARBÂSSÎ M.S., *Muʿǧam anṣâr al-Ḥusayn – al-nisâʾ*, 2009: 337–8.

[198] al-Baḥrânî., *ʿAwâlim al-ʿulûm wa-l-maʿârif al-aḥwâl min al-âyât wa-l-aḫbâr wal-aqwâl*, vol. XI, bb. 1, n. 3: 947. Precisely the same phrase (رَأَيْتُ الْبَارِحَةَ رُؤْيَا) is used by al-Ḥusayn's daughter Sukayna, as she describes to Yazîd a vision she has had of a castle in Paradise.

[199] Cf. for e.g. al-Ḥâkim al-Nîsâbûrî., *Kitâb (Talḫîs) al-mustadrak ʿalâ al-ṣaḥîḥayn*, vol. III (*Kitâb maʿrifat al-ṣaḥâba*): 160, Ibn ʿAsâkir., *Târîḫ Dimashq*, vol. XLII, bb. 4933 (*ʿAlî b. Abî Ṭâlib*): 65, al-Ğawzî., *Kitâb al-mawḍûʿât min al-aḥâdîṯ al-marfûʿa*, vol. II: 5, al-Ḏahabî., *Mîzân al-iʿtidâl fî tarâğim al-riğâl*, Part 4: 237, Ibn ʿAsâkir., *Târîḫ madînat Dimashq*, vol XIV, bb. 1566 (*al-Ḥusayn b. ʿAlî b. Abî Ṭâlib*): 168, al-Ṣaffûrî., *Nuzhat al-mağâlis wa-muntaḫab al-nafâʾis*, vol. II, bb. *manâqib Fâṭima al-Zahrâʾ*: 179–80.

as 'one'."[200] This, like many other pious stories, is not found in the classical Shîʿî sources.

Yaḥyâ b. Salîm al-Mâzanî[201] points out her chastity and refinement during the period of her early childhood and her maidenhood, saying:

> I was close to the Commander of the Faithful for a long time and in the vicinity of the house[202] in which his daughter Zaynab lived, and by God, I never saw a person with her or heard a sound from her. Whenever she wanted to go out to visit[203] her grandfather the Messenger of God, she would go out at night with al-Ḥasan on her right, and al-Ḥusayn on her left, and the Commander of the Faithful in front of her. Whenever she came near to the noble tomb, the Commander of the Faithful would precede her and extinguish the light of the lamps. Al-Ḥasan once asked him about this, and ʿAlî replied: "I fear that someone will look upon the person of your sister Zaynab."[204]

---

[200] KARBÂSSÎ M.S., *Muʿǧam anṣâr al-Ḥusayn – al-nisâʾ*, 2009: 338, SHAHIN B., *Lady Zaynab*, 2002: 63.

[201] Martyred with al-Ḥusayn at Karbalâʾ.

[202] The ground-floor room, notes the author in a footnote.

[203] The text uses the word *ziyâra*, indicating that these visits were in the form of a pilgrimage to sites associated with her grandfather, such as his tomb.

[204] KARBÂSSÎ M.S., *Muʿǧam anṣâr al-Ḥusayn – al-nisâʾ*, 2009: 338–9. This is, at best, an anachronistic text, for while as a pious story it attempts to highlight the modesty and devoutness of Zaynab, it is at variance with other pictures we have of her; al-Ṭabarî's ostensibly eyewitness accounts of her vigorous and visible presence at Karbalâʾ, for example, and later, contemporary interpretations of Zaynab (by scholars like Shariati) as the exemplar of the modern woman taking her place in society. Furthermore, as certainly as there are scholars who would support an active role for women in contemporary society, others might employ a story like this to reinforce the need for female seclusion and invisibility. As it stands, Karbâssî is unable to refer us to any classical texts, and this story is carried

Karbâssî recounts another well-known story; one day, Zaynab questions her father, saying: "My father, do you love us?" ʿAlî responds: "How could I not love you, when you are the fruit of my heart?" She replies: "My father, love is for God Most High, and for us, tenderness!"[205]

It is reported that she had achieved a high level of intelligence by the time she had reached her fifth year, when her grandfather Muḥammad died, in 11/632, followed approximately six months later by the death of Zaynab's mother Fâṭima. Al-Kâshânî, like Karbâssî quoting the threads of his story from al-Baḥrânî's *ʿAwâlim al-ʿulûm*, notes in his hagiography that all of Zaynab's upbringing and education were within the prophetic household; she grew up in the 'house of the prophecy', was "suckled with the milk of revelation from the breast of al-Zahrâʾ,[206] the Virgin, and with food from the hand of the nephew of the Messenger."[207] Says al-Kâshânî: "She was raised with a holy upbringing and educated with a spiritual education, clothed in the garments of sublimity and majesty and clad in the cloak of modesty and timidity."[208] He goes on to say that it was the five 'companions of the cloak' (*aṣḥâb al-ʿabâʾ*)[209] who

---

only by a late source, al-Baḥrânî (al-Baḥrânî., *ʿAwâlim al-ʿulûm wa-l-maʿârif al-aḥwâl min al-âyât wa-l-aḫbâr wal-aqwâl*, vol. XI, bb. 7: 955).

205 KARBÂSSÎ M.S., *Muʿǧam anṣâr al-Ḥusayn – al-nisâʾ*, 2009: 339, SHAHIN B., *Lady Zaynab*, 2002: 63.

206 In the case of Fâṭima, the appellation al-Zahrâʾ ('the Radiant') is directly connected with the themes of light that are suffused throughout her story. Some descriptions of her conception augment the accounts, with depictions of light emanating from God to Muḥammad and then to Fâṭima and ʿAlî. This light passed from her to her sons and subsequently to the other Imâms. Cf. CLOHESSY C., *Fatima, Daughter of Muhammad*, 2009: 94–96.

207 AL-KÂSHÂNÎ A., *250 Karâma li-l-sayyida Zaynab wa-sayyidât bayt al-nubuwwa*, 2008: 14.

208 Ibid.

209 The famous 'report of the cloak' (*ḥadîṯ al-kisâʾ*), transmitted by numerous Sunnî and Shîʿî texts, on the occasion of the revelation of Q. 33: 3, when Muḥammad spread his cloak over ʿAlî, Fâṭima, al-Ḥasan and al-Ḥusayn and stated: "These are the members of my Household, and

were concerned with her education, her instruction and her training.[210]

Al-Kâshânî refers us to a number of works; he quotes Ibn Ḥağar al-ʿAsqalânî's *al-Iṣâba* that she was intelligent (*ʿâqila*) and abundantly understanding (*labîba*).[211] He directs us to al-ʿAllâma al-Baraġânî writing in his *Mağâlis al-muttaqîn*,[212] who notes that the cognitive dignities specific to Zaynab (*al-muqâmât al-ʿifâniyya al-ḫâṣṣa bi-zaynab*) come close to the dignities of the Imamate; and that Zaynab, when she saw the condition of her nephew Zayn al-ʿÂbidîn, who had seen the bodies of his father, brothers, closest relatives and the people of his house felled on the ground, butchered like blood sacrifices, his heart agitated and his face pale, set about consoling him. Al-Baraġânî reports that it is transmitted in *aḥâdîṯ* from Umm Ayman that it was God Most High who commissioned this from her.[213]

God has purified them of all uncleanness." Among the Sunnî transmissions, cf. for e.g. Ibn Ḥanbal., *Musnad*, vol. I, *Musnad ʿAbd Allâh b. al-ʿAbbâs b. ʿAbd al-Muṭṭalib*, n. 3062: 708–709, vol. VI, *Ḥadîṯ Wâṯala b. al-ʿAsqaʿ*, n. 16985: 45, vol. X, *Ḥadîṯ Umm Salama*, n. 26570: 177, n. 26612: 186–187, n. 26659: 197, n. 26808: 228, al-Tirmiḏî., *Sunan*, vol. IX, bk. 50 (*Kitâb al-manâqib*), *Manâqib ahl bayt al-nabî*, bb. 77, n. 3789: 341–342, vol. IX, bk. 50 (*Kitâb al-manâqib*), bb. *fî faḍl Fâṭima bt. Muḥammad*, n. 3870: 388, al-Ḥâkim al-Nîsâbûrî., *Kitâb (Talḫîs) al-mustadrak ʿalâ al-ṣaḥîḥayn*, vol. II, Part 2, bk. 27 (*Kitâb al-tafsîr*), *Tafsîr sûrat al-aḥzâb*, nn. 3615, 3616: 489, vol. III, Part 3, bk. 31 (*Kitâb maʿrifat al-ṣaḥâba*), *Manâqib amîr al-muʾminîn ʿAlî b. Abî Ṭâlib*, n. 4639: 125, Ibn ʿAsâkir., *Târîḫ madînat Dimashq*, vol. XLII, bb. 4933 (*ʿAlî b. Abî Ṭâlib*): 98, 100, 112, 114, Ibn al-Aṯîr., *Usd al-ġâba fî maʿrifat al-ṣaḥâba*, vol. VI, bb. 7175 (*Fâṭima bt. Rasûl Allâh*): 225, al-Suyûṭî., *al-Durr al-manṯûr fî al-tafsîr bi-l-maʾṯûr*, vol. V, *Sûrat al-aḥzâb*, v. 33: 377.

210 Cf. al-Baḥrânî., *ʿAwâlim al-ʿulûm wa-l-maʿârif al-aḥwâl min al-âyât wa-l-aḫbâr wal-aqwâl*, vol. XI, bb. 5: 949. These sentiments are not found in early sources.

211 al-ʿAsqalânî., *al-Iṣâba fî tamyîz al-ṣaḥâba*, vol. IV, n. 510: 314–315.

212 Muḥammad Taqî al-Baraġânî, d. 1263/1847. A prominent Shîʿî cleric in Qajar Persia, his work details the sufferings of the Imâms.

213 AL-KÂSHÂNÎ A., *250 Karâma li-l-sayyida Zaynab wa-sayyidât bayt al-nubuwwa*, 2008: 15.

Al-Kâshânî points us to a work entitled *al-Ṭirâẓ al-Muḏḏahab*,[214] which offers a list of the interior cognizance and spiritual dignities of Zaynab; her virtues, her benefactions, her traits, her sublimity, her knowledge, her way of acting, her impeccability, her modesty, her light, her brightness her nobility and her beauty, all of which follow those of her mother and proxy. He also takes note of a work entitled *Ğannât al-ḫulûd*;[215] Zaynab, in her eloquence, her abstemiousness, her management and her courage, was close to her father and her mother. The arrangement of the affairs of the *ahl al-bayt* and even of the Hâshimids after the martyrdom of al-Ḥusayn was under her counsel and management. [216]

Al-Kâshânî makes reference to Ibn ʿInaba's *Ansâb al-Ṭâlibîyîn*, which informs us that Zaynab was distinguished by her abundant kindliness, her sublime qualities, her praiseworthy, traits, her radiant characteristics, her conspicuous good deeds and her pure virtues.[217] He refers to al-Suyûṭî's *al-Risâlat al-Zaynabiyya*, which claims that Zaynab was born in the lifetime of her grandfather, the Messenger of God, was abundantly understanding, intelligent and powerful of heart, and that al-Ḥasan was born eight years before

---

214 *Kitâb al-ṭirâẓ al-muḏḏahab fî aḫbâr al-sayyida Zaynab* by ʿAbbâs al-Mustawfî. Shahin ascribes this work to al-Râwandî, but without further details.

215 *Kitâb ğannât al-ḫulûd* by Muḥammad Riḍâ b. Muḥammad Mu'min Imâmî Ḫâtûn Âbâdî Iṣfahânî.

216 AL-KÂSHÂNÎ A., *250 Karâma li-l-sayyida Zaynab wa-sayyidât bayt al-nubuwwa*, 2008: 16.

217 "Among the most virtuous of all women," says al-ʿÂmilî, describing her virtue as more renowned and distinct even than all that is remembered and written about her. He notes especially that Zaynab was aware of the majesty of her circumstances, the greatness of her standing, the power of her argument, the agility of her intelligence, the persistence of her tragedy, the fluency of her tongue and the eloquence of her speech. cf. al-ʿÂmilî., *Aʿyân al-Shîʿa*, vol. VII: 137.

Muḥammad's 11/632 death, al-Ḥusayn seven and Zaynab five (and thus in 6/627).[218]

He directs us to a work by al-Nîsâbûrî entitled *al-Risalat al-ʿAlawiyya*;[219] here we are told that in her eloquence, her fluency, her abstemiousness and her worship, Zaynab was the daughter of ʿAlî, and just like her father al-Murtaḍâ and her mother al-Zahrâʾ. He refers us to the work *Fâṭima bint Muḥammad* by ʿUmar Abû al-Naṣr al-Lubnânî, published in Beirut, in which he claims that Zaynab demonstrated that she was one of the greatest of the *ahl al-bayt* in terms of courage, eloquence and fluency. Her renown was spread, not only by her behaviour on the day of Karbalâʾ, but also after it, with the example she gave by argument, power, courage and eloquence; the chroniclers of history and the books bear witness to her.[220]

In another didactic story not found in any classical text, Karbâssî recounts that Zaynab used to recite parts of the Qurʾân within earshot of her father ʿAlî, and it seemed proper to her to ask him about the exegesis (*tafsîr*) of some of the verses. This she did, and ʿAlî, as a result of her luminous intelligence, went on to allude to some of the perils and dangers awaiting her in the future, in order to strengthen her so that she would not be dismayed by them. Zaynab, serious and composed, informed him that she already knew of these things, having been informed of them by her mother Fâṭima, in order to prepare her for her future.[221]

---

218 AL-KÂSHÂNÎ A., *250 Karâma li-l-sayyida Zaynab wa-sayyidât bayt al-nubuwwa*, 2008: 16. However, I do not find these details in the al-Suyûṭî text.

219 Neither Sezgin nor Brockelmann attribute a work by this name to Muḥammad b. ʿAbd Allâh b. Muḥammad al-Ḥâkim al-Nîsâbûrî b. al-Bayyiʿ (d. 404/914: cf. GAL S. I: 276), if this is in fact the al-Nîsâbûrî to whom al-Kâshânî is referring. There is such a work written by Abû al-Fatḥ Muḥammad b. ʿAbd al-Raḥmân b. ʿUṯmân al-Karâǧakî al-Shîʿî (d. 499/1057: cf. GAL S. I: 602), although not accredited to him by either Sezgin or Brockelmann.

220 AL-KÂSHÂNÎ A., *250 Karâma li-l-sayyida Zaynab wa-sayyidât bayt al-nubuwwa*, 2008: 16.

221 KARBÂSSÎ M.S., *Muʿǧam anṣâr al-Ḥusayn – al-nisâʾ*, 2009: 339.

In speaking of her intelligence, her virtue and her knowledge (*maʿrifa*), al-Kâshânî refers us to Ibn Abî Ṭâhir Ṭayfûr's work *Balâġât al-nisâʾ*;[222] Ṭayfûr transmits a *ḥadîṯ* from Aḥmad b. Ǧaʿfar b. Sulaymân al-Hâshimî reporting Zaynab as saying: "The one who intends to have creatures as his intercessors before God, let him praise Him. Do you not listen to His words: God hears the one who praises him? So, fear God for His power over you and be shy before Him for His closeness to you."[223] While the *ḥadîṯ* is found in works such as *Balâġât al-nisâʾ* and *Aʿyân al-shîʿa*, Karbâssî notes that he is unable to find this extant in the biographies either of Zaynab or of Umm Kulṯûm.[224] It is transmitted in popular hagiographies, but in few classical texts.

Karbâssî recounts another popular story:

> One day in Medina, al-Ḥasan and al-Ḥusayn were sitting, remembering something they had heard from their grandfather:[225] 'The lawful (*al-ḥalâl*) is evident and the unlawful (*al-ḥarâm*) is evident, but between them there are obscure matters about which many people have no knowledge. Whoever protects himself from these obscure things purifies his religion and his honour. Whoever falls into these obscure things is like a shepherd pasturing around the prohibited herbage (*al-ḥimâ*),

---

[222] Abû al-Faḍl Aḥmad b. Abî Ṭâhir Ṭayfûr (d. 280/893: cf. GAL S. I: 210). Brockelmann transcribes the work incorrectly as *Balâġat al-nisâʾ*.

[223] Cf. al-ʿÂmilî., *Aʿyân al-Shîʿa*, vol. VII: 140, SHAHIN B., *Lady Zaynab*, 2002: 64, AL-KÂSHÂNÎ A., *250 Karâma li-l-sayyida Zaynab wa-sayyidât bayt al-nubuwwa*, 2008: 17, Ibn Abî Ṭâhir Ṭayfûr., *Balâġât al-nisâʾ*: 62.

[224] KARBÂSSÎ M.S., *Muʿǧam anṣâr al-Ḥusayn – al-nisâʾ*, 2009: 358.

[225] This *ḥadîṯ* is found in, among others, al-Buḫârî., *Ṣaḥîḥ*, vol. I, ch. 2 (*Kitâb al-imân*), bb. 39, n. 52: 83, Abû Dâwûd., *Sunan*, vol. IV, ch. 22 (*Kitâb al-buyûʿ*), bb. 3, nn. 3329, 3330: 60–2, al-Tirmiḏî., *Ǧâmiʿ*, vol. III, ch. 12 (*Abwâb al-buyûʿ*), bb. 1, n. 1205: 21, al-Nasâʾî., *al-Sunan al-kubrâ*, vol. VI, ch. 51 (*Kitâb al-ashraba*), bb. 50, n. 5713: 363–4. However, Karbâssî in his transmission has left out a number of crucial words, so that the *ḥadîṯ* loses it sense. Instead, it is reproduced here from al-Buḫârî. Cf. KARBÂSSÎ M.S., *Muʿǧam anṣâr al-Ḥusayn – al-nisâʾ*, 2009: 341. It is to be noted that the classical Shîʿî sources do not recount this story concerning Zaynab and her brothers.

on the verge of falling into it. Beware! Every king has a prohibited herbage! Beware! The prohibited herbage of God on His earth is His forbidden things. Beware! In the body there is a piece of flesh; when it is healthy, the whole body is healthy and when it is corrupt the whole body is corrupt. Beware! It is the heart!' When Zaynab heard their conversation, she intervened, saying: "Listen, Ḥasan and Ḥusayn! Your grandfather, the Messenger of God was well instructed[226] in the morals of God. God instructed[227] him and perfected His instruction. He himself said: My Lord instructed me and perfected my instruction, as he was prepared in this manner by the Lord of the worlds for bearing the message of religion and the bidding to the worship of God the Mighty, whom "*Naught is as His likeness; and He is the Hearer, the Seer*".[228] Who is like my grandfather, the Prophet, the Arab, the Hâshimî, the Qurayshî, whom God Most High preferred[229] and whom He chose to make evident to the people the path of life, of good and evil, in his agreeable and pleasant way and his elevated, gratifying explanation, overflowing with mildness, sympathy, affection and compassion." Then she gave herself free reign, saying: "The lawful is evident and the unlawful is evident, but between them there are obscure matters, so that there are three degrees in religion,

---

[226] The Arabic *adab* means 'manners', 'etiquette', 'right conduct' or 'norms of right conduct'; pre-Islamic Arabs used the word to mean 'a praiseworthy habit', 'a hereditary norm of conduct', 'a custom', learned from the ancestors who were looked upon as models. Islam would refine the pre-Islamic Arab meaning, which then became 'high quality of soul', 'good upbringing', 'urbanity', and 'courtesy'. To be *mu'addab*, as Zaynab here describes her grandfather Muḥammad, is to be 'well-mannered', 'civil', 'urbane'.

[227] The verb is the second-form *addaba-yu'addibu*, meaning 'to teach someone the disciple of the mind and the acquisition of good qualities of mind or soul'; cf. LANE E.W., *An Arabic-English Lexicon*, vol. I, 1968: 34.

[228] Q. 42: 11.

[229] The verb for 'preferred' is the eighth form *iṣṭafâ-yaṣṭafî*, meaning 'to choose, select'. In Q. 3: 42, the same verb is used twice in the same verse of Maryam.

the lawful, the unlawful and the ambiguous. The lawful is what God Most High has declared permissible, in that the noble Qur'ân came to permit it, and the Messenger made it evident in his *Sunna*; such as the exoneration of buying and selling, or the performance of the prayer (*al-ṣalât*) at its appointed times, or the almsgiving (*al-zakât*) the fasting (*ṣawm*) of Ramaḍân, and the pilgrimage (*ḥağğ*) to the House for those in a position to do so, and the abandonment of falsehood, hypocrisy and faithlessness.[230] The unlawful is what the Qur'ân prohibits, and is contrary to the lawful, while the ambiguous is something that is neither lawful nor unlawful. The believer who desires for himself happiness in the world and felicity in the Hereafter is obliged to discharge what God has made incumbent upon him, and travel on the road of the wise Qur'ân, and emulate my grandfather the Prophet, taking him as model, and keep away from the path of uncertainties as far as he is able. The one who is on guard against uncertainties purifies his religion and his honour; his religion and his honour become sound, and his honour immaculate and pure. He serves his Lord with pure worship and "*Surely pure religion is for Allah only*".[231] However, the one travels on the road of uncertainties will not be safe from his foot slipping and falling into what God has forbid-

[230] This sounds like Zaynab catechizing her brothers in the tenets of their religion, as she lists four of what would eventually be definitively established as the five 'pillars' (*arkân al-islâm*) of Sunnî Islam, omitting the first, the 'bearing witness' (*shahâda*). It would be long after the death of Zaynab that the *iṯnâ ʿasharî* Shîʿa would define their five central pillars, as noted by Haider, as the belief in one God (*tawḥîd*), in Muḥammad as the last Prophet (*nubuwwa*), in the Day of Judgment (*yawm al-dîn*), in God being just in a manner humans can rationally understand (*ʿadl*) and in the essentiality of the divinely-inspired *aʾimma* (Imâms) descended from Muḥammad. Cf. HAIDER N., *Shiʾi Islam: An Introduction*, 2014: 1. To these they add ten primary duties, which include not only the four pillars mentioned by Zaynab, but also the concepts of enjoining the good (*amr bi-l-maʿrûf*) and forbidding what is evil (*naḥî ʿan al-munkar*), both of which find a resonance in this story.

[231] Q. 39: 3.

> den. Every king has a prohibited herbage within the realm of his dominion, and the prohibited herbage of the King of kings, Creator of the heavens and the earth and what they contain, is His forbidden things. For this reason (the Messenger) said: 'Avoid the forbidden things and you will be the most worshipful of the people'.[232] Therefore, God has given man a piece of flesh and a refined jewel; when it is healthy, the whole body is healthy, pure from filth and malady and disobedience of the Creator, the Greatest, Lord of the worlds. This is the heart. When the heart is sound, its adherent is vigilant in the affairs of his religion and the principles of its law and sees all the happiness in the keeping to the guidance of the Qur'ân and the *Sunna.* On the Day of Judgment, he will be among the victorious. Our life on earth is a stage of the journey leading man either to Paradise or to the Fire. There is neither censure after death nor home after the world except for Paradise or the Fire."[233]

Karbâssî recounts that that sometime in 56/676, Zaynab made a pilgrimage to the tomb of her grandfather Muḥammad, and there overheard Umayyad governor ʿAmr b. Saʿîd al-Ashdaq saying: "The lawful is evident and the unlawful is evident, but between them there are obscure matters about which many people have no knowledge." At once she challenged him, saying: "But, are you Nuʿmân b. Bashîr?' When he replied in the negative, she ordered him to be silent and not speak, saying that should he want to speak, he should say: "On the authority of Nuʿmân b. Bashîr, the Messenger of God said: The lawful (*al-ḥalâl*) is evident."[234]

ʿAbd Allâh b. al-ʿAbbâs transmitted that Zaynab recited the words of the Most High: "O thou wrapped up in thy raiment! Keep vigil the night long, save a little – A half thereof, or abate a little thereof, Or add (a little) thereto – and chant the Qur'an in

---

232 A truncated version of a *ḥadîṯ* found in al-Tirmiḏî: "Guard against forbidden things and you will be the most worshipful of the people" (al-Tirmiḏî., *Ǧâmiʿ*, vol. IV, ch. 34 (*Abwâb al-zuhd*), bb. 2, n. 2305: 343.

233 KARBÂSSÎ M.S., *Muʿǧam anṣâr al-Ḥusayn – al-nisâ'*, 2009: 341–3.

234 Op. cit.: 354.

measure"[235] as far as the words of the Most High: "as do a party of those with thee".[236] Then she said: "We share with our grandfather in the words of the Most High: "as do a party of those with thee". We, by God's favour, are members of that party."[237] Al-Ḥasan responded to his sister by saying: "How blessed you are, pure one (al-ṭâhira)! Truly, you are a branch of the two youths from the blessed tree of prophecy and of the treasure trove of the noble message."[238]

Karbâssî in fact attributes to Zaynab a number of incidents, which in other sources are attributed to her sister; he transmits from al-Mufîd's *Kitâb al-irshâd*, for example, but after the name 'Umm Kulṯûm', he inserts in brackets the name 'Zaynab'. However, al-Mufîd is quite clear that there are two daughters, and since he transmits information about Zaynab, we can presume that when he uses the name Umm Kulṯûm, he means Zaynab al-Ṣuġrâ. Thus, Karbâssî greatly increases the bulk of sayings of and encounters with Zaynab al-Kubrâ, but greatly diminishes the status and import of Umm Kulṯûm. These incidents are especially around the three days leading up to the assassination of ʿAlî and the immediate aftermath. So, for example, Karbâssî carries a long transmission from *Biḥâr al-anwâr* about ʿAlî breaking his fast in the house of Umm Kulṯûm on the 19th night of Ramaḍân; while Karbâssî insists that it is Zaynab, *Biḥâr al-anwâr* does not, and Ladak thinks this is Umm Kulṯûm, not Zaynab.[239]

This is, mostly, hagiography, carried by standard works, but with few substantial references to the classical texts of Sunnî and Shîʿî Islam. Nonetheless, hagiography is not without value, expressing as it does important elements of popular piety. As Ayoub notes:

---

[235] Q. 73: 1–4.

[236] Q. 73: 20.

[237] KARBÂSSÎ M.S., *Muʿǧam anṣâr al-Ḥusayn – al-nisâʾ*, 2009: 354.

[238] Op. cit.: 343. This title (*maʿdin al-risâla*) is one of the theological names that Zaynab confers upon al-Ḥusayn during her Kûfa address.

[239] al-Maǧlisî., *Biḥâr al-anwâr*, vol. XLII, bb. 127: 276, LADAK J., *The Hidden Treasure. Lady Umm Kulthum, Daughter of Imam Ali and Lady Fatima*, 2011: n.p.

> What criterion, then, must the historian, and especially the historian of religion, use in examining the various traditions purporting to relate an event of great significance for the religious life of so many people over so many centuries...? It will not do...to limit ourselves to the bare facts as we see them, because even they have to be arbitrarily chosen. Nor can we, to be sure, take all traditions to be factual data. We must, however, choose our facts, often including those facts which, while to us they do not seem historically valid, were nonetheless considered as such by the community...[240]

Since the aim and scope of this work is an attempt to construct a theology and spirituality through an examination of Zaynab's life at the level of the texts, I have treated them specifically as religious texts and sacrosanct documents, which, read together, espouse a purposely numinous language to forge an enticing and attractive picture of Zaynab. Nevertheless, it will be by means of the more definitive and eye-witness events around Karbalâʾ, to which we must now turn, that we will fashion a Zaynabian theology and spirituality.

[240] AYOUB M., *Redemptive Suffering in Islam. A Study of the Devotional Aspects of ʿAshura in Twelver Shiʿism*, Mouton Publishers, The Hague 1978: 137.

CHAPTER TWO. THE PRE-KARBALÂʾ NARRATIVES

In terms of a chronology of the events around Karbalâʾ in which we are able to situate the person of Zaynab, al-Ṭabarî in his *Kitâb aḫbâr al-rusul wa-l-mulûk* provides the following schema:[1]

1. He omits Zaynab's pre-Karbalâʾ vision al-Ḫuzaymiyya.

2. Zaynab hears the clamour of battle on the afternoon of Thursday 9th Muḥarram.

3. al-Ḥusayn sends his brother al-ʿAbbâs b. ʿAlî to request a respite from the enemy forces, now fast advancing under pressure from Ibn Ziyâd, so that the night of the 9th could be spent in prayer. A delay is granted by ʿUmar b. Saʿd, who is commanding the battle.

4. A dirge sung by al-Ḥusayn in front of his tent is heard by ʿAlî b. al-Ḥusayn and Zaynab.

5. After the morning prayer on Friday 10th Muḥarram, battle is enjoined. Both al-Ṭabarî and his editor are wrong; it was a Friday, rather than a Wednesday or a Saturday, as confirmed by other transmitters such as al-Fattâl al-Nîsâbûrî.[2]

6. al-Ḥusayn sends his brother al-ʿAbbâs b. ʿAlî and his son ʿAlî b. al-Ḥusayn to calm the women, who have been seized by panic at a farewell address delivered by al-Ḥusayn.

---

[1] HOWARD I.K.A., (trans.), *The History of al-Ṭabarî*, vol. XIX, 1990: 112–164.

[2] al-Fattâl al-Nîsâbûrî., *Rawḍat al-wâʿiẓîn wa-tabṣirat al-muttaʿiẓîn*: 419. Cf. also Sibṭ al-Ǧawzî., *Taḏkirat ḫawâṣṣ al-umma bi-ḏikr ḫaṣâʾiṣ al-aʾimma*: 212, 216.

7. The threat by Shimr b. Ḏî al-Ǧawshan to burn the tents of the women and children.

8. The death of ʿAlî al-Akbar b. al-Ḥusayn b. ʿAlî, ostensibly al-Ḥusayn's eldest son, and the emergence of a grieving Zaynab onto the battlefield.

9. The emergence of a young boy, whose face is like the first splinter of the moon. He is armed with a sword, and is wearing a shirt and waistcloth, and a pair of sandals, one of the straps of which (the left) is broken. He dies crying out "Uncle!" Al-Ḥusayn's reaction to his death is intense. The boy is named al-Qâsim b. al-Ḥasan b. ʿAlî b. Abî Ṭâlib; curiously, Zaynab is not recorded as reacting his death.

10. The killing of al-Ḥusayn's infant son, ʿAbd Allah b. al-Ḥusayn, sitting on his father's knee; some accounts include Zaynab in the story.

11. The emergence and killing of an unidentified young man from the family of al-Ḥusayn; clutching a tent pole and wearing a waistcloth and a shirt, he is patently frightened, looking anxiously to the right and left. There are two pearls in his ears, which swing at every movement of his head.

12. The emergence of the boy whom Zaynab, despite an order from al-Ḥusayn, is unable to restrain. He is killed by Baḥr b. Kaʿb, crying for his mother; al-Ḥusayn calls him 'nephew'.

13. The death of al-Ḥusayn, possibly killed by Sinân b. Anas, although others, especially Shimr b. Ḏî al-Ǧawshan, are named as chief culprit.

14. The young and sickly ʿAlî b. al-Ḥusayn has his life saved by Ḥumayd b. Muslim, who dissuades Shimr b. Ḏî al-Ǧawshan from murdering 'a boy'.

15. Sinân b. Anas, described as 'a poet' and 'slightly insane', goes to ʿUmar b. Saʿd's tent and sings an appalling poem about being rewarded for killing al-Ḥusayn. He is severely chastised by ʿUmar b. Saʿd, suggesting the somber mood that prevails immediately after the battle.

16. On the same day (Friday 10th Muḥarram), al-Ḥusayn's head is despatched with Ḫawalî b. Yazîd and Ḥumayd b. Muslim al-Azdî to Ibn Ziyâd. The next day (Saturday 11th Muḥarram) the bodies of

the dead are buried. By all accounts, on Sunday 12th Muḥarram the departures from Karbalâ' to Kûfa with the women take place.

17. Zaynab's great lament as the departing women pass the graves or the battle litter (rather than the actual corpses) of al-Ḥusayn and his companions; in fact, al-Ṭabarî has already reported that the bodies had been buried on the previous day by members of the Banû Asad.

1. A NIGHT AT AL-ḪUZAYMIYYA

The night voices heard by Zaynab at al-Ḫuzaymiyya comprise, for all intents and purposes, the first significant moment in the story of al-Ḥusayn's sister at Karbalâ' and fit methodically into an already well-established pattern of dreams and auguries that began before al-Ḥusayn's birth and continued after his martyrdom. The incident is found in, among others, the narratives of al-Ḫawârizmî and Ibn Shahrâshûb, and is transmitted by al-Mağlisî and al-ʿÂmilî.[3] It is missing, however, from the accounts of al-Ṭabarî, even though he dedicates a substantial amount of energy to describing al-Ḥusayn's journey from Mecca to Karbalâ', and to some of the well-meaning supporters (such as ʿAbd Allâh b. ʿAbbâs, ʿAbd Allâh b. al-Zubayr and ʿAbd Allâh b. Ğaʿfar b. al-Muṭṭalib) who tried to dissuade him from continuing. Al-Mufîd and Ibn Ṭâ'ûs also omit the account.

Al-Ḥusayn is still *en route* from Mecca to Karbalâ', a 913–mile (1470 kilometres) journey, and arrives a place called al-Ḫuzamiyya, not quite halfway to Karbalâ', where he encamps for a day and a night. It is difficult to determine Zaynab's mindset at this stage of the journey, although some of her words and reactions suggest strongly that she has not yet fully grasped the outcome of these events. This is not to suggest that Zaynab had forgotten the numerous predictions of her brother's eventual martyrdom; what is not certain is whether she realized that his envisioned end would come as Karbalâ'. Some people had certainly attempted to dissuade

---

[3] al-Ḫawârizmî., *Maqtal al-Ḥusayn*, bk. 1, bb. *fî ḫurûğ al-Ḥusayn min Makka ilâ al-ʿIrâq*: 323–4, Ibn Shahrâshûb., *Manâqib âl Abî Ṭâlib*, vol. IV, *faṣl fî maqtali-hi*: 95, al-Mağlisî., *Biḥâr al-anwâr*, vol. XLIV, bb. 37, n. 2: 372, al-ʿÂmilî., *Aʿyân al-Shîʿa*, vol. VII: 137.

al-Ḥusayn from undertaking the journey; one of these was Zaynab's husband ʿAbd Allâh b. Ǧaʿfar, in bad health and who, unsuccessful in deterring al-Ḥusayn, would send his wife Zaynab and two of their sons, ʿAwn and Muḥammad, to accompany him.[4]

It is here, at al-Ḫuzamiyya, that an agitated Zaynab tells her brother that she has heard a voice or voices calling in the night in a lament she does not understand:

> O eye, truly, be extravagant in effort, for who will weep over the martyrs after me, over[5] a people conveyed by death, precisely to the achievement of a promise sworn?

Al-Ḥusayn's response is a laconic declaration that all that has been decreed will come to be.

A lament on the night air by unknown voices is a prevalent genre in the Karbalâʾ story. In his *Kâmil al-ziyârât* for example, al-Qummî dedicates an entire chapter to the lament of the *ǧinn* for al-Ḥusayn after his death.[6] These dirges consist of pithy verses, put on the lips of the *ǧinn* by al-Qummî and most often heard in the night. A number of these are transmitted on the authority of Umm Salama: "I heard the *ǧinn* lamenting over al-Ḥusayn," she is reported to have said, and, in another version: "Since the death of the Prophet, I never heard the lament of the *ǧinn* except at night…"[7]

---

[4] al-Maǧlisî., *Biḥâr al-anwâr*, vol. XLIV, bb. 37: 366.

[5] al-Ḫawârizmî's text reads, correctly, *ʿalâ*, compared to some others which read *ilâ*.

[6] Ibn Qûlûya al-Qummî., *Kâmil al-ziyârât*, bb. 28, n. 23: 187, bb. 29, n.n. 1–10: 189–197. A collective noun, of disputed origin but possibly from the Latin *genius*, *ǧinn* refers to corporeal beings made of mist or flame (although they can take on different visible forms), endowed with intellect and imperceptible to the senses (the Arabic root *ǧanna* carries the sense of concealment). Belief in these sometimes mischievous, sometimes malevolent spirit creatures predates Islam, and they form part of those whom Muḥammad is sent to save (cf. Q. 51: 56).

[7] Cf. for e.g. Ibn ʿAsâkir., *Târîḫ madînat Dimashq*, vol. XIV, bb. 1566: 242 for a *ḥadîṯ* in which similar lamentation poetry is put into the mouth of "a caller who cried out at night." Cf. also al-Haytamî., *Maǧmaʿ al-zawâʾid wa-manbaʿ al-fawâʾid*, vol. IX, bb. 95 (*Manâqib al-Ḥusayn*), n.n. 15179, 15180

Two things cause the al-Ḫuzamiyya incident to stand out: the first is that it is sparsely transmitted in the classical texts, even among the Shîʿa, and the second is that the dirge is particularly close to similar laments heard by Umm Salama and others after al-Ḥusayn's death at Karbalâʾ. Al-Qâḍî al-Nuʿmân, Ibn Qûlûya al-Qummî, al-Fattâl al-Nîsâbûrî, Ibn Shahrâshûb (transmitting from al-Nîsâbûrî and al-Ṭûsî), Ibn Namâ al-Ḥillî, al-Baḥrânî, al-Maǧlisî and al-Baḥrânî[8] all place this verse in the mouths of the *ǧinn*, whom Umm Salama (or sometimes other people in Medina) hear in the night after Karbalâʾ. Al-Ḫawârizmî, Ibn Shahrâshûb, al-Ǧazâʾirî, al-Maǧlisî and al-Baḥrânî[9] also place the verse on the lips of an un-

---

(Maymûna, not Umm Salama), 15181: 234, al-Mufîd., *al-Amâlî li-l-Mufîd*, n. 7: 350, al-Ṭûsî., *al-Amâlî fî al-ḥadîṯ*, bb. 3, n. 50–131: 91, al-Ṭabarsî., *Kitâb al-iḥtiǧâǧ ʿalâ ahl al-liǧâǧ*, vol. II: 305, Ibn Shahrâshûb., *Manâqib âl Abî Ṭâlib*, vol. IV, bb. *fî âyâti-hi baʿda wafâti-hi*: 69–70, al-Maǧlisî., *Biḥâr al-anwâr*, vol. XLIV, bb. 37: 378, vol. XLV, bb. 39: 147, bb. 43: 236–237, bb. 44: 276 for similar accounts of unidentified speakers.

[8] al-Nuʿmân b. Muḥammad b. Manṣûr b. Aḥmad b. Ḥayyûn al-Tamîmî al-Qâḍî Abû Ḥanîfa al-Shîʿa (d. 363/974: cf. GAL S. I: 324, although Brockelmann names the work differently) in his *Sharḥ al-aḫbâr fî faḍâʾil al-aʾimma*, vol. III, n. 1107: 167, Ibn Qûlûya al-Qummî., *Kâmil al-ziyârât*, bb. 29, n. 1: 93, al-Fattâl al-Nîsâbûrî., *Rawḍat al-wâʿiẓîn wa-tabṣirat al-muttaʿiẓîn*, vol. I, n. 3 [409]: 388, Ibn Shahrâshûb., *Manâqib âl Abî Ṭâlib*, vol. IV, bb. *faṣl fî âyâti-hi*: 62, Ibn Namâ al-Ḥillî., *Muṯîr al-aḥzân wa munîr subul al-ashǧân*: 107, Hâshim b. Sulaymân b. Ismâʿîl b. ʿAbd al-Ǧawâd b. ʿAbd al-Raḥmân al-Ḥusaynî al-Baḥrânî (d. 1107/1695: cf. GAL S. II: 506, 533) in his *Madînat al-maʿâǧiz fî muǧâʾiz al-aʾimma al-aṭhâr*, vol. IV: 121, 194, al-Maǧlisî., *Biḥâr al-anwâr*, vol. XLV, bb. 43, n. 8: 238, vol. LX, bb. 2, n. 3: 65, al-Baḥrânî., *ʿAwâlim al-ʿulûm wa-l-maʿârif al-aḥwâl min al-âyât wa-l-aḫbâr wal-aqwâl*, vol. IV, n. 3: 482, transmitting from al-Ṣadûq (cf. al-Ṣadûq., *Kitâb al-amâlî fî-l-aḥâdîṯ wa-l-aḫbâr*, n. 2: 139).

[9] al-Ḫawârizmî., *Maqtal al-Ḥusayn*, bk. 1, bb. *fî ḫurûǧ al-Ḥusayn min Makka ilâ al-ʿIrâq*, n. 7: 323–324, Ibn Shahrâshûb., *Manâqib âl Abî Ṭâlib*, vol. IV, bb. *faṣl fî maqtali-hi*: 95, Niʿmat Allâh al-Ǧazâʾirî (d. 1112/1701) in his *Riyâḍ al-abrâr fî manâqib al-aʾimma al-aṭhâr*, vol I: 217, al-Maǧlisî., *Biḥâr al-anwâr*, vol. XLIV, bb. 37: 372, al-Baḥrânî., *ʿAwâlim al-ʿulûm wa-l-maʿârif al-aḥwâl min al-âyât wa-l-aḫbâr wal-aqwâl*, vol. II, n. 12: 961, vol. IV: 223.

known person or people, possibly *ǧinn*, although this is not clarified, heard by Zaynab on the night at al-Ḫuzamiyya.

In his *Maqtal*, al-Muqarram, while ascribing this verse to an unknown voice heard by Zaynab on the night air in al-Ḫuzamiyya and referring us to Ibn Namâ's *Muṯîr al-aḥzân*, attributes a remarkably similar verse heard recited by a voice on the night of al-Ḥusayn's death by Umm Salama, and directs us to Ibn ʿAsâkir, al-Hayṯamî and al-Suyûṭî:

> O eyes! This is a day for your tears,
> So cry hard and spare not.
> Who after me shall the martyrs mourn,
> Over folks led by their fates
> To a tyrant in the reign of slaves?[10]

What, then, did Zaynab hear on the night air? In the al-Ḫuzamiyya narratives, there is no indication, as there is in the Umm Salama accounts, of whose voice has called out. It is not unreasonable to imagine that she heard what a number of others would report having heard; unidentified voices on the night air, bewailing al-Ḥusayn's fate. Judging by this and by later events, it is fair to say that Zaynab has not yet fully grasped the extreme jeopardy of her brother's situation. This will be seen especially in her growing sense of panic during these pre-Karbalâ' days. A failure to appreciate this trepidation would be to do her a disservice. Zaynab is embarking upon a twofold journey. The physical journey to Karbalâ' is the outer shell; the more decisive journey is the existential one, in which Zaynab is becoming Zaynab, that is, she is being forged into that woman who, standing in front of Ibn Ziyâd and Yazîd, will draw on all her inner strength and help her brother to save and to lead Islam. To negate her fear and doubt is to deny that crucial existential journey, which is far more common to the lives of most people than is the physical one.

---

[10] Ibn ʿAsâkir., *Târîḫ madînat Dimashq*, vol XIV, bb. *al-Ḥusayn b. ʿAlî b. Abî Ṭâlib*: 241, al-Hayṯamî., *Maǧmaʿ al-zawâ'id wa-manbaʿ al-fawâ'id*, vol. IX, bb. 95 (*Manâqib al-Ḥusayn*), n. 15181: 234, al-Suyûṭî., *al-Ḫaṣâ'iṣ al-kubrâ*, vol. II: 215. Cf. AL-JIBOURI Y.T., (trans.), *Maqtal al-Ḥusain*, 2014: 238–9.

There are people who have turned Zaynab into a fearless superheroine, tenacious and assured. This may be useful for some political discourse or social narrative, but it is not a true representation of the Zaynab of the texts. The Zaynab of al-Ḫuzamiyya is a woman who has not yet fully comprehended the final outcome of the Karbalâʾ event. As already noted, while there is a whole genre of dreams, visions and angelic visitations, to some of which Zaynab is privy, of the martyrdom of al-Ḥusayn, those that pinpoint Karbalâʾ as the place of his death of fewer. While Zaynab may have been aware of his impending death, some of her words and actions, noted through the course this text suggest that hers was a swelling realization that the hour of his martyrdom had arrived. As the journey progresses there will be a growing cognizance that there is no turning back, again, seen especially in some of the words she speaks and some of her reactions to incidents. However, the Zaynab of al-Ḫuzamiyya is a markedly different woman from the one who will stand before Ziyâd, or who will volunteer to be killed before anyone harms the new Imâm, or who tells Yazîd what a savage he was. That is the Zaynab still to come.

2. RUMOURS OF WAR

A second decisive pre-battle moment for Zaynab, in which we are offered a clear picture of a genuinely distressed woman, is transmitted by al-Ṭabarî, who carries Abû Miḫnaf's report from the Shîʿî traditionist ʿAbd Allâh b. Sharîk al-ʿÂmirî.[11] Hearing the noise of the approaching army on the day before the battle, Zaynab comes up to al-Ḥusayn, seated in front of his tent. She asks him if he has heard the distant noise; in reply, he tells her that he has had a vision, while asleep, of Muḥammad, who informed him: "You are coming to us." Zaynab is distraught, crying out: "Woe is me!" Her brother replies: "Woe is not for you, sister."

---

[11] ʿAbd Allâh b. Sharîk al-ʿÂmirî (narrated from Imâms or their Companions and died in the first half of the 2nd/8th century). Cf. HOWARD I.K.A., (trans.), *The History of al-Ṭabarî*, vol. XIX, 1990: 111–112.

The story is recounted by many of the Sunnî historians, who place it sometime after the *ʿaṣr* prayer[12] on the day before the battle, therefore 9th Muḥarram. Al-Ḥusayn is sitting in front of his tent, legs drawn up and garment around him, ostensibly cleaning his sword and preparing it for battle, but in fact dozing off, his head dropping drowsily. His sister Zaynab hears the threatening noise of the approaching army, and goes to wake him, since he has not been roused by the clamour that so disturbs his sister – that of an arriving enemy force – to ask if he has not heard how near they are. "Do you not hear the sounds coming closer?"[13] she asks. Al-Ḥusayn lifts his head and says: "I saw the Messenger of God while asleep, and he said to me: You are coming to us!" She strikes her face and cries out: "My woe!" Al-Ḥusayn replies: "Woe is not for you, my sister. Calm down and may the Merciful be merciful to you!"[14]

In al-Fattâl al-Nîsâbûrî's transmission,[15] the sister is unnamed, but we may presume her to be Zaynab. Ibn Ṭâʾûs, on the other hand, changes the chronology, putting the whole scene of al-Ḥusayn dozing later than the other transmitters, separating it from Zaynab hearing the sound of the approaching army and from her grieving over the dirge her brother sings. According to his narration, al-Ḥusayn is seated in front of his tent sleeping. He awakens and says to Zaynab: "My sister, I have just seen my grandfather Muḥammad and my father ʿAlî and my mother Fâṭima al-Zahrâʾ and my brother al-Ḥasan, and they said: Ḥusayn, you are coming to us soon" (in some transmitters, he notes, 'tomorrow').[16] In practically all the other transmitters, al-Ṭabarî, Ibn al-Aṯîr, Ibn Kaṯîr, as well as numerous Shîʿî authors,[17] this incident occurs just after the

---

[12] Thus, somewhere between the midday prayer and sunset.

[13] al-Fattâl al-Nîsâbûrî., *Rawḍat al-wâʿiẓîn wa-tabṣirat al-muttaʿiẓîn*: 183.

[14] Ibn al-Aṯîr., *al-Kâmil fî al-târîḫ*, vol. II: 416–418 (who also notes that all his sisters wept upon hearing the dirge), Ibn Kaṯîr., *al-Bidâya wa-l-nihâya*, vol. XII: 529.

[15] al-Fattâl al-Nîsâbûrî., *Rawḍat al-wâʿiẓîn wa-tabṣirat al-muttaʿiẓîn*: 416.

[16] Ibn Ṭâʾûs., *Kitâb al-luhûf fî qatlâ al-ṭufûf*: 55.

[17] Cf. HOWARD I.K.A., (trans.), *The History of al-Ṭabarî*, vol. XIX, 1990: 112, al-Mufîd., *al-Irshâd fî maʿrifat ḥuǧaǧ Allâh ʿalâ al-ʿibâd*, vol. II, bb.

ʿaṣr prayer on the afternoon of 9th Muḥarram. Except for al-Ḫawârizmî, who puts it after the lament al-Ḥusayn has sung in front of his tent[18] and Ibn Ṭâ'ûs, who separates it from Zaynab hearing a noise,[19] the transmitters are agreed upon almost all the details.

In the moments he was asleep, al-Ḥusayn has had a vision of his grandfather Muḥammad, or perhaps all of the 'people of the cloak', whom Muḥammad, in a moment that is pivotal for the theology of Shîʿî Islam, once gathered about him and proclaimed: "These are the people of my house."[20] Al-Ṭabarî, al-Mufîd, al-

---

nuzûl al-Imâm al-Ḥusayn fî Karbalâ': 89–90, al-Fattâl al-Nîsâbûrî., *Rawḍat al-wâʿiẓîn wa-tabṣirat al-muttaʿiẓîn*: 183, al-Ṭabarsî., *Iʿlâm al-warâ bi-aʿlâm al-hudâ*: 235, Ibn al-Aṯîr., *al-Kâmil fî al-târîḫ*, vol. II: 415–417, Ibn Kaṯîr., *al-Bidâya wa-l-nihâya*, vol. XI: 529, al-Maǧlisî., *Biḥâr al-anwâr*, vol. XLIV, bb. 37, n. 2: 391, al-ʿÂmilî., *Aʿyân al-Shîʿa*, vol. VII: 137 (from al-Mufîd and Ibn al-Aṯîr).

18 al-Ḫawârizmî., *Maqtal al-Ḥusayn*, bk. 1, bb. *fî ḫurûǧ al-Ḥusayn min Makka ilâ al-ʿIrâq*: 353.

19 Ibn Ṭâ'ûs., *Kitâb al-luhûf fî qatlâ al-ṭufûf*: 55.

20 The concept of the 'people of the house' (*ahl al-bayt*) is one of the key poles (side by side with the specific designation of ʿAlî) around which the whole of the Shîʿî ethos is structured. The phrase is found twice in the Qur'ân: in *sûrat al-Aḥzâb*, it is in reference to the family of Muḥammad, in the so-called 'verse of purification' (*âyat al-taṭhîr*), so decisive for the Shîʿa: «*Allah's wish is but to remove uncleanness far from you, O Folk of the household, and cleanse you with a thorough cleansing*» (Q. 33: 33). Basing their argument on the *aḥâdîṯ* narrated by Muḥammad's Companions and recorded in both Shîʿî and Sunnî sources, the Shîʿî scholars, as well as some of the Sunnî, consider the 'people of the house' cited in this verse to refer to Muḥammad, ʿAlî, Fâṭima, al-Ḥasan and al-Ḥusayn, excluding all Muḥammad's other wives, offspring and grandchildren. The Shîʿî and Sunnî collections transmit accounts of the *ahl al-bayt*, grouping the *aḥâdîṯ* in a number of strands, including the crucial *ḥadîṯ* of 'the two weighty things' (*al-ṯaqalayn*) and that of 'the boat' (*al-safîna*). The *ḥadîṯ* of 'the cloak' (*al-kisâ'*) stands at the head of these strands. Sunnî transmitters of the *ḥadîṯ al-kisâ'* (*ḥadîṯ* of the cloak), already listed earlier in this work, have judged it to be authentic. Ibn Ḥanbal, in his *Musnad*, quotes Umm Salama as saying: "The Holy Prophet was in my house. Fâṭima came to her father…the Holy Prophet

Fattâl al-Nîsâbûrî, al-Ṭabarsî, Ibn al-Aṯîr, Ibn Kaṯîr and al-Mağlisî all transmit that al-Ḥusayn saw the Messenger of God (*rasûl Allâh*) and no one else in his dream. Al-Ḫawârizmî, Ibn Ṭâʾûs (and al-Mağlisî transmitting from him) add ʿAlî, Fâṭima and al-Ḥasan, the other core members of the *ahl al-bayt.*[21] All the key members together would clearly establish al-Ḥusayn's legitimacy and authority, on the eve of the martyrdom his momentous decision will bring about, as one of the *maʿṣûmûn* and an indispensible member of the *ahl al-bayt*.

In his conversation with his interlocutor(s) al-Ḥusayn has been informed of his imminent death – it is 'soon' in most texts, although some narrations, notes Ibn Ṭâʾûs, use the word 'tomorrow'. Zaynab's reaction is strongly physical; she is deeply peturbed,

---

stated: Invite your husband and two sons to come as well. ʿAlî, al-Ḥasan, and al-Ḥusayn also came there and all sat down to eat. Then, the Holy Prophet was sitting on a cloak in his resting place and I was reciting the prayer in the chamber. At this time, God revealed the verse "*Allah's wish is but to remove uncleanness far from you, O Folk of the household, and cleanse you with a thorough cleansing*". The Holy Prophet covered ʿAlî, Fâṭima, al-Ḥasan, and al-Ḥusayn with the cloak and then stretched his hand toward the sky and said: O God! These are the Members of my Household, so purify them of all uncleanness. Umm Salama said: I asked him: Am I also with you? He stated: You have your own place, you are virtuous (but did not say that you are a member of my Household)." Cf. Ibn Ḥanbal., *Musnad*, vol. I, *Musnad ʿAbd Allâh b. al-ʿAbbâs b. ʿAbd al-Muṭṭalib*, n. 3062: 708–709, vol. VI, *Ḥadîṯ Wâṯala b. al-ʿAsqaʿ*, n. 16985: 45, vol. X, *Ḥadîṯ Umm Salama*, n. 26570: 177, n. 26612: 186–187, n. 26659: 197, n. 26808: 228.

21 HOWARD I.K.A., (trans.), *The History of al-Ṭabarî*, vol. XIX, 1990: 112, al-Mufîd., *al-Irshâd fî maʿrifat ḥuğağ Allâh ʿalâ al-ʿibâd*, vol. II, bb. *nuzûl al-Imâm al-Ḥusayn fî Karbalâʾ*: 90, al-Fattâl al-Nîsâbûrî., *Rawḍat al-wâʿiẓîn wa-tabṣirat al-muttaʿiẓîn*: 183, al-Ṭabarsî., *Iʿlâm al-warâ bi-aʿlâm al-hudâ*: 235, Ibn al-Aṯîr., *al-Kâmil fî al-târîḫ*, vol. II: 415, Ibn Kaṯîr., *al-Bidâya wa-l-nihâya*, vol. XI: 529, al-Mağlisî., *Biḥâr al-anwâr*, vol. XLIV, bb. 37, n. 2: 391. Cf. al-Ḫawârizmî., *Maqtal al-Ḥusayn*, bk. 1, bb. *fî ḫurûğ al-Ḥusayn min Makka ilâ al-ʿIrâq*: 352, Ibn Ṭâʾûs., *Kitâb al-luhûf fî qatlâ al-ṭufûf*: 55, al-Mağlisî., *Biḥâr al-anwâr*, vol. XLIV, bb. 37, n. 2: 391.

crying out 'woe is me' or 'my woe' and, in some texts,[22] striking her face. The texts offer three possible responses from her brother: 'Woe is not for you, sister',[23] in almost all the texts, an exhortation and wish ('calm down, and may the Merciful be merciful to you'),[24] and, only in Ibn Ṭâʾûs and al-Mağlisî's transmission from him, a second exhortation ('Be calm! Do not cause the people to rejoice in our misfortune').[25] Zaynab has now heard from her brother's own mouth that he will die; but judging by later words and reactions, she still has not grasped the gravity of the situation.

3. THE DIRGE

This third incident takes place on the night before al-Ḥusayn's death, sometime after Zaynab's hearing the noise of an arriving army, and is carried by a number of transmitters, both Sunnî and Shîʿî. Included among the group, which comprises a significant number of historians, are al-Balâḏurî, al-Yaʿqûbî, al-Ṭabarî, al-Iṣfahânî, al-Mufîd, al-Fattâl al-Nîsâbûrî, al-Ḫawârizmî, Ibn Shahrâshûb, Ibn al-Aṯîr, Ibn Namâ al-Ḥillî, Ibn Kaṯîr, al-Mağlisî

---

[22] al-Mufîd., *al-Irshâd fî maʿrifat ḥuğağ Allâh ʿalâ al-ʿibâd*, vol. II, bb. *nuzûl al-Imâm al-Ḥusayn fî Karbalâʾ*: 90, al-Fattâl al-Nîsâbûrî., *Rawḍat al-wâʿiẓîn wa-tabṣirat al-muttaʿiẓîn*: 183, al-Ṭabarsî., *Iʿlâm al-warâ bi-aʿlâm al-hudâ*: 235, Ibn al-Aṯîr., *al-Kâmil fî al-târîḫ*, vol. II: 415, Ibn Ṭâʾûs., *Kitâb al-luhûf fî qatlâ al-ṭufûf*: 55, Ibn Kaṯîr., *al-Bidâya wa-l-nihâya*, vol. XI: 529, al-Mağlisî., *Biḥâr al-anwâr*, vol. XLIV, bb. 37, n. 2: 391.

[23] HOWARD I.K.A., (trans.), *The History of al-Ṭabarî*, vol. XIX, 1990: 112, al-Mufîd., *al-Irshâd fî maʿrifat ḥuğağ Allâh ʿalâ al-ʿibâd*, vol. II, bb. *nuzûl al-Imâm al-Ḥusayn fî Karbalâʾ*: 90, al-Fattâl al-Nîsâbûrî., *Rawḍat al-wâʿiẓîn wa-tabṣirat al-muttaʿiẓîn*: 183, Ibn al-Aṯîr., *al-Kâmil fî al-târîḫ*, vol. II: 415, Ibn Kaṯîr., *al-Bidâya wa-l-nihâya*, vol. XI: 529, al-Mağlisî., *Biḥâr al-anwâr*, vol. XLIV, bb. 37, n. 2: 391.

[24] al-Mufîd., *al-Irshâd fî maʿrifat ḥuğağ Allâh ʿalâ al-ʿibâd*, vol. II, bb. *nuzûl al-Imâm al-Ḥusayn fî Karbalâʾ*: 89–90, al-Fattâl al-Nîsâbûrî., *Rawḍat al-wâʿiẓîn wa-tabṣirat al-muttaʿiẓîn*: 183, al-Ṭabarsî., *Iʿlâm al-warâ bi-aʿlâm al-hudâ*: 235, Ibn al-Aṯîr., *al-Kâmil fî al-târîḫ*, vol. II: 415, Ibn Kaṯîr., *al-Bidâya wa-l-nihâya*, vol. XI: 529.

[25] Ibn Ṭâʾûs., *Kitâb al-luhûf fî qatlâ al-ṭufûf*: 55, al-Mağlisî., *Biḥâr al-anwâr*, vol. XLIV, bb. 37, n. 2: 391.

and al-ʿÂmilî. Each of them relates the story with generally few substantial differences in the details he gives. Al-Ḫawârizmî in his *Maqtal* and Ibn Ṭâʾûs in his *Kitâb al-luhûf* are the lone voices of dissent, situating the incident much earlier than the other transmitters do; around the second or third day of Muḥarram rather than the evening of the 9th, and thus shortly after the arrival of the group at Karbalâʾ. Al-Ḥusayn asks the name of the land, and when told it is Karbalâʾ, prays a prayer of refuge in God from distress (*al-karb*) and tribulation (*al-balâʾ*). Ibn Ṭâʾûs then recounts the story of the lament and Zaynab's reaction.[26]

Abû Miḫnaf has al-Ḥusayn's son, ʿAlî b. al-Ḥusayn b. ʿAlî, relate the incident, and most of the transmissions follow this; al-Balâḏurî, contrastingly, places the story on the lips of a servant called Ḥuwayy (so named by Abû Miḫnaf and Ibn Kaṯîr),[27] and who is with al-Ḥusayn, helping him to prepare his sword before battle and make it serviceable. While al-Iṣfahânî, al-Ṭabarsî, al-Ḫawârizmî, Ibn Ṭâʾûs, Ibn Namâ al-Ḥillî, (and, consequently, al-Mağlisî at times) name this servant as Ğawn,[28] al-Mufîd names him Ğuwayn,[29] and Ibn Ṭâʾûs thinks his name might be ʿAwn.[30] Others, like al-Ṭabarî, make no mention of

---

[26] Ibn Ṭâʾûs., *Kitâb al-luhûf fî qatlâ al-ṭufûf*: 49. Cf. al-Ḫawârizmî., *Maqtal al-Ḥusayn*, bk. 1, bb. *fî ḫurûğ al-Ḥusayn min Makka ilâ al-ʿIrâq*: 338–339.

[27] al-Balâḏurî., *Kitâb ansâb al-ashrâf*, vol. III: 393, Abû Miḫnaf., *Waqʿat al-Ṭaff*, bb. *al-Imâm laylat ʿÂshûrâʾ*: 200, Ibn Kaṯîr., *al-Bidâya wa-l-nihâya*, vol. XI: 531. Cf. also al-ʿÂmilî., *Aʿyân al-Shîʿa*, vol. VII: 138.

[28] al-Iṣfahânî., *Maqâtil al-ṭâlibîyyîn*: 113, al-Ṭabarsî., *Iʿlâm al-warâ bi-aʿlâm al-hudâ*: 239, al-Ḫawârizmî., *Maqtal al-Ḥusayn*, bk. 1, bb. *fî ḫurûğ al-Ḥusayn min Makka ilâ al-ʿIrâq*: 338, Ibn Ṭâʾûs., *Kitâb al-luhûf fî qatlâ al-ṭufûf*: 64–65, Ibn Namâ al-Ḥillî., *Muṯîr al-aḥzân wa munîr subul al-ashğân*, Part 2: 63, al-Mağlisî., *Biḥâr al-anwâr*, vol. XLV, bb. 37: 22, 71.

[29] al-Mufîd., *al-Irshâd fî maʿrifat ḥuğağ Allâh ʿalâ al-ʿibâd*, vol. II, bb. *ḫuṭbat al-Ḥusayn bi-aṣḥâbi-hi*: 93, al-Baḥrânî., *ʿAwâlim al-ʿulûm wa-l-maʿârif al-aḥwâl min al-âyât wa-l-aḫbâr wa-l-aqwâl*, vol. XI, bb. 12: 962 (from al-Mufîd).

[30] Ibn Ṭâʾûs., *Kitâb al-iqbâl bi-l-aʿmâl al-ḥasana*, vol. II: 713.

him, or simply refer to him as 'a person' (*fulân*)[31] although all the transmitters mention that he is in fact the retainer of Abû Ḏarr al-Ġifârî, greatly venerated by the Sunnî and the Shîʿa alike.[32] Al-Ḫawârizmî, Ibn Ṭâʾûs and Ibn Namâ al-Ḥillî will all go on to record Ğawn's death on the field of Karbalâʾ.[33]

According to Abû Miḫnaf's account,[34] on the evening before the day on which his father would be killed, the sickly ʿAlî b. al-Ḥusayn b. ʿAlî recounts that he was being nursed by his aunt Zaynab, on account of whatever illness it was that would finally prevent him fighting and, eventually, help to save him from being killed. These elements are omitted by some of the transmitters;[35] in some, the dirge forms part of a longer prayer, without the details of ʿAlî being nursed by Zaynab.[36] However, in the majority of trans-

---

[31] al-Fattâl al-Nîsâbûrî., *Rawḍat al-wâʿiẓîn wa-tabṣirat al-muttaʿiẓîn*, vol. I: 184 (although he also notes the name Ğuwayn), al-Mağlisî., *Biḥâr al-anwâr*, vol. XLV, bb. 37, n. 2: 2, al-Baḥrânî., *ʿAwâlim al-ʿulûm wa-l-maʿârif al-aḥwâl min al-âyât wa-l-aḫbâr wa-l-aqwâl*, vol. VII: 245.

[32] Modarressi notes that Abû Ḏarr al-Ġifârî was one of the more senior Companions of Muḥammad who retained and special devotion to the members of Muḥammad's household; he is one of those, therefore, considered by the Shîʿa to be a member of their first generation. Cf. MODARRESSI H., *Crisis and Consolidation in the Formative Period of Shiʿite Islam*, Darwin Press, Princeton, NJ: 1993: 1.

[33] al-Ḫawârizmî., *Maqtal al-Ḥusayn*, bk. 2, bb. *fî maqtal al-Ḥusayn*: 23, Ibn Ṭâʾûs., *Kitâb al-luhûf fî qatlâ al-ṭufûf*: 64–65, Ibn Namâ al-Ḥillî., *Muṯîr al-aḥzân wa munîr subul al-ashğân*, Part 2: 63.

[34] HOWARD I.K.A., (trans.), *The History of al-Ṭabarî*, vol. XIX, 1990: 117–118.

[35] al-Ṣadûq., *Kitâb al-amâlî fî-l-aḥâdîṯ wa-l-aḫbâr*, *mağlis* 30: 156, Ibn Shahrâshûb., *Manâqib âl Abî Ṭâlib*, vol. IV, bb. *faṣl fî maqtali-hi*: 99, Ibn Ṭâʾûs., *Kitâb al-luhûf fî qatlâ al-ṭufûf*: 49–50, Ibn Namâ al-Ḥillî., *Muṯîr al-aḥzân wa munîr subul al-ashğân*, Part 1: 49, al-Mağlisî., *Biḥâr al-anwâr*, vol. XLIV, bb. 37: 316, al-Ğazâʾirî., *Riyâḍ al-abrâr fî manâqib al-aʾimma al-aṭhâr*, vol I: 221, al-Baḥrânî., *ʿAwâlim al-ʿulûm wa-l-maʿârif al-aḥwâl min al-âyât wa-l-aḫbâr wa-l-aqwâl*, vol. XIV: 165.

[36] al-Ṣadûq., *Kitâb al-amâlî fî-l-aḥâdîṯ wa-l-aḫbâr*, *mağlis* 30: 156, Ibn Ṭâʾûs., *Kitâb al-luhûf fî qatlâ al-ṭufûf*: 49–50, al-Mağlisî., *Biḥâr al-anwâr*, vol.

missions, both ʿAlî b. al-Ḥusayn and Zaynab hear al-Ḥusayn reciting an elegy about his approaching death. Al-Ḥusayn is seated in front of his tent,[37] being helped by Ǧawn to ready his sword for battle.[38] Two or three times, notes his son, al-Ḥusayn repeats the lament, "until I knew it by heart"[39] or, in other texts, until the boy could not but understand what they meant:[40]

> Time, shame on you as friend! By sunrise and late afternoon, how many a companion or seeker will be yours, fallen? But time will not be content with the alternative, and the matter is with the Majestic, for every living creature is a traveller on a path!

Lost in the translation is the splendid rhythm and rhyme of the verse:

> *Yâ dahr, uff laka min ḫalîl*
> *Kam laka bi-l-ishrâq wa-l-aṣîl*

XLIV, bb. 37: 316, al-Ǧazâʾirî., *Riyâḍ al-abrâr fî manâqib al-aʾimma al-aṭhâr*, vol I: 201.

37 While most of the transmitters (cf. for e.g. al-Mufîd., *Kitâb al-irshâd*, vol. II, bb. *ḫuṭbat al-Ḥusayn bi-aṣḥâbi-hi*: 93, al-Fattâl al-Nîsâbûrî., *Rawḍat al-wâʿiẓîn wa-tabṣirat al-muttaʿiẓîn*: 184, al-Ṭabarsî., *Iʿlâm al-warâ bi-aʿlâm al-hudâ*, *faṣl* 4: 239, Ibn Shahrâshûb., *Manâqib âl Abî Ṭâlib*, vol. IV, bb. *faṣl fî maqtali-hi*: 99) place al-Ḥusayn in front of his tent, Ibn Kaṯîr has him secluded within his tent with his companions: cf. Ibn Kaṯîr., *al-Bidâya wa-l-nihâya*, vol. XII: 531.

38 In al-Iṣfahânî, al-Ḥusayn was working on an arrow, the text reading *sihâm*, which is an arrow or a dart. Cf. al-Iṣfahânî., *Maqâtil al-ṭâlibîyyîn*: 113.

39 al-Balâḏurî., *Kitâb ansâb al-ashrâf*, vol. III: 393 (although the narrator here is not clearly ʿAlî), al-Ḫawârizmî., *Maqtal al-Ḥusayn*, bk. 1, bb. *fî ḫurûǧ al-Ḥusayn min Makka ilâ al-ʿIrâq*: 338.

40 Abû Miḫnaf., *Waqʿat al-Ṭaff*, b. *al-Imâm laylat ʿÂshûrâʾ*: 200, al-Yaʿqûbî., *Târîḫ* vol. II: 243, al-Mufîd., *al-Irshâd fî maʿrifat ḥuǧaǧ Allâh ʿalâ al-ʿibâd*, vol. II, bb. *ḫuṭbat al-Ḥusayn bi-aṣḥâbi-hi*: 93, al-Fattâl al-Nîsâbûrî., *Rawḍat al-wâʿiẓîn wa-tabṣirat al-muttaʿiẓîn*: 184, al-Ṭabarsî., *Iʿlâm al-warâ bi-aʿlâm al-hudâ*, vol. I: 239, 452, Ibn Kaṯîr., *al-Bidâya wa-l-nihâya*, vol. XI: 531, al-Maǧlisî., *Biḥâr al-anwâr*, vol. XLV, bb. 37, n. 2: 2.

Min ṣâḥib wa ṭâlib qatîl
Wa-l-dahru la yaqnaʿu bi-l-badîl
Wa innamâ al-amru ilâ al-Ǧalîl
Wa kullu ḥayy sâlik sabîl

Whether she was, as in most transmissions, nursing her nephew, or, as in others, sitting in the tents with the other women,[41] the reaction of Zaynab is stark, and far removed from that of the composed and forceful woman who a few days later would coerce Ibn Ziyâd to back down and reduce Yazîd to a crestfallen silence. While ʿAlî b. al-Ḥusayn is 'choked' with tears ("I knew that affliction had come down"),[42] Zaynab is overwrought, a reaction which her nephew explains by saying: "As for my aunt, she heard what I heard, but she is a woman, and weakness[43] and grief[44] are the [qualities] of women; she could not control herself."[45] Zaynab leaps to her feet, tearing at her clothes and veil, and goes, bareheaded, to her brother. Al-Ṭabarî, transmitting in his *Kitâb aḫbâr al-rusul wa-l-mulûk* from Abû Miḫnaf, and closely followed by al-Balâḏurî, al-

---

[41] Ibn Ṭâ'ûs., *Kitâb al-luhûf fî qatlâ al-ṭufûf*: 50.

[42] al-Yaʿqûbî., *Târîḫ*, vol. II: 243–4, al-Fattâl al-Nîsâbûrî., *Rawḍat al-wâʿiẓîn wa-tabṣirat al-muttaʿiẓîn*: 184, Ibn Kaṯîr., *al-Bidâya wa-l-nihâya*, vol. XI: 531. In al-Iṣfahânî he does not hold the tears back as in other narrations: al-Iṣfahânî., *Maqâtil al-ṭâlibîyyîn*: 113.

[43] The Arabic *al-riqqa* carries the sense of 'delicacy', 'sensitivity of feeling' or 'weakness of resistance'. Cf. LANE E.W., *An Arabic-English Lexicon*, vol. III, 1968: 1131.

[44] The Arabic *al-ǧaziʿ* carries the sense of 'restless', 'apprehensive', 'uneasy', 'worried' or 'sad'. WEHR H., *A Dictionary of Modern Written Arabic*, Librairie du Liban, Beirut 1980: 147. The same words (*al-riqqa* and *al-ǧaziʿ*) are used by almost all the transmitters: cf. for e.g. Abû Miḫnaf., *Waqʿat al-Ṭaff*, bb. *al-Imâm laylat ʿÂshûrâ'*: 200, al-Mufîd., *al-Irshâd fî maʿrifat ḥuǧaǧ Allâh ʿalâ al-ʿibâd*, vol. II, bb. *ḫuṭbat al-Ḥusayn bi-aṣḥâbi-hi*: 93, al-Ṭabarsî., *Iʿlâm al-warâ bi-aʿlâm al-hudâ*: 239, al-Maǧlisî., *Biḥâr al-anwâr*, vol. XLV, b. 37, n. 2: 3, al-Baḥrânî., *ʿAwâlim al-ʿulûm wa-l-maʿârif al-aḥwâl min al-âyât wa-l-aḫbâr wa-l-aqwâl*, vol. XI: 962.

[45] HOWARD I.K.A., (trans.), *The History of al-Ṭabarî*, vol. XIX, 1990: 118. In al-Iṣfahânî, 'anxiety' and 'weakness' (*raqqa*) 'clung to her'. Cf. al-Iṣfahânî., *Maqâtil al-ṭâlibîyyîn*: 113.

Ḫawârizmî (in a second of two narrations), Ibn Kaṯîr and al-Mağlisî (transmitting from al-Mufîd), recounts the basic details, as narrated by ʿAlî b. al-Ḥusayn. Howard's translation reads:

> Unveiled she went to him. She said to him, "I will lose a brother! Would that death had deprived me of life today! My mother Fāṭimah is dead, and my father ʿAlī, and my brother al-Ḥasan. You are the successor (khalīfah) of those who have passed away and the guardian of those who remain!" Al-Ḥusayn said to her as he looked at her, "Sister! Don't let Satan take away your forbearance." She replied, "I swear by my father and mother, Abū Abdallāh (i.e., al-Ḥusayn)! You have exposed yourself to death. May God accept my life for yours!" Choking back his grief and with his eyes full of tears, he said, "If the sand grouse are left at night, they will sleep." She lamented, "My grief! Your life will be violently wrenched from you, and that is more wounding to my heart and harsher to my soul." She struck at her face and bent down to her dress and tore it. Then she fell down in a faint. Al-Ḥusayn got up and bathed her face with water. Then he said to her, "Sister, fear God and take comfort in the consolation of God. Know that the people of the earth will die and the inhabitants of heaven will not continue to exist forever, '...for everything will be destroyed except the face of God', Who created earth by His power, Who sends forth creatures and causes them to return, Who is unique and alone. My father was better than I, my mother was better than I, and my brother was better than I. I and every Muslim have an ideal model in the Apostle of God." By this and the like he tried to console her and he said, "Sister, I swear to you – so keep my oath – that you must not tear your clothes, nor scratch your face, nor cry out with grief and loss when I am destroyed." Then he brought her and made her sit with me.[46]

[46] HOWARD I.K.A., (trans.), *The History of al-Ṭabarî*, vol. XIX, 1990: 118. Cf. al-Balâḏurî., *Kitâb ansâb al-ashrâf*, vol. III: 393, al-Yaʿqûbî., *Târîḫ* vol. II: 243–4, Ibn Kaṯîr., *al-Bidâya wa-l-nihâya*, vol. XI: 531, al-Ḫawârizmî., *Maqtal al-Ḥusayn*, bk. 1, bb. *fî ḫurûğ al-Ḥusayn min Makka ilâ al-ʿIrâq*: 338, al-

Some of these details vary or are missing in other transmissions,[47] but as a whole, the text merits some analysis. Zaynab's immediate

---

Mağlisî., *Biḥâr al-anwâr*, vol. XLV, bb. 37, n. 2: 1–2 (transmitting from al-Mufîd, as told by ʿAlî b. al-Ḥusayn). Cf. also al-Ṭabarsî, *Ḫâtimat mustadrak al-wasâ'il*, vol. II, b. 71, n. 2442: 452. Although it is far outside the scope of this work, the grief-stricken actions of Zaynab, and her brother's words to her, raise the issue of one of the most tangible, precarious symbols, heavily debated both within and outside of the Shîʿî community; those physical actions which include the self-infliction of wounds and the drawing of blood. It is crucial to note that the ʿÂshûrâ memorials are not primarily about inflicting pain on the individual. However, in these physical actions, under the broad headings of *ma'tam* and *laṭm*, active participation rather than passive observance by the devotee is seen in a more stark way. These rituals of self-mortification have noticeably increased in the intensity of their violence, and yet remain a sensitive and compelling Shîʿî mark of identity (cf. CALMARD J. & J., "Muharram Ceremonies in Tehran" in P. Chelkowski (ed.), *Ta'ziyeh: Ritual and Drama in Iran*, New York University Press, New York 1979: 59). While there are clearly many who insist that such dramatic and physical acts of mourning were clearly forbidden by Muḥammad (not to mention al-Husayn, ostensibly, in his words to his sister), the practitioners of such rituals employ a variety of arguments to justify their actions, arguing, for example, that the self-infliction of physical suffering demonstrates the readiness of the mourners to suffer for and with al-Ḥusayn, so that in these actions, a continuity is created with his own physical suffering. Much of the criticism is aimed at those more instrumental rites in which blood is drawn (a ritual action not entirely unknown in Western Christianity); again, its adherents regard it as a proclamation that had they been in Karbalâ', they would have spilled their blood. Some members of the Shîʿî community posit that emulating al-Ḥusayn's spiritual life or ethical code is a better way to honour his legacy, instead of actions that bring down accusations of fanaticism upon Shîʿî Islam and which may even, through the shedding of blood, render the participant ritually impure. Cf. CLOHESSY C., "Some Notes on mağlis and taʿziya" in *Encounter*, vol. 41/1 (2016), Pontificio Istituto di Studi Arabi e d'Islamistica, Rome: 108–109.

[47] Sibṭ al-Ğawzî, for example, appears to combine the two events – the noise of war and the dirge of al-Ḥusayn – into one single instant, re-

preoccupation is that having lost her parents (ʿAlî and Fâṭima) and her brother (al-Ḥasan), she is now about to lose al-Ḥusayn, and wishes instead that she were dead, echoing the Qurʾânic wish of Maryam.[48] Her mother Fâṭima had died young, inconsolable at the death of her father Muḥammad, her own death hastened by events immediately after Muḥammad's demise in 11/632. ʿAlî had himself been assassinated in the mosque at Kûfa in January 40/661 by ʿAbd al-Raḥmân b. Mulǧam al-Murâdî. Zaynab's brother al-Ḥasan too had been killed, with Shîʿî (and some Sunnî) historians insisting that he was poisoned by his wife at the instigation of the caliph Muʿâwiya. Martyrdom is understood as part of the role of the Imâm, who gives his very self for the good of the Islamic community, and so provides the pattern of suffering and protest that guides and inspires the Shîʿa; but this is of little consolation to Zaynab in the moment. Her words 'I will lose a brother' are decisive, since they suggest that she is only now beginning to realize fully the implications of what is happening around her.

Addressing al-Ḥusayn as 'the successor of those who have passed away and the guardian of those who remain', (*ḫalîfat al-mâḍîn wa ṯimâl al-bâqîn*)[49] seems to be an attempt to persuade him not to die, since it would mean that those who remain would be without guardianship. Her brother attempts to comfort her, urging that she not allow Satan to steal her 'composure' (*ḥilm*). Although the Arabic word carries a primary sense of 'clemency', that is, the quality by which one forgives and forgets, Lane notes that it also refers to the way one manages one's soul and temper on the occasion of

---

cording few of the details aside from Zaynab's stark reaction. Cf. Sibṭ al-Ǧawzî., *Taḏkirat ḫawâṣṣ al-umma bi-ḏikr ḫaṣâʾiṣ al-aʾimma*: 211.

48 "*She said: Oh, would that I had died ere this and become a thing of naught, forgotten*" (Q. 19: 23). Zaynab's mother Fâṭima expresses similar sentiments after the death of her father, in her struggles with Abû Bakr over the land of Fadak.

49 al-Balâḏurî., *Kitâb Kitâb ansâb al-ashrâf*, vol. III: 1319, al-Iṣfahânî., *Maqâtil al-ṭâlibîyyîn*: 113, al-Ṭabarsî., *Iʿlâm al-warâ bi-aʿlâm al-hudâ*: 239, Ibn Ṭâʾûs., *Kitâb al-luhûf fî qatlâ al-ṭufûf*: 49–50, Ibn Namâ al-Ḥillî., *Muṯîr al-aḥzân wa munîr subul al-ashǧân*, Part 1: 49, Ibn Kaṯîr., *al-Bidâya wa-l-nihâya*, vol. XI: 531, al-Maǧlisî., *Biḥâr al-anwâr*, vol. XLV, bb. 37, n. 2: 2.

excitement, emotion or anger, or maintains tranquillity on such an occasion. It is thus probably best translated here as 'calm' or 'composure' rather than 'forbearance'.[50]

The proverb about the sandgrouse, which only serves to intensify Zaynab's distress, is extant only in a handful of transmitters.[51] The sense of the maxim is that of being provoked into action; that even if one does not desire it, one must strike the one who causes or prompts something detestable, and that once one is roused to action, there is no going back. Al-Ṭabarî refers us to Ibn Manẓûr's *Lisân al-ʿArab*,[52] while al-Mağlisî draws our attention to al-Maydânî, who tells the story of one ʿAmr b. Mâma, who takes up lodging among the Murâd tribe. They come to him by night, and in doing so provoke the sandgrouse from their places. His wife sees this as an omen, and awakens her husband, who says: "But they are just sandgrouse!" His wife replies: "If the sandgrouse had been left alone at night, it would have slept."[53] This is not the only occasion

---

[50] LANE E.W., *An Arabic-English Lexicon*, vol. II, 1968: 632.

[51] Cf. for e.g. al-Iṣfahânî., *Maqâtil al-ṭâlibîyyîn*: 113, al-Mufîd., *al-Iršâd fî maʿrifat ḥuğağ Allâh ʿalâ al-ʿibâd*, vol. II, bb. *ḫuṭbat al-Ḥusayn bi-aṣḥâbi-hi*: 93, al-Ṭabarsî., *Iʿlâm al-warâ bi-aʿlâm al-hudâ*: 239, al-Ḫawârizmî., *Maqtal al-Ḥusayn*, bk. 1, bb. *fî ḫurûğ al-Ḥusayn min Makka ilâ al-ʿIrâq*: 338, Ibn Shahrâshûb., *Manâqib âl Abî Ṭâlib*, vol. IV, bb. *faṣl fî maqtali-hi*: 99, Ibn Ṭâʾûs., *Kitâb al-luhûf fî qatlâ al-ṭufûf*: 50, Ibn Namâ al-Ḥillî., *Muṯîr al-aḥzân wa munîr subul al-ashğân*, Part 1: 49, al-Mağlisî., *Biḥâr al-anwâr*, vol. XLV, bb. 37, n. 2: 2, al-ʿÂmilî., *Aʿyân al-Shîʿa*, vol. VII: 138.

[52] Ibn Manẓûr., *Lisân al-ʿArab*, vol. XI: 233.

[53] Recorded by Abû al-Faḍl Aḥmad b. Muḥammad b. Aḥmad b. Ibrâhîm al-Maydânî (d. 518/1124, cf. GAL S. I: 506) in his collection of proverbs. Cf. al-Maydânî., *Mağmaʿ al-amṯâl*, vol. III: 97. If the meaning of the proverb is clear enough, the details of the Ibn Mâma story are less lucid without some context. The Murâd were an eastern Yemeni Arab tribe; according to some scholars, their correct name was Yuḥâbir, but they were nicknamed 'Murâd' because of their rebelliousness (*tamarrada* – 'to rebel'), and the mountains of Murâd and their inhabitants were well-known for outlaws and bandits. While Levi Della Vida regards this as a less than satisfactory etymology, it would explain the initial nervousness of

on which this proverb is placed on the lips of al-Ḥusayn. Al-Maǧlisî recounts the moment when al-Ḥusayn, the only survivor on the field, turns to the women's tents and offers them greetings peace; a conversation ensues with his daughter Sukayna.[54] She begs him to return to the sanctuary of Muḥammad, and he quotes the sand-grouse proverb.[55]

However, Zaynab is inconsolable, striking her face,[56] tearing her garments and, before falling into a faint, exclaiming: "My grief! Your life will be violently wrenched from you, and that is more wounding to my heart and harsher to my soul." Al-Ḥusayn revives her and, quoting a fragment of Q. 28: 88,[57] tries again to encourage her:

> "Sister, fear God and take comfort in the consolation of God. Know that the people of the earth will die and the inhabitants of heaven will not continue to exist forever, "*everything will perish save His countenance*", Who created earth by His power."

While al-Yaʿqûbî is more succinct ("My sister! Fear God! Death comes down inevitably!"), al-Balâḏurî reports that al-Ḥusayn recites Q. 44: 20–21 ("*And lo! I have sought refuge in my Lord and your Lord lest ye stone me to death. And if ye put no faith in me, then let me go*"); his sisters weep at this, and he has to calm them down.[58]

In response to her grief over the loss of her family, al-Ḥusayn urges her to reflect more deeply on the lives of ʿAlî, Fâṭima and al-

---

Ibn Mâma's wife. Cf. LEVI DELLA VIDA G., "Murād" in *The First Encyclopaedia of Islam*, E.J. Brill, Leiden 1987: 726.

[54] Wrongly called 'Sakîna' by the English translators of this volume; cf. SARWAR M., (trans.), *Behar al-anwar*, 2014: 304.

[55] al-Maǧlisî., *Biḥâr al-anwâr*, vol. XLV, bb. 37, n. 2: 47.

[56] The text uses the Arabic verb *laṭama-yalṭimu*, from which derives *laṭam*, used to describe a particular ritual action employed by some Shîʿî adherents during the ʿÂshûrâ commemorations.

[57] The whole verse reads: "*And cry not unto any other god along with Allah. There is no Allah save Him. Everything will perish save His countenance. His is the command, and unto Him ye will be brought back*".

[58] al-Yaʿqûbî., *Târîḫ* vol. II: 243–4, al-Balâḏurî., *Kitâb ansâb al-ashrâf*, vol III: 397/1323.

Ḥasan, reminding her that in Muḥammad, every Muslim has an ideal exemplar, and insisting that when he is killed, she should neither tear her clothes, nor beat her face, nor wail and lament. Ibn Kaṯîr records the event quite fully:

> So, I will lose him! Would that death had deprived me of life the day my mother Fâṭima died, and my father ʿAlî and my brother Ḥasan, successor of those passed away, the helper of those remaining." Al-Ḥusayn looked at her and said: "My sister, Satan must not carry off your forbearance!" She replied: "May my father and mother be ransomed for you, Abû ʿAbd Allâh, I would risk my very self for you!" She struck her face and ripped the collar of her robe, falling to the ground in a faint. Al-Ḥusayn went to her, pouring water on her face, and said: "My sister, fear God and take comfort in the consolation of God. Know that the people of the earth will die and the inhabitants of heaven will not continue to exist forever, for "*everything will perish save His countenance*", Who created creation by His power, and brings them to die by His vanquishing and his might. His is matchless in his unity. Know that my father is better than me, my mother is better than me, my brother is better than me; I and they and every Muslim has the Messenger of God as an excellent exemplar." Then he forbade her to do any of this after his death, and taking her by the hand, he brings her back to ʿAlî b. al-Ḥusayn.[59]

Ibn Ṭâʾûs tells the story differently in his *Kitâb al-luhûf*; al-Ḥusayn is seated in front of his tent, but there is no mention either of ʿAlî b. al-Ḥusayn or of Ǧawn the retainer, and the dirge is, in fact, part of a longer prayer. Ibn Ṭâʾûs transmits his account in two strands; in the first, Zaynab hears the poem and goes to al-Ḥusayn and says: "My brother, this is the talk of one who is certain he will be killed!"[60] When he replies in the affirmative, she says: "So, I will lose him! Al-Ḥusayn himself announces his own the death to me!" The women weep, striking their cheeks and ripping the upper

---

[59] Ibn Kaṯîr., *al-Bidâya wa-l-nihâya*, vol. XII: 531.

[60] Cf. also al-Ḥurr al-ʿÂmilî., *Iṯbât al-hudât bi-l-nuṣûṣ wa-l-muʿǧizât*, vol. IV: 51.

opening (collars) of their garments. Umm Kulṯûm begins to wail and al-Ḥusayn comforts her with words in most other transmitters addressed to Zaynab, saying:

> "My sister, be fortified by the consolation of God! The inhabitants of the heavens will pass away and all the people of the earth will die, and all of creation will perish." Then he said: "My sister, Umm Kulṯûm, and you Zaynab, and you Fâṭima, and you Rubâb,[61] see that when I am killed, that you do not rip a garment for me or scratch a face for me, and do not use unseemly language on my behalf."

In the second strand, transmitted, says Ibn Ṭâ'ûs from a different path, Zaynab is in another place, in seclusion with the women and the girls, when she hears the content of the verses. She emerges, unveiled and trailing her robe, and stands before al-Ḥusayn, saying:

> "So, I will lose him! Would that death had deprived me of life the day my mother Fâṭima died, and my father ʿAlî and my brother al-Ḥasan, successor of those who are gone, and support of those remaining." Al-Ḥusayn looked at her and said: "My sister, Satan must not carry off your forbearance." She replied: "I swear by my father and my mother! I would let myself be killed for you as a ransom." A groan broke forth from al-Ḥusayn, his eyes filled with tears and he said: "If the sandgrouse had been left alone at night, it would have slept." She answered: "My grief! Will your life not be forcibly taken from you? That is more wounding to my heart, more calamitous for my soul." Then she reached for the collar of her garment and ripped it, and fainting, she sank to the ground. Standing, al-Ḥusayn poured water over her until she regained consciousness. Then he tried his utmost to console her, reminding her of the calamity of the death of his father and his grandfather.[62]

Al-Ḫawârizmî also relates the incident in two strands. In the first, al-Ḥusayn is sitting in his tent repairing his sword with Ǧawn; he

---

[61] One of al-Ḥusayn's wives, and the mother of his daughter Sukayna.

[62] Ibn Ṭâ'ûs., *Kitâb al-luhûf fî qatlâ al-ṭufûf*: 49–50.

declaims the verses of the dirge. ʿAlî b. al-Ḥusayn narrates that his father repeated these verses, that he memorized them from his father and was choked with tears, but that he kept silence as far as he was able. However, his aunt Zaynab, when she heard the dirge, shed tears and wept, for she was delicate (*ḍaʿîfa*) of heart, and was manifestly affected by sorrow and anxiety. Dragging the hems of her garment, she draws near to al-Ḥusayn, whom she addresses as 'coolness of my eye'. The conversation continues as in other transmissions, with al-Ḥusayn quoting Q. 28: 70, 88 ("*everything will perish save His countenance. His is the command, and unto Him ye will be brought back*")[63] and citing the example of ʿAlî and Muḥammad: "for where are my father and my grandfather, who are better than me? In them, for me and for every Muslim, is an excellent exemplar!" He returns her to her quarters, but not without the warning about no wailing or violence done to self after his death.

Al-Ḫawârizmî then offers a second strand. Some of the details are familiar, but there is uncertainty as to whether the character involved, referred to as al-Ḥusayn's 'sister', and who hears the dirge and reacts to it, is Zaynab or Umm Kulṯûm; both are named in the text and both would be old enough for the reaction recorded. In fact, it is of note that al-Iṣfahânî in his *Maqâtil* does not actually name Zaynab in the text, while al-Ṣadûq records the dirge, but neither recounts any of the familiar context nor mentions Zaynab or her intervention.[64] Upon hearing the verses, the unnamed sister in al-Ḫawârizmî[65] goes to her brother and says: "My brother, this is the speech of one who is who certain of death." In fact, this is a strand transmitted in similar form about Zaynab by Ibn Ṭâ'ûs,[66] although in less detail. Al-Ḥusayn replies: "Yes, my sister." She responds: "In that case, take us back to the sanctuary of our grand-

---

[63] Q. 28: 70, 88.

[64] al-Iṣfahânî., *Maqâtil al-ṭâlibîyyîn*: 113, al-Ṣadûq., *Kitâb al-amâlî fî-l-aḥâdîṯ wa-l-aḫbâr, maǧlis* 30: 156.

[65] Also unnamed in al-Iṣfahânî. Cf. al-Iṣfahânî., *Maqâtil al-ṭâlibîyyîn*: 113 and al-Baḥrânî., *ʿAwâlim al-ʿulûm wa-l-maʿârif al-aḥwâl min al-âyât wa-l-aḫbâr wa-l-aqwâl*, vol. XI: 962, vol. VII: 245 (although after the words 'my aunt', 'Zaynab' is added in parentheses).

[66] Ibn Ṭâ'ûs., *Kitâb al-luhûf fî qatlâ al-ṭufûf*: 49.

father." Al-Ḥusayn responds with the sandgrouse proverb, and she answers: "So, I will lose him! Would that death had deprived me of life! My grandfather, the Messenger of God, died, my father ʿAlî died, my mother Fâṭima died, my brother al-Ḥasan died! There remains the support of the people of the house, and today he announces his own death!" She weeps then, "as do the other women", with the striking of cheeks and ripping of robes. Then, al-Ḫawârizmî tells us, al-Ḥusayn's sister, although we are not sure whether it the same one or another, cries out loudly: "My Muḥammad! Father of al-Qâsim! The day my grandfather Muḥammad died! My father, my ʿAlî. The day my father ʿAlî died! My mother! My Fâṭima! The day my mother Fâṭima died! My brother! My Ḥasan! The day my brother al-Ḥasan died! My brother! My Ḥusayn! What a loss for us after you, Father of ʿAbd Allâh!" Al-Ḥusayn fortifies her and urges patience, saying:

> "My sister! Be fortified by the consolation of God and be content with the divine decree of God; the people of heaven will vanish, and the people of the earth will die, and none of the creatures will continue to exist, for "*everything will perish save His countenance*", and blessed be God to whom all creation will return! It is He who created all creatures by His power and brings them to nought by His will and calls them forth by His volition! Sister! My grandfather, my father, my mother and my brother were better than me, and more excellent, and they have undergone death and the dust has gathered them. For me, and for you and for every believer, there is, in the Messenger of God, an excellent exemplar." Then he said: "Zaynab! Umm Kulṯûm! Fâṭima! Rubâb! See when I am killed that there is no ripping (the collar of) the garment for me and no scratching the face for me, and do not use unseemly language on my behalf!"[67]

---

[67] al-Ḫawârizmî., *Maqtal al-Ḥusayn*, bk. 1, bb. *fî ḫurûǧ al-Ḥusayn min Makka ilâ al-ʿIrâq*: 338–339.

Ibn Shahrâshûb is worth noting; he is transmitting from a number of sources,[68] including al-Ṣadûq, who records the dirge, but neither recounts any of the familiar context nor mentions Zaynab or her intervention.[69] That being said, Ibn Shahrâshûb's transmission is truncated and lacks many of the better-known elements, such as ʿAlî b. al-Ḥusayn being nursed by Zaynab.[70] ʿAlî b. al-Ḥusayn narrates that he was sitting on the night before his father was killed, and his father recited the dirge. Zaynab responded: "It is as if you know well that your life will be taken by force!" to which her brother replied by quoting the sandgrouse proverb.[71] Ibn Namâ's narration makes no mention of ʿAlî b. al-Ḥusayn or of Abû Ḏarr al-Ġifârî's retainer, but otherwise seems to be a mix of the two strands of Ibn Ṭâ'ûs.[72]

Of equal interest is al-Fattâl al-Nîsâbûrî in his *Rawḍat al-wâʿiẓîn*, who narrates all the familiar events with one exception; there is no mention of Zaynab's reaction. Considering that al-Fattâl al-Nîsâbûrî is transmitting from a number of key Shîʿî texts (such as al-Kulaynî's *al-Kâfî*, al-Ṣadûq's *al-Amâlî*, *Kitâb al-ḫiṣâl*, *ʿUyûn aḫbâr al-Riḍâ* and *Maʿânî al-aḫbâr*, and al-Mufîd's *al-Amâlî* and *al-Irshâd*), this is an enigmatic omission. In fact, he goes on to omit almost all the battlefield details of Zaynab.[73] Like al-Iṣfahânî, writing his *Maqâtil* more than a century before him, al-Fattâl does not hesitate

---

68 al-Ṣadûq's *Kitâb al-amâlî fî-l-aḥâdîṯ wa-l-aḫbâr*, ʿAlî al-Fattâl al-Nîsâbûrî's *Rawḍat al-wâʿiẓîn wa-tabṣirat al-muttaʿiẓîn*, al-Iṣfahânî's *Maqâtil al-ṭâlibîyyîn*, al-Mufîd's *al-Irshâd fî maʿrifat ḥuǧaǧ Allâh ʿalâ al-ʿibâd*, al-Yaʿqûbî's *Târîḫ*, al-Ṭabarṣî's *Iʿlâm al-warâ bi-aʿlâm al-hudâ* and al-Ṭabarî's *Kitâb aḫbâr al-rusul wa-l-mulûk*.

69 al-Ṣadûq., *Kitâb al-amâlî fî-l-aḥâdîṯ wa-l-aḫbâr*, *maǧlis* 30: 156.

70 Ibn Shahrâshûb., *Manâqib âl Abî Ṭâlib*, vol. IV, bb. *faṣl fî maqtali-hi*: 99. Cf. also al-Ǧazâ'irî., *Riyâḍ al-abrâr fî manâqib al-a'imma al-aṭhâr*, vol. I: 217.

71 Ibn Shahrâshûb., *Manâqib âl Abî Ṭâlib*, vol. IV, bb. *faṣl fî maqtali-hi*: 99.

72 Ibn Namâ al-Ḥillî., *Muṯîr al-aḥzân wa munîr subul al-ashǧân*, Part 1: 49.

73 al-Fattâl al-Nîsâbûrî., *Rawḍat al-wâʿiẓîn wa-tabṣirat al-muttaʿiẓîn*: 418.

to use 'moral qualifiers',[74] regularly inviting the curse of God on the perpetrators.

Just hours before battle is engaged, Zaynab has been given a clear intimation by her brother of what lies ahead. For the rest of the night, she is confined to her quarters with the other women and the children. When she emerges onto the field at a fateful mo-

---

74 HUSSEIN A.J., *A Developmental Analysis of Depictions of the Events of Karbalā' in Early Islamic History*, 2001: 21. In his *Kitâb Sulaym b. Qays*, Ibn Qays al-Hilâlî (d. c. 80/662: cf. MODARRESSI H., *Tradition and Survival,* 2003: 82, 424), used the moral qualifier 'may God curse him' (لعنه الله) against Iblîs, against those who attacked the house of Fâṭima, against Ibn Mulǧam, killer of ʿAlî, against Muʿâwiya and against Yazîd (al-Hilâlî., *Kitâb Sulaym b. Qays*, vol. II: 579, 586, 588, 671, 774, 866). Kohlberg notes that the *Kitâb Sulaym b. Qays* was named after its supposed author, the pro-ʿAlid Sulaym b. Qays al-Hilâlî al-ʿÂmirî, who died during the governorship of the Umayyad al-Haǧǧâǧ b. Yûsuf (75/694 – 95/714). The Shîʿî bibliographer Ibn al-Nadîm (d. 385/995 or 388/998) regarded it as the first Shîʿî work, but later Shîʿî scholars took a much more skeptical view (shared by Goldziher), and some openly declare it a fabrication. Cf. KOHLBERG E., "Shīʿī *Hadīth*" in A.F.L. Beeston et al., (eds.), *Arabic Literature to the End of the Umayyad Period*, Cambridge University Press, Cambridge 1983: 301. The qualifier occurs in a few other early texts, most regularly against Iblîs; Imâm al-Riḍâ (d. 202/818) in his *al-Fiqh al-mansûb* and in the *Ṣaḥîfat al-Imâm al-Riḍâ* uses it against the enemies of the Imâms, while al-Qummî in the *Tafsîr* attributed to him (alive in 307/1440, claims Modarressi, but the work is not by him; MODARRESSI H., *Tradition and Survival,* 2003: xvii, 410) employs it against various enemies of Muḥammad such as Abû Ǧahl, as well as against Yazîd (al-Qummî., *Tafsîr*, vol. I, *sûrat al-Baqara*: 45, *sûrat Âl ʿImrân*: 119, 124, *sûrat al-Aʿraf*: 242, vol. II, *sûrat as-Isrâ'*: 13, *sûrat al-Ḥaǧǧ*: 84). In two other early texts it is used against al-Haǧǧâǧ (al-Barqî., *al-Maḥâsin*, vol. I, bb. 3: 203) and against ʿUmar b. Saʿd, Ibn Ziyâd and Yazîd, the principle enemies involved in the Karbalâ' event, in a chapter about the words of Zaynab (Ibn Abî Ṭâhir Ṭayfûr., *Balâġât al-nisâ'*: 34). By the time Imâm al-ʿAskarî's companion al-Ṣaffâr (d. 290/903) was composing his *Baṣâi'r al-daraǧât* in the 3rd/9th century, the Karbalâ' narratives had increased exponentially and the moral qualifier was becoming more common against the enemies of the *ahl al-bayt*, and especially those see as responsible for the death of al-Ḥusayn.

ment of the conflict the next morning, it will be as a woman transfigured; no less anguished by the murder of her family, but with an audacity and assurance drawn from some hidden source and inconcealable to the eyewitnesses of Karbalâʾ.

CHAPTER THREE. ON THE FIELD OF KARBALÂ᾿

According to al-Ṭabarî's chronology, the battle of Karbalâ᾿ was engaged on the morning of 10th Muḥarram, after *ṣalât al-faǧr* (the morning prayer). It was not fought in any manner familiar to conventional warfare, with two armies facing each other. Rather, individual members of al-Ḥusayn's small band of around seventy-two men went out, mostly individually and often reciting poetry, to face the might of the opposing army (at least five thousand, but possibly more)[1] led by al-Ḥurr b. Yazîd al-Tamîmî (until his dramatic and emotional defection to the tents of al-Ḥusayn), with ʿUmar b. Saʿd b. Abî Waqqâṣ appointed to command the actual battle (until a querulous Ibn Ziyâd replaced him with Shimr b. Ḏî al-Ǧawshan).[2]

---

[1] al-Ṭabarî, al-Ṣadûq and al-Mufîd mention at least five thousand (one thousand with al-Ḥurr b. Yazîd al-Tamîmî and four thousand with ʿUmar b. Saʿd). However, the number varies dramatically, with some claiming up to twenty or thirty thousand. Cf. HOWARD I.K.A., (trans.), *The History of al-Ṭabarî*, vol. XIX, 1990: 93, 103, al-Ṣadûq., *Kitâb al-amâlî fî-l-aḥâdîṯ wa-l-aḫbâr*, *maǧlis* 30: 154–155, al-Mufîd., *al-Irshâd fî maʿrifat ḥuǧaǧ Allâh ʿalâ al-ʿibâd*, vol. II, bb. *wâqiʿ Karbalâ᾿ wa baṭûla Imâm al-Ḥusayn wa aṣḥâbi-hi*: 106.

[2] Shimr (or Shamir) b. Ḏî al-Ǧawshan b. Shuraḥbîl b. al-Aʿwar b. ʿUmar b. Muʿâwiya al-ʿÂmir; he had fought, notes Howard, on ʿAlî's side at the battle of Ṣiffîn but later switched sides and would be assassinated in retribution for the role he played in al-Ḥusayn's death. (Cf. HOWARD I.K.A., (trans.), *The History of al-Ṭabarî*, vol. XIX, 1990, nt. 192: 49). Shîʿî Islam clearly place the responsibility of al-Ḥusayn's death on the shoulders of two men. One is al-Ziyâd, Yazîd's governor in Kûfa. The other is Shimr; for it was this military man who had urged al-Ziyâd to deal puni-

Al-Ḥusayn had taken great pains to ensure that not only were the women and children confined to their tents, but that they were almost entirely inaccessible to the enemy; at one stage in the battle, a threat by Shimr b. Ḏî al-Ǧawshan to burn the tents and their occupants was met with disbelief by an appalled al-Ḥusayn. In the course of the hours that followed, al-Ḥusayn was destined to lose almost all the male members of his family; he would be the last to die, so that he endured the prolonged agony of seeing his sons and nephews killed one by one.

Almost all the transmitters agree that the first of al-Ḥusayn's immediate family to die was ʿAlî al-Akbar b. al-Ḥusayn b. ʿAlî, born to al-Ḥusayn by his wife Laylâ bt. Abî Murrah b. ʿUrwah b. Masʿûd al-Ṯaqafî.[3] Both his age and his identity are, as noted in an appendix to this work, considerably problematic in the sources; for the moment, it is his death that concerns us, since it brings Zaynab out of the confines of her tent and onto the field of Karbalâʾ for the first time. Transmitting from Abû Miḫnaf, al-Ṭabarî tells the story of how this boy steps in front of the opposing army with the words: "I am ʿAlî, son of Ḥusayn, son of ʿAlî! We are, by the Lord of the House, first in respect of the Prophet! No son of a bastard will pass judgment on us!"[4] He is killed, although al-Ṭabarî omits

---

tively with al-Ḥusayn and had incited an Umayyad army more than a little reluctant to take up arms against the Muḥammad's grandson. If al-Ziyâd's culpability is somewhat tempered by his distance from the battlefield (and the subsequent regret he expresses, apparently treating the survivors quite well, at least at the beginning), Shimr will be ever despised by Shîʿî Muslims.

[3] Cf. for e.g. al-Balâḏurî., *Kitâb ansâb al-ashrâf*, vol III: 361–362, 406, Ibn al-Aṯîr., *al-Kâmil fî al-târîḫ*, vol. II: 428, Ibn Kaṯîr., *al-Bidâya wa-l-nihâya*, vol. XI: 545, al-Maǧlisî., *Biḥâr al-anwâr*, vol. XLV, b. 37, n. 2: 43, 45. The texts give a variety of names when reporting the first to die, but a distinction should be maintained between ʿAlids, members of the *ahl al-bayt* and al-Ḥusayn's immediate family members.

[4] al-Ṭabarî., *Kitâb aḫbâr al-rusul wa-l-mulûk*, vol. V: 446. Cf. also Abû Miḫnaf., *Waqʿat al-Ṭaff*, bb. *al-Imâm laylat ʿÂshûrâʾ*: 242, al-Mufîd., *al-Irshâd fî maʿrifat ḥuǧaǧ Allâh ʿalâ al-ʿibâd*, vol. II, bb. *wâqiʿ Karbalâʾ wa baṭûla Imâm al-Ḥusayn wa aṣḥâbi-hi*: 106, al-Ṭabarsî., *Iʿlâm al-warâ bi-aʿlâm al-hudâ*: 246,

an important detail; he dies in his father's arms, crushed less by his wounds than by his agonizing thirst,[5] one of the enduring themes of the Karbalâ᾿ tragedy.

1. THE RISING SUN

It is at this instant, reports Abû Miḫnaf, that Ḥumayd b. Muslim al-Azdî[6] sees a woman hurrying from her tent. It is worth noting that Ḥumayd is a pivotal eyewitness to the Karbalâ᾿ events, attentive as he is to numerous small details. Among other things, he is on hand when Ibn Ziyâd sends a missive ordering that al-Ḥusayn and his men be barred from access to water, as well as when Ibn Ziyâd sends the brutal Shimr to take control of a situation that seems to be slipping under the vacillating ʿUmar b. Saʿd. He witnesses the first shot fired in battle and mortified, challenges Shimr who is threatening to burn the tents of the women as, after the battle, he will challenge him a second time when he wants to kill the ailing ʿAli b. al-Ḥusayn (who lives to thank him for his intervention). He is witness to the death of al-Ḥusayn's eldest son as well as that of an unknown nephew, and Zaynab's intervention on both occasions. He notes the radiant qualities of Zaynab's face, and the broken sandal strap of a boy with a face like the moon as he wanders onto the field. He is able to describe exactly the clothing that al-Ḥusayn is wearing as he dies and observes the killing of al-Ḥusayn and the plundering of his corpse. He serves as a messenger for ʿUmar b. Saʿd after the battle, accompanying al-Ḥusayn's head to Ibn Ziyâd, where he sees its ill-treatment. He is a crucial bystander

---

Ibn Shahrâshûb., *Manâqib âl Abî Ṭâlib*, vol. IV, bb. *faṣl fî maqtali-hi*: 106, 109 (slightly extended), Ibn Namâ al-Ḥillî., *Muṯîr al-aḥzân wa munîr subul al-ashğân*, Part 1: 68, al-Mağlisî., *Biḥâr al-anwâr*, vol. XLV, bb. 37: 43, 65 (from Ibn Shahrâshûb), vol. XCVIII, bb. 19: 269, al-Ğazâ'irî., *Riyâḍ al-abrâr fî manâqib al-a᾿imma al-aṭhâr*, vol. I: 314, al-Baḥrânî., *ʿAwâlim al-ʿulûm wa-l-maʿârif al-aḥwâl min al-âyât wa-l-aḫbâr wa-l-aqwâl*, vol. XIV: 286.

[5] al-Ḫawârizmî., *Maqtal al-Ḥusayn*, bk. 2, bb. *fî maqtal al-Ḥusayn*: 35, Ibn Namâ al-Ḥillî., *Muṯîr al-aḥzân wa munîr subul al-ashğân*, Part 2: 68.

[6] Written 'Ḥulayd' in the Arabic text, but this is certainly an error. Howard designates him an eyewitness of the battle. Abû Miḫnaf posits he was a member of Shimr's army.

during the ʿAlî-Ibn Ziyâd dialogues and overhears the governor branding both al-Ḥusayn and ʿAlî b. Abî Ṭâlib as liars.[7]

The woman Ḥumayd has noticed comes from her tent "like the rising sun" and crying "my brother, my nephew!" He asks after her identity and is informed that this is Zaynab, the daughter of Fâṭima. She throws herself on the body of the young ʿAlî, and her brother al-Ḥusayn comes, takes her by the hand and leads her back to her tent.

Al-Iṣfahânî recounts a Zaynab emerging with slightly different words on her lips: "O my love, O son of my brother," she cries as she comes and leans over the boy's lifeless body, before being led away by al-Ḥusayn. Al-Ḫawârizmî and al-Mağlisî also put a slightly different wording to her grief ("Oh my love, fruit of my heart, light of my eyes!"), while a number of key transmitters – Abû Miḫnaf, al-Mufîd, Ibn Ṭâʾûs and Ibn Namâ, for example – omit any reference to the imagery of the sun rising.[8] Still others, like al-Balâḏurî, omit any reference at all to Zaynab in the incident.[9]

---

[7] Cf. HOWARD I.K.A., (trans.), *The History of al-Ṭabarî*, vol. XIX, 1990: 107–167, WELLHAUSEN J., *Die religiös-politischen Oppositionsparteien in alten Islam*, Weidmannsche Buchhandlung, Berlin 1901: 87.

[8] Abû Miḫnaf., *Waqʿat al-Ṭaff*, bb. *al-Imâm laylat ʿÂshûrâʾ*: 242, al-Iṣfahânî., *Maqâtil al-ṭâlibîyyîn*: 115, al-Mufîd., *al-Irshâd fî maʿrifat ḥuğağ Allâh ʿalâ al-ʿibâd*, vol. II, bb. *wâqiʿ Karbalâʾ wa baṭûla Imâm al-Ḥusayn wa aṣḥâbi-hi*: 112, al-Ḫawârizmî., *Maqtal al-Ḥusayn*, bk. 2, bb. *fî maqtal al-Ḥusayn*: 35, Ibn Ṭâʾûs., *Kitâb al-luhûf fî qatlâ al-ṭufûf*: 68, Ibn Namâ al-Ḥillî., *Muṯîr al-aḥzân wa munîr subul al-ashğân*, Part 2: 68, al-Mağlisî., *Biḥâr al-anwâr*, vol. XLV, bb. 37: 44.

[9] al-Balâḏurî., *Kitâb ansâb al-ashrâf*, vol III: 361–362, 406. Curiously, Ibn ʿAsâkir transmits a version of this incident in which it is Zaynab daughter of al-Ḥusayn and not Zaynab daughter of ʿAlî who emerges 'like the sun' at the death of ʿAlî al-Akbar, crying out 'my brother!' Ibn ʿAsâkir himself notes that he does not find such a recollection about Zaynab bt. al-Ḥusayn in the *Kitâb al-nasab* of al-Zubayr. His reference is to the partially extant work by al-Zubayr b. Bakkâr al-Zubayrî (d. 256/870). Cf. Ibn ʿAsâkir., *Târîḫ madînat Dimashq*, vol. LXIX, bb. 9349 (*Zaynab bt. al-Ḥusayn b. ʿAlî b. Abî Ṭâlib*): 169, JUDD S. & SCHEINER J., (eds.), *New Perspectives on Ibn ʿAsākir in Islamic Historiography*, Brill, Leiden 2017: 191.

The three problematic texts are al-Mufîd, al-Ḫawârizmî and Ibn Namâ, specifically because while al-Mufîd puts the boy at nineteen years of age and al-Ḫawârizmî at eighteen, Ibn Namâ merely says that he was 'older than ten'.[10] Such statements create difficulties not only in determining the age of al-Ḥusayn's successor as Imâm, but also in establishing which of his sons it was that survived him. This issue is dealt with briefly in the appendix to this work.

One of Zaynab's biographers notes that "when the tragedy of Karbala befell her in her mid-fifties she was forced to go out uncovered. It was then that some people remarked that she appeared as a 'shining sun' and a 'piece of the moon'."[11] This seems a banal and minimalist interpretation; this is not the only time that this particular eyewitness, Ḥumayd b. Muslim, will use such language. He will witness a boy, identified as Qâsim b. al-Ḥasan b. ʿAlî b. Abî Ṭâlib, al-Ḥusayn's nephew, who emerges onto the field with a broken sandal strap and a face "like the first splinter of the moon" and takes his stand.[12] In both cases, Ḥumayd seems to be describing a distinct transfiguration; the small boy with his otherwise inexplicable courage and Zaynab, transformed from the frightened woman of the day before. Ibn Kaṯîr, for example, describes Zaynab, despite her being in her fifties, as "a girl, who was like the sun in loveliness", suggesting some sort of metamorphosis that made her

---

[10] al-Mufîd., *al-Irshâd fî maʿrifat ḥuǧaǧ Allâh ʿalâ al-ʿibâd*, vol. II, bb. *wâqiʿ Karbalâ' wa baṭûla Imâm al-Ḥusayn wa aṣḥâbi-hi*: 106, al-Ḫawârizmî., *Maqtal al-Ḥusayn*, bk. 2, bb. *fî maqtal al-Ḥusayn*: 34, Ibn Namâ al-Ḥillî., *Muṯîr al-aḥzân wa munîr subul al-ashǧân*, Part 2: 68.

[11] Cf. BILGRAMI M.H., *The Victory of Truth: The Life of Zaynab bint 'Ali*, 1986: 'Womanhood', n.p.

[12] al-Ṭabarî., *Kitâb aḫbâr al-rusul wa-l-mulûk*, vol. V: 446, al-Iṣfahânî., *Maqâtil al-ṭâlibîyyîn*: 115 (from al-Ṭabarî), al-Mufîd., *al-Irshâd fî maʿrifat ḥuǧaǧ Allâh ʿalâ al-ʿibâd*, vol. II, bb. *wâqiʿ Karbalâ' wa baṭûla Imâm al-Ḥusayn wa aṣḥâbi-hi*: 107, al-Ḫawârizmî., *Maqtal al-Ḥusayn*, bk. 2, bb. *fî maqtal al-Ḥusayn*: 31, Ibn Namâ al-Ḥillî., *Muṯîr al-aḥzân wa munîr subul al-ashǧân*, Part 2: 69. Cf. also HOWARD I.K.A., (trans.), *The History of al-Ṭabarî*, vol. XIX, 1990: 152–153.

barely recognizable at that moment.[13] Bearing in mind those *aḥâdîṯ* that insist upon the superiority of the moon when it is full, or over all the other celestial bodies,[14] the phrase 'first splinter of the moon' has mystical and eschatological undertones, and links Zaynab intimately to her grandfather, since it used by a handful of transmitters to describe Muḥammad. A number of *aḥâdîṯ* tell of his face being like the moon when it is full, or like a piece of the moon,[15] or that his face was like the moon whenever he was happy.[16] Others relate that when Muḥammad was seen in the darkness of night, his face had a light 'like the first splinter of the moon'.[17] Moreover, the first group of believers to enter Paradise is described as glittering like the moon, an image used throughout the books of *aḥâdîṯ* to describe people's faces on the Day of Resurrection.[18] In the course of the famous *ḥadîṯ al-kisâ'*, Fâṭima describes her father's face as being like the full moon;[19] and she herself is said to have

[13] Ibn Kaṯîr., *al-Bidâya wa-l-nihâya*, vol. XI: 545.

[14] Abû Dâwûd., *Sunan*, bk. 24 (*Awwal kitâb al-ʿilm*), bb. 1, n. 3641: 207, bk. 39 (*Abwâb al-ʿilm*), bb. 19, n. 2682: 77–78.

[15] al-Buḫârî., *Ṣaḥîḥ*, bk. 61 (*Kitâb al-manâqib*), bb. 23, n. 3552: 460, Muslim, *Ṣaḥîḥ*, bk. 43 (*Kitâb al-faḍâ'il*), bb. 30, n. 6084: 190, Abû Dâwûd., *Sunan*, bk. 46 (*Abwâb al-manâqib*), bb. 8, n. 3636: 331.

[16] al-Buḫârî., *Ṣaḥîḥ*, bk. 61 (*Kitab al-manâqib*), bb. 23, n. 3556: 461, bk. 64 (*Kitâb al-maġâzi*), bb. 80, n. 4418: 432, bk. 65 (*Kitâb al-tafsîr*), bb. 18, n. 4677: 154, Muslim, *Ṣaḥîḥ*, bk. 49 (*Kitâb al-tawba*), bb. 9, n. 7016: 156, Abû Dâwûd., *Sunan*, bk. 46 (*Abwâb tafsir al-qur'an*), bb. 9, n. 3102: 409.

[17] Cf. for e.g. al-Kulaynî., *al-Kâfî fî ʿilm al-dîn*, vol. I, bb. *mawlid al-nabî*, n. 20: 446, al-Ṭabarsî., *Makârim al-aḫlâq*: 24, al-Kâshânî., *Kitâb ǧâmiʿ al-wâfî*, vol. III: 904, al-Maǧlisî., *Biḥâr al-anwâr*, vol. XIV, bb. 8: 190.

[18] al-Buḫârî., *Ṣaḥîḥ*, bk. 59 (*Kitâb bad' al-ḫalq*), bb. 18, nn. 3245–7: 292–293, n. 3254: 295, bk. 60 (*Kitâb al-aḥâdîṯ al-anbiyâ'*), bb. 1, n. 3327: 326–327, bk. 77 (*Kitâb al-libâs*), bb. 18, n. 5811: 387, bk 81 (*Kitâb al-riqâq*), bb. 50, nn. 6542–3: 294–295, n. 6554: 298, Muslim, *Ṣaḥîḥ*, bk. 1 (*Kitâb al-îmân*), bb. 94, n. 523: 346, n. 526: 347, bk. 51 (*Kitâb al-ǧanna*), bb. 6, n. 7147: 230, n. 7149: 230–231, n. 7150: 231, bb. 7, n. 7151: 232.

[19] al-Baḥrânî., *ʿAwâlim al-ʿulûm wa-l-maʿârif al-aḥwâl min al-âyât wa-l-aḫbâr wa-l-aqwâl*, vol. XI: 935.

had a face radiant as the moon.[20] Al-ʿAbbâs, half-brother to al-Ḥusayn and Zaynab, and whose martyrdom on the Karbalâ' field came at the end of an act of superhuman strength and courage, is referred to as 'the moon of the Banû Hâshim' (*qamar banî hâshim*).[21] Later, in Kûfa, Zaynab, from her carriage, will catch sight of al-Ḥusayn's head, which seemed to her as a 'radiant, moonlike…a rising moon' (*zuhrî qamarî…qamar tâliʿ*).

2. A Boy

It is the tenacious stand and death of another child that brings Zaynab out onto the field for a second time. From the tents of the women emerges a boy, whom most of the texts observe is 'not yet an adolescent' (said of more than one victim at Karbalâ') and who, resisting all attempts to stop him, takes his stand next to al-Ḥusayn, where he will be badly wounded and die within minutes. Al-Ṭabarî, transmitting from Abû Miḫnaf's account, does not name the boy, and notes that his identity is uncertain, since the man named as his killer is not known to have killed any of al-Ḥusayn's nephews;[22] nor do al-Balâḏurî, al-Iṣfahânî (who, like al-Ṭabarî, refers to him 'a boy from the family') or Ibn al-Aṯîr name him.[23] However, besides the fact that al-Ḥusayn addresses him as 'son of my brother', and he in turn refers to al-Ḥusayn as 'my uncle', a number of the texts give us his name; he is almost certainly ʿAbd Allâh b. al-Ḥasan and, as son of al-Ḥasan, nephew both to al-Ḥusayn and to Zaynab.

These are the bare bones of a more elaborate and evocative story. As the boy emerges, Zaynab, urged on by al-Ḥusayn, pursues

---

[20] al-Ṭabarî., *Dalâ'il al-imâma*, n. 63, 151, Ibn Shahrâshûb., *Manâqib âl Abî Ṭâlib*, vol. III, bb. *faṣl fî ḥilyati-hâ*: 356, al-Mağlisî., *Biḥâr al-anwâr*, vol. XLIII, bb. 6, n. 7: 6.

[21] Ibn Shahrâshûb., *Manâqib âl Abî Ṭâlib*, vol. IV, bb. *faṣl fî maqtali-hî*: 108, al-Mağlisî., *Biḥâr al-anwâr*, vol. XLV, bb. 37: 39–40.

[22] HOWARD I.K.A., (trans.), *The History of al-Ṭabarî*, vol. XIX, 1990: 158.

[23] al-Iṣfahânî., *Maqâtil al-ṭâlibîyyîn*: 116, Ibn al-Aṯîr., *al-Kâmil fî al-târîḫ*, vol. II: 431. Al-Balâḏurî relates the story very briefly, with few of the usual details and with no mention of Zaynab; al-Balâḏurî., *Kitâb ansâb al-ashrâf*, vol. III: 408.

him from the tents in an attempt to prevent him from taking the field. The boy puts up a fierce resistance: "By God," he says, "I will not be separated from my uncle," giving us a first clue to his identity. Within minutes of his arrival at al-Ḥusayn's side, an enemy soldier, whose identity is disputed, plunges at al-Ḥusayn, sword in hand. Al-Ṭabarî names the soldier as Baḥr b. Kaʿb b. ʿUbayd Allâh, the man who would later go on to rob the dead body of al-Ḥusayn. Ibn al-Aṯîr and Ibn Namâ concur, while al-Iṣfahânî and al-Mufîd both call him Abǧar b. Kaʿb and Ibn Ṭâʾûs refers to him as Ḥarmala b. Kâhil. Al-Maǧlisî notes two of the possibilities, Abǧar b. Kaʿb or Ḥarmala b. Kâhil.

The youthful ʿAbd Allâh b. al-Ḥasan, standing by his uncle's side, calls his killer by a different name; 'Ibn al-Ḫabîṯa' – 'son of an abominable woman' (the suggestion being that he was born out of wedlock, impacting both upon him and upon his mother). "Would you kill my uncle?" he shouts, attempting to shield al-Ḥusayn from the blows, almost losing his arm in the process and receiving a mortal wound. In Ibn Ṭâʾûs, to whom we shall return shortly, the wounded boy is then killed by an arrow while in the arms of his uncle, seemingly fired by Ḥarmala b. al-Kâhil, a detail missing from most other transmissions.[24] It may be that Ibn Ṭâʾûs is here conflating two different deaths, for this is how al-Ḥusayn's infant son will be killed while in his father's arms.

At this stage, his attacker appears to step back; the boy, crying out "O my mother" (in most texts) dies in al-Ḥusayn's arms as his uncle tries to console him, urging him to be patient in his sufferings, and promising that soon he will be reunited with his righteous ancestors. Some texts name them, although not always in the same order, as the Messenger of God, ʿAlî, Ḥamza, Ǧaʿfar and al-Ḥasan.

As it stands, the story is carried with minor variants by al-Ṭabarî, al-Iṣfahânî, al-Mufîd, al-Ṭabarsî, Ibn al-Aṯîr, Ibn Ṭâʾûs, Ibn Namâ al-Ḥillî and al-Maǧlisî.[25] Ibn Namâ al-Ḥillî, in whose narra-

---

[24] Ibn Ṭâʾûs., *Kitâb al-luhûf fî qatlâ al-ṭufûf*: 72.

[25] HOWARD I.K.A., (trans.), *The History of al-Ṭabarî*, vol. XIX, 1990: 158, al-Iṣfahânî., *Maqâtil al-ṭâlibîyyîn*: 116, al-Mufîd., *al-Irshâd fî maʿrifat ḥuǧaǧ Allâh ʿalâ al-ʿibâd*, vol. II, bb. *wâqiʿ Karbalâʾ wa baṭûla Imâm al-Ḥusayn wa aṣḥâbi-hi*: 110, al-Ṭabarsî., *Iʿlâm al-warâ bi-aʿlâm al-hudâ*: 249, Ibn al-Aṯîr., *al-*

tive the story is immediately preceded by the death of al-Ḥusayn's oldest son, changes two details; he does not record al-Ḥusayn ordering Zaynab to restrain the boy, and the boy dies crying out for his uncle rather than for his mother. Al-Ḫawârizmî, and Ibn Ṭâ᾿ûs writing one hundred years or so after Ibn Namâ, are worth examining, for while both have a chronology at odds with the other transmitters, al-Ḫawârizmî omits the incident entirely, replacing it with a similar one and Ibn Ṭâ᾿ûs transmits it with disparate details.

The incident is preceded by three, in some transmitters four, key events: in al-Ṭabarî, al-Mufîd and Ibn Ṭâ᾿ûs, the death of al-Ḥusayn's son ʿAlî b. al-Ḥusayn, already examined and, shortly afterwards, the curious emergence onto the field and subsequent death of al-Qâsim b. al-Ḥasan, the boy with a face like the moon. Al-Ḫawârizmî reverses the order of these two boys' deaths but keeps most of the details. The third event, transmitted by al-Ṭabarî, al-Mufîd, al-Ḫawârizmî and Ibn Ṭâ᾿ûs (with some added details) is the killing of the infant son of al-Ḥusayn and the fourth – only in al-Ṭabarî and, with a different chronology, al-Iṣfahânî – is the story of the boy with the pearl earrings. Schematically, the sources adhere to the following order:

1. al-Ṭabarî (death of ʿAlî al-Akbar, death of the moon-faced al-Qâsim, death of al-Ḥusayn's infant son, death of the boy with the pearl earrings, death of the unrestrainable boy)
2. al-Iṣfahânî (death of ʿAlî al-Akbar, death of the unrestrainable boy, death of the boy with the pearl earrings)
3. al-Mufîd (death of ʿAlî al-Akbar, death of the moon-faced al-Qâsim, death of al-Ḥusayn's infant son, death of the unrestrainable boy)
4. al-Fattâl al-Nîsâbûrî (death of ʿAlî al-Akbar, death of the moon-faced al-Qâsim, death of al-Ḥusayn's infant son)

Kâmil fî al-târîḫ, vol. II: 431, Ibn Ṭâ᾿ûs., *Kitâb al-luhûf fî qatlâ al-ṭufûf*: 72, Ibn Namâ al-Ḥillî., *Muṯîr al-aḥzân wa munîr subul al-asḥgân*, Part 2: 73, al-Mağlisî., *Biḥâr al-anwâr*, vol. XLV, bb. 37: 53–54.

5. al-Ḫawârizmî (death of ʿAlî al-Akbar, death of the moon-faced al-Qâsim, emergence and restraining of ʿAlî b. al-Ḥusayn, the future fourth Imâm, death of al-Ḥusayn's infant son)

6. Ibn Ṭâʾûs (death of ʿAlî al-Akbar, death of the moon-faced al-Qâsim, death of al-Ḥusayn's infant son, death of the unrestrainable boy)

7. Ibn Namâ al-Ḥillî (death of ʿAlî al-Akbar, death of the moon-faced al-Qâsim, death of al-Ḥusayn's infant son, death of the unrestrainable boy)

Al-Ḫawârizmî omits entirely the narrative of the boy whom Zaynab was unable to restrain, thus setting himself apart from al-Ṭabarî, al-Mufîd and Ibn Ṭâʾûs. Instead, he turns his attention to ʿAlî b. al-Ḥusayn, identified in his narrative as Zayn al-ʿÂbidîn, who emerges from his tent, undeterred by his father's strict prohibition; he was, notes the text, smaller than his brother recently killed, and was sick. He would be the one, says al-Ḫawârizmî, who would continue the family of Muḥammad, but at this stage he was not strong enough even to carry his sword. From behind him, his aunt Umm Kulṯûm shouts: "My child, come back!" He replies: "My aunt! Let me fight in front of the son of the Messenger of God!" At this point al-Ḥusayn intervenes, telling Umm Kulṯûm to seize hold of the boy and return him to his tent, since the earth could not continue devoid of the progeny of the family of Muḥammad, that is, without the members of the *ahl al-bayt*. As the only surviving son, ʿAlî b. al-Ḥusayn will be the only one who can continue the line and the Imamate.

This story is intensely similar to the story of the boy who would not be restrained, omitted by al-Ḫawârizmî, although here, Zaynab is substituted by Umm Kulṯûm and the boy (ʿAbd Allâh b. al-Ḥasan b. ʿAlî) by al-Ḥusayn's own son, with a wholly different outcome. Shahin, in his biography, notes that in bidding his final farewell to the women, al-Ḥusayn had ordered Zaynab to prevent ʿAlî b. al-Ḥusayn from fighting, and that she does this quite forcefully; Shahin gives no references to any classical text and does not repeat the story told by al-Ḫawârizmî.[26]

Al-Ḫawârizmî precedes the narrative of Zayn al-ʿÂbidîn's emergence onto the field with a highly poignant story, also carried by al-Ṭabarî. It is not a story that in any way involves Zaynab, but is worth telling, since it falls into a common Karbalâʾ genre of boys, often pre-adolescent, dying in the battle. It is of a young boy who emerges onto the field, wearing, an onlooker notes, earrings in his ears. It is one of those minor details, like the broken sandal strap of Qâsim, observed by eyewitnesses and which lends a powerful credibility to the narrative. The boy is quite patently terrified, looking anxiously to right and to left, his earrings swinging from side to side. He is killed almost at once by a soldier named Hânî b. Baʿîṯ.[27] His earrings are of note, since at a later stage in the battle, Zaynab will be noticed for her earrings, swinging violently as she emerges, resolute, onto the field for a third and last time.

Al-Ṭabarî, having related the death of al-Ḥusayn's infant son, ʿAbd Allah b. al-Ḥusayn, while sitting on his father's knee, follows the account with the emergence and killing of this unidentified boy from the family of al-Ḥusayn; besides the 'two pearls' in his ears, al-Ṭabarî notes that he is clutching a stick from the tents and wearing a waistcloth and a shirt. Al-Ṭabarî names the eyewitness himself, Hânî b. Ṯubayt al-Ḥaḍramî, as the killer, noting that years later, as an old man, Hânî would deny it. It is then that al-Ṭabarî relates the death of the boy whom Zaynab could restrain, called 'nephew' by al-Ḥusayn and who dies crying for his mother.[28]

Between the death of the moon-faced al-Qâsim b. al-Ḥasan and the emergence of the boy who would not be restrained, following the chronology of al-Mufîd and to a lesser extent al-Ṭabarî, Ibn

---

[26] SHAHIN B., *Lady Zaynab*, 2002: 184.

[27] al-Ḫawârizmî., *Maqtal al-Ḥusayn*, bk. 2, bb. *fî maqtal al-Ḥusayn*: 36. Cf. al-Maǧlisî., *Biḥâr al-anwâr*, vol. XLV, bb. 37: 45–46, who places it where al-Ṭabarî does, before the incident of the boy whom Zaynab could not restrain.

[28] HOWARD I.K.A., (trans.), *The History of al-Ṭabarî*, vol. XIX, 1990: 155–156.

Ṭâʾûs[29] recounts the gruesome death of al-Ḥusayn's infant son. Al-Ḥusayn, almost all his companions now slain and aware that he will be next, goes to the tent and asks Zaynab to bring his infant son, Abd Allâh b. Ḥusayn b. ʿAlî b. Abî Ṭâlib, whose mother was Rubâb, so that he might say his farewells. As al-Ḥusayn embraces him, the infant is struck in the throat by an arrow, fired, says Ibn Ṭâʾûs, by Ḥarmala b. al-Kâhil. Al-Ḥusayn thrusts him back into the arms of Zaynab, scoops up some of his blood and flings it heavenwards. In the other transmissions, Zaynab is not involved in this incident.

It is after this that Ibn Ṭâʾûs recounts the story of ʿAbd Allâh b. al-Ḥasan, the boy who would not be held back, but with a detail missing in the other transmitters; that he is killed by an arrow while already dying in the arms of his uncle, seemingly also fired by Ḥarmala b. al-Kâhil. As already noted, while Ibn Ṭâʾûs involves Zaynab in the death of the infant ʿAbd Allâh, he omits any order from al-Ḥusayn to Zaynab to restrain the boy who would not be deterred, just as he omits any reference to Zaynab's appearance 'like the rising sun'.[30]

In Ibn Namâʾs account, the deaths of the infant son and then of the unrestrainable boy are separated by the death of al-ʿAbbâs, al-Ḥusayn's last surviving brother.[31] After the death of the moon-faced al-Qâsim b. al-Ḥasan, his narrative reports al-Ḥusayn going to the women's tent and asking to see his infant son ʿAbd Allâh (also known as ʿAlî), who is subsequently shot and killed in his father's arms. In Ibn Namâʾs narration, Zaynab makes no appearance in this pericope.[32]

Al-Ḫawârizmî narrates the death of Muḥammad b. ʿAbd Allâh b. Ǧaʿfar b. Abî Ṭâlib followed by ʿAwn b. ʿAbd Allâh b. Ǧaʿfar b. Abî Ṭâlib. He does not mention that these are the two sons of Zaynab, although in other cases (such as that of Abû Bakr b. ʿAlî, ʿUṯmân b. ʿAlî and the other brothers of al-Ḥusayn) he does indeed

---

[29] Ibn Ṭâʾûs., *Kitâb al-luhûf fî qatlâ al-ṭufûf*: 69–72.

[30] Ibid.

[31] Ibn Namâ al-Ḥillî., *Muṯîr al-aḥzân wa munîr subul al-ashǧân*, Part 2: 71.

[32] Ibn Ṭâʾûs., *Kitâb al-luhûf fî qatlâ al-ṭufûf*: 69–70.

report the name of the deceased's mother. However, he is uncertain who emerges next, noting that according to some transmitters, the next to come out and die was ʿAbd Allâh b. al-Ḥasan b. ʿAlî b. Abî Ṭâlib and according to other transmitters, al-Qâsim b. al-Ḥasan, the latter described as a boy who had not yet reached puberty. When al-Ḥusayn sees him, he embraces him and both are overwhelmed with weeping. The boy then asks permission to fight; his uncle al-Ḥusayn refuses to permit it, but the boy persists, standing resolutely in front of him until it is given. He then enters into battle and is killed, and al-Ḫawârizmî relates how his face was like a 'half-moon'. Al-Ḫawârizmî immediately narrates Ḥumayd b. Muslim al-Azdî's eyewitness account of a boy, describing his shirt and his broken sandal strap, and whom Ḥumayd attempts unsuccessfully to prevent his being killed.[33]

3. A CHALLENGE

One last time, Zaynab makes an appearance on the Karbalâʾ field. While a number of her biographers record her anguish upon hearing of the gallant death of her half-brother al-ʿAbbâs, ("O, for my brother! O, for al-ʿAbbâs! We have certainly lost everything as we lost you"), this intervention is not carried by the classical texts.[34] It is now virtually the end of the battle; al-Ḥusayn, exhausted, all his companions dead, is surrounded by enemy soldiers. Al-Ṭabarî and a number of other transmitters note a general tone of reluctance; few of the soldiers attacking al-Ḥusayn seem eager to kill him, and they hold back in the hope that this task would fall to someone else. Ultimately, al-Ḥusayn will be killed because an irritated and impatient Shimr harangues and intimidates his troops. Whoever it was who ultimately struck the death blow,[35] there is no one who bears responsibility for al-Ḥusayn's death more than Shimr.

---

[33] Cf. al-Ḫawârizmî., *Maqtal al-Ḥusayn*, bk. 2, bb. *fî maqtal al-Ḥusayn*: 30–32.

[34] AL-JIBOURI Y.T., (trans.), *Maqtal al-Ḥusain*, 2014: 221, SHAHIN B., *Lady Zaynab*, 2002: 183.

[35] Sibṭ al-Ğawzî names five possibilities, with Sinân in first place and Shimr in fifth. Cf. Sibṭ al-Ğawzî., *Taḏkirat ḫawâṣṣ al-umma bi-ḏikr ḫaṣâʾiṣ al-aʾimma*: 214.

It is while al-Ḥusayn is being attacked from all sides that Zaynab emerges one last time from her tent, at an extremely perilous moment in the battle and in a defiant intervention recorded even by al-Balâḏurî, although he omits almost all other references to her in his Karbalâʾ account.[36] One eyewitness reports a seeing her earrings "bobbing between her ears and her shoulders,"[37] not the first time a bystander has taken note of such a small detail. On her lips is a lament of harrowing despair: "My brother! My master! People of my house! Would that the heaven covered the earth, and that the mountains were levelled on the plain!"[38] is Ibn Ṭâʾûs' rendition. In other transmitters, it is a more succinct "would that the heaven covered the earth,"[39] while al-ʿIṣâmî has her emerge 'calling out', although he records no actual lament.[40] When she catches sight of ʿUmar b. Saʿd,[41] commander of the enemy forces, she accosts him, demanding to know whether he is going to do nothing more than look on while her brother is being killed. According to the narrator ʿAmmâr, ʿUmar turns his head from her, weeping.

---

[36] al-Balâḏurî., *Kitâb ansâb al-ashrâf*, vol. III: 409, HOWARD I.K.A., (trans.), *The History of al-Ṭabarî*, vol. XIX, 1990: 160–161, al-Mufîd., *al-Irshâd*, vol. II, bb. *wâqiʿ Karbalâʾ wa baṭûla Imâm al-Ḥusayn wa aṣḥâbi-hi*: 112, al-Ḫawârizmî., *Maqtal al-Ḥusayn*, bk. 2, bb. *fî maqtal al-Ḥusayn*: 40, Ibn al-Aṯîr., *al-Kâmil fî al-târîḫ*, vol. II: 431–2, Ibn Ṭâʾûs., *Kitâb al-luhûf fî qatlâ al-ṭufûf*: 73, Ibn Kaṯîr., *al-Bidâya wa-l-nihâya*, vol. XI: 548, al-ʿIṣâmî., *Simṭ al-nuǧûm al-ʿawâlî*, vol. III: 71, al-Maǧlisî., *Biḥâr al-anwâr*, vol. XLIV, bb. 36: 306, vol. XLV, bb. 37: 55, al-ʿÂmilî., *Aʿyân al-Shîʿa*, vol. VII: 138.

[37] ʿAbd Allâh b. ʿAmmâr al-Bâriqî, a witness to the battle and to the death of al-Ḥusayn.

[38] Ibn Ṭâʾûs., *Kitâb al-luhûf fî qatlâ al-ṭufûf*: 73, al-Maǧlisî., *Biḥâr al-anwâr*, vol. XLV, bb. 37: 54.

[39] al-Ḫawârizmî., *Maqtal al-Ḥusayn*, bk. 2, bb. *fî maqtal al-Ḥusayn*: 40, Ibn al-Aṯîr., *al-Kâmil fî al-târîḫ*, vol. II: 431–2, Ibn Kaṯîr., *al-Bidâya wa-l-nihâya* vol. XI: 548, al-ʿIṣâmî., *Simṭ al-nuǧûm al-ʿawâlî*, vol. III: 71, al-Maǧlisî., *Biḥâr al-anwâr*, vol. XLV, bb. 37: 55.

[40] al-ʿIṣâmî., *Simṭ al-nuǧûm al-ʿawâlî*, vol. III: 71.

[41] Son of Saʿd b. Abî al-Waqqâṣ, one of the Companions of Muḥammad.

As al-Mufîd recounts it, al-Ḥusayn's sister Zaynab came to the door of the tent and called out to ʿUmar b. Saʿd: "Woe to you, ʿUmar! Is Abû ʿAbd Allâh being killed while you watch?" However, ʿUmar does nothing to help, and Zaynab cries out in desperation: "Woe upon all of you! Is there not a Muslim among you?" But no one responds to her plea. Al-Mufîd omits the detail of her lament and the tearful reaction of ʿUmar b. Saʿd, but adds the second appeal, in the face of ʿUmar's failure to respond, to all the other soldiers. It is immediately after this second appeal that, in al-Mufîd's narration, Shimr berates the troops for not finishing the job.[42]

The challenge to ʿUmar b. Saʿd and his subsequent tears of mortification are omitted by Ibn Ṭâʾûs, but recorded by al-Ṭabarî, al-Ḫawârizmî, Ibn al-Aṯîr, Ibn Kaṯîr and al-ʿIṣâmî. In al-Mufîd's narrative, it appears to be a desperate appeal for help which, when it fails, causes Zaynab to turn to others. In Ibn Kaṯîr, it is clearly a moral rebuke: "Are you satisfied that Abû ʿAbd Allâh is being killed while you watch?"[43] If it is indeed that – a moral upbraiding more than a desperate appeal – it marks yet another crucial stage in the transformation of Zaynab, preparing her for the two critical encounters that now lie ahead of her on a different field of battle.

4. TO KÛFA

The immediate aftermath of al-Husayn's death is a frenzy of rapid events, although the chronology is not always straightforward. According to al-Ṭabarî, on the same day that he was killed (in this narrative, by Sinân b. Anas),[44] that is, 10th Muḥarram, al-Ḥusayn's head was despatched with Ḫawalî b. Yazîd and Ḥumayd b. Muslim al-Azdî to Ibn Ziyâd.[45] The next day (11th Muḥarram), the bodies

[42] al-Mufîd., *al-Irshâd*, vol. II, bb. *wâqiʿ Karbalâʾ wa baṭûla Imâm al-Ḥusayn wa aṣḥâbi-hi*: 112.

[43] Ibn Kaṯîr., *al-Bidâya wa-l-nihâya*, vol. XI: 548.

[44] al-Ṭabarî., *Kitâb aḫbâr al-rusul wa-l-mulûk*, vol. V: 453.

[45] While some agree with al-Ṭabarî (cf. for e.g. Ibn al-Aṯîr., *al-Kâmil fî al-târîḫ*, vol. II: 434), others think it was with Ḫawalî b. Yazîd alone (cf. for e.g. al-Ḫawârizmî., *Maqtal al-Ḥusayn*, bk. 2, bb. *fî maqtal al-Ḥusayn*: 44, Ibn Shahrâshûb., *Manâqib âl Abî Ṭâlib*, vol. IV, bb. *fî maqtali-hi*: 111).

of al-Ḥusayn and his companions were buried. By all accounts, on 12th Muḥarram the departure to Kûfa with the women and children took place.[46] Somewhere in these three days, between al-Ḥusayn's death and the withdrawal from Karbalâ', but from a chronological point of view almost certainly on 10th Muḥarram and not later than that, there were a number of other events: the looting of the women and their tents (with the intervention of ʿUmar b. Saʿd), the attempt to kill ʿAlî b. al-Ḥusayn (with the intervention of Ḥumayd b. Muslim) and the lament of Zaynab (and others) upon seeing the bodies of the dead.

The looting of the dead body of al-Ḥusayn and, immediately after that, of the women and their tents, is described by many transmitters. Ibn al-Aṯîr notes that al-Ḥusayn's body was stripped of everything, and that the women's robes were literally torn from them, leaving them unveiled and with almost nothing.[47] A number of transmitters record the extremely callous looting of one of al-Ḥusayn's daughters, usually unnamed, but identified by Ibn Namâ al-Ḥillî as Fâṭima.[48] In the midst of this brutality, ʿUmar b. Saʿd, to whom Zaynab had so fruitlessly appealed a short while before, arrives at the women's tents. The women, horrified by the appearance of a senior army commander, begin to shriek with fear; in fact, ʿUmar b. Saʿd intervenes and stops the looting. The women petition him that their possessions be returned, and ʿUmar b. Saʿd complies by ordering: "Do not enter into even one of the houses of these women…whoever takes anything from their belongings must return it." However, note the texts laconically, nobody returned anything.[49]

---

[46] HOWARD I.K.A., (trans.), *The History of al-Ṭabarî*, vol. XIX, 1990: 163–4. Cf. Ibn al-Aṯîr., *al-Kâmil fî al-târîḫ*, vol. II: 434.

[47] Ibn al-Aṯîr., *al-Kâmil fî al-târîḫ*, vol. II: 432–3. Cf. also al-Ḫawârizmî., *Maqtal al-Ḥusayn*, bk. 2, bb. *fî maqtal al-Ḥusayn*: 43.

[48] Ibn Namâ al-Ḥillî., *Muṯîr al-aḥzân wa munîr subul al-ashǧân*, Part 2: 76.

[49] al-Mufîd., *al-Irshâd*, vol. II, bb. *wâqiʿ Karbalâ' wa baṭûla Imâm al-Ḥusayn wa aṣḥâbi-hi*: 113, al-Fattâl al-Nîsâbûrî., *Rawḍat al-wâʿiẓîn wa-tabṣirat al-muttaʿiẓîn*: 428, al-Ḫawârizmî., *Maqtal al-Ḥusayn*, bk. 2, bb. *fî maqtal al-Ḥusayn*: 43, Ibn al-Aṯîr., *al-Kâmil fî al-târîḫ*, vol. II: 432–3, Ibn Ṭâ'ûs., *Kitâb*

It is Shimr who, coming upon the ailing ʿAlî b. al-Ḥusayn in the tents of the women, wants to kill him, and Ḥumayd b. Muslim ("Glory be to God! Would you kill the youth?")[50] and ʿUmar b. Saʿd who intervene to save the life of the next Imâm. Transmitting from Abû Miḫnaf, Ibn Kaṯîr narrates:

> "Shimr b. Ḏî al-Ğawshan intended to kill ʿAlî b. al-Ḥusayn al-Aṣġar Zayn al-ʿÂbidîn, who was young and sick, but was dissuaded from doing that by one of his companions, Ḥumayd b. Muslim. ʿUmar b. Saʿd came and said: 'No one is to enter upon these women, and no one is to kill this youth.'"[51]

Two days after the death of al-Ḥusayn, notes Ibn al-Aṯîr,[52] and thus 12th Muḥarram, the journey from Karbalâ' to Kûfa commences. The women, bareheaded and in full view, are mounted in litters on female camels, and entrusted by ʿUmar b. Saʿd to someone to guard and protect them.[53] In Abû Miḫnaf's account[54] from, among others, Qurra b. Qays al-Ḥanẓalî al-Tamîmî, an eyewitness at Karbalâ',[55] it is ʿUmar b. Saʿd who orders the departure, taking

al-luhûf fî qatlâ al-ṭufûf: 77–78, Ibn Namâ al-Ḥillî., *Muṯîr al-aḥzân wa munîr subul al-ashğân*, Part 2: 76, Ibn Kaṯîr., *al-Bidâya wa-l-nihâya*, vol. XI: 550, al-Mağlisî., *Biḥâr al-anwâr*, vol. XLV, bb. 37: 58.

[50] Ibn al-Aṯîr., *al-Kâmil fî al-târîḫ*, vol. II: 432–3. Quite clearly, this happens before Ḥumayd leaves the scene bearing the head of al-Ḥusayn.

[51] HOWARD I.K.A., (trans.), *The History of al-Ṭabarî*, vol. XIX, 1990: 161–2, al-Mufîd., *al-Irshâd*, vol. II, bb. *wâqiʿ Karbalâ' wa baṭûla Imâm al-Ḥusayn wa aṣḥâbi-hi*: 113, al-Fattâl al-Nîsâbûrî., *Rawḍat al-wâʿiẓîn wa-tabṣirat al-muttaʿiẓîn*: 428, al-Ḫawârizmî., *Maqtal al-Ḥusayn*, bk. 2, bb. *fî maqtal al-Ḥusayn*: 43, Ibn al-Aṯîr., *al-Kâmil fî al-târîḫ*, vol. II: 432–3, Sibṭ al-Ğawzî., *Taḏkirat ḫawâṣṣ al-umma bi-ḏikr ḫaṣâ'iṣ al-a'imma*: 218, Ibn Kaṯîr., *al-Bidâya wa-l-nihâya*, vol. XI: 550.

[52] Ibn al-Aṯîr., *al-Kâmil fî al-târîḫ*, vol. II: 434.

[53] Ibn Kaṯîr., *al-Bidâya wa-l-nihâya*, vol. XI: 560.

[54] HOWARD I.K.A., (trans.), *The History of al-Ṭabarî*, vol. XIX, 1990: 164–167.

[55] Qurrah b. Qays al-Ḥanẓalî al-Tamîmî, an eyewitness of the battle and member of the opposing forces, who witnessed the severing of the heads.

with him the daughters and sisters of the dead al-Ḥusayn, the children with them and the sick ʿAlî b. al-Ḥusayn.[56] There were also female servants in the retinue.[57] Al-Haytamî, transmitting from Ibn Saʿd, provides a list of the survivors who were moved from the site of the battle and sent to Ibn Ziyâd; he names ʿAlî b. al-Ḥusayn, Fâṭima bt. al-Ḥusayn and Sukayna bt. al-Ḥusayn. Curiously, Zaynab is omitted from the list, although admittedly, al-Haytamî seems to be interested here primarily in al-Ḥusayn's children. He notes that ʿAlî b. al-Ḥusayn, who was despatched with the others, was a boy who had already reached puberty; it is an important detail for the later questions that Ibn Ziyâd will raise about his manhood.[58]

It is at the very start of this exodus from the battle site, at least according to some of the transmitters (al-Balâḏurî, al-Ṭabarî, al-Ḫawârizimî, Ibn al-Aṯîr, Ibn Kaṯîr, al-ʿÂmilî), that Zaynab raises a lamentation upon seeing the dead bodies of her brother, his family and his companions. This introduces a problem of chronology; for despite the words of Zaynab about bodies under the open sky, al-Ṭabarî has reported that the bodies of al-Ḥusayn and his companions had been buried by members of the Banû Asad the previous day, 11th Muḥarram.[59] It may be that al-Ṭabarî has inserted an Abû Miḫnaf report about the lament after his description of the burials without thought for timing; or, it may be that when Ibn Kaṯîr[60] notes that they saw al-Ḥusayn and his companions 'on the ground', it is a reference to the freshly-dug graves or even to battle litter, rather than the actual corpses. However, the most likely explana-

---

56 Cf. also al-Ḫawârizmî., *Maqtal al-Ḥusayn*, bk. 2, bb. *fî maqtal al-Ḥusayn*: 44, Ibn al-Aṯîr., *al-Kâmil fî al-târîḫ*, vol. II: 434, Ibn Ṭâʾûs., *Kitâb al-luhûf fî qatlâ al-ṭufûf*: 77–78, Ibn Namâ al-Ḥillî., *Muṯîr al-aḥzân wa munîr subul al-ashǧân*, Part 2: 75.

57 al-Dînawarî., *Kitâb al-aḫbâr al-ṭiwâl*: 270.

58 al-Haytamî., *Maǧmaʿ al-zawâʾid wa-manbaʿ al-fawâʾid*, vol. IX, bb. 95 (*Manâqib al-Ḥusayn*), n. 15148: 227.

59 HOWARD I.K.A., (trans.), *The History of al-Ṭabarî*, vol. XIX, 1990: 163. Cf. Ibn Shahrâshûb., *Manâqib âl Abî Ṭâlib*, vol. IV, bb. *fî maqtali-hi*: 111.

60 Ibn Kaṯîr., *al-Bidâya wa-l-nihâya*, vol. XI: 560.

tion is that it is transmitters like Ibn Ṭâʾûs[61] and Ibn Namâ al-Ḥillî who have gotten it correct; that the lament was not sung by Zaynab as the survivors were leaving Karbalâʾ on 12th Muḥarram, but two days earlier, immediately after the death of al-Ḥusayn, when the women were being driven from their burning tents.

The length and wording of the lament differ in various transmissions, as noted by, among others, al-ʿÂmilî in his *Aʿyân al-Shîʿa*.[62] As they pass the remains of al-Ḥusayn and the other dead, notes al-Ṭabarî, the women shriek and tear at their faces. Qurrah b. Qays remarks that he had never seen women as beautiful:[63] "By God," he remarks, "they were more beautiful than the wild cows at Yabrîn."[64] He then reports the exquisite lament of Zaynab as she passes the dead body of her brother:

> "O Muḥammad! O Muḥammad! May the angels[65] of heaven bless you. Here is Ḥusayn in the open, stained[66] with blood

---

[61] Curiously, al-ʿÂmilî, transmitting from Ibn Ṭâʾûs, still puts the lament on the wrong day. Cf. al-ʿÂmilî., *Aʿyân al-Shîʿa*, vol. VII: 138.

[62] al-ʿÂmilî., *Aʿyân al-Shîʿa*, vol. VII: 138.

[63] Literally, "I never ever saw a sight of women that was more beautiful than the sight I saw of them that day."

[64] These details are not in Abû Miḫnaf. Yabrîn refers to an oasis in Saudi Arabia, near the town of al-Ḫunn.

[65] While al-Balâḏurî uses 'sovereign' (*malik*), al-Ṭabarî uses *malâʾika* ('angels'); al-Ḫawârizimî and Ibn Shahrâshûb, writing two-and-a-half centuries after al-Ṭabarî, transmit the word as *malîk*, which means 'sovereign' or 'king'. Forty years after Ibn Shahrâshûb, Ibn al-Aṯîr returns to *malâʾika*; so does one of his contemporaries, Ibn Ṭâʾûs, while another, Sibṭ al-Ğawzî, changes it to 'the God of heaven' (Sibṭ al-Ğawzî., *Taḏkirat ḫawâṣṣ al-umma bi-ḏikr ḫaṣâʾiṣ al-aʾimma*: 216–217). Writing a few years later, Ibn Namâ, although he follows very closely the Ibn Ṭâʾûs narrative, reverts to *malîk*; a century after him, Ibn Kaṯîr uses *malâʾika*. Al-Mağlisî, transmitting from Ibn Shahrâshûb, retains his use of *malîk*. It seems, therefore, unlikely that this is merely a mistake in transmission, with the Arabic for angel (*malak* or *malâk*, with its plural *malâʾika*) devolving into *malîk*. Instead, I have chosen to follow the possibility that these are two different strands, and following the definition given by Arthur Jeffery, I have translated the word *malîk*, not as a corruption of the Arabic for 'angel' or 'angels', but as

> and limbs torn off. O Muḥammad! Your daughters are prisoners, your progeny killed, and the east wind blows dust over them."[67]

Many transmitters add the reaction of those standing around: "By God, she caused enemy and friend alike to weep."[68] This will not be the last time that groups of people will weep upon hearing Zaynab speak. It is a Zaynab who is less distraught; her words are becoming more measured and restrained, as the metamorphosis from the terrified woman at al-Ḫuzaymiyya to the woman who confutes Ibn Ziyâd and Yazîd continues.

A number of transmissions provide longer, more detailed and quite diverse laments.[69] Al-Ḫawârizmî writes in his *Maqtal* that when the survivors (al-Ḥusayn's daughters, sisters, ʿAlî b. al-

---

'sovereign'. Cf. JEFFERY A., "The Foreign Vocabulary of the Qur'ān" in G Böwering and J D McAuliffe (eds.), *Texts and Studies of the Qur'ān*, Brill, Leiden 2007: 269.

[66] al-Ṭabarî's text (like others after him such as Sibṭ al-Ğawzî's) employs the term *murammal*, different from the *muzammal* of al-Balâḏurî, and which Howard translates as 'stained'. In all other places, I have chosen to translate this word as 'soiled'. Al-Ḫawârizmî, Ibn al-Aṯîr and Ibn Kaṯîr, transmitting some centuries after al-Ṭabarî, have read the word as *muzammal*, which I have rendered as 'wrapped'.

[67] al-Balâḏurî., *Kitâb ansâb al-ashrâf*, vol. III: 411–412, HOWARD I.K.A., (trans.), *The History of al-Ṭabarî*, vol. XIX, 1990: 164. Cf. also al-Ḫawârizmî., *Maqtal al-Ḥusayn*, bk. 2, bb. *fî maqtal al-Ḥusayn*: 44–45 (with a slight variation in the wording), Ibn al-Aṯîr., *al-Kâmil fî al-târîḫ*, vol. II: 434, Sibṭ al-Ğawzî., *Taḏkirat ḫawâṣṣ al-umma bi-ḏikr ḫaṣâʾiṣ al-aʾimma*: 216–217, Ibn Kaṯîr., *al-Bidâya wa-l-nihâya*, vol. XI: 560.

[68] HOWARD I.K.A., (trans.), *The History of al-Ṭabarî*, vol. XIX, 1990: 164. Cf. also al-Ḫawârizmî., *Maqtal al-Ḥusayn*, bk. 2, bb. *fî maqtal al-Ḥusayn*: 44–45, Ibn al-Aṯîr., *al-Kâmil fî al-târîḫ*, vol. II: 434, Ibn Kaṯîr., *al-Bidâya wa-l-nihâya*, vol. XI: 560.

[69] al-Ḫawârizmî., *Maqtal al-Ḥusayn*, bk. 2, bb. *fî maqtal al-Ḥusayn*: 44–5 (with only slight changes), Ibn Ṭâʾûs., *Kitâb al-luhûf fî qatlâ al-ṭufûf*: 78–79, Ibn Shahrâshûb., *Manâqib âl Abî Ṭâlib*, vol. IV, bb. *fî maqtali-hi*: 113, Ibn Namâ al-Ḥillî., *Muṯîr al-aḥzân wa munîr subul al-ashğân*, Part 2: 77, 84, al-Mağlisî., *Biḥâr al-anwâr*, vol. XLV, bb. 37: 58–59.

Ḥusayn and their offspring – al-Ḫawârizmî fails to mention the wives of al-Ḥusayn, but they were surely present) pass the bodies of al-Ḥusayn and his companions, the women cry out and strike faces. Zaynab exclaims:

> "O Muḥammad! The Sovereign[70] of heaven bless you! Here is Ḥusayn in the open air, wrapped with blood, begrimed with dust, dismembered of limbs! O Muḥammad! Your daughters, captives of the army, your offspring killed, the sand scattered over them, this son of yours, head cut off at the nape; he is neither absent and anticipated, nor wounded and curable." She was still speaking when her listeners, friend and foe alike, began to weep.

Ibn Ṭâʾûs records a slightly longer dirge by Zaynab, following the looting of the women's tents. Stripped of head covering and barefoot, their tents on fire, the captured women see the dead of Karbalâʾ lying on the ground. Ibn Ṭâʾûs transmits from the narrator Ḥumayd b. Muslim; this is a crucial detail, for it places the lament before his departure for Kûfa, which al-Ṭabarî says is 10th Muḥarram. Ḥumayd says:

> By God! I will never forget Zaynab daughter of ʿAlî, bewailing al-Ḥusayn, and crying with a sad voice and grief-stricken heart: "O Muḥammad! May the angels of heaven bless you! This is Ḥusayn, soiled with blood, dismembered of limbs, and your daughters, captives. To God, this complaint, to Muḥammad al-Muṣṭafâ (the Chosen), to ʿAlî al-Murtaḍâ (the Approved), to Fâṭima al-Zahrâʾ (the Radiant) and to Ḥamza, master of the martyrs. O Muḥammad! This is Ḥusayn in the open air, the wind covering him with sand, killed by the children of harlots. The grief of it! The torment of it! Today my grandfather the Messenger of God has died! Companions of Muḥammad! These are the offspring of the Chosen, driven like the driving of captives."[71]

---

[70] The Arabic *malîk*.

[71] Ibn Ṭâʾûs., *Kitâb al-luhûf fî qatlâ al-ṭufûf*: 78, al-Mağlisî., *Biḥâr al-anwâr*, vol. XLV, bb. 37: 59.

Ibn Ṭâ'ûs follows this with a second, longer narration, which combines elements from many of the others and is followed immediately by an account of the looting of al-Ḥusayn after his death:

> "O Muḥammad! Your daughters are captives, your offspring killed, the wind spreading sand upon them! This is Ḥusayn, head cut from the nape, turban and gown plundered. May my father be[72] ransomed for his army plundered on Monday! May my father be ransomed for his tent, its ties lacerated! May my father be ransomed for the one who is not absent and expected back, not wounded and treatable. May my father be ransomed for the one for whom my soul is a ransom! May my father be ransomed for the one grief-stricken until he was killed! May my father be ransomed for the one thirsty until he departed! May my father be ransomed for the one whose beard drips with blood May my father be ransomed for the one whose grandfather is Muḥammad al-Muṣṭafâ! May my father be ransomed for the one whose grandfather is the Messenger of the God of heaven! May my father be ransomed for the one who is the grandson of the prophet of guidance! May my father be ransomed for Muḥammad al-Muṣṭafâ! May my father be ransomed for Ḫadîǧa al-Kubrâ! May my father be ransomed for ʿAlî al-Murtaḍâ! May my father be ransomed for Fâṭima al-Zahrâ', Mistress of the women of the worlds! May my father be ransomed for whom the sun went back until he had prayed."[73] The transmitter said: By God, she made every enemy and friend weep.[74]

---

[72] The Arabic *bi abî* here is, ostensibly, a shortened version of a longer formula, *bi abî anta wa ummî* (lit. 'you are to me as my father and mother'). The sense is sacrificial; had I something as precious as my own mother and father to offer as a ransom for you, I would do so. Muhammad Sarwar suggests "how earnestly I wish to sacrifice something as dear, beloved and extremely important to me as my father for..." Cf. SARWAR M., (trans.), *Behar al-anwar*, vol. 43, 2015: 317.

[73] It is reported that on two occasions, once during the life of Muḥammad and once after his death, ʿAlî caused (through prayer) the sun to return to its earlier position. On one of these occasions, on the authori-

Ibn Shahrâshûb's *Manâqib* seems little concerned with chronology; Zaynab eulogizes her brother, using the lament found in al-Ḫawârizmî and in extended form in al-Mağlisî, but adding a number of phrases from a longer lament in Ibn Ṭâ'ûs and later in al-Mağlisî. Ibn Shahrâshûb gives little indication of timing; he notes that the bodies were buried one day after they were killed,[75] but in his narration, Zaynab's lament is squeezed between a list of those killed and the account of Sinân arriving with al-Ḥusayn's head at the palace of Ibn Ziyâd.[76]

In Ibn Namâ al-Ḥillî, Zaynab and the other women are driven bareheaded from their burning tents; upon passing the body of al-Ḥusayn on the ground, she laments for him in an anguished voice and with a wounded heart, in the words of Ibn Ṭâ'ûs' first narration. The narrator notes that at her words, hardened hearts and 'coarse faces melted', and that in another (less trustworthy) manuscript, 'coarse faces were broken'.[77] Ibn Namâ uses 'Sovereign' instead of 'angels'; he omits the name of Muḥammad, transmitting the phrase "To God, this complaint, to ʿAlî al-Murtaḍâ, to Fâṭima al-Zahrâ' and to Ḥamza, master of the martyrs." He also changes 'the children of harlots' (*al-bağâyâ*) to 'the children of imposters' (*al-adʿiyâ'*), although this word can also mean 'bastards'. Then, based on the account of Qurra b. Qays, Ibn Namâ records a second version of the complaint (*shakwâ*) of Zaynab to her grandfather Muḥammad about the slaying of the people of his house:

---

ty of well-known transmitters like Umm Salama, al-Anṣârî and al-Ḫudrî, Muḥammad was resting on ʿAlî's thigh and receiving revelation, so that ʿAlî was unable to make the afternoon prayer. Muḥammad tells him to ask God to send the sun back for him, so that he may pray the prayer standing and at its proper time. This he does. Cf. al-Mufîd., *al-Irshâd*, vol. I, bb. *fî radd al-shams li-ʿAlî maratayn*: 346.

[74] Ibn Ṭâ'ûs., *Kitâb al-luhûf fî qatlâ al-ṭufûf*: 78–79.

[75] Ibn Shahrâshûb., *Manâqib âl Abî Ṭâlib*, vol. IV, bb. *fî maqtali-hi*: 111.

[76] Op. cit.: 112–113.

[77] Ibn Namâ al-Ḥillî., *Muṯîr al-aḥzân wa munîr subul al-ashğân*, Part 2: 77.

> Qurra b. Qays said: "I will never forget the words of Zaynab, daughter of ʿAlî, as she passed by her brother on the ground. She said: 'O Muḥammad, the Sovereign of heaven bless you! This is Ḥusayn in the open air, soiled with blood, dismembered of limbs! O Muḥammad, your daughters, captive, your offspring killed, the sand scattered over them!" Friend and foe alike wept at these words.[78]

It is noteworthy that in this version, Qurra b. Qays' words ('I will never forget the words of Zaynab') are, with a small variation, the same opening words attributed by Ibn Ṭâʾûs to Ibn Ḥumayd b. Muslim ('I will never forget Zaynab').

Ultimately, it is in Ibn Ṭâʾûs and al-Mağlisî that we find the longest laments. Al-Mağlisî begins by transmitting from Ibn Ṭâʾûs the dirge of Zaynab, immediately after the looting of the women's tents, as bareheaded and barefoot, their tents on fire, the captured women see the dead of Karbalâʾ lying on the ground. The lament is narrated by Ḥumayd b. Muslim who, as already noted and if al-Ṭabarî is correct, was not there by the time the survivors left for Kûfa, so that the lament had to be earlier than 12th Muḥarram.[79] Al-Mağlisî follows this with a longer, more detailed lament which, he says, is found in 'some transmitters' (*fî baʿḍ al-ruwâyât*) but without identifying them. Besides the fact that Ibn Shahrâshûb inserts bits of it into the lament he records from Zaynab, and which Ibn Ṭâʾûs carries it in almost the same form, it is not transmitted in this complete form by any major Shîʿî author:

> And in some transmitters: "O Muḥammad! Your daughters are captives, your offspring killed, the wind spreading sand upon them! This is Ḥusayn, head cut from the nape, turban and gown plundered! May my father be ransomed for his army plundered on Monday! May my father be ransomed for his tent, its ties lacerated! May my father be ransomed for the one who is not absent and expected back, not wounded and treatable. May my father be ransomed for the one for whom my soul

---

[78] Ibn Namâ al-Ḥillî., *Muṯîr al-aḥzân wa munîr subul al-ashğân*, Part 3: 83–84.

[79] al-Mağlisî., *Biḥâr al-anwâr*, vol. XLV, bb. 37: 58–59.

> is a ransom! May my father be ransomed for the one grief-stricken until he was killed! May my father be ransomed for the one thirsty until he departed! May my father be ransomed for the one whose beard drips with blood! May my father be ransomed for the one who grandfather is the Messenger of the God of heaven! May my father be ransomed for the one who is the grandson of the prophet of guidance. May my father be ransomed for Muḥammad al-Muṣṭafâ! May my father be ransomed for Ḫadîǧa al-Kubrâ! May my father be ransomed for ʿAlî al-Murtaḍâ! May my father be ransomed for Fâṭima al-Zahrâ', mistress of the women! May my father be ransomed for whom the sun went back until he had prayed!"[80]

Shahin in his biography records a prayer uttered by Zaynab as she passes the body of her brother: "God, accept this offering and reward him for his deed." He gives no references for the prayer, and in fact it is not transmitted by the major Shîʿî sources. It is, Shahin notes, prayed at the very moment that the *ahl al-bayt* is being removed by force from the political arena of Islam.[81]

There are two addenda to the account of Zaynab's lament and the departure to Kûfa. The first is that in his history, al-Ṭabarî transmits a bizarre incident involving Sinân b. Anas, sometimes named as al-Ḥusayn's killer (and if not, certainly present at the moment of his death), and described by al-Balâḏurî and al-Ṭabarî as 'a poet' and 'a bit insane'. He goes to ʿUmar b. Saʿd's tent and sings a song for which he will be severely chastised:

> "Fill my saddlebags with silver and gold, for I have killed the hidden sovereign! I have killed the best of people as regards his mother and father, and the best of them when they speak of lineage."[82]

The song is compelling not only for its callousness, but also because its singer and the place it is sung are substantially disputed in

---

[80] Op. cit., vol. XLV, bb. 37: 59.

[81] SHAHIN B., *Lady Zaynab*, 2002: 43.

[82] al-Balâḏurî., *Kitâb ansâb al-ashrâf*, vol. III: 410, HOWARD I.K.A., (trans.), *The History of al-Ṭabarî*, vol. XIX, 1990: 162.

the texts. Ibn al-Aṯîr[83] and Ibn Kaṯîr follow the al-Ṭabarî narrative, including the stern reaction provoked by the verses. ʿUmar b. Saʿd orders Sinân brought into the tent, and when he enters, ʿUmar flings his whip at him and shouts: "Woe to you, you are mad! By God, had Ibn Ziyâd heard you say this, he would have had you beheaded!"[84] Ibn Shahrâshûb, al-Fattâl al-Nîsâbûrî and al-Ṣadûq, on the other hand, have Sinân b. Anas actually reciting these words to Ibn Ziyâd, who replies: "Woe to you! If you knew he was the best of people as regards his mother and father, why in that case did you kill him?" and orders Sinân's execution.[85]

In his *Usd al-ġâba fî maʿrifat al-ṣaḥâba*,[86] Ibn al-Aṯîr places the verses on the lips of one of those regarded as the killer of al-Ḥusayn, either Shimr or ʿUmar b. Saʿd, and has them sung to Ibn Ziyâd by the killer when he brings to Ziyâd the head of al-Ḥusayn. His contemporary, Sibṭ al-Ğawzî, grandson of the more famous Ibn al-Ğawzî, places the words on the lips of either Sinân or Shimr, and has them sung at the door of ʿUmar's tent.[87] Others, like Ibn ʿAsâkir and al-Ḫawârizmî, report the verse being recited by Ḫawalî b. Yazîd al-Aṣbaḥî, tasked with transporting the head to Ibn Ziyâd. Ziyâd reacts angrily to the poem ("if you knew he was so great, why did you kill him?") and has the reciter executed.[88] Whatever

---

83 Ibn al-Aṯîr., *al-Kâmil fî al-târîḫ*, vol. II: 433. Ibn al-Aṯîr describes Sinân as 'courageous' (*shuğâʿ*), 'a poet' (*shâʿir*) but 'a little crazy' (*bi-hi lûṯa*). The first two terms will crop again later, in a conversation between Zaynab and Ibn Ziyâd.

84 Ibn Kaṯîr., *al-Bidâya wa-l-nihâya*, vol. XI: 551.

85 al-Fattâl al-Nîsâbûrî., *Rawḍat al-wâʿiẓîn wa-tabṣirat al-muttaʿiẓîn*: b. *Maqtal al-Ḥusayn*, n. 8 [414]: 429, al-Ṣadûq., *Kitâb al-amâlî fî-l-aḥâdîṯ wa-l-aḫbâr*: 144, Ibn Shahrâshûb., *Manâqib âl Abî Ṭâlib*, vol. IV, bb. *fî maqtali-hi*: 113.

86 Ibn al-Aṯîr., *Usd al-ġâba fî maʿrifat al-ṣaḥâba*, vol. I, bb. 1173 (*al-Ḥusayn b. ʿAlî*): 570.

87 Sibṭ al-Ğawzî., *Taḏkirat ḫawâṣṣ al-umma bi-ḏikr ḫaṣâʾiṣ al-aʾimma*: 215.

88 Ibn ʿAsâkir., *Târîḫ madînat Dimashq*, vol. XIV, bb. 1566 (*al-Ḥusayn b. ʿAlî b. Abî Ṭâlib b. ʿAbd al-Muṭṭalib b. Hâshim b. ʿAbd al-Manâf*): 252, al-Ḫawârizmî., *Maqtal al-Ḥusayn*, bk. 2, bb. *fî maqtal al-Ḥusayn*: 45.

the details of the poem in terms of the reciter and his fate and the recipient of the verses, it is a crucial anecdote recorded by the Sunnî scholars, indicating as it does that in the immediate aftermath of Karbalâ᾿, the authorities knew that something terrible had transpired. This realization is clearly seen in the vacillations and mood swings of Ibn Ziyâd and Yazîd.

A second addendum is the curious tangent taken by al-Ṣadûq in his *Kitâb al-amâlî* and al-Fattâl al-Nîsâbûrî in his *Rawḍat al-wâʿiẓîn*. Al-Ṣadûq recounts the instant of al-Ḥusayn's death; at that moment, it is, in al-Ṣadûq's narrative, Umm Kulṯûm, daughter of al-Ḥusayn, who emerges, bareheaded, her hands on her head, and laments with words that most other authors have put into the mouth of Zaynab: "O Muḥammad! This is al-Ḥusayn in the open air, robbed of turban and outer garment!"[89] In fact, this is not the only time that al-Ṣadûq put words that traditionally belong to Zaynab into someone else's mouth. He records another incident, also found in al-Iṣfahânî, in which Ibn Ziyâd sends a delegate (*qâṣid*) to Umm Kulṯûm. The text here is uncertain and offers the possibility that this is either al-Ḥusayn's sister or his daughter; in this case, considering the age of al-Ḥusayn's daughter, his and Zaynab's sister seems the more likely candidate. The delegate, in words reminiscent of those Ibn Ziyâd would speak to Zaynab, says: "Praise be to God, who has killed your men! How do you see what He has done to you?" Umm Kulṯûm replies:

> "Ibn Ziyâd, if indeed you are delighted by the killing of al-Ḥusayn, how often did his grandfather not delight in him, kissing him and kissing his lips and placing him on his shoulder! Ibn Ziyâd! Consider his grandfather in answering, for on a future day he will be your adversary!"[90]

Al-Fattâl al-Nîsâbûrî also recounts the story of al-Ḥusayn's horse; it drew near, bespattered with his fragrance (the author notes that other texts say 'soiled with his blood'), the front of its head stained with the blood of al-Ḥusayn. It is galloping and whinnying, and

---

[89] al-Ṣadûq., *Kitâb al-amâlî fî-l-aḥâdîṯ wa-l-aḫbâr*, *maǧlis* 30: 163.

[90] Op. cit.: 164. Also in al-Iṣfahânî., *Maqâtil al-ṭâlibîyyîn*, bb. *maqtal al-Ḥusayn*, n. 8 [414]: 469–470.

hearing these sounds, the womenfolk ('the daughters of the prophet') emerge. Seeing the riderless horse, they realize at once that al-Ḥusayn is dead. This causes Umm Kulṯûm, whom, like al-Ṣadûq, the author names as daughter of al-Ḥusayn, one of the women who has emerged bareheaded, to place her hands on her head and begin a lament, using words that most other authors have put into the mouth of Zaynab: "O Muḥammad! This is al-Ḥusayn in the open air, robbed of turban and outer garment!"[91]

Besides the questions about which Umm Kulṯûm this is, and whether Zaynab's words have, mistakenly, been put into her mouth, it is a curious text; it appears to mark the moment of realization by the women that al-Ḥusayn is dead; the women, that is, aside from Zaynab, whom the texts quite patently reveal to be an eyewitness to his death, in the very last moments challenging his killers. The death of her brother marks Zaynab's final intervention on the field of Karbalâʾ; transformed and empowered by the example of the martyrs, Zaynab will now take the leading role in defending the justice of al-Ḥusayn's cause and making Karbalâʾ the indestructible paradigm of struggle that it has become for every generation of the Shîʿa.

---

[91] al-Fattâl al-Nîsâbûrî., *Rawḍat al-wâʿiẓîn wa-tabṣirat al-muttaʿiẓîn*: 428.

CHAPTER FOUR. IN THE HALLS OF THE KINGS

1. THE FIRST PROTEST

It is a journey of approximately 46 miles (79.4 kilometres) from Karbalâʾ to Kûfa; al-Ṭabarî in his history gives no indication of how long it took the survivors and their captors to cover this distance. However, it is upon their arrival, in a busy market square crowded with inquisitive onlookers, that Zaynab delivers the first of two momentous protests. Her words are carried, with some slight variations, by a number of transmitters;[1] al-Mufîd in his *al-Amâlî*, for example, is reporting from Ḥaḏlam b. Satîr,[2] who says: "I arrived in Kûfa in Muḥarram of the year 61, with the departure

---

[1] al-Mufîd., *al-Amâlî li-l-Mufîd*, *mağlis* 38: 321–323, al-Ṭûsî., *al-Amâlî fî al-ḥadît*, *mağlis* 3: 92–93, al-Ṭabarsî., *Kitâb al-iḥtiğâğ ʿalâ ahl al-liğâğ*, vol. II: 304, al-Ḫawârizmî., *Maqtal al-Ḥusayn*, bk. 2, bb. *fî maqtal al-Ḥusayn*: 45, Ibn Shahrâshûb., *Manâqib âl Abî Ṭâlib*, vol. IV, bb. *fî maqtali-hi*: 115, Ibn Ṭâʾûs., *Kitâb al-luhûf fî qatlâ al-ṭufûf*: 86–87, Ibn Namâ al-Ḥillî., *Muṯîr al-aḥzân wa munîr subul al-ashğân*, Part 3: 86, al-Mağlisî., *Biḥâr al-anwâr*, vol. XLV, bb. 39, n. 1: 108–110 (from Ibn Ṭâʾûs), vol. XLV, bb. 39: 163–164 (from al-Ṭabarsî), vol. XLV, bb. 39, n. 1: 108–110 (from al-Mufîd and al-Ṭûsî), al-Shablanğî., *Nûr al-abṣâr fî manâqib âl bayt al-nabî al-muḫtâr*: 20, al-ʿÂmilî., *Aʿyân al-Shîʿa*, vol. VII: 138.

[2] The editor notes he is called Ḥaḏlam b. Bashîr in other texts, Ḥaḏîm Ibn Sharîk al-Asadî in al-Ṭabarsî (al-Ṭabarsî., *Kitâb al-iḥtiğâğ ʿalâ ahl al-liğâğ*, vol. II: 304), Bashîr b. Ḥaḏlam in Ibn Namâ al-Ḥillî and in al-Mağlisî (Ibn Namâ al-Ḥillî., *Muṯîr al-aḥzân wa munîr subul al-ashğân*: 112, al-Mağlisî., *Biḥâr al-anwâr*, vol. XLV, bb. 39: 147), and Bashîr b. Ḫazîm al-Asadî in al-Ḫawârizmî and Ibn Ṭâʾûs (al-Ḫawârizmî., *Maqtal al-Ḥusayn*, bk. 2, bb. *fî maqtal al-Ḥusayn*: 45, Ibn Ṭâʾûs., *Kitâb al-luhûf fî qatlâ al-ṭufûf*: 86).

of ʿAlî b. al-Ḥusayn with the women from Karbalâʾ, and with them the soldiers guarding them. The people went to look at them." Then Ḥaḏlam catches sight of Zaynab: "I had never seen such a modest one[3] more articulate than her; it was as though she was cast[4] from the tongue of the Commander of the Faithful." Zaynab[5] motions to the crowd to be quiet, and their voices[6] fall silent as the people literally hold their breath. Then she begins her declaration:

> "Praise be to God and blessing upon my grandfather the Messenger of God.[7] O people of Kûfa! O people of deception and desertion![8] Let the tears not cease flowing or the cry subside. Your similarity is nothing but "*like unto her who unravelleth the*

---

[3] 'A shy woman' notes the editor.

[4] 4th form verb *afraġa-yufriġu*; cf. LANE E.W., *An Arabic-English Lexicon*, vol. VI, 1968: 2381, al-ʿÂmilî., *Aʿyân al-Shîʿa*, vol. VII: 137. Al-Maǧlisî, transmitting from Ibn Ṭâʾûs, employs the 2nd for verb *farraʿa-yufarriʿu*, which could carry the sense of 'to be superior to' (LANE E.W., *An Arabic-English Lexicon*, vol. VI, 1968: 2378). Al-Ḫawârizmî adds the verb *naṭaqa-yanṭuqu* "as if she spoke with the tongue of the Commander of the Faithful ʿAlî b. Abî Ṭâlib and was cast from it" (al-Ḫawârizmî., *Maqtal al-Ḥusayn*, bk. 2, bb. *fî maqtal al-Ḥusayn*: 45).

[5] It must be noted that Ibn Abî Ṭâhir Ṭayfûr places almost the same protest, with much the same detail (including the narration by one who he names Ḥiḏâm al-Asadî) on the lips of Umm Kulṯûm, ostensibly the sister of Zaynab. He has not mixed up the two women, since he has a chapter dedicated to each, although while he clearly identifies Zaynab as daughter of ʿAlî, he does do the same for Umm Kulṯûm. It seems certain enough that he means Zaynab's sister; to her, he attributes what others attribute to Zaynab, that is, the protest at Kûfa. He then goes on to record Zaynab's protest before Yazîd. Cf. Ibn Abî Ṭâhir Ṭayfûr., *Balâġât al-nisâʾ*: 38–39.

[6] In al-Mufîd, 'voices' (*al-aṣwât*), but in al-Ṭabarsî, al-Ḫawârizmî, Ibn Ṭâʾûs, Ibn Namâ al-Ḥillî (and also Ibn Abî Ṭâhir Ṭayfûr, recounting the story about Umm Kulṯûm), '(animal) bells' (*al-aǧrâs*).

[7] al-Ḫawârizmî adds: 'and upon his pure and righteous family, the family of God' (al-Ḫawârizmî., *Maqtal al-Ḥusayn*, bk. 2, bb. *fî maqtal al-Ḥusayn*: 46).

[8] al-Ḫawârizmî, Ibn Ṭâʾûs and Ibn Namâ al-Ḥillî add here: 'Do you weep?'

thread, after she hath made it strong, to thin filaments, making your oaths[9] *a deceit between you*".[10] Is there nothing among you but conceit, the stain of vice, the hateful heart? Cowards in the encounter, powerless against the enemies, faithless in allegiance, neglecters of the covenant![11] What wretchedness your souls have sent ahead of you, that God is angry with you and you will remain forever in torment![12] Do you weep?[13] Yes, by God, weep a great deal and laugh little! Already you are dismayed[14] by its ignominy and its disgrace, and you will never ever wash its stain from yourselves! You have deserted and turned from[15]

---

[9] Wrongly transcribed in both al-Ḫawârizmî and Ibn Ṭâ'ûs as 'your faith' (*îmâni-kum*) instead of 'your oaths' (*aymâni-kum*), as in the other texts. Al-Ḫawârizmî changes the last part of the Qur'ânic citation, turning it into a question: "Do you make your oaths a deceit between you?", but this is not how it reads in the Qur'ânic text (cf. al-Ḫawârizmî., *Maqtal al-Ḥusayn*, bk. 2, bb. *fî maqtal al-Ḥusayn*: 46).

[10] Q. 16: 92. Referring their readers to a number of classical works of exegesis (al-Maḥallî and al-Suyûṭî's *Tafsîr al-Ğalâlayn*, al-Râzî's *al-Tafsîr al-kabîr* and al-Ṭabarî's *Ğâmi' al-bayân 'an ta'wîl al-qur'ân*) the editors of 'The Study Quran' suggest that "weaving strands of yarn together to form a strong thread, only to senselessly unravel it, was reportedly the practice of a mentally impaired woman in Makkah, who did this as a regular habit. In this verse, it is used as a metaphor for those who take oaths to form strong bonds of alliance, only to break those oaths and undo those bonds when they seem to have lost their political expediency…" Cf. NASR S.H. et al., (eds.), *The Study Quran*, HarperOne, New York 2015: 682.

[11] This phrase is also found in al-Ṭûsî (al-Ṭûsî., *al-Amâlî fî al-ḥadît, mağlis* 3: 92) but is missing from al-Ḫawârizmî, Ibn Ṭâ'ûs, al-Ṭabarsî, Ibn Namâ al-Ḥillî and Ibn Shahrâshûb.

[12] Cf. Q. 5: 80. Similar words were spoken by Fâṭima on her deathbed.

[13] al-Ṭabarsî reads: "Do you weep over my brother? Yes, by God, weeping is most appropriate for you!" (al-Ṭabarsî., *Kitâb al-iḥtiğâğ 'alâ ahl al-liğâğ*, vol. II: 304).

[14] al-Ṭabarsî reads 'tested', while al-Ḫawârizmî, Ibn Ṭâ'ûs, and Ibn Namâ al-Ḥillî read 'destroyed'.

[15] al-Ṭabarsî, al-Ḫawârizmî, Ibn Ṭâ'ûs and Ibn Namâ al-Ḥillî read 'in what way will you wash away the killing…'

> the scion of the seal of the prophecy, the leader of the youths of the people of paradise, the shelter in your confusion, the refuge in your calamity, the sign of your destination and the spokesman of your proof! Is it not an evil that you have taken upon yourselves, and wretchedness and degeneration! The endeavour is dashed, hands are covered with dust, the deal is forfeited, and you have been "*visited with wrath from Allah*" "*and humiliation and wretchedness were stamped upon*" you.[16] Alas for you! Are you aware which side of Muḥammad you have split lengthwise, and which blood of his you have shed and which precious thing of his you have deceived? "*Assuredly ye utter a disastrous thing whereby almost the heavens are torn, and the earth is split asunder and the mountains fall in ruins*"[17] filling the earth and the heaven – does it astonish you that the sky drips blood? Truly, the torment of the Afterlife is more ignominious. Let not leisure cheer you, for haste does not induce Him, nor does He fear that vengeance will slip by. No, for "*Lo! thy Lord is ever watchful*".[18]

Al-Ṭûsî transmits closely from al-Mufîd, but two centuries after al-Mufîd, Ibn Ṭâ'ûs' transmission contains some noticeable differences:[19]

> Bashîr b. Ḫuzaym al-Asadî said: "On that day, I looked at Zaynab, daughter of ʿAlî, and by God I have not seen such a reserved person more eloquent than her; it was as though she

---

[16] A paraphrase of Q. 2: 61 "*And humiliation and wretchedness were stamped upon them and they were visited with wrath from Allah*", repeated, although with a different word order, in Q. 3: 112 "*They have incurred anger from their Lord, and wretchedness is laid upon them*". In the latter verse, aside from the change in word order, Pickthall is incorrect in his translation of the Arabic '*Allâh*' as 'their Lord'.

[17] Q. 19: 89–90. Cf. also Q. 42: 5.

[18] Q. 89: 14.

[19] Ibn Ṭâ'ûs., *Kitâb al-luhûf fî qatlâ al-ṭufûf*: 86–87.

surpassed[20] the eloquence of the Commander of the Faithful, ʿAlî b. Abî Ṭâlib. She motioned to the people to become quiet; breathing was reduced, the bells became still. Then she said: 'Praise be to God and blessings upon my father Muḥammad and upon his pure and righteous family. O people of Kûfa! People of deception and desertion! Do you weep? May the tears not cease to flow, the lament[21] not abate![22] Truly, your likeness is similar "*unto her who unravelleth the thread, after she hath made it strong, to thin filaments, making your oaths a deceit between you*".[23] Is there among you anything except conceit, the stain of vice, the hating heart, the flattering of slaves,[24] the winking[25] of the enemies, like grassland over a ruin or like silver[26] over a grave?[27] Is it not an evil[28] that your souls have sent ahead of

---

[20] In al-Mufîd, al-Ṭabarsî, al-Ḫawârizmî and Ibn Namâ, the verb is *tafarraġa* ('to be cast from'). Ibn Ṭâʾûs (and al-Maǧlisî transmitting from him), uses *tafarraʿa* ('to surpass').

[21] al-Ṭabarsî and Ibn Shahrâshûb read 'sighs' (*al-ẓafra*).

[22] Here, al-Shablanǧî adds 'or the sighs' (*al-ẓafra*).

[23] Q. 16: 92.

[24] al-Shablanǧî reads in the singular 'the (female) slave' (*al-ama*) rather than the plural *al-imâʾ*: cf. al-Shablanǧî., *Nûr al-abṣâr fî manâqib âl bayt al-nabî al-muḫtâr*: 203.

[25] al-Shablanǧî reads 'prevention' or 'containment' (*ḥaǧz*); cf. al-Shablanǧî., *Nûr al-abṣâr fî manâqib âl bayt al-nabî al-muḫtâr*: 203.

[26] al-Ḫawârizmî reads 'gypsum' (*qaṣṣa* or *qiṣṣa*), with a footnote explaining that this is a type of plaster; cf. al-Ḫawârizmî., *Maqtal al-Ḥusayn*, bk. 2, bb. *fî maqtal al-Ḥusayn*: 46 and LANE E.W., *An Arabic-English Lexicon*, vol. VII, 1968: 2527.

[27] The phrase from 'the flattering of slaves' until 'like silver over a grave', is entirely omitted by al-Mufîd, who replaces it with: 'cowards in the encounter' (*ḫawwârûn fî-l-liqâʾ*), 'powerless before the enemy' (*ʿâǧizûn ʿan al-aʿdâʾ*), 'faithless to the allegiance' (*nâkiṯûn li-l-bayya*) and 'neglecters of the covenant' (*muḍayyiʿûn li-l-ḏimma*): cf. al-Mufîd., *al-Amâlî li-l-Mufîd*, *maǧlis* 38: 322.

[28] al-Ṭabarsî and Ibn Shahrâshûb read 'wretchedness'.

you,[29] that God is angry with you and that you will remain forever in anguish? Do you weep and lament? Yes, by God, weep a great deal and laugh little! Certainly, its ignominy and its disgrace[30] have destroyed you, and you will never wash it with any ablution after this. In what way will you wash away the killing of the descendant of the seal of the prophethood,[31] the treasure trove[32] of the message, the leader of the youths of the people of paradise,[33] the shelter of your confusion,[34] the refuge of your calamity,[35] the minaret of your proof[36] and the spokesman[37] of your *sunna*?[38] Is it not an evil that you take[39]

---

29 At this point, Ibn Shahrâshûb's narration changes quite dramatically from that of Ibn Ṭâ'ûs. Al-Shablanǧî reads: "Is it not an evil that you have taken upon yourselves?" which is a later phrase in al-Ḫawârizmî and Ibn Ṭâ'ûs. Cf. al-Shablanǧî., *Nûr al-abṣâr fî manâqib âl bayt al-nabî al-muḫtâr*: 203.

30 While most of the texts read 'disgrace' (*shanâr*), al-Maǧlisî reads 'hatred' (*shan'ân*) (cf. al-Maǧlisî., *Biḥâr al-anwâr*, vol. XLV, bb. 39, n. 1: 109). He notes the alternative reading in works such as al-Ṣadûq's *Kitâb al-ḫiṣâl*.

31 Also in al-Ṭabarsî, al-Ḫawârizmî, al-Maǧlisî and al-Shablanǧî. Al-Ḫawârizmî and al-Maǧlisî read 'the prophets' (*al-anbiyâ'*) rather than 'the prophecy' (*al-nubuwwa*) of Ibn Ṭâ'ûs (Ibn Ṭâ'ûs., *Kitâb al-luhûf fî qatlâ al-ṭufûf*: 87), Ibn Namâ (Ibn Namâ al-Ḥillî., *Muṯîr al-aḥzân wa munîr subul al-ashǧân*, Part 3: 86) and al-Shablanǧî (al-Shablanǧî., *Nûr al-abṣâr fî manâqib âl bayt al-nabî al-muḫtâr*: 203).

32 The Arabic *ma'din* means the 'place of the origin or source of some treasure'. Also in al-Ṭabarsî and al-Shablanǧî.

33 Also in al-Ṭabarsî, al-Ḫawârizmî, al-Maǧlisî and al-Shablanǧî.

34 Transcribed in al-Ḫawârizmî and al-Maǧlisî as *ḫayrati-kum* ('your treasure') and in Ibn Ṭâ'ûs as *ḥayrati-kum* ('your bewilderment').

35 Also in al-Ṭabarsî, al-Ḫawârizmî and al-Maǧlisî.

36 Also in al-Ḫawârizmî and al-Maǧlisî.

37 Mistakenly transcribed in Ibn Ṭâ'ûs, and should read *midrah*, as in al-Ḫawârizmî.

38 Also in al-Maǧlisî. While both he and Ibn Ṭâ'ûs read 'your *sunna*', al-Ḫawârizmî reads 'your tongues' (*alsinati-kum*), with an editorial footnote that clarifies that this ought to be understood as 'accentuating' or 'stress-

upon yourselves, a far removal for you, and crushing?[40] Certainly, the course has already failed, the hands have perished,[41] the deal is forfeited, and you have been "*visited with wrath from Allah*" "*and humiliation and wretchedness were stamped upon*" you. Alas for you, people of Kûfa! Are you aware[42] which side of the Messenger of God you have split lengthwise, and which precious thing of his you have exposed, and which blood of his you have shed,[43] and which holiness of his you have desecrated?[44] You have brought them,[45] bald-headed,[46] white

---

ing'. Al-Ṭabarsî, as will be noted in the main text, adds a number of names that are not found in our other authors.

[39] Mistaken transcription in al-Ḫawârizmî, which should read *taẓirûna*.

[40] Here, al-Shablanǧî reads instead: "Alas for you, people of Kûfa! Is it not an evil into which your souls have seduced you, that God is angry with you and that you will remain forever in anguish?" Cf. al-Shablanǧî., *Nûr al-abṣâr fî manâqib âl bayt al-nabî al-muḫtâr*: 43.

[41] al-Mufîd reads 'have become dusty' in the sense of suffering an enormous loss, such as from riches to poverty (cf. al-Mufîd., *al-Amâlî li-l-Mufîd*, *maǧlis* 38: 323).

[42] Omitted by al-Maǧlisî.

[43] These two phrases are reversed in al-Ḫawârizmî and al-Shablanǧî. Al-Ḫawârizmî adds: "And which sacred precinct of his you have assaulted?"

[44] Here, al-Ḫawârizmî and al-Shablanǧî insert a Qur'ânic verse: "*Assuredly ye utter a disastrous thing, Whereby almost the heavens are torn, and the earth is split asunder and the mountains fall in ruins*" (Q. 19: 89–90).

[45] The heads of al-Ḥusayn and his martyred companions.

[46] That is, without turbans, which were stripped from the dead during the post-Karbalâ' looting of the bodies. Al-Ṭabarî takes note in his history that al-Ḥusayn was wearing his turban in the run-up to the battle, that he put a turban back on after receiving a head wound, and that he was wearing it at his death (HOWARD I.K.A., (trans.), *The History of al-Ṭabarî*, vol. XIX, 1990: 92, 153, 160). As noted earlier in this work, her brother being stripped of his gown and turban forms part of Zaynab's lament.

necked,[47] blackened,[48] distorted (and some of them) clumsy and misshapen,[49] as though sufficient for filling the earth or like the gathering[50] of heaven.[51] Were you astonished that the heavens rained blood? Truly, the affliction of the Afterlife is far worse,[52] and you will not be helped. Do not let leisure[53] make you estimate it lightly, for haste does not induce[54] Him, nor

---

[47] Literally, 'long-necked', with special reference to the whiteness of neck of a bird of legend such as the griffon; but the root also carries a sense of 'calamity'. Cf. LANE E.W., *An Arabic-English Lexicon*, vol. V, 1968: 2177–2178, HAVA J.G., *Arabic English Dictionary for Advanced Learners*, 2008: 497.

[48] Mistaken transcription in al-Ḫawârizmî, which should read *sawdâʾ*. Al-Mağlisî reads *sawwâʾ*, which seems to be an error in transcription.

[49] In the Arabic text, this list of adjectives has a poetic sequence: *ṣalʿâʾ*, *ʿanqâʾ*, *sawdâʾ*, *faqmâʾ*, *ḫarqâʾ* and *shawhâʾ*. Ibn Namâ, Ibn Shahrâshûb and al-Shablanğî omit all but the last two.

[50] According to Lane, a 'gathering', with specific reference to nobles, chiefs or principle persons. Cf. LANE E.W., *An Arabic-English Lexicon*, vol. VII, 1968: 2792. Al-Shablanğî omits this phrase.

[51] Most of this phrase is omitted by al-Mufîd.

[52] al-Ḫawârizmî: "Truly, the affliction of the Afterlife is worse and viler…"

[53] That is, of the arrival of the Afterlife with its concomitant reward or punishment.

[54] I have followed al-Mufîd, al-Ṭabarsî, al-Ḫawârizmî and Ibn Ṭâʾûs in their *lâ yaḥfizu-hu al-bidâr* ("haste does not induce Him"). Ibn Shahrâshûb and al-Shablanğî both employ the verb *ḥaqara* ('to scorn, disdain') while Ibn Namâ uses instead the verb *ḥafara* ('to watch over, protect' or, alternatively, 'to be shy, diffident, bashful'). Ibn Namâ also uses *al-badra*, while the other texts employ *al-bidâr* ('haste').

> does He fear that vengeance[55] will slip by. "*Lo! thy Lord is ever watchful*".'[56]
>
> The transmitter said: By God, truly, I saw the people that day, bewildered, weeping, putting their hands over their mouths. I saw an old man standing at my side, weeping until his beard was soaked. He said: 'May my parents be ransomed for you! Your elders are the best of elders, your youth the best of youth, and your women the best of women. They will be neither disgraced nor overcome.'"

While al-Ṭabarsî and al-Ḫawârizmî list three accusations made by Zaynab again the people of Kûfa – 'deception' (*al-ḫatl*, which he clarifies as *ḫidâʿ*), 'treachery' (*al-ġadr*) and 'desertion' (*al-ḫadl*)[57] – Ibn Shahrâshûb records five: they have committed 'betrayal' (*al-ḫatr*), 'treachery' (*al-ġadr*), 'deception' (*al-ḫatl*), 'desertion' (*al-ḫadl*) and 'cunning' (*al-makr*).[58] Ibn Ṭâʾûs maintains only 'deception' (*al-ḫatl*) and 'treachery' (*al-ġadr*) (as, therefore, does al-Maǧlisî transmitting from him) while al-Mufîd, Ibn Namâ and al-Shablanǧî catalogue only deception' (*al-ḫatl*) and 'desertion' (*al-ḫadl*).[59]

Later in the text, al-Mufîd and Ibn Ṭâʾûs list a further three indictments – 'conceit' (*al-ṣalaf*), 'being stained with vices or crimes'

---

55 Mistaken transcription in al-Ḫawârizmî, which should read *ṯaʾr*. The editor of *Muṯîr al-aḥzân* notes that some transmitters render this as *al-nâr* (the Fire). As in in al-Ḫawârizmî, Ibn Namâ's text reads *al-ṯâr* instead of *al-ṯaʾr* ('vengeance').

56 Q. 89: 14. Al-Ḫawârizmî adds here a curious phrase "and they awaited the first of *al-Naḥl* and the last of *Ṣâd*", meaning the first verse of *sûrat a-Naḥl*, "*The commandment of Allah will come to pass, so seek not ye to hasten it. Glorified and Exalted be He above all that they associate (with Him)*" (Q. 16: 1) and the last verse of *sûrat Ṣâd*, "*And ye will come in time to know the truth thereof*" Q. 38: 88.

57 al-Ṭabarsî., *Kitâb al-iḥtiǧâǧ ʿalâ ahl al-liǧâǧ*, vol. II: 304, al-Ḫawârizmî., *Maqtal al-Ḥusayn*, bk. 2, bb. *fî maqtal al-Ḥusayn*: 46.

58 Ibn Shahrâshûb., *Manâqib âl Abî Ṭâlib*, vol. X, bb. *fî maqtali-hi*: 378.

59 al-Mufîd., *al-Amâlî li-l-Mufîd*, *maǧlis* 38: 321, Ibn Namâ al-Ḥillî., *Muṯîr al-aḥzân wa munîr subul al-ashǧân*, Part 3: 86, al-Shablanǧî., *Nûr al-abṣâr fî manâqib âl bayt al-nabî al-muḫtâr*: 203

(*al-naṭaf*) and 'the hating heart' (*al-ṣadr al-shanaf*).[60] Al-Ṭabarsî and Ibn Shahrâshûb list four: 'conceit' (*al-ṣalaf*), 'vanity' (*al-ʿuǧb*), 'enmity' (*al-shanaf*) and 'deceit' (*al-kiḏb*).[61] Al-Ḫawârizmî also lists four, but different: 'conceit', 'intrinsically corrupt' (*al-ṭanaf* or *al-ṭanif*), 'hatred' and 'being stained with vices or crimes'. An editor's footnote defines the first as 'insolence', the second as 'a rottenness of morals', the third as 'enmity' and the fourth as 'impurity'.[62] Al-Shablanǧî lists 'conceit', *al-ṣanaf*, which may be a mistaken transcription of 'intrinsically corrupt' (*al-ṭanaf* or *al-ṭanif*) and 'the disease of the hating heart' (*dâʾ al-ṣadr al-shanaf*).[63] Al-Maǧlisî, transmitting from Ibn Ṭâʾûs, omits 'the hating heart', maintaining only 'conceit' and 'being stained with vices or crimes'.[64] Ibn Namâ lists 'conceit' and 'being stained with vices or crimes', adding 'the ignominy of the hating servant' (*ḏull al-ʿabd al-shanaf*).[65]

In spite of the severity of these charges, they pale in comparison to Zaynab's devastating quotation from Q. 19: 89–90; the verse is omitted by Ibn Ṭâʾûs and Ibn Namâ, but carried by al-Mufîd, al-Ṭûsî, al-Ṭabarsî, al-Ḫawârizmî and Ibn Shahrâshûb. The context of Q. 19: 89–90 is the accusation of ascribing to God a son:

> "*And they say: The Beneficent hath taken unto Himself a son. Assuredly ye utter a disastrous thing whereby almost the heavens are torn, and the earth is split asunder and the mountains fall in ruins, that ye ascribe unto the Beneficent a son, when it is not meet for (the Majesty of) the Beneficent that He should choose a son*" (Q. 19: 88–92).

---

60 al-Mufîd., *al-Amâlî li-l-Mufîd*, *maǧlis* 38: 322, Ibn Ṭâʾûs., *Kitâb al-luhûf fî qatlâ al-ṭufûf*: 87

61 al-Ṭabarsî., *Kitâb al-iḥtiǧâǧ ʿalâ ahl al-liǧâǧ*, vol. II: 304, Ibn Shahrâshûb., *Manâqib âl Abî Ṭâlib*, vol. IV, bb. *fî maqtali-hi*: 115.

62 al-Ḫawârizmî., *Maqtal al-Ḥusayn*, bk. 2, bb. *fî maqtal al-Ḥusayn*: 46. Cf. STEINGASS F., *Learner's Arabic English Dictionary*, 1993: 1128.

63 al-Shablanǧî., *Nûr al-abṣâr fî manâqib âl bayt al-nabî al-muḫtâr*: 203.

64 al-Maǧlisî., *Biḥâr al-anwâr*, vol. XLV, bb. 39, n. 1: 109.

65 Ibn Namâ al-Ḥillî., *Muṯîr al-aḥzân wa munîr subul al-ashǧân*, Part 3: 86.

The implicit suggestion is that Zaynab regards the murder of al-Ḥusayn as being on the same level as the sin of *shirk*, the ascribing of a partner to God, described by Q. 4: 48 as unforgivable. While the possibility of forgiveness for al-Ḥusayn's killers remains a debated question, on the Day of Judgment Fâṭima will stand before God holding in her hand the bloodied shirt of her son and demand that his killers be punished.[66]

One could understand that between them, the texts propose a Zaynabian theology, that is, a number of 'beautiful names' or theological titles for al-Ḥusayn articulated by his sister as she paints a portrait of him. He is 'the scion of the seal of the prophethood' (*salîl ḫâtim al-nubuwwa*),[67] 'the treasure trove of the message' (*maʿdin al-risâla*),[68] 'the leader of the youths of the people of paradise' (*sayyid shabâb ahl al-ğanna*),[69] 'the shelter for your confusion' (*malâḏ ḥayrati-kum*)[70] or of 'your good deed' (*malâḏ ḫayrati-kum*),[71] 'the shelter for your warfare' (*malâḏ ḥarbi-kum*),[72] 'the refuge of your party' (*maʿâḏ*

---

66 CLOHESSY C., *Fatima, Daughter of Muhammad*, 2009: 176–178.

67 In al-Ṭabarsî, al-Ḫawârizmî, Ibn Ṭâʾûs, Ibn Namâ, al-Mağlisî and al-Shablanğî. Al-Mufîd transcribes *al-risâla* rather than *al-nubuwwa*.

68 In al-Ṭabarsî, Ibn Ṭâʾûs, Ibn Namâ and al-Shablanğî.

69 In al-Mufîd, al-Ṭabarsî, al-Ḫawârizmî, Ibn Ṭâʾûs, Ibn Namâ, al-Mağlisî and al-Shablanğî. In a well-known *ḥadîṯ* carried both by Sunnî and Shîʿî transmitters, al-Ḥasan and al-Ḥusayn, the two sons of ʿAlî and Fâṭima, are named by Muḥammad as 'the leaders of the youths of paradise' (*sayyidâ shabâb al-ğanna*). Cf. for e.g. Ibn Ḥanbal., *Musnad*, vol. IX, *Ḥadîṯ Ḥuḏîfa*, n. 23389: 91, Ibn Mâğa., *Sunan*, vol. I, *al-Muqaddima*, bb. 11 (*Faḍâʾil aṣḥâb rasûl Allâh, Faḍl ʿAlî b. Abî Ṭâlib*), n. 118: 44, al-Tirmiḏî., *Sunan*, vol. IX, bk. 50 (*Kitâb al-manâqib*), bb. *manâqib al-Ḥasan wa-l-Ḥusayn*, n. 3771: 331, al-Ṭabarî., *Kitâb aḫbâr al-rusul wa-l-mulûk*, vol. V: 168, al-Ḫawârizmî., *Maqtal al-Ḥusayn*, bk. 1, bb. *faḍâʾil Fâṭima al-Zahrâʾ bt. rasûl Allâh*, n. 42: 108–109, n. 66: 125, Ibn ʿAsâkir., *Taʾrîḫ madînat Dimashq*, vol. XIV, bb. 1566 (*al-Ḥusayn b. ʿAlî b. Abî Ṭâlib b. ʿAbd al-Muṭṭalib b. Hâshim b. ʿAbd al-Manâf*): 130, 132, al-Shablanğî., *Nûr al-abṣâr fî manâqib âl bayt al-nabî al-muḫtâr*: 43.

70 In Ibn Ṭâʾûs.

71 In al-Mufîd, al-Ḫawârizmî and al-Mağlisî.

72 In al-Ṭabarsî.

ḥizbi-kum),[73] 'the abode of your peace' (*maqarr silmi-kum*),[74] 'the sorrow of your speech' (*âsî kalimi-kum*),[75] 'the refuge for your calamity' (*mafza*ʿ *nâzilati-kum*),[76] 'the minaret of your proof' (*manâr ḥuğğati-kum*),[77] 'the spokesman of your *sunna*' (*midrah sunnati-kum*),[78] 'the spokesman of your tongues' (*midrah alsinati-kum*),[79] 'the minaret of your destination' (*manâr maḥağğati-kum*),[80] 'the spokesman of your arguments' (*midrah ḥuğaği-kum*)[81] and 'the one to whom to turn in your struggle' (*al-marğa*ʿ *ilay-hi* ʿ*ind muqâtalati-kum*).[82] While a number of these appellations are unique to al-Ṭabarsî, and some could even represent transcription errors rather than actual names, they nonetheless fashion an image of al-Ḥusayn in popular piety.

Ibn Namâ's transmission is missing a number of words from the end of the sermon,[83] while Ibn Shahrâshûb[84] too offers a slightly altered text, omitting a number of lines:

> Until her speech ultimately reached her statement: "Is it not an evil that you have sent ahead for yourselves, an evil that you have taken upon yourselves) to the day of your resurrection, and wretchedness, wretchedness, and degeneracy, degeneracy! The course has already failed, the hands have perished, the deal

[73] In al-Ṭabarsî.

[74] In al-Ṭabarsî.

[75] In al-Ṭabarsî.

[76] In al-Mufîd, al-Ṭabarsî, al-Ḫawârizmî, Ibn Ṭâʾûs and al-Mağlisî.

[77] In al-Mufîd (who reads *madrağa*), al-Ḫawârizmî, Ibn Ṭâʾûs, Ibn Namâ (who reads *midrah* rather than *manâr*) and al-Mağlisî.

[78] In Ibn Ṭâʾûs and al-Mağlisî.

[79] In al-Ḫawârizmî.

[80] In al-Ṭabarsî, Ibn Namâ and al-Shablanğî. Al-Mufîd transcribes *amâra* ('sign', 'token', 'mark') rather than *manâr*.

[81] In al-Ṭabarsî. Al-Mufîd transcribes *madraga* ('course', 'way', 'road').

[82] In al-Ṭabarsî.

[83] Ibn Namâ al-Ḥillî., *Muṯîr al-aḥzân wa munîr subul al-ashğân*, Part 3: 86.

[84] Ibn Shahrâshûb., *Manâqib âl Abî Ṭâlib*, vol. IV, bb. *fî maqtali-hi*: 115. Cf. al-Mufîd's *al-Amâlî li-l-Mufîd*, al-Ṭûsî's *al-Amâlî fî al-ḥadîṯ*, al-Ṭabarṣî's *Kitâb al-iḥtiğâğ* ʿ*alâ ahl al-liğâğ* and al-Ḫawârizmî's *Maqtal al-Ḥusayn*.

> is forfeited, you have been contaminated with anger from God! Vileness and avarice have struck you. Are you aware, alas for you, which side of Muḥammad you have split lengthwise? And which commitment have you violated? And which precious thing of his you have exposed, and which blood of his you have shed? "*Assuredly ye utter a disastrous thing, Whereby almost the heavens are torn, and the earth is split asunder and the mountains fall in ruins*".[85] You have come with them, misshapen, clumsy, sufficient for the filling earth and heaven. Were you astonished that the heavens rain blood? Truly, the affliction of the Afterlife will suffice, and they will not be helped. Do not let leisure excite you to levity, for haste does not disdain Him, mighty and lofty, nor does He fear that vengeance will slip by. No indeed, "*Lo! thy Lord is ever watchful*" over us and over them."[86]

Al-Ṭabarsî records ʿAlî b. al-Ḥusayn telling his aunt to quieten down after the sermon, saying to her: "Among those remaining, there is esteem in respect to those who have passed away. You, by the praise of God, are erudite without a teacher, discerning without instruction. Weeping and yearning do not bring back what destiny has caused to pass away."[87]

These are not the only words Zaynab will speak in front of the people of Kûfa. Al-Mağlisî[88] reports that at a particular moment, ostensibly after the public protest but before the appearance before Ibn Ziyâd, the heads of the murdered men are brought into view, and Zaynab, in her carriage, catches sight of al-Ḥusayn's head which seems to her 'radiant, moonlike…a rising moon' (*zuhrî*

---

[85] Q. 19: 89–90.

[86] A paraphrase of Q. 89: 14.

[87] al-Ṭabarsî., *Kitâb al-iḥtiğâğ ʿalâ ahl al-liğâğ*, vol. II: 305, al-Mağlisî., *Biḥâr al-anwâr*, vol. XLV, bb. 39: 164. Cf. SHAHIN B., *Lady Zaynab*, 2002: 65. Al-Mufîd's editor notes this, but it is not included in al-Mufîd's narration: cf. al-Mufîd., *al-Amâlî li-l-Mufîd*, *mağlis* 38: 323.

[88] al-Mağlisî., *Biḥâr al-anwâr*, vol. XLV, bb. 39, n. 1: 115. Cf. also al-Ğazâʾirî., *Riyâḍ al-abrâr fî manâqib al-aʾimma al-aṭhâr*, vol. I: 342, al-Baḥrânî., *ʿAwâlim al-ʿulûm wa-l-maʿârif al-aḥwâl min al-âyât wa-l-aḫbâr wal-aqwâl*, vol. II, bb. 15: 975, vol. XVII: 373.

qamarî...qamar tâliʿ). She strikes her head against the front side of the carriage, causing blood to follow, and gestures with a piece of rug at her brother's head, saying:

> "O new moon, when it is complete, perfect
> Its cloud snatches it unawares
> And setting, it is revealed!
> I never imagined, O half of my heart
> That this was foreordained, written.
> My brother! Fâṭima *al-saġîra*; talk to her!
> Her heart is on the point of melting!
> My brother, your heart was affectionate to us
> What is wrong with it, stern and become hard?
> My brother, were you to see ʿAlî among the captives, with the orphans!
> He cannot bear what is imposed!
> Whenever he is hurt with beating, he calls out to you in degradation,
> dwindling away, from tears poured out.
> My brother, embrace him to yourself and bring him close!
> Calm his frightened heart!
> What an abasement for an orphan, that calling upon his father
> He finds in him no answer."

This lament is carried by no major transmitter, and al-Maġlisî gives few clues as to where he found it.

2. ʿUBAYD ALLÂH B. ZIYÂD

If indeed Zaynab functions as an archetype of defiant resistance against injustice in its manifold forms, it is in the moment she steps into the presence of ʿUbayd Allâh b. Ziyâd that this role becomes incontestable. A man close to thirty years of age at the time of Karbalâʾ, Ibn Ziyâd would die a matter of six or seven years after his encounter with this daughter of ʿAlî. Standing before him, she would not only competently defend her father and her brother but would save the life of ʿAlî b. al-Ḥusayn, throwing herself over him in a maternal embrace. It would be her words, together with this dauntless action, that would be pivotal in preserving both the truth about Karbalâʾ and the future of the Imamate. The account of the Zaynab-Ibn Ziyâd confrontation is carried by numerous Sunnî and Shîʿî transmitters,[89] but al-Ṭabarî serves as our base text for the chronology of events, since his history preserves much of the verbal skirmish. Al-Ṭabarî presents a drama that unfolds in a number of acts.

In the first, the heads of the slain and the survivors are brought before Ibn Ziyâd. It is not entirely apparent in al-Ṭabarî's account whether they were all brought before him together, or whether the head of al-Ḥusayn was already in Ibn Ziyâd's palace when the women and children were led in. This latter possibility is Ibn Ṭâʾûs' reading of it.[90] According to al-Ṭabarî, the head was despatched to Ibn Ziyâd immediately after the battle; by all accounts it arrived on the night of ʿÂshûrâ, but since the palace gates were locked, it remained overnight with the luckless Ḫawalî b. Yazîd as-Aṣbaḥî (whose wife, appalled that her returning warrior husband had brought not silver or gold, but the head of the Prophet's grandson, banished him from the marriage bed) and was only

---

[89] al-Balâḏurî., *Kitâb ansâb al-ashrâf*, vol. III: 412 (in a much less detailed narrative than the other transmitters), HOWARD I.K.A., (trans.), *The History of al-Ṭabarî*, vol. XIX, 1990: 165–167, al-Ṣadûq., *Kitâb al-amâlî fî-l-aḥâdîṯ wa-l-aḫbâr*, *mağlis* 31: 165, al-Mufîd., *al-Irshâd fî maʿrifat ḥuğağ Allâh ʿalâ al-ʿibâd*, vol. II, bb. *mâ ğarâ fî-l-Kûfa baʿda qatli Imâm al-Ḥusayn*: 115, al-Fattâl al-Nîsâbûrî., *Rawḍat al-wâʿiẓîn wa-tabṣirat al-muttaʿiẓîn*, vol. I: 190, al-Ṭabarsî., *Iʿlâm al-warâ bi-aʿlâm al-hudâ*: 252, al-Ḫawârizmî., *Maqtal al-Ḥusayn*, bk. 2, bb. *fî maqtal al-Ḥusayn*: 47–48, Ibn ʿAsâkir., *Târîḫ madînat Dimashq*, vol. XLI, bb. 4875 (*ʿAlî b. al-Husayn b. ʿAlî b. Abî Ṭâlib b. Hâshim b. ʿAbd al-Manâf*): 367, Ibn Aṯîr., *al-Kâmil fî al-târîḫ*, vol. II: 434–5, Ibn Ṭâʾûs., *Kitâb al-luhûf fî qatlâ al-ṭufûf*: 93–95, Ibn Namâ al-Ḥillî., *Muṯîr al-aḥẓân wa munîr subul al-ashğân*, Part 3: 90–91, al-Irbilî., *Kashf al-ğumma fî maʿrifat al-aʾimma*, vol. II: 64, Ibn Kaṯîr, *al-Bidâya wa-l-nihâya*, vol. XII: 560, al-ʿAsqalânî., *Tahḏîb al-tahḏîb*, vol II, (*Ḥusayn b. ʿAlî b. Abî Ṭâlib*): 323, al-ʿIṣâmî., *Simṭ al-nuğûm al-ʿawâlî*, vol. III: 58–87, al-Mağlisî., *Biḥâr al-anwâr*, vol. XLV, bb. 39: 116, n. 3: 154, al-ʿÂmilî., *Aʿyân al-Shîʿa*, vol. VII: 138–139.

[90] Ibn Ṭâʾûs., *Kitâb al-luhûf fî qatlâ al-ṭufûf*: 93.

the next day brought to Ibn Ziyâd.[91] It is unlikely that the survivors would have arrived before or even simultaneously with heads. Al-Ṭabarî, transmitting from Abû Miẖnaf, notes that the head of al-Ḥusayn[92] was brought, together with his children, sisters and womenfolk, to Ibn Ziyâd.[93] Ibn Ṭâ'ûs, on the other hand, writes that Ibn Ziyâd was seated in his palace for a public meeting; the head of al-Ḥusayn was placed before him, and al-Ḥusayn's women and children were ushered into his presence.[94] Whether it was brought with them, or whether it was already there, it would have been a gruesome spectacle; the caliph Yazîd b. Muʿâwiya would prove more amenable to protecting the children from such a sight than would his governor Ibn Ziyâd.

The second act begins with Zaynab, disguised in shabby clothes, sitting among her maids. Three times Ibn Ziyâd will demand to know who she is and will receive no answer. Al-Ṭabarî intimates that he noticed her because she sat down in his presence ("who is that woman who is sitting down?" he asks).[95] Al-Ḫawârizmî's text suggests the same, although a little more provocatively; Zaynab comes in, throws a look towards Ibn Ziyâd, and then sits.[96] He responds by demanding to know who the seated woman is. Others adduce that it was because she had segregated herself and her maidservants from everyone else.[97] It is not always easy to tell whether Ibn Ziyâd directs his questions to her expressly,

---

91 Cf. for e.g. al-Balâḏurî., *Kitâb ansâb al-ashrâf*, vol. III: 411.

92 Despatched from Karbalâ' with Ḫawalî b. Yazîd as-Aṣbaḥî and Ḥumayd b. Muslim al-Azdî to Ibn Ziyâd and left for the night under a washtub in his house by Ḫawalî (having found the palace door locked).

93 HOWARD I.K.A., (trans.), *The History of al-Ṭabarî*, vol. XIX, 1990: 165.

94 Ibn Ṭâ'ûs., *Kitâb al-luhûf fî qatlâ al-ṭufûf*: 93.

95 HOWARD I.K.A., (trans.), *The History of al-Ṭabarî*, vol. XIX, 1990: 165.

96 al-Ḫawârizmî., *Maqtal al-Ḥusayn*, bk. 2, bb. *fî maqtal al-Ḥusayn*: 47.

97 Cf. for e.g. al-Mufîd., *al-Irshâd fî maʿrifat ḥuǧaǧ Allâh ʿalâ al-ʿibâd*, vol. II, bb. *mâ ǧarâ fî-l-Kûfa baʿda qatli Imâm al-Ḥusayn*: 115, al-Ṭabarsî., *Iʿlâm al-warâ bi-aʿlâm al-hudâ*: 252, al-Irbilî., *Kashf al-ġumma fî maʿrifat al-a'imma*, vol. II: 64.

or merely asks about her; in some of the texts, like al-Ṭabarî, we are told quite distinctly that Zaynab did not respond to him, and nor did anyone else. Finally, a maid will tell him that this is Zaynab daughter of Fâṭima. In almost all the texts, she is referred to more than once as 'the daughter of Fâṭima' rather than 'the daughter of ʿAlî'. In an earlier encounter, before the arrival of the women and children, when Zayd b. Arqam had challenged Ibn Ziyâd for poking at al-Ḥusayn's teeth with his staff, al-Ḥusayn too is referred to as 'the son of Fâṭima'. In itself, this suggests something evocative and powerful about the status of the daughter of Muḥammad, and the influence of her memory; more so, it is a considered and brazen provocation of the dictator, as the unidentified maid indelicately reminds him whose grandchildren he is ill-treating, clearly linking this badly-dressed prisoner with God's Messenger and his daughter.

Although al-Ṣadûq omits the details of a disguise in dirty clothes and the questions of the governor, al-Mufîd and those like al-Ṭabarsî and al-Irbilî who transmit from him, fill out the picture. The survivors are brought into the presence of Ibn Ziyâd; Zaynab, named as 'the sister of al-Ḥusayn' enters as part of the group, but in disguise, wearing the worst of her robes, and proceeds to sit on the side of the palace hall, surrounded by her handmaids. Ibn Ziyâd asks who this is, who has segregated herself on the side with her women, but Zaynab makes no answer. A second and third time he asks about her, and one of her handmaids informs him that this is Zaynab, now named as 'daughter of Fâṭima', daughter of the Messenger of God. The conversation, which we will examine shortly, now proceeds almost exactly as recorded by al-Ṣadûq and numerous other transmitters.[98]

---

[98] HOWARD I.K.A., (trans.), *The History of al-Ṭabarî*, vol. XIX, 1990: 165, al-Mufîd., *al-Irshâd fî maʿrifat ḥuǧaǧ Allâh ʿalâ al-ʿibâd*, vol. II, bb. *mâ ǧarâ fî-l-Kûfa baʿda qatli Imâm al-Ḥusayn*: 115, al-Ṭabarsî., *Iʿlâm al-warâ bi-aʿlâm al-hudâ*: 252, Ibn Aṯîr., *al-Kâmil fî al-târîḫ*, vol. II: 435, al-Irbilî., *Kashf al-ġumma fî maʿrifat al-aʾimma*, vol. II: 64, al-ʿIṣâmî., *Simṭ al-nuǧûm al-ʿawâlî*, vol. III: 72 (who does not relay the conversation in detail), Ibn Kaṯîr., *al-Bidâya wa-l-nihâya*, vol. XII: 560. Ibn Kaṯîr does not make any mention of Zaynab before Ibn Ziyâd in his main text, but in a long footnote records how she enters before him disguised in her vilest robe and surrounded by

Ibn Ṭâ'ûs, followed closely by Ibn Namâ (although a substantial amount of the detail provided by Ibn Ṭâ'ûs is missing from his account) transmits that Zaynab sits disguised, and asking about her, Ibn Ziyâd is informed that this is Zaynab, daughter of ʿAlî (in Ibn Namâ, 'daughter of ʿAlî b. Abî Ṭâlib'). All our other texts have named her as the daughter of her mother Fâṭima. Ibn Namâ omits Ibn Ṭâ'ûs' details about Ibn Ziyâd being in his palace, noting that Zaynab appears before Ibn Ziyâd disguised in her 'vilest dress', and that three times Ibn Ziyâd asks who she is. Ibn Namâ reports that she refuses to speak, suggesting the possibility that the questions are addressed directly to her, rather than merely about her. Eventually, someone whose rank or status is not identified, tells him that she is Zaynab, daughter of ʿAlî b. Abî Ṭâlib.[99]

In his 'Reliving Karbala', Syed Akbar Hyder recounts a sermon he heard preached in Damascus in 1996 by Rashid Turabi, in which the preacher reshaped this moment, placing it in the court of Yazîd rather than that of Ibn Ziyâd, and putting a fiesty response onto the lips of Zaynab:

> Among the captives, Yazid noticed a woman, encircled by other women, whose very demeanor signified defiance. Yazid lashed out, asking, "Who is this arrogant woman?" A surreal silence enveloped the court. The defiant woman rose to respond to this question, and made her way through the women who surrounded her. Finally, face to face with Yazid, she retorted: "Why are you asking them [the women]? Ask me. I'll tell you [who I am] I am Muhammad's granddaughter. I am Fatima's daughter. Ask me, Yazid."[100]

The third act of the drama then begins, initiated by Ibn Ziyâd's first verbal encounter with Zaynab; he commences with the words 'praise to be God', as does Zaynab in her rebuttal. He asks his

---

her maids. He asks after her but no one replies, until finally one of her maids says: "That is Zaynab, daughter of Fâṭima."

[99] Ibn Ṭâ'ûs., *Kitâb al-luhûf fî qatlâ al-ṭufûf*: 93–94, Ibn Namâ al-Ḥillî., *Muṯîr al-aḥzân wa munîr subul al-ashğân*, Part 3: 90–91.

[100] HYDER S.A., *Reliving Karbala. Martyrdom in South Asian Memory*, Oxford University Press, Oxford 2006: 97.

goading question, 'how do you see things now?' to which Zaynab makes her magnificent reply, diversely recorded in the texts, but which greatly affronts Ibn Ziyâd. Al-Ṣadûq's transmission of the dialogue reads:[101]

> Zaynab, the daughter of ʿAlî was among them, and Ibn Ziyâd said: "Praise be to God, who has disgraced you, and killed you, and given the lie to your fables."[102] Zaynab replied: "Praise be to God, who has honoured us with Muḥammad and has cleansed us[103] "*with a thorough cleansing*".[104] Instead, God disgraces the dissolute[105] and gives the lie to the deviant."[106] (Ibn Ziyâd) answered: "How do you see what God has done with

---

[101] al-Ṣadûq., *Kitâb al-amâlî fî-l-aḥâdîṯ wa-l-aḫbâr, maǧlis* 31: 165.

[102] al-Ṣadûq and al-Fattâl al-Nîsâbûrî use the word *aḥâdîṯ*, which includes a range of meanings such as 'speech', 'telling lies or fables', 'gossip' or 'tale', and can carry the sense of an 'innovation' or 'invention'. The other transmitters employ *uḥdûṯa*, which carries the same range of meaning; it can signify 'a wonderful thing told or narrated', with some insisting that it refers specifically to a story in which there is no profit. Cf. LANE E.W., *An Arabic-English Lexicon*, vol. II, 1968: 529.

[103] Here, al-Mufîd, as well as those transmitting from him (al-Ṭabarsî and al-Irbilî) adds "from filth" (*al-riǧs*).

[104] Cf. Q. 33: 33.

[105] *Fâsiq* (pl. *fussâq*, *fasaqa*) from the verb *fasaqa-yafsuqu* or *yafsiqu*, meaning 'to stray from the right course, to stray, deviate, to act unlawfully, sinfully, immorally, to lead a dissolute life'. The primary meaning is 'to go forth from another thing in a bad or corrupt manner'. Cf. LANE E.W., *An Arabic-English Lexicon*, 1997, vol. VI: 2398.

[106] *Fâǧir* (pl. *fuǧǧâr* or *faǧara*), from the verb *faǧara-yafǧuru*, the primary meaning of which is 'to cleave, dig up, break up (ground), cut, divide, break open'. It also means 'to incline, decline, lean, deviate, to err or lie, to commit a foul deed, an unlawful action, to act immorally, unrighteously, wickedly or sinfully, to transgress, to quit or depart from the way of truth or the right road'. Cf. LANE E.W., *An Arabic-English Lexicon*, 1997, vol. VI: 2340. Here, al-Mufîd and Ibn Namâ add "and he is other than us, praise be to God"; cf. al-Mufîd., *al-Irshâd fî maʿrifat ḥuǧaǧ Allâh ʿalâ al-ʿibâd*, vol. II, bb. *mâ ǧarâ fî-l-Kûfa baʿda qatli Imâm al-Ḥusayn*: 115, Ibn Namâ al-Ḥillî., *Muṯîr al-aḥzân wa munîr subul al-ashǧân*, Part 3: 90–91.

> you, people of the house?"[107] She replied: "To be killed was prescribed for them and they have gone forth to the places where they were to lie.[108] God will bring you and them together[109] and you will summon one another before Him."[110]

There are a number of textual issues that bear a closer look. Zaynab's quote of Q. 33: 33 ("*Allah's wish is but to remove uncleanness far from you, O Folk of the Household, and cleanse you with a thorough cleansing*") firmly roots the victims of Karbalâʾ, both those killed and the surviving prisoners, into this crucial verse about Muḥammad's family. It is, like the titles of al-Ḥusayn and Zaynab as 'son' and 'daughter' of Fâṭima, a stark reminder to Ibn Ziyâd of who he is maltreating; those of whom Muḥammad spoke when, at the moment Q. 33: 33 was revealed, he wrapped ʿAlî, Fâṭima, al-Ḥasan and al-Ḥusayn in a cloak and and prayed: "O God! These are the members of my Household, so purify them of all uncleanness."[111]

---

[107] al-Mufîd reads "what God has done to the people of your house."

[108] A slightly paraphrased Q. 3: 154 ("*those appointed to be slain would have gone forth to the places where they were to lie*").

[109] al-Ṭabarsî, transmitting from the al-Mufîd narrative, adds: "on the Day of Resurrection." Cf. al-Ṭabarsî., *Iʿlâm al-warâ bi-aʿlâm al-hudâ*: 252.

[110] al-Mufîd reads "you will plead excuses with Him and contend before Him"; cf. al-Mufîd., *al-Irshâd fî maʿrifat ḥuǧaǧ Allâh ʿalâ al-ʿibâd*, vol. II, bb. *mâ ǧarâ fî-l-Kûfa baʿda qatli Imâm al-Ḥusayn*: 115. Additionally, in Sibṭ al-Ǧawzî in a truncated form; cf. Sibṭ al-Ǧawzî., *Taḏkirat ḫawâṣṣ al-umma bi-ḏikr ḫaṣâʾiṣ al-aʾimma*: 218.

[111] Cf. Ibn Ḥanbal., *Musnad*, vol. I, *Musnad ʿAbd Allâh b. al-ʿAbbâs b. ʿAbd al-Muṭṭalib*, n. 3062: 708–709, vol. VI, *Ḥadîṯ Wâṯala b. al-ʿAsqaʿ*, n. 16985: XLV, vol. X, *Ḥadîṯ Umm Salama*, n. 26570: 177, n. 26612: 186–187, n. 26659: 197, n. 26808: 228. Cf. also al-Ṭabarî., *Ǧâmiʿ al-bayân ʿan taʾwîl al-qurʾân*, vol. XXII, Part 22, *sûrat al-Aḥzâb*, v. 33: 6–7. Cf. also al-Suyûṭî., *al-Durr al-manṯûr fî al-tafsîr bi-l-maʾṯûr*, vol. V, *sûrat al-Aḥzâb*, v. 33: 376. Cf. also Ibn al-Aṯîr., *Usd al-ġâba fî maʿrifat al-ṣaḥâba*, vol. V, bb. *ḥarf al-fâʾ*: 521–522.

A further point of note is the use by some transmitters of verbs in different voices; in al-Mufîd (and al-Ṭabarsî and al-Irbilî from him), Ibn Ṭâ'ûs (and al-Mağlisî from him) and Ibn Namâ, these verbs are in the passive: "the dissolute is disgraced, and the lie is given to the deviant." In al-Ṭabarî and al-Ṣadûq, it is more clearly God Himself who digraces the dissolute and gives the lie to the deviant.

Of further interest is that al-Ṭabarî, al-Mufîd, al-Ṭabarsî, Ibn al-Aṯîr, Ibn Namâ, Ibn Kaṯîr and al-Irbilî read, "how do you judge what God has done to the people of your house", while al-Ḫawârizmî, Ibn Ṭâ'ûs and al-Mağlisî transmitting from him read "what God has done to your brother and to the people of your house?" Al-Ṣadûq and al-Fattâl al-Nîsâbûrî rephrase the question: "what God has done to you (pl.), people of the house?" Although the possibilty exists that Ibn Ziyâd is, at this moment, asking the question of the whole group of survivors, the context suggests that ostensibly it is addressed to Zaynab alone. The implication is that at this moment, she encompasses within her person and in some sense carries the whole of the *ahl al-bayt.* Only three of our major transmitters record the famous answer of Zaynab, which has been deeply woven into popular piety and the retelling of the events: "I see nothing but beauty!"[112]

Finally, there is the issue of the eventual outcome, since each transmitter presents one or more consequences on the Day of Judgment. Al-Ṭabarî, al-Mufîd, al-Ṭabarsî, al-Ḫawârizmî and al-Irbilî all read "you (pl.) will dispute" with God (*tuḥâğğûna*), while al-Mufîd, al-Ṭabarsî, al-Ḫawârizmî, Ibn al-Aṯîr and al-Irbilî have "you (pl.) will quarrel" (*taḫtaṣimûna* or *tuḫâṣimûna*). Al-Ṣadûq reads "you (pl.) will summon one another" (*tataḥâkamûna*) while al-Fattâl al-Nîsâbûrî reads "they will summon one another" (*yataḥâkamûna*). Only Ibn Ṭâ'ûs and Ibn Namâ keep the verbs in the singular, as referring to Ibn Ziyâd alone; "You will dispute and you will argue," read their texts, "but watch (that day) to whom belongs victory!

112 al-Ḫawârizmî., *Maqtal al-Ḥusayn*, bk. 2, bb. *fî maqtal al-Ḥusayn*: 47, Ibn Ṭâ'ûs., *Kitâb al-luhûf fî qatlâ al-ṭufûf*: 93, Ibn Namâ al-Ḥillî., *Muṯîr al-aḥzân wa munîr subul al-ashğân*, Part 3: 90. Cf. also al-ʿÂmilî., *Aʿyân al-Shîʿa*, vol. VII: 139.

Your mother will be bereaved of you, Ibn Marǧâna!"[113] This title, which is placed on someone's lips more than once during the Karbalâ᾿ event, is a not uncommon but damning reference, attributing him to his mother and thus recalling his apparent birth out of wedlock and, consequently, to a woman of loose morals.

It is of note that al-Fattâl al-Nîsâbûrî, transmitting from Imâm al-Bâqir[114] (who notes that he himself was present at these proceedings) and who follows al-Ṣadûq word for word, begins his narrative with a curious detail, found also in al-Ṣadûq and al-Iṣfahânî's *Maqâtil.* Ibn Ziyâd sends a message to Umm Kulṯûm, daughter of al-Ḥusayn, saying: "Praise be to God who has killed your men! How do you judge what God has done to you?" She replies: "Ibn Ziyâd, if indeed you are delighted by the killing of al-Ḥusayn, how often did his grandfather not delight in him, kissing him and kissing his lips and placing him on his shoulder! Ibn Ziyâd! Consider his grandfather (in) answering, for on a future day he will be your adversary!"[115] As already noted, it seems likely that if such a message had been sent, it would have been to Umm Kulṯûm, sister of Zaynab, rather than to the very young daughter of al-Ḥusayn.

The fourth act of this drama opens with the anger of Ibn Ziyâd to Zaynab's response; he is so enraged, some texts note, that

---

113 Cf. al-Ḫawârizmî., *Maqtal al-Ḥusayn*, bk. 2, bb. *fî maqtal al-Ḥusayn*: 47, Ibn Ṭâ᾿ûs., *Kitâb al-luhûf fî qatlâ al-ṭufûf*: 93, Ibn Namâ al-Ḥillî., *Muṯîr al-aḥzân wa munîr subul al-ashǧân*, Part 3: 90. Ibn Ziyâd would be referred to by this name more than once, by Zayd b. Arqam, by ʿAbd Allâh b. ʿAfîf al-Azdî al-Ġâmadî (a devout partisan of ʿAlî who heard Ibn Ziyâd refer to al-Ḥusayn as 'the liar and son of the liar') and by Yazîd himself. Cf. al-Balâḏurî., *Kitâb ansâb al-ashrâf*, vol. III: 413, HOWARD I.K.A., (trans.), *The History of al-Ṭabarî*, vol. XIX, 1990: 165, 167, 171. Sibṭ al-Ǧawzî has ʿAbd Allâh b. ʿAfîf al-Azdî turn on Ibn Ziyâd, saying: "No, Ibn Marǧâna, it is you and your father who are the liar and the son of the liar!" Cf. Sibṭ al-Ǧawzî., *Taḏkirat ḫawâṣṣ al-umma bi-ḏikr ḫaṣâ᾿iṣ al-a᾿imma*: 218.

114 al-Fattâl al-Nîsâbûrî., *Rawḍat al-wâʿiẓîn wa-tabṣirat al-muttaʿiẓîn*, vol. I: 190.

115 Ibn Namâ al-Ḥillî., *Muṯîr al-aḥzân wa munîr subul al-ashǧân*, Part 3: 90, al-Ṣadûq., *Kitâb al-amâlî fî-l-aḥâdîṯ wa-l-aḫbâr, maǧlis* 30: 164, al-Iṣfahânî., *Maqâtil al-ṭâlibîyyîn*, bb. *maqtal al-Ḥusayn*, n. 8 [414]: 469–470.

he 'had evil designs' (*hamma bi-hâ*) and ʿAmr b. Ḥurayṯ is forced to intervene and calm him down. ʿAmr b. Ḥurayṯ al-Maḫzûmî played an ambiguous role in the Karbalâʾ event. Both al-Ṭabarî and Ibn Saʿd claim he was chief of police, although Abû Miḫnaf names another, al-Ḥusayn b. Tamîm, in this postition. Whatever he was, it is difficult to imagine that ʿAmr should be particularly worried over the fate of Zaynab. Appointed by Ibn Ziyâd (after the arrival of al-Ḥusayn in Karbalâʾ) to manage the affairs of Kûfa, it was ʿAmr who played a substantial role in preventing people from joining al-Ḥusayn; he was, without doubt, responsible for a number of ʿAlid deaths, and would continue to play a significant role in Kûfa until his death in 78/697 or 85/704–5.[116] In the fifth volume of his *Kitâb aḫbâr al-rusul wa-l-mulûk*, al-Ṭabarî records the event:

> Ibn Ziyâd became angry and fumed with rage. ʿAmr b. Ḥurayṯ said to him: "May God prosper the governor! She is just a woman! Can a woman be censured for something in her logic? Really, do not censure her for words, or blame her for prattle!" Ibn Ziyâd said to her: "God has cured my soul from your tyrant and the seditious members of your family." Zaynab wept, and then she said: "By my life! You have killed my mature men, defamed[117] my family, cut my young branches to pieces and uprooted my lineage! If this cures you, then you are cured!" ʿUbayd Allâh said to her: 'By my life! This is bravery! Your father was brave, a poet!" She answered: "What has a woman to do with bravery? I am too distracted for bravery, but what I speak is my very soul."[118]

---

[116] Cf. HOWARD I.K.A., (trans.), *The History of al-Ṭabarî*, vol. XIX, 1990: 21, 53, Ibn Saʿd., *Kitâb al-ṭabaqât al-kabîr*, vol. VI: 14.

[117] Ibn al-Aṯîr's editor has a footnote to say that al-Ṭabarî's transmission reads 'you have defamed' (*abarta*) and that this is clearer than Ibn al-Aṯîr's reading, which is 'you have exposed' (*abrazta*). Probably, 'defamed' is a better translation that 'ruined', which is Howard's translation of *abarta.* Cf. LANE E.W., *An Arabic-English Lexicon*, 1968, vol. I: 5, Ibn al-Aṯîr., *al-Kâmil fî al-târîḫ*, vol. II: 435.

[118] al-Ṭabarî., *Kitâb aḫbâr al-rusul wa-l-mulûk*, vol. V: 457. In al-Mufîd's account: "but, my heart gives voice to what I say!"

Ibn Katîr, (in a long footnote), follows al-Ṭabarî exactly, but stops abruptly after the advice of ʿAmr b. Ḥurayṯ and does not continue the conversation.[119] Al-Ṣadûq, on the other hand, followed by al-Fattâl al-Nîsâbûrî, has a much shorter version. He notes, as does al-Ḫawârizmî,[120] that Ibn Ziyâd had evil designs on Zaynab, but omits entirely the words of ʿAmr b. Ḥurayṯ,[121] the malicious verbal assault by Ibn Ziyâd, the weeping of Zaynab and the discussion about bravery:

> Ibn Ziyâd, may God curse him, grew angry with her and planned to deal with her, but ʿAmr b. Ḥurayṯ calmed him, and Zaynab said: "O Ibn Ziyâd, are you satisfied with what you have perpetrated against us? You have killed our men, severed our lineage, made our sanctum public property, taken our women and our progeny captive. If this is the seeking of a cure, then you are cured!"[122]

Al-Mufîd follows al-Ṭabarî quite closely, except for one noticeable change in the response of Ibn Ziyâd to Zaynab; she answers his taunts articulately and with immense courage, and, according to Abû Miḫnaf, al-Mufîd, al-Ṭabarsî, al-Ḫawârizmî, Ibn Ṭâʾûs, Ibn Namâ and al-Irbilî, he responds in words that suggest a tempering of his anger or even a change of heart: "This is rhymed prose (*saǧǧâʿa*)! By my life, your father was one who spoke in rhymed prose (*saǧǧâʿ*), a poet (*shâʿir*)!" Al-Ṭabarî, Ibn al-Aṯîr and al-ʿIṣâmî record the words as: "This is courage (*shaǧâʿa*)! Your father was courageous, (*shuǧâʿ*) a poet (*shâʿir*). The editor of Abû Miḫnaf seems to suggest that perhaps al-Ṭabarî has recorded the words wrongly, and that the *saǧǧâʿa-saǧǧâʿ* reading is more appropriate and suitable in terms of context. In this case, the error in transcription has been handed down from one transmitter to the next.[123]

---

119 Ibn Kaṯîr., *al-Bidâya wa-l-nihâya*, vol. XII: 561.

120 al-Ṣadûq., *Kitâb al-amâlî fî-l-aḥâdîṯ wa-l-aḫbâr*, *maǧlis* 31: 165–166, al-Ḫawârizmî., *Maqtal al-Ḥusayn*, bk. 2, bb. *fî maqtal al-Ḥusayn*: 47.

121 As does Ibn al-Aṯîr: cf. Ibn al-Aṯîr., *al-Kâmil fî al-târîḫ*, vol. II: 435.

122 al-Ṣadûq., *Kitâb al-amâlî fî-l-aḥâdîṯ wa-l-aḫbâr*, *maǧlis* 31: 165.

123 Cf. LIMBA M., (trans.), *The Event of Taff, the Earliest Historical Account of the Tragedy of Karbala*, Ahlul Bayt Digital Islamic Library Project,

In the final act of this drama in the courts of Ibn Ziyâd, he turns his attention, abruptly, to the young ʿAlî b. al-Ḥusayn, until now a silent presence, symbolic of the quietude that will pervade his entire life; this moment perhaps marks the beginning of his rightful assumption of the Imamate after his father. Ibn Ziyâd expresses doubt over whether he has reached manhood and has him examined in a crude and invasive manner. When it is determined that he has indeed matured, Ibn Ziyâd orders him killed, and ʿAlî b. al-Ḥusayn persuasively challenges this sentence. He is, in these moments, strongly reminiscent of the Christian gospel figure of Jesus, silent before Pilate, physically and verbally abused but employing an economy of words.

There follows a curious interlude in two strands. In the first, Abû Miḫnaf, transmitting from al-Muğâlid b. Saʿîd al-Hamdânî,[124] says that Ibn Ziyâd looks at the young ʿAlî b. al-Ḥusayn and demands that one of his police officials check him (i.e. his genitals) to see if he has attained manhood; when his manhood is confirmed, his execution is ordered. ʿAlî b. al-Ḥusayn breaks his silence to respond with Qurʾânic quotes, further enraging Ibn Ziyâd and provoking his doubts about ʿAlî b. al-Ḥusayn's boyhood; the ability to quote the text seems to Ibn Ziyâd to be a sign of maturity. ʿAlî then tells Ibn Ziyâd that since there is kinship between Ibn Ziyâd and the women, it would fall upon his shoulders to find someone to care for them: "If there is any kinship between you and these women," Ibn Kaṯîr has him saying, "dispatch a man with them to

2012: n.n., HOWARD I.K.A., (trans.), *The History of al-Ṭabarî*, vol. XIX, 1990: 165, al-Mufîd., *al-Irshâd fî maʿrifat ḥuğağ Allâh ʿalâ al-ʿibâd*, vol. II, bb. *mâ ğarâ fî-l-Kûfa baʿda qatli Imâm al-Ḥusayn*: 116, al-Ṭabarsî., *Iʿlâm al-warâ bi-aʿlâm al-hudâ*: 252, al-Ḫawârizmî., *Maqtal al-Ḥusayn*, bk. 2, bb. *fî maqtal al-Ḥusayn*: 48, Ibn Aṯîr., *al-Kâmil fî al-târîḫ*, vol. II: 435, Ibn Ṭâʾûs., *Kitâb al-luhûf fî qatlâ al-ṭufûf*: 94, al-ʿIṣâmî., *Simṭ al-nuğûm al-ʿawâlî*, vol. III: 72, Ibn Namâ al-Ḥillî., *Muṯîr al-aḥzân wa munîr subul al-ashğân*, Part 3: 90, al-Irbilî., *Kashf al-ġumma fî maʿrifat al-aʾimma*, vol. II: 64–65, al-Mağlisî., *Biḥâr al-anwâr*, vol. XLV, bb. 39, n. 2: 116.

124 Al-Muğâlid b. Saʿîd al-Hamdânî, a renowned Kûfan historian (d. 144/762).

watch over them." At this, Ibn Ziyâd relents.[125] In al-Balâḏurî's account, when ʿAlî says to him, "if there is any kinship between you and these women, you will send a man with them to watch over them," Ibn Ziyâd replies: "You are the man!"[126] Symbolically, in this moment, the Imamate is secured.

Al-Ṭabarî's second, variant strand is a longer and more detailed transmission about the Ibn Ziyâd-ʿAlî b. al-Ḥusayn encounter; a substantial conversation between a volatile governor and a taciturn young Imâm, in which ʿAlî's silence profoundly annoys an already irate Ibn Ziyâd. According to Abû Miḫnaf's account, from Sulaymân b. Abî Rashîd on the authority of Ḥumayd b. Muslim al-Azdî:

> I was standing by Ibn Ziyâd when ʿAlî b. al-Ḥusayn was displayed before him. Ibn Ziyâd said to him: "What is your name?" and he replied: "I am ʿAlî b. al-Ḥusayn." Ibn Ziyâd retorted: "Except, did God not kill ʿAlî b. al-Ḥusayn?" He remained silent, so Ibn Ziyâd said to him: "What is the matter with you that you do not speak?" He replied: "I had a brother, who was also called ʿAlî b. al-Ḥusayn, but the people killed him." Ibn Ziyâd replied: "In truth, God killed him." ʿAlî remained silent, so Ibn Ziyâd said to him: "What is the matter with you that you do not speak?" He answered: ""*Allah receiveth (men's) souls at the time of their death*":[127] "*No soul can ever die except by Allah's leave*"."[128] Ibn Ziyâd said: "By God, you are one of them! Woe to you! Have a look;[129] has he reached maturity? By

---

[125] HOWARD I.K.A., (trans.), *The History of al-Ṭabarî*, vol. XIX, 1990: 165, Ibn Kaṯîr., *al-Bidâya wa-l-nihâya*, vol. XII: 567, al-ʿAsqalânî., *Tahḏîb al-tahḏîb*, vol II, (*Ḥusayn b. ʿAlî b. Abî Ṭâlib*): 323, al-ʿIṣâmî., *Simṭ al-nuǧûm al-ʿawâlî*, vol. III: 72 (a less detailed account).

[126] al-Balâḏurî., *Kitâb ansâb al-ashrâf*, vol. III: 413. Cf. also Sibṭ al-Ǧawzî., *Taḏkirat ḫawâṣṣ al-umma bi-ḏikr ḫaṣâʾiṣ al-aʾimma*: 218.

[127] Q. 39: 42. Al-Maǧlisî, transmitting from Ibn Ṭâʾûs and Ibn Nâma, adds the second part of Q. 39: 42, omitted by most other texts: "*and that (soul) which dieth not (yet) in its sleep*". Cf. al-Maǧlisî., *Biḥâr al-anwâr*, vol. XLV, bb. 39: 117.

[128] Q. 3: 145.

[129] In the plural, and thus addressed to a group of police or officials.

> God, I believe he is a man!" Murrî b. Muʿâḏ al-Aḥmarî uncovered him, and said: "Yes, he has reached maturity," to which Ibn Ziyâd replied: "Kill him!" ʿAlî b. al-Ḥusayn spoke up: "Who will you put in charge of these women?" Zaynab his aunt clung to him and said: "Ibn Ziyâd! Have we not satisfied you? Have you slaked your thirst with our blood?[130] Will you spare even one of us?" She threw her arms around ʿAlî's neck and said: "I ask you by God, if you are a believer, if you kill him, then kill me with him!" ʿAlî called to him, saying: "Ibn Ziyâd! If there is kinship between you and them, send a righteous man with them to accompany them with the companionship of Islam." Ibn Ziyâd looked at him for a while, and then looked at the people and said: "What an astonishing thing kinship is! By God, I think she really wishes that if I kill him, I would kill her with him! Leave the boy! Depart with your women!"[131]

Both Ibn Kaṯîr and al-ʿIṣâmî are closer to al-Ṭabarî's first strand, although Ibn Kaṯîr makes changes in the word order and al-ʿIṣâmî adds Zaynab's insistence that if ʿAlî is to be killed, she should be killed with him, followed immediately by ʿAlî's appeal to kinship. Ibn Kaṯîr's text, which adds 'Zayn al-ʿÂbidîn' to ʿAlî's name, is incorrect, reading 'on the authority of al-Muǧâlid, on the authority of Saʿîd' instead of 'on the authority of al-Muǧâlid b. Saʿîd'. While al-ʿIṣâmî offers a reduced narrative, giving only bare details of the

---

[130] The word occurs here, as in a number of other places, in the plural; 'bloods'. Although unusual in English, this poses little problem for the Semitic languages. In both Hebrew and in Greek, for example, the word 'blood' is used in the plural to describe the discharge of blood after an act of violence, as in murder or battle.

[131] al-Ṭabarî., *Kitâb aḫbâr al-rusul wa-l-mulûk*, vol. V, 1973: 457–458, Ibn ʿAsâkir., *Târîḫ madînat Dimashq*, vol. XLI, bb. 4875 (*ʿAlî b. al-Husayn b. ʿAlî b. Abî Ṭâlib b. Hâshim b. ʿAbd al-Manâf*): 367 (with fewer details), Ibn al-Aṯîr., *al-Kâmil fî al-târîḫ*, vol. II: 434–6, Sibṭ al-Ǧawzî., *Taḏkirat ḫawâṣṣ al-umma bi-ḏikr ḫaṣâʾiṣ al-aʾimma*: 218 (in truncated form; simply as a response to Ibn Ziyâd wondering how ʿAlî has survived, Zaynab asks whether he is still not satisfied with their blolod and that if he kill the boy, he kill her with her), Ibn Kaṯîr., *al-Bidâya wa-l-nihâya*, vol. XI: 561.

strands of conversation, Ibn Kaṯîr goes on to transmit al-Ṭabarî's second strand, with a slight variation in Zaynab's words: "Ibn Ziyâd! Are you not (yet) satisfied with what you have done to us, that you have slaked your thirst with our blood? Will you spare even one of us?"[132]

Transmitting the event in *al-Irshâd*, al-Mufîd, followed by al-Ṭabarsî and later by al-ʿÂmilî[133] does not record the silences on the part of ʿAlî b. al-Ḥusayn, or the quotation of Q. 39: 42. He also has a variance in some of the words that pass between Ibn Ziyâd and Zaynab. After the quotation of Q. 3: 145, Ibn Ziyâd grows heated and rebukes ʿAlî: "You have an audacity in answering me and within you is the residue of opposition against me!"[134] Ibn Ziyâd then summons his police, ordering them: "Take him way and behead him!" Zaynab intervenes, clinging to her nephew: "Ibn Ziyâd, our blood is sufficient for you! She throws her arms around ʿAlî's neck and says: "By God, I will not be parted from him! If you kill him, then kill me."[135] In some texts, Zaynab's words seem to be less of a threat ('if you kill him you will have to kill me first')[136] and more a request ('if you are going to kill him, then I ask you to kill me with him').

Like al-Mufîd, Ibn Namâ and al-Irbilî do not record the silences of the young Imâm and omit the quotation of the second Qurʾânic verse (Q. 39: 42), as well as Zaynab's declaration ("By God, I will not be parted from him"), but in her other words, they more or less follow al-Mufîd.[137] Ibn Namâ al-Ḥillî makes a slight

---

[132] Ibn Kaṯîr., *al-Bidâya wa-l-nihâya*, vol. XI: 561, al-ʿIṣâmî., *Simṭ al-nuǧûm al-ʿawâlî*, vol. III: 72.

[133] al-Ṭabarsî., *Iʿlâm al-warâ bi-aʿlâm al-hudâ*: 252, al-ʿÂmilî., *Aʿyân al-Shîʿa*, vol. VII: 139.

[134] Cf. also al-ʿÂmilî., *Aʿyân al-Shîʿa*, vol. VII: 139.

[135] al-Mufîd., *al-Irshâd fî maʿrifat ḥuǧaǧ Allâh ʿalâ al-ʿibâd*, vol. II, bb. *mâ ǧarâ fî-l-Kûfa baʿda qatli Imâm al-Ḥusayn*: 116, al-ʿÂmilî., *Aʿyân al-Shîʿa*, vol. VII: 139.

[136] Cf. for e.g. al-Ḏahabî., *Siyar aʿlâm al-nubalâʾ*, vol. III, bb. 48: 309–310. Al-Ḏahabî offers an extremely truncated version of the events.

[137] Ibn Namâ al-Ḥillî., *Muṯîr al-aḥzân wa munîr subul al-ashǧân*, Part 3: 90, al-Irbilî., *Kashf al-ġumma fî maʿrifat al-aʾimma*, vol. II: 66–67.

change of wording in Ibn Ziyâd's accusation: "You have a liveliness (*ḥarâk*) in answering me!"[138]

Al-Ḫawârizmî and Ibn Ṭâ'ûs offer narrations containing substantially different details. Al-Ḫawârizmî follows al-Ṭabarî closely, with some changes; he includes the silence after the first question (but not the second), notes the discrepancy in the text, which can read 'the people killed him' or 'they killed him' and adds to ʿAlî b. al-Ḥusayn's words a phrase about his older brother and the men who killed him: "He has a claim on them on the Day of Resurrection." When Ibn Ziyâd replies, No, rather, God!' (missing but presuming as understood the words 'killed him' as found in Ibn Ṭâ'ûs), ʿAlî quotes the two Qur'ânic verses, adding to Q. 3: 145 the words "*at a term appointed*" omitted by most other transmitters. Al-Ḫawârizmî omits Ibn Ziyâd's rebuke about an insolent answer, and names the police official who who inspected him as Marwân b. Muʿâḏ al-Aḥmarî. Zaynab is named 'daughter of ʿAlî', but not immediately identified as ʿAlî b. al-Ḥusayn's aunt as in the other texts; al-Ḫawârizmî also omits the words 'if you are a believer' in Zaynab's appeal to Ibn Ziyâd, as well as Zaynab's talk of 'our blood' and Ibn Ziyâd's praising of kinship.

Where al-Ḫawârizmî makes a radical departure from most other transmitters is in his inclusion of an instruction by ʿAlî b. al-Ḥusayn to his aunt to be quiet, so that he can talk to Ibn Ziyâd. It is made immediately after Zaynab's appeal: "I ask you by God, Ibn Ziyâd, if you kill him, that you kill me with him." ʿAlî b. al-Ḥusayn now turns to Zaynab and says: "Aunt, be quiet, so that I can speak to him."[139]

In Ibn Ṭâ'ûs' *Kitâb al-luhûf*, Ibn Ziyâd's question is asked about ʿAlî b. al-Ḥusayn rather than posed directly to him: "He said: who is this? He was told: ʿAlî b. al-Ḥusayn". It is remarkably similar to his noticing Zaynab and asking about her; quite patently, these two figures stand out among the rest. The second question,

---

[138] Ibn Namâ al-Ḥillî., *Muṯîr al-aḥzân wa munîr subul al-ashǧân*, Part 3: 90.

[139] al-Ḫawârizmî., *Maqtal al-Ḥusayn*, bk. 2, bb. *fî maqtal al-Ḥusayn*: 48, Ibn Ṭâ'ûs., *Kitâb al-luhûf fî qatlâ al-ṭufûf*: 95, al-Mağlisî., *Biḥâr al-anwâr*, vol. XLV, bb. 39: 164, al-ʿÂmilî., *Aʿyân al-Shîʿa*, vol. VII: 139.

about God killing ʿAlî b. al-Ḥusayn is directed to and answered by ʿAlî directly. Ibn Ṭâʾûs records the quotation of Q. 39: 42 but not of Q. 3: 145, and omits Zaynab's reference to the blood of the *ahl al-bayt*. He does, however, include ʿAlî b. al-Ḥusayn asking his aunt to be quiet. It is a consummate moment, marking the end of Zaynab's protective role and ʿAlî b. al-Ḥusayn taking his legitimate place as Imâm. Zaynab will make one final protest; when Ibn Ziyâd orders that these surviving members of the *ahl al-bayt* be lodged in a house near the mosque, Zaynab says: "No Arab woman except for a slave girl (*umm walad* and *mamlûka*) should enter, because they are captives just as we are!"[140]

Three times Zaynab is asked to be quiet; by her brother al-Ḥusayn, when she breaks down after hearing his dirge,[141] by her nephew ʿAlî b. al-Ḥusayn when people break down after her Kûfa protest,[142] and again by ʿAlî b. al-Ḥusayn in front of Ibn Ziyâd.[143] Never is there, in these texts, any hint of harshness or impatience towards her. A later incident will describe Yazîd telling Zaynab to speak and she herself deferring to ʿAlî b. al-Ḥusayn, saying: "He is the speaker."[144]

Despite sparing their lives, Ibn Ziyâd still then enters the pulpit for the *ṣalât* and says in his *ḫuṭba*: 'Praise be to God, who has revealed the truth and its adherents, and who has assisted the Commander of the Faithful, Yazîd and his party, and has killed the liar and son of the liar, al-Ḥusayn b. ʿAlî, and his Shîʿa'.

---

[140] Ibn Ṭâʾûs., *Kitâb al-luhûf fî qatlâ al-ṭufûf*: 95. Cf. al-Mağlisî., *Biḥâr al-anwâr*, vol. XLV, bb. 39: 117, al-ʿÂmilî., *Aʿyân al-Shîʿa*, vol. VII: 139.

[141] al-Mufîd., *al-Irshâd fî maʿrifat ḥuğağ Allâh ʿalâ al-ʿibâd*, vol. II, bb. *nuzûl Imâm al-Ḥusayn fî Karbalâʾ*: 90, al-Fattâl al-Nîsâbûrî., *Rawḍat al-wâʿiẓîn wa-tabṣirat al-muttaʿiẓîn*: 183, al-Ṭabarsî., *Iʿlâm al-warâ bi-aʿlâm al-hudâ*: 239, al-Mağlisî., *Biḥâr al-anwâr*, vol. XLIV, bb. 37: 391.

[142] al-Ṭabarsî., *Kitâb al-iḥtiğâğ ʿalâ ahl al-liğâğ*, vol. II: 305, al-Mağlisî., *Biḥâr al-anwâr*, vol. XLV, bb. 39: 164.

[143] al-Ḫawârizmî., *Maqtal al-Ḥusayn*, bk. 2, bb. *fî maqtal al-Ḥusayn*: 48, Ibn Ṭâʾûs., *Kitâb al-luhûf fî qatlâ al-ṭufûf*: 95, al-Mağlisî., *Biḥâr al-anwâr*, vol. XLV, bb. 39: 164.

[144] Cf. Ibn Aṯîr., *al-Kâmil fî al-târîḫ*, vol. II: 439, al-Mağlisî., *Biḥâr al-anwâr*, vol. XLV, bb. 39, n. 22: 175.

There is one addendum to this incident worth noting; in his *Maqâtil*, al-Iṣfahânî attributes the whole of this conversation to Yazîd instead of Ibn Ziyâd, moving it from the governor's residence to the caliph's palace. Yazîd asks ʿAlî b. al-Ḥusayn his name, and when he is told "ʿAlî", remarks: "Did God not kill ʿAlî b. al-Ḥusayn?" ʿAlî speaks his heartrending line: "I had an older brother called ʿAlî, but they killed him," to which Yazîd replies: "No, God killed him." This marks the start of an exchange of Qurʾânic verses. ʿAlî begins with the first phrase of Q. 39: 42 ("*Allah receiveth (men's) souls at the time of their death*") and Yazîd responds with Q. 42: 30 ("*Whatever of misfortune striketh you, it is what your right hands have earned*"), but, as in Ibn al-Aṯîr, omitting the last phrase: "*And He forgiveth much*". ʿAlî replies with Q. 57: 22–23 ("*Naught of disaster befalleth in the earth or in yourselves but it is in a Book before we bring it into being – Lo! that is easy for Allah – That ye grieve not for the sake of that which hath escaped you, nor yet exult because of that which hath been given. Allah loveth not all prideful boasters*". In response, Yazîd quotes Q. 42: 30 ("*Whatever of misfortune striketh you, it is what your right hands have earned*"). At this moment, the narrative moves to the intervention by a Syrian man. Notes Hussein:

> Al-Isfahānī then inserts his own narrative voice directly into the text, providing the explanation that no such scenario ever occurred at 'Ubaydullah b. Ziyad's court, and that historians prior to him have mistakenly attributed the rhetorical confrontations with Yazxd to 'Ubaydullah b. Ziyad instead. Although not impossible, it seems that this explanation is unsatisfactory, especially when considering numerous other aspects that betray the highly manipulated nature of Isfahānī's work as a whole.[145]

3. YAZÎD B. MUʿÂWIYA

Once again, the journey from Kûfa to Damascus is a drama that unfolds in a number of acts. Al-Ṭabarî's chronology is a useful skeleton, although he omits a number of crucial details:

---

[145] HUSSEIN A.J., *A Developmental Analysis of Depictions of the Events of Karbalāʾ in Early Islamic History*, 2001: 112.

1. The head is despatched; Yazîd expresses a certain distress in seeing it, leading us to ask whether this would temper his treatment of the survivors. He expresses his distress in lament and poetry.

2. Ibn Ziyâd orders the survivors be made ready for travel.

3. Yazîd's reacts angrily to the insults against the arriving prisoners, specifically from Muḥaffiz al-Ṯaʿlaba.

4. The survivors are summoned into the presence of Yazîd and the Syrian nobles he has gathered.

5. He addresses ʿAlî, who answers with Qurʾânic quotes; Yazîd orders his own son to match these, but he proves unable to do so.

6. Yazîd looks at the survivors and is distressed by their condition, expressing some criticism of Ibn Ziyâd; this could be an attempt to extricate himself from the appalling results of Karbalâʾ, putting the immediate blame on his governor. There is an apparent regret for what has happened, or at the least, a growing realization of how serious it is.

7. The intervention of a Syrian, and Zaynab's response; her first words before Yazîd.

9. The Zaynab-Yazîd encounter and his dismissal of the Syrian.

10. The preparations for departure.

11. Yazîd's fixation with ʿAlî.

12. Fâṭima bt. ʿAlî suggests to her sister Zaynab that their Syrian guard be rewarded.

Zaynab and the other survivors from among al-Ḥusayn's followers, a remnant comprised almost entirely of women and children, were marched to Damascus, Yazîd's capital, where they were arrayed before him. Tradition says that Zaynab, already in anguish due to the death of her brother al-Ḥusayn and other family members, was once again forced to march unveiled, an extraordinary affront to the granddaughter of Muḥammad.

Yazîd, a man of about thirty-four at his encounter with Zaynab, is only a few years older than his governor Ibn Ziyâd and will die within three years of Karbalâʾ. He shows himself a capricious dictator whose moods swing rapidly from enraged violence to an almost repentant kindness. As Zaynab's personality is transforming from grief to courage, Yazîd is moving from defiance to discomfiture.

Most of the transmitters agree that Ibn Ziyâd ordered the move to Damascus and made the necessary arrangements.[146] Al-Ṭabarî sets the scene by jumping ahead in his narrative to Yazîd's palace prior to the arrival of the prisoners. A messenger (Zaḥr b. Qays, according to al-Ṭabarî and al-Balâḏurî, but Shimr according to al-Dînawarî) gives the caliph a graphic description of the battle[147] and Yazîd is reduced to tears, lamenting the death of al-Ḥusayn:

> I would have been satisfied with your obedience without killing al-Ḥusayn. May God curse Ibn Sumayya. By God, if it had been I who had accompanied him, I would have let him off. May God have mercy on al-Ḥusayn.[148]

Yazîd displays an intensifying realization of the gravity of what has happened and a concomitant remorse; he subtly shifts blame onto his governor, calling him 'Ibn Sumayya', a public reminder that Ibn Ziyâd's mother was a woman of ill-repute, and expressing his regret by asking that the same God who curses Ibn Ziyâd should be merciful to al-Ḥusayn; the enemy has become the ally and the ally the enemy.

Al-Ṭabarî now returns us to the palace of Ibn Ziyâd; according to his account, the governor ordered the women and children to be prepared for the journey, ʿAlî b. al-Ḥusayn with a chain around his neck.[149] ʿAlî is, seemingly, now perceived as a threat

---

146 HOWARD I.K.A., (trans.), *The History of al-Ṭabarî*, vol. XIX, 1990: 165, Ibn al-Aṯîr., *al-Kâmil fî al-târîḫ*, vol. II: 436.

147 In Ibn al-Aṯîr, this description is given by Zaḥr after the arrival of the survivors. Cf. Ibn al-Aṯîr., *al-Kâmil fî al-târîḫ*, vol. II: 436.

148 al-Balâḏurî., *Kitâb ansâb al-ashrâf*, vol. III: 415, al-Dînawarî., *Kitâb al-aḫbâr al-ṭiwâl*: 272 (Ibn Ziyâd is addressed in his text as Ibn Marǧâna rather than Ibn Sumayya), HOWARD I.K.A., (trans.), *The History of al-Ṭabarî*, vol. XIX, 1990: 169, Ibn al-Aṯîr., *al-Kâmil fî al-târîḫ*, vol. II: 437.

149 al-Balâḏurî., *Kitâb ansâb al-ashrâf*, vol. III: 416, HOWARD I.K.A., (trans.), *The History of al-Ṭabarî*, vol. XIX, 1990: 169, Ibn Kaṯîr., *al-Bidâya*

after his vigorous verbal encounter with Ibn Ziyâd; the texts note that he is silent throughout the journey, as he will be for much of his life. The survivors are despatched after the heads and separately from them, and among the men who accompany them are two of note; the brutal Shimr b. Ḏî al-Ǧawshan, who threatened to burn the women's tents and tried to kill ʿAlî b. al-Ḥusayn and seems almost certainly to be al-Ḥusayn's murderer, and Muḥaffiz[150] b. Ṭaʿlaba al-ʿÂʾiḏî, who is about to earn a stinging rebuke from Yazîd. As they reach the door of Yazîd's palace, Muḥaffiz announces himself in a strident voice, and informs the caliph that he has brought him 'the shameless ignobles' (*al-liʾâm al-fağara*). Yazîd in turn chastises Muḥaffiz: "What the mother of Muḥaffiz gave birth to is evil and ignoble!"[151] This defence of the prisoners' status, parallel with his weeping and anguish, suggests a swelling remorse; but his frequently swinging mood hints at a certain instability. A second time, al-Ṭabarî interrupts his own narrative to describe Yazîd's reaction to the heads being placed before him; once more, it is lament and tears over these men "dear to us" but none-

wa-l-nihâya, vol. XI: 561. Ibn al-Aṯîr says around his hands as well; Ibn al-Aṯîr., *al-Kâmil fî al-târîḫ*, vol. II: 436.

150 al-Mufîd names him 'Muğfir' (al-Mufîd., *al-Irshâd*, vol. II, bb. *masîr al-sabâyâ ilâ al-Shâm*: 119), al-Ṭabarsî as 'Miḥfir' and Ibn Namâ al-Ḥillî and al-Mağlisî as 'Muḫfir' (Ibn Namâ al-Ḥillî., *Muṯîr al-aḥzân wa munîr subul al-ashğân*, Part 2: 96, 98, al-Mağlisî., *Biḥâr al-anwâr*, vol. XLV, bb. 39: 124, 130–131.

151 al-Balâḏurî., *Kitâb ansâb al-ashrâf*, vol. III: 416, HOWARD I.K.A., (trans.), *The History of al-Ṭabarî*, vol. XIX, 1990: 169–170, al-Ḫawârizmî., *Maqtal al-Ḥusayn*, bk. 2, bb. *fî maqtal al-Ḥusayn*: 65, al-Ḏahabî., *Siyar aʿlâm al-nubalâʾ*, vol. III, bb. 48: 315, Ibn Kaṯîr., *al-Bidâya wa-l-nihâya*, vol. XI: 561. In Ibn al-Aṯîr's narrative, Muḥaffiz shouts: "We have come with the head of the most foolish of the people and the basest of them!" Yazîd replies: "What the mother of Muḥaffiz gave birth to is more foolish and baser than him, even though he is cut off and tyrannical." Ibn al-Aṯîr., *al-Kâmil fî al-târîḫ*, vol. II: 437.

theless "disobedient and oppressive." Yazîd again insists that he himself would never have killed al-Ḥusayn.[152]

All of this provides our context for Yazîd's encounter with Zaynab, ʿAlî b. al-Ḥusayn and the other survivors. Unlike Ibn Ziyâd, who begins with Zaynab and then notices ʿAlî, Yazîd starts with the young, enchained Imâm, for whom he develops an enigmatic fascination and who, in these moments, is reminiscent of the figure of Jesus in the Christian gospel, moving as a prisoner between the governor Pontius Pilate and the High Priest. There are two strands; in the first (al-Balâḏurî, al-Ṭabarî, Ibn al-Aṯîr, Ibn Kaṯîr), Yazîd initiates the conversation. In the second (al-Ḏahabî, al-Haytamî), ʿAlî begins it, reacting angrily to Yazîd's poking at the teeth of al-Ḥusayn by quoting Qurʾânic texts.

Al-Balâḏurî's narrative is less compact than that of al-Ṭabarî, and he interrupts the Yazîd accounts for a discussion of who killed al-Ḥusayn. He then returns to Yazîd: "When ʿAlî b. al-Ḥusayn was brought in to Yazîd, he said: 'My dear, your father broke my kinship and ill-treated me, and you have seen what God has done to him!'" ʿAlî responds by quoting Q. 57: 22: "*Naught of disaster befalleth in the earth or in yourselves but it is in a Book before we bring it into being*", omitting the last phrase, "*Lo! that is easy for Allah*". Yazîd then turns to his son Ḫâlid, telling him to answer ʿAlî, but the boy seems not to know what to say and has to be coached by his father: "Say to him: "*Whatever of misfortune striketh you, it is what your right hands have earned. And He forgiveth much*"."[153] Zaynab makes no appearance in this part of the al-Balâḏurî narrative.

Al-Ṭabarî and Ibn Kaṯîr tell an almost identical story but add that Yazîd's quotation from the Qurʾân silences ʿAlî ('for a while', adds Ibn Kaṯîr tersely).[154] Al-Haytamî tells a different tale; the bag-

---

152 HOWARD I.K.A., (trans.), *The History of al-Ṭabarî*, vol. XIX, 1990: 169, Ibn al-Aṯîr., *al-Kâmil fî al-târîḫ*, vol. II: 436, 438.

153 al-Balâḏurî., *Kitâb ansâb al-ashrâf*, vol. III: 419–420. The Qurʾânic quote is Q. 42: 30, although there are miniscule differences in the transcription of text in al-Balâḏurî compared to the Qurʾânic text.

154 HOWARD I.K.A., (trans.), *The History of al-Ṭabarî*, vol. XIX, 1990: 170–171, Ibn Kaṯîr., *al-Bidâya wa-l-nihâya*, vol. XI: 561–562. Ibn

gage (presumably both material and human) of al-Ḥusayn was brought in to Yazîd, and the head placed in front of him. Yazîd weeps and says: "We have split the skulls of men beloved to us; however, they were most disobedient and oppressive! But by God, had I been your companion, I would never have killed you." At this, ʿAlî b. al-Ḥusayn speaks up: "It is not like that! Yazîd replies: "How, then, O son of my mother?"[155] ʿAlî then quotes Q. 57: 22, including the last phrase, "*Lo! that is easy for Allah*".[156]

Ibn al-Aṯîr changes the chronology, placing Yazîd's encounter with ʿAlî b. al-Ḥusayn after the women are brought into his presence, and the incident between the Syrian, Yazîd and Zaynab. He notes that Yazîd takes care to shield Fâṭima and Sukayna, daughters of al-Ḥusayn, from the grisly sight of their father's head. In spite of this, Fâṭima will challenge him about the daughters of the Messenger of God being in chains. When ʿAlî b. al-Ḥusayn is brought before him, he too complains about the chains:

> "Had the Messenger of God seen us chained he would have untied us!" Yazîd replied: "You speak the truth," and he ordered that his chains be struck from him. Then ʿAlî said: "Had the Messenger of God seen us standing at a distance, he would have wanted to bring us close!" Yazîd ordered that he be brought close to him. Then Yazîd said to him: "ʿAlî b. al-Ḥusayn, your father is the one who broke my kinship, was ignorant of my due and disputed my authority with me, and you have seen what God has done to him."[157]

It is at this moment that ʿAlî quotes Q. 57: 23–22:

Kaṯîr relates this account not in a footnote, but in the main body of his text.

[155] In other words, 'you are like a brother to me'. I have followed Pickthall (Q. 20: 94) in the translation of the phrase *ya umma.*

[156] al-Hayṯamî., *Mağmaʿ al-zawâʾid wa-manbaʿ al-fawâʾid*, vol. IX, bb. 95 (*Manâqib al-Ḥusayn*), n. 15176: 233. Cf. also al-Ḏahabî., *Siyar aʿlâm al-nubalâʾ*, vol. III, bb. 48: 319–320, where it is ʿAlî who quotes Q. 57: 22 and Q. 42: 30.

[157] Ibn al-Aṯîr., *al-Kâmil fî al-târîḫ*, vol. II: 439.

> "*Naught of disaster befalleth in the earth or in yourselves but it is in a Book before we bring it into being – Lo! that is easy for Allah – That ye grieve not for the sake of that which hath escaped you, nor yet exult because of that which hath been given. Allah loveth not all prideful boasters*".

In response, Yazîd quotes Q. 42: 30 ("*Whatever of misfortune striketh you, it is what your right hands have earned*") but omitting the last phrase: "*And He forgiveth much*".

Al-Haytamî, following Ibn Saʿd, records a more detailed dialogue, combining in one narrative many of the elements scattered throughout the other transmitters. Curiously, he takes note of the presence of Fâṭima and Sukayna but makes no mention of Zaynab. He writes of how ʿAlî b. Ḥusayn (whom, he observes, had reached boyhood), Fâṭima bt. Ḥusayn and Sukayna bt. Ḥusayn were 'rushed' to ʿUbayd Allâh b. Ziyâd. He in turn despatches them to Yazîd b. Muʿâwiya, who orders that Sukayna be placed behind his throne – lest she see the head of her father and those of her kin – while ʿAlî b. Ḥusayn remains shackled. The head of al-Ḥusayn is set down and Yazîd strikes at the teeth, saying: "We have split the skulls of men beloved to us; however, they were most disobedient and oppressive." At this, ʿAlî b. Ḥusayn speaks up, quoting Q. 57: 22. Al-Haytamî notes that 'it weighed heavily' on Yazîd that he had quoted a verse of poetry and ʿAlî b. Ḥusayn had responded with a verse from the Qur'ân, so Yazîd himself quotes from the second half of Q. 42: 30: "*It is for what your hands have earned, but He pardons much*". ʿAlî then makes his protest about what the Messenger of God would do were he to see them in chains and kept at a distance.[158]

It is now that Zaynab's story commences; it will begin with the intervention of a man from Syria who is looking for a slave-girl and will end with Zaynab turning Yazîd against one of his own nobles. Al-Ṭabarî narrates the story from Abû Miḫnaf, although, as we shall see, there are some textual problems with his narrative.

---

158 al-Haytamî., *Mağmaʿ al-zawâ'id wa-manbaʿ al-fawâ'id*, vol. IX, bb. 95 (*Manâqib al-Ḥusayn*), n. 15148: 227.

Abû Miḫnaf is reporting from al-Ḥâriṯ b. Kaʿb al-Wâlibî, who says that according to a narration of Fâṭima, daughter of ʿAlî:

> When we were made to sit in front of Yazîd b. Muʿâwiya, he showed pity to us, ordered things for us and was kind to us. Then a Syrian man with a ruddy complexion stood up before Yazîd and said: "Commander of the Faithful, give me this one." He meant me, for I was a radiant girl. I trembled and was dismayed, for I thought that this might be permissable for them. I caught hold of the skirt of my sister Zaynab, since my sister Zaynab was older and cleverer than I, and she knew that this could not happen. She said: "You lie, by God, and are sordid! Such a thing is not for you, nor for him!" Yazîd grew angry and said: "It is *you* who have lied, and by God, it *is* for me – and had I wanted to do it, I would have done it!" She answered: "Never, by God! God would never concede this to you unless you departed our faith and professed belief in another religion." Yazîd grew increasingly angry and agitated, and said: "You dare confront me with this? Your father and your brother departed from the religion!" Zaynab replied: "You, your father and your grandfather have been guided by the religion of God, the religion of my father and the religion of my brother and my grandfather." He responded: "You lie, enemy of God!" She replied: "You, a commander who has authority, vilify unjustly and oppress with your authority." (The narrator said): By God! It was as if he were ashamed, and he grew silent. The Syrian repeated: "Commander of the Faithful, give me that girl." Yazîd said to him, "Stay a bachelor! May God grant you a dreadful death!"[159]

The narrator of the text, who is herself the girl desired by the red-faced Syrian, cannot be Fâṭima, daughter of ʿAlî, as stated by a number of transmitters,[160] but must in fact be Fâṭima, daughter of

---

[159] al-Ṭabarî., *Kitâb aḫbâr al-rusul wa-l-mulûk*, vol. V. 461–462. Al-ʿÂmilî omits a number of the details but relates the most important elements of the encounter; cf. al-ʿÂmilî., *Aʿyân al-Šîʿa*, vol. VII: 139.

[160] Besides Abû Miḫnaf (LIMBA M., (trans.), *The Event of Taff, the Earliest Historical Account of the Tragedy of Karbala*, 2012) and al-Ṭabarî, also

al-Ḥusayn. Howard notes this in his translation of al-Ṭabarî's *Kitâb aḫbâr al-rusul wa-l-mulûk*, referring the reader to the opinion of al-Mufîd in his *al-Irshâd.* Al-Ḫawârizmî agrees,[161] and the editor of Abû Miḫnaf adds that al-Ǧawzî thinks so too, even though the text reads 'daughter of ʿAlî'. Most of the Shîʿî transmitters follow al-Mufîd's opinion that the girl in question is al-Ḥusayn's daughter;[162] curiously, al-Ṣadûq[163] does not. The girl addresses Zaynab as 'sister', but, as with her being nominated 'sister of ʿAlî', this seems unlikely; it is more probably the skirt of her aunt, and not of her sister, that this young girl seizes. Al-Ḫawârizmî adds the confusing and clearly erroneous narrative that in her fear, the girl "grabbed hold of the robe of my sister and my aunt Zaynab." Her 'aunt' then addresses Yazîd with words always attributed to Zaynab, sister of al-Ḥusayn.[164] The very fact that she describes herself as a 'radiant girl' means she could not have been Zaynab's sister, who by that stage would have been in her fifties. Ibn Kaṯîr, in the second of his two transmissions of the incident, does not name her at all, and nor does al-ʿAsqalânî in his; one of the Syrians present before Yazîd to

---

Ibn ʿAsâkir., *Târîḫ madînat Dimashq*, vol. LXIX, bb. 9353 (*Zaynab al-Kubrâ bt. ʿAlî b. Abî Ṭâlib b. ʿAbd al-Muṭṭalib b. Hâshim b. ʿAbd al-Manâf*): 177, Ibn al-Aṯîr., *al-Kâmil fî al-târîḫ*, vol. II: 438, who calls her 'sister' of Zaynab, Ibn Kaṯîr., *al-Bidâya wa-l-nihâya*, vol. XI: 562 (transmitting from Abû Miḫnaf). In a second, truncated narrative, he leaves the girl unnamed (Ibn Kaṯîr., *al-Bidâya wa-l-nihâya*, vol. XI: 567).

161 al-Ḫawârizmî., *Maqtal al-Ḥusayn*, bk. 2, bb. *fî maqtal al-Ḥusayn*: 69.

162 al-Ṭabarsî., *Iʿlâm al-warâ bi-aʿlâm al-hudâ*: 254, *Kitâb al-iḥtiǧâǧ ʿalâ ahl al-liǧâǧ*, vol. II: 31, Ibn Ṭâʾûs., *Kitâb al-luhûf fî qatlâ al-ṭufûf*: 108, Ibn Namâ al-Ḥillî., *Muṯîr al-aḥzân wa munîr subul al-ashǧân*, Part 3: 100, al-Maǧlisî., *Biḥâr al-anwâr*, vol. XLV, bb. 39: 136, al-ʿÂmilî., *Aʿyân al-Shîʿa*, vol. VII: 139.

163 al-Ṣadûq., *Kitâb al-amâlî fî-l-aḥâdîṯ wa-l-aḫbâr*, *maǧlis* 31: 167. Al-Fattâl al-Nîsâbûrî, who in his *Rawḍat* is transmitting from al-Ṣadûq, changes this detail from 'daughter of ʿAlî to 'daughter of al-Ḥusayn', and while al-Ṣadûq says the Syrian man's name is Aḥmar, al-Fattâl offers a few more possibilities: cf. al-Fattâl al-Nîsâbûrî., *Rawḍat al-wâʿiẓîn wa-tabṣirat al-muttaʿiẓîn*, vol. I: 192.

164 al-Ḫawârizmî., *Maqtal al-Ḥusayn*, bk. 2, bb. *fî maqtal al-Ḥusayn*: 69.

congratulate him on his victory, a man with ruddy complexion and blue eyes, looking at what he seems to think is a maid or serving girl (*waṣîfa*) among the women, asks that she be given to him. Zaynab speaks up at once and says: "No, by God, there is no such honour for you or for him, other than he leave the religion of God!" The Syrian repeats his request and is told by Yazîd: "Stay a bachelor! And God grant you a dreadful death!"[165]

Sibṭ al-Ǧawzî, who correctly identifies the girl as Fâṭima, daughter of al-Ḥusayn, records Zaynab's bruising response to Yazîd's suggestion that he can do as he pleases: "Pray towards a *qibla* other than ours, and submit to a religious community other than ours, and you can do what you like!" Yazîd then lapses into a churlish silence.[166]

In a number of the texts, the Syrian is described as being 'ruddy of complexion' (*aḥmar*).[167] Al-Fattâl al-Nîsâbûrî suggests that he is not ruddy of complexion, but that his name is in fact Ḥamr or

---

[165] Op. cit.: 70 (where he adds the words: 'God curse you'), Ibn Kaṯîr., *al-Bidâya wa-l-nihâya*, vol. XI: 562, 567, al-ʿAsqalânî., *Tahḏîb al-tahḏîb*, vol II, (*Ḥusayn b. ʿAlî b. Abî Ṭâlib*): 353. The Arabic imperative (*uzub*) could be read as 'remain unmarried' or, as in the case of al-Ḫawârizmî, 'distance yourself from me' (*uzub ʿannî*). Al-Ḫawârizmî adds a further sentence from Yazîd to the Syrian: "Woe to you! Do not say such a thing! This is the daughter of ʿAlî and Fâṭima! They are the people of the house!" In Ibn Namâ's *Muṯîr*, a 'decisive' or 'unequivocal' (*qâṭiʿ*) death is wished. In other texts, notes the editor of his text, the same, but with the sense of 'lethal' (*qâḍiʿ*): cf. Ibn Namâ al-Ḥillî., *Muṯîr al-aḥzân wa munîr subul al-ashǧân*, Part 3: 101.

[166] Sibṭ al-Ǧawzî., *Taḏkirat ḫawâṣṣ al-umma bi-ḏikr ḫaṣâʾiṣ al-aʾimma*: 222.

[167] al-Ṭabarî., *Kitâb aḫbâr al-rusul wa-l-mulûk*, vol. V: 461–462, al-Ṣadûq., *Kitâb al-amâlî fî-l-aḥâdîṯ wa-l-aḫbâr*, *maǧlis* 31: 167, al-Mufîd., *al-Irshâd fî maʿrifat ḥuǧaǧ Allâh ʿalâ al-ʿibâd*, vol. II, bb. *masîr al-sabâyâ ilâ al-Shâm*: 121, al-Ṭabarsî., *Kitâb al-iḥtiǧâǧ ʿalâ ahl al-liǧâǧ*, vol. II: 31, al-Ḫawârizmî., *Maqtal al-Ḥusayn*, bk. 2, bb. *fî maqtal al-Ḥusayn*: 69, Ibn Namâ al-Ḥillî., *Muṯîr al-aḥzân wa munîr subul al-ashǧân*, Part 3: 100, Ibn Kaṯîr., *al-Bidâya wa-l-nihâya*, vol. XI: 562, 567, al-Maǧlisî., *Biḥâr al-anwâr*, vol. XLV, bb. 39: 136, n. 3: 156.

Aḥmar or Aḥmad.[168] Still others add that he is also 'blue eyed' (*azraq*),[169] a feature, notes one author, "considered unfortunate by the ancient Arabs" and which "finds an echo in Q 20: 102, according to which the wicked will rise on the day of resurrection with shiny (or blue) eyes."[170]

Aside from the issue of wrongly identifying Fâṭima and some cosmetic details, this narrative reads very much the same in all the Shîʿî and Sunnî transmitters, making it a useful text in attempting to construct biographical details for Zaynab.[171] Her speech, notes Ibn al-Aṯîr (despite his misidentification of the Fâṭima in the text) is widely known and celebrated, demonstrating her wisdom and strength of heart.[172]

Ibn Ṭâʾûs offers a reading that does have some substantial differences. He begins by narrating that the head of al-Ḥusayn is placed in front of Yazîd, who makes the women (not just the

---

[168] al-Fattâl al-Nîsâbûrî., *Rawḍat al-wâʿiẓîn wa-tabṣirat al-muttaʿiẓîn*, vol. I: 192. In other editions of the *Rawḍat*, his name is also suggested as Aḥmar or Aḥmad.

[169] Ibn Namâ al-Ḥillî., *Muṯîr al-aḥzân wa munîr subul al-ashǧân*, Part 3: 100, Ibn Kaṯîr., *al-Bidâya wa-l-nihâya*, vol. XI: 567, al-ʿAsqalânî., *Tahḏîb al-tahḏîb*, vol II, (*Ḥusayn b. ʿAlî b. Abî Ṭâlib*): 353.

[170] Cf. BAR-ASHER M.M., "Shīʿism and the Qurʾān" in J D McAuliffe (ed.), *Encyclopaedia of the Qurʾān*, vol. 4, Brill, Leiden 2004: 599.

[171] If the protagonist is indeed Fâṭima daughter of ʿAlî rather than Fâṭima daughter of al-Ḥusayn, her words "she was older than me" seem more pertinant to a sister than to an aunt. On the other hand, it seems anomalous that the Syrian would want possession of a woman approaching sixty, when there were younger girls in the group of survivors. Abû Miḫnaf is reporting from al-Ḥâriṯ b. Kaʿb al-Wâlibî who, Miḫnaf's editors claim, was narrating from ʿAlî b. al-Ḥusayn. Al-Ṭabarî takes the account from Abû Miḫnaf, repeating what is ostenibly an error; his editor refers the reader to *Shayḫ* al-Mufîd's andf Ibn al-Ǧawzî's correction, but also notes that al-Ḥâriṯ b. Kaʿb al-Wâlibî is an unknown (HOWARD I.K.A., (trans.), *The History of al-Ṭabarî*, vol. XIX, 1990, nt. 228: 66).

[172] Ibn al-Aṯîr., *Usd al-ġâba fî maʿrifat al-ṣaḥâba*, vol. VI, bb. 6961 (*Zaynab bt. ʿAlî b. Abî Ṭâlib*): 137.

daughters of al-Ḥusayn) sit behind him so that they do not look upon it; but when Zaynab, in spite of Yazîd's best efforts, catches sight of her brother's head, she pulls at her robe, and with grief-stricken heart cries out in a sad voice: "Ḥusayn! Beloved of the Messenger of God! Son of Mecca and Minâ! Son of Fâṭima al-Zahrâ', Mistress of the women! Son of the daughter of al-Muṣṭafâ!"[173] The narrator notes that everyone in the gathering wept while Yazîd remained in stony silence. Ibn Namâ is a little more effusive:

> Then she cried out in a sad voice that wounded the heart and weakened the strong: "My Ḥusayn! Beloved of his grandfather the Messenger! Fruit of the heart of the Radiant, the Virgin![174] Son of the daughter of the Chosen! Son of Mecca and Minâ! Son of ʿAlî the Approved!" [175]

Ibn Ṭâ'ûs, having recounted Zaynab's second major protest, only then records the intervention of the Syrian man. When the Syrian, whose features he does not describe, makes his demand, Fâṭima turns to her aunt Zaynab and says: "I have been orphaned, and now I am to be enslaved?"[176] Zaynab speaks up: "No, there is no such distinction for this profligate!" The Syrian asks: "Who is this young girl?" Yazîd replies: "This is Fâṭima, daughter of al-Ḥusayn, and that is Zaynab, daughter of ʿAlî b. Abî Ṭâlib." The Syrian clarifies: "Al-Ḥusayn son of Fâṭima and ʿAlî b. Abî Ṭâlib?" When Yazîd answers in the affirmative, the Syrian calls down God's curses on the caliph for killing the family of the Prophet and imprisoning his

---

173 al-Ṭabarsî., *Kitâb al-iḥtiğâğ ʿalâ ahl al-liğâğ*, vol. II: 307, Ibn Ṭâ'ûs., *Kitâb al-luhûf fî qatlâ al-ṭufûf*: 104, Ibn Namâ al-Ḥillî., *Muṯîr al-aḥzân wa munîr subul al-ashğân*, Part 3: 90, al-Mağlisî., *Biḥâr al-anwâr*, vol. XLV, bb. 39: 132.

174 In numerous *aḥâdîṯ* and theological writings, Fâṭima, daughter of Muḥammad, is described as *al-ʿaḏrâ'*, meaning 'virgin', a designation expressed more frequently by the use of the term *al-batûl*. For some of the theology behind these titles, cf. CLOHESSY C., *Fatima, Daughter of Muhammad*, 2009: 103–133.

175 Ibn Namâ al-Ḥillî., *Muṯîr al-aḥzân wa munîr subul al-ashğân*, Part 3: 100.

176 Ibid.

offspring: "By God," he says, "I was under the delusion that they were Byzantine captives!" In other accounts, Yazîd wishes the Syrian perpetual bachelorhood and a miserable death for his persistance in asking, especially since his request has brought a fresh, humiliating attack from Zaynab. In Ibn Ṭâ'ûs, he is ordered killed for cursing Yazîd.[177]

This event is also recorded in al-Iṣfahânî's *Maqâtil*, but in a somewhat condensed form. He takes note of two men who intervene: the first, a Syrian, asks permission to kill ʿAlî b. al-Ḥusayn for his impertinence, and Zaynab recites to him the same verse that that ʿAlî b. al-Ḥusayn had just recited to Yazîd (Q. 57: 22–23). A second man, not identified as a Syrian, then stands and asks to be given an unnamed girl – al-Iṣfahânî refers us to Ibn al-Aṯîr (where she is named as Fâṭima, but later qualified as 'sister' of Zaynab) and to al-Ṭabarî.[178] Zaynab says to him: "No, no such distinction, not for you!" Then, presumably addressing Yazîd: "Not unless he leaves the religion of God!" In most other narrations, the concept of 'leaving' religion is directed at Yazîd, Zaynab's suggestion being that he would only be able to give Fâṭima to the man were he himself to abandon his religion and find another. Yazîd tells the man to sit down. Then Zaynab approaches Yazîd and says to him: "Yazîd! Our blood is sufficient for you!" In fact, as noted previously, al-Iṣfahânî has mixed up his narratives; Zaynab's declaration about the blood is almost certainly to Ibn Ziyâd, and not to Yazîd.

Among the Sunnî historians, Ibn ʿAsâkir offers two very different narrative; the first, from Fâṭima bt. ʿAlî, recounts all the details we now know, with Fâṭima's terror, the fierce exchange of words beyween Zaynab and Yazîd, and Yazîd's peremptory dismissal of the Syrian. In the second narrative, a Syrian man stands before Yazîd and says: "Their women are permissible (*ḥalâl*) for us!"[179] ʿAlî b. al-Ḥusayn responds: "You lie! That is not (possible) for you unless you leave our community!" In this substantially long chapter, Ibn ʿAsâkir gives numerous details about the *ahl al-bayt*

---

[177] Ibn Ṭâ'ûs., *Kitâb al-luhûf fî qatlâ al-ṭufûf*: 108–109.

[178] al-Iṣfahânî., *Maqâtil al-ṭâlibîyyîn*: 120.

[179] Cf. also Sibṭ al-Ǧawzî., *Taḏkirat ḫawâṣṣ al-umma bi-ḏikr ḫaṣâ'iṣ al-a'imma*: 221.

(such as the *ḥadîṯ* of the cloak and the 'verse of purification'), the predictions of al-Ḥusayn's death (such as the dreams of Umm Salama) and the cosmic consequences of his death (such as the signs in the heavens and the weeping of the *ǧinn*). To the battle itself, he gives little attention, at least in the range of well-attested incidents in the life of Zaynab. Here, before Yazîd, there is no mention of Zaynab; perhaps unwittingly, Ibn ʿAsâkir seems to be presenting a Zaynab already stepping back so that the young Imâm can take his rightful place.[180]

Some of the texts record a certain ambivalence in Yazîd's behaviour towards the survivors. Transmitting from a number of authorities, al-Ṭabarî takes careful note of Yazîd's words and gestures; using lament and poetry, the caliph expresses a certain distress in seeing the head of al-Ḥusayn, leading us to ask whether this would moderate his treatment of the survivors. He weeps at the news of al-Ḥusayn's death, stating that he would have preferred his not being killed and more than once insisting that he himself would never have killed the Prophet's grandson.[181] He curses Ibn Ziyâd – Ibn Sumayya – and asks that the same God who should curse his governor should have mercy on al-Ḥusayn; this could be an attempt to extricate himself from the appalling results of Karbalâ', by putting the blame on Ibn Ziyâd. He turns savagely on Muḥaffiz b. Ṯaʿlaba al-ʿÂʾiḏî, who arrogantly announces his presence by insulting the survivors, and refers to the martyrs of Karbalâʾ as "those dear to us." He is horrified by the appearance of the women and children, again cursing Ibn Ziyâd, whom this time he refers to as 'Ibn Marǧâna', for his lack of empathy and concern.[182] All of this leads

---

180 Ibn ʿAsâkir., *Târîḫ madînat Dimashq*, vol. LXIX, bb. 9353 (*Zaynab al-Kubrâ bt. ʿAlî b. Abî Ṭâlib b. ʿAbd al-Muṭṭalib b. Hâshim b. ʿAbd al-Manâf*): 178, vol. XLI, bb. 4875 (*ʿAlî b. al-Husayn b. ʿAlî b. Abî Ṭâlib b. Hâshim b. ʿAbd al-Manâf*): 367.

181 Cf. for e.g. al-Ḫawârizmî., *Maqtal al-Ḥusayn*, bk. 2, bb. *fî maqtal al-Ḥusayn*: 63, Sibṭ al-Ǧawzî., *Taḏkirat ḫawâṣṣ al-umma bi-ḏikr ḫaṣâʾiṣ al-aʾimma*: 220.

182 al-Ḫawârizmî., *Maqtal al-Ḥusayn*, bk. 2, bb. *fî maqtal al-Ḥusayn*: 63, 69, Ibn Kaṯîr., *al-Bidâya wa-l-nihâya*, vol. XI: 562.

Zaynab's sister Fâṭima to remark on Yazîd's kindness[183] and Sukayna, al-Ḥusayn's daughter, to observe that she had never come across an unbeliever who was a better person that Yazîd. Yazîd displays a particular concern for the women; he orders the careful preparations for their journey back to Medina and their lodging while in Damascus, and when challenged by al-Ḥusayn's daughter Fâṭima, attempts to persuade her of his regret, addressing her as 'cousin' and promising some sort of restituiton. Al-Hayṯamî is not the only one to note that Yazîd orders that the young Sukayna be seated behind his throne, lest her catching sight of the head of her father cause her kinship with Yazîd to be weakened.[184] Yazîd has a particular fixation with ʿAlî b. al-Ḥusayn, consistently inviting him to meals,[185] cursing Ibn Ziyâd, and assuring the young Imâm that had he been with al-Ḥusayn, he would have protected him from death even "through the destruction of some of my own children" and would have granted him any favour he asked. He urges ʿAlî b. al-Ḥusayn to remain in contact and to "report everything that you need."[186]

Whether there was in Yazîd a genuine regret for what has happened, or merely a growing realization of how serious Karbalâʾ was, Sukayna, daughter of al-Ḥusayn swiftly put paid to any such thought of a change of heart in the caliph. Noting that the women were housed by Yazîd, Ibn al-Aṯîr records the words of Sukayna, daughter of al-Ḥusayn, about the caliph: "I never saw a disbeliever (*kâfir*) in God more charitable (*ḫayr*) than Yazîd b. Muʿâwiya."

---

183 Ibn ʿAsâkir., *Târîḫ madînat Dimashq*, vol. LXIX, bb. 9353 (*Zaynab al-Kubrâ bt. ʿAlî b. Abî Ṭâlib b. ʿAbd al-Muṭṭalib b. Hâshim b. ʿAbd al-Manâf*): 178.

184 Ibn Namâ al-Ḥillî., *Muṯîr al-aḥzân wa munîr subul al-ashǧân*, Part 3: 99, al-Ḏahabî., *Siyar aʿlâm al-nubalâʾ*, vol. III, bb. 48: 319–320, al-Hayṯamî., *Mağmaʿ al-zawâʾid wa-manbaʿ al-fawâʾid*, vol. IX, bb. 95 (*Manâqib al-Ḥusayn*), n. 15148: 227.

185 al-Dînawarî., *Kitâb al-aḫbâr al-ṭiwâl*: 272, Ibn ʿAsâkir., *Târîḫ madînat Dimashq*, vol. LXIX, bb. 9353 (*Zaynab al-Kubrâ bt. ʿAlî b. Abî Ṭâlib b. ʿAbd al-Muṭṭalib b. Hâshim b. ʿAbd al-Manâf*): 177.

186 Cf. HOWARD I.K.A., (trans.), *The History of al-Ṭabarî*, vol. XIX, 1990: 169–176.

Since the phrase is not unlike being damned with faint praise – he may have been charitable, but he was still being accused of *kufr* – it is hard to know why Ibn al-Aṯîr includes it. He is certainly sympathetic towards the survivors of the massacre and does not fail to record moments of regret on the part of the perpetrators. However, to record words of one who labels the Commander of the Faithful an 'ingrate' or 'disbeliever', in spite of the sympathy he may feel, is at the very least unusual. Nonetheless, this narrative is dramatically different in *Rawḍat al-wâʿiẓîn*; here, Sukayna says of Yazîd: "I have never seen a heart harsher than Yazîd's, nor have I ever seen a disbeliever (*kâfir*) or polytheist (*mushrik*) more evil than him or anyone more brutish!"[187] His guilt is tempered neither by his distance from the battlefield, nor by his reported kind treatment of the survivors of the *ahl al-bayt.*

Writing in his *Târîḫ madînat Dimashq*, Ibn ʿAsâkir notes a tradition from Abû Bakr b. al-Anbârî, that on the day al-Ḥusayn was killed, his sister Zaynab stuck her head out of her tent and declaimed in a loud voice the verses which begin: "What will you say if the Prophet asks you…"[188] Ibn Kaṯîr notes the same verse, adding, in terms of its origin, that 'only God knows', unsurprisingly so, because although some like al-Shablanǧî attribute these words to Zaynab, sister of al-Ḥusayn, and others to ʿAlî b. al-Ḥusayn before Yazîd,[189] most sources attribute them to another Zaynab, daughter of ʿAqîl,[190] who recited them as the survivors finally arrived in Medina. Ibn ʿAsâkir, noting the discrepancies, himself transmits a second strand which correctly attributes this verse to Zaynab bt. ʿAqîl.

---

187 al-Ṣadûq., *Kitâb al-amâlî fî-l-aḥâdîṯ wa-l-aḫbâr, maǧlis* 31, n. 3: 167, Ibn al-Aṯîr., *al-Kâmil fî al-târîḫ*, vol. II: 439, al-Fattâl al-Nîsâbûrî., *Rawḍat al-wâʿiẓîn wa-tabṣirat al-muttaʿiẓîn*, bb. *maqtal al-Ḥusayn*, vol. I: 191.

188 Ibn ʿAsâkir., *Târîḫ madînat Dimashq*, vol. LXIX, bb. 9353 (*Zaynab al-Kubrâ bt. ʿAlî b. Abî Ṭâlib b. ʿAbd al-Muṭṭalib b. Hâshim b. ʿAbd al-Manâf*): 178.

189 al-Ḫawârizmî., *Maqtal al-Ḥusayn*, bk. 2, bb. *fî maqtal al-Ḥusayn*: 71.

190 Cf. for e.g. al-Balâḏurî., *Kitâb ansâb al-ashrâf*, vol. III: 4120, Sibṭ al-Ǧawzî., *Taḏkirat ḫawâṣṣ al-umma bi-ḏikr ḫaṣâʾiṣ al-aʾimma*: 225, al-Haytamî., *Maǧmaʿ al-zawâʾid wa-manbaʿ al-fawâʾid*, vol. IX, bb. 95 (*Manâqib al-Ḥusayn*), n. 15183: 234–235.

Al-ʿAsqalânî writes that the survivors are moved to Medina, and it is upon their arrival there that a bareheaded woman from the women of ʿAbd al-Muṭṭalib, unnamed by al-ʿAsqalânî, meets them with the verses:

> "What will you say if the Prophet asks you; what have you, the last of the communities, done with my offspring and my family after my departure? Among them are prisoners and among them, those stained with blood. After I have given you good advice, what reward is this for me, that you should repay me with evil to my blood relations?"[191]

A substantial number of Shîʿî transmitters carry this verse; some attribute it to Zaynab, sister of al-Ḥusayn, attaching it to the Kûfa sermon,[192] others to Umm Luqmân, daughter of ʿAqîl, who, upon hearing the announcement of al-Ḥusayn's death, emerges bareheaded with her sisters Umm Hâniʾ, Asmâʾ, Ramla and Zaynab and sings the dirge,[193] some to Zaynab bt. ʿAqîl,[194] some to ʿAlî b. al-Ḥusayn before Yazîd[195] and some to the *ğinn*, whose voices are

---

[191] al-Ḫawârizmî., *Maqtal al-Ḥusayn*, bk. 2, bb. *fî maqtal al-Ḥusayn*: 84 (attributed to Zaynab bt. ʿAqîl), Ibn ʿAsâkir., *Târîḫ madînat Dimashq*, vol. LXIX, bb. 9353 (*Zaynab al-Kubrâ bt. ʿAlî b. Abî Ṭâlib b. ʿAbd al-Muṭṭalib b. Hâshim b. ʿAbd al-Manâf*): 178, Ibn Kaṯîr., *al-Bidâya wa-l-nihâya*, vol. XI: 567, al-ʿAsqalânî., *Tahḏîb al-tahḏîb*, vol II, (*Ḥusayn b. ʿAlî b. Abî Ṭâlib*): 353, al-Shablanğî., *Nûr al-abṣâr fî manâqib âl bayt al-nabî al-muḫtâr*: 202.

[192] al-Ṭabarsî., *Kitâb al-iḥtiğâğ ʿalâ ahl al-liğâğ*, vol. II: 305, Ibn Shahrâshûb., *Manâqib âl Abî Ṭâlib*, vol. IV, bb. *fî maqtali-hi*: 115, al-Mağlisî., *Biḥâr al-anwâr*, vol. XLV, bb. 39: 163.

[193] al-Mufîd., *al-Irshâd*, vol. II, bb. *fî wuṣûl ḫabar istishhâd al-Imâm al-Ḥusayn*: 124, al-Fattâl al-Nîsâbûrî., *Rawḍat al-wâʿiẓîn wa-tabṣirat al-muttaʿiẓîn*, vol. I: 193, al-Irbilî., *Kashf al-ġumma fî maʿrifat al-aʾimma*, vol. II: 68, Ibn Ṭâʾûs., *Kitâb al-luhûf fî qatlâ al-ṭufûf*: 99, al-Mağlisî., *Biḥâr al-anwâr*, vol. XLV, bb. 39: 123.

[194] Ibn Namâ al-Ḥillî., *Muṯîr al-aḥẓân wa munîr subul al-ashğân*, Part 2: 95.

[195] al-Mağlisî., *Biḥâr al-anwâr*, vol. XLV, bb. 39: 136.

heard lamenting al-Ḥusayn.[196] There are some variations in the wording between the different transmitters.

Finally, the texts record, Yazîd directs that the women be lodged in a secluded house, and with them in the house their brother ʿAlî b. al-Ḥusayn (although he was not brother to all the women). He further commands that preparations be made for the survivors to return to Medina. He orders that one al-Nuʿmân b. Bashîr make the arrangements and provide them with all that would be practical or useful. This would include finding a trustworthy Syrian man to travel with them and the supplying of horses.[197] While neither al-Ṭabarî nor Ibn ʿAsâkir nor Ibn al-Aṯîr identity the trustworthy Syrian as al-Nuʿmân b. Bashîr, Abû Miḫnaf and Ibn Kaṯîr do. In Abû Miḫnaf, Yazîd orders him to send a righteous and trustworthy person, and Nuʿmân ends up going himself.[198] Al-Dînawarî notes that, besides lodging the women and calling ʿAlî b. al-Ḥusayn to meals with him, Yazîd releases the fourth Imâm with the surviving women, ordering that he be the one to see them safely back to their own home country, and dispatches with him thirty horsemen to journey with them and guard them until they reach Medina.[199] It had been ʿAlî b. al-Ḥusayn who had insisted that Ibn Ziyâd send a 'pure' or 'righteous' man to accompany the woman; consciously or not, both Ibn Ziyâd (as noted by al-Balâḏurî) and Yazîd (as noted by al-Dînawarî) seem to think that ʿAlî is that man.

---

196 Ibn Qûlûya al-Qummî., *Kâmil al-ziyârât*: 95, al-Mağlisî., *Biḥâr al-anwâr*, vol. XLV, bb. 43: 237.

197 HOWARD I.K.A., (trans.), *The History of al-Ṭabarî*, vol. XIX, 1990: 172, Ibn ʿAsâkir., *Târîḫ madînat Dimashq*, vol. LXIX, bb. 9353 (*Zaynab al-Kubrâ bt. ʿAlî b. Abî Ṭâlib b. ʿAbd al-Muṭṭalib b. Hâshim b. ʿAbd al-Manâf*): 178.

198 LIMBA M., (trans.), *The Event of Taff, the Earliest Historical Account of the Tragedy of Karbala*, 2012: n.n., HOWARD I.K.A., (trans.), *The History of al-Ṭabarî*, vol. XIX, 1990: 172, Ibn ʿAsâkir., *Târîḫ madînat Dimashq*, vol. LXIX, bb. 9353 (*Zaynab al-Kubrâ bt. ʿAlî b. Abî Ṭâlib b. ʿAbd al-Muṭṭalib b. Hâshim b. ʿAbd al-Manâf*): 177–178, Ibn al-Aṯîr., *al-Kâmil fî al-târîḫ*, vol. II: 440–441, Ibn Kaṯîr., *al-Bidâya wa-l-nihâya*, vol. XI: 562.

199 al-Dînawarî., *Kitâb al-aḫbâr al-ṭiwâl*: 272.

As they are leaving, reports al-Ṭabarî, Yazîd engages in one final, almost pleading conversation with ʿAlî b. al-Ḥusayn:

> "God curse Ibn Marjanah, if I had been with your father, he would never have asked a favor from me without my granting it to him; I would have protected him from death with all my power, even through the destruction of some of my own children. But God has decreed what you have seen. Write to me from Medina and report everything that you need." He presented clothes to them, and entrusted them to the messenger.[200]

In the end, then, there almost certainly is a Syrian, even if not clearly identifiable. Al-Ṭabarî notes that the messenger went with them, never letting the group out of his sight, guarding, prtotecting and shielding them at every instant, constantly asking about their needs and treating them with great gentleness. At the end of the journey, in an incident omitted by Abû Miḫnaf but reported by al-Ṭabarî, Fâṭima bt. ʿAlî remarks to her sister Zaynab that this unnamed Syrian has been good to them and should be rewarded ("have you something with which we can bless him?"). Zaynab replies: "By God, we have nothing with which to bless him except for our jewellery!" Perhaps she means trinkets, considering the insistence that the women's possessions had been looted as far as stripping a gold anklet off Fâṭima. Alternatively, this might represent jewelry given them by Yazîd, who had both promised and given restitution.[201] The Syrian responds to the gifts and the accompanying apology for their meagreness by insisting that he would have been pleased with reward had he done this for worldly reasons, but that he had done it for God and by reason of their relationship to Muḥammad.[202]

Here ends the account of Zaynab in al-Ṭabarî. Knowingly or not, he has presented a daughter of ʿAlî who plays a vital role at a

---

200 HOWARD I.K.A., (trans.), *The History of al-Ṭabarî*, vol. XIX, 1990: 175.

201 Ibid.

202 Op. cit. 173, Ibn al-Aṯîr., *al-Kâmil fî al-târîḫ*, vol. II: 440–441. Cf. also al-ʿÂmilî., *Aʿyân al-Shîʿa*, vol. VII: 140.

crucial juncture in Shîʿî history, and then steps back into the shadows of history as the fourth Imâm takes his place. But her story is not quite finished.

4. THE SECOND PROTEST

According to al-Ṭabarsî,[203] Zaynab's second major address – he calls it a 'protest' (*iḥtiǧâǧ*) – which is transmitted by a substantially smaller group of Shîʿî scholars and barely any of their Sunnî counterparts,[204] was provoked by a poem recited by Yazîd, as he took jabs at the head al-Ḥusayn with his staff. "The protest of Zaynab, daughter of ʿAlî b. Abî Ṭâlib, upon seeing Yazîd, may God curse him, poking the teeth of al-Ḥusayn with a staff," begins al-Ṭabarsî's account, and he then goes on to relay the verses of the caliph:

> "Hâshim played with the dominion, and no news came, no revelation descended. Would that my elders at Badr had witnessed the apprehension of the Ḫazraǧ at the tumbling of the spears![205] They would have invoked God's name, beaming joyfully, and would have said: O Yazîd, may you not be paralyzed! We have been requited by it in similar manner as Badr. I would not be of the Ḫandaf if I did not take revenge on the offspring of Aḥmad for what was done."

The poem that Yazîd recites – "would that my elders at Badr had witnessed the apprehension of the Ḫazraǧ" – is not his own; he quotes it, as noted by a number of transmitters, from Ibn Zibaʿrî (in some texts Ibn Zabaʿrî or Ibn Zubaʿrî), spoken on the day of

---

203 al-Ṭabarsî., *Kitâb al-iḥtiǧâǧ ʿalâ ahl al-liǧâǧ*, vol. II: 308–309. Cf. also al-ʿÂmilî., *Aʿyân al-Shîʿa*, vol. VII: 139.

204 Besides al-Ṭabarsî, cf. also Ibn Abî Ṭâhir Ṭayfûr., *Balâġât al-nisâʾ*: 35–36, Ibn Ṭâʾûs., *Kitâb al-luhûf fî qatlâ al-ṭufûf*: 105–108, Ibn Namâ al-Ḥillî., *Muṯîr al-aḥzân wa munîr subul al-ashǧân*, Part 3: 101–102, al-Maǧlisî., *Biḥâr al-anwâr*, vol. XLV, bb. 39: 133–135 (from Ibn Ṭâʾûs), vol. XLV, bb. 39: 157–160 (from al-Ṭabarsî). Among the Sunnî, cf. al-Ḫawârizmî., *Maqtal al-Ḥusayn*, bk. 2, bb. *fî maqtal al-Ḥusayn*: 71–4.

205 Cf. LANE E.W., *An Arabic-English Lexicon*, vol. I, 1968: 59.

the battle of Uḥud.[206] The Shîʿî transmitters offer a diversity both in length and in wording, and place the recital of the poem in a variety of circumstances; for some, it is the catalyst for ʿAlî b. al-Ḥusayn's quoting Qur'ânic verses at Yazîd, for others, the incentive for Zaynab's cutting protest, in which she refers back to some of the sentiments expressed by the poem. In both these instances, Yazîd recites it while poking at the teeth of al-Ḥusayn.[207] Al-Ṣadûq, followed by al-Fattâl al-Nîsâbûrî, prefaces the recital with a comment by Sukayna on Yazîd which we have already seen.[208] Al-Râwandî records it just after al-Ḥusayn's killer has told Yazîd to 'fill my saddlebags with silver and gold' as a reward for his deed, a sentiment which Yazîd strongly rejects.[209] Al-Ṭabarsî's version is

---

[206] al-Tabarî., *Kitâb al-mustarshid fî imâmat ʿAlî b. Abî Tâlib*: 510, al-Ḫawârizmî., *Maqtal al-Ḥusayn*, bk. 2, bb. *fî maqtal al-Ḥusayn*: 64, Ibn Shahrâshûb., *Manâqib âl Abî Ṭâlib*, vol. IV, (*faṣl fî maqtali-hi*): 114, Ibn Ṭâ'ûs., *Kitâb al-luhûf fî qatlâ al-ṭufûf*: 105, Ibn al-Ḥadîd., *Sharḥ nahğ al-balâġa*, vol. XIV: 279, Ibn Namâ al-Ḥillî., *Muṯîr al-aḥzân wa munîr subul al-ashğân*, Part 2: 101, al-Irbilî., *Kashf al-ġumma fî maʿrifat al-a'imma*, vol. II: 21, al-Mağlisî., *Biḥâr al-anwâr*, vol. XLV, bb. 39: 133, 156. The 624 Battle of Badr ended in victory for the Muslim army, fighting a substantially larger Meccan force. Nine months later, a second clash at Uḥud, saw the defeat of the Muslims by the Meccans, in an engagement aimed at avenging Badr and the securing of the vital trade route.

[207] Cf. for e.g. Ibn Abî Ṭâhir Ṭayfûr., *Balâġât al-nisâ'*: 73, al-Ṭabarsî., *Kitâb al-iḥtiğâğ ʿalâ ahl al-liğâğ*, vol. II: 307, Ibn Shahrâshûb., *Manâqib âl Abî Ṭâlib*, vol. IV, bb. *fî maqtali-hi*: 114 where it prefaces Zaynab's first protest, not her second), Ibn Ṭâ'ûs., *Kitâb al-luhûf fî qatlâ al-ṭufûf*: 105, al-Baḥrânî., *al-Burhân fî tafsîr al-qur'ân*, vol. III, n. 7413: 905, al-Mağlisî., *Biḥâr al-anwâr*, vol. XLV, bb. 39: 157, 167 (from the *Tafsîr* of al-Qummî).

[208] al-Ṣadûq., *Kitâb al-amâlî fî-l-aḥâdîṯ wa-l-aḫbâr*, *mağlis* 31: 167, al-Fattâl al-Nîsâbûrî., *Rawḍat al-wâʿiẓîn wa-tabṣirat al-muttaʿiẓîn*, vol. I: 191 (he quotes the whole poem), al-Mağlisî., *Biḥâr al-anwâr*, vol. XLV, bb. 39: 155–156.

[209] al-Râwandî., *al-Ḫarâ'iğ wa-l-ğarâ'iḥ fî al-muʿğiẓât*, vol. II: 580, al-Mağlisî., *Biḥâr al-anwâr*, vol. XLV, bb. 39: 186.

slightly different from most other texts; for example, this is the narration of Ibn Katîr:[210]

> "Would that my elders at Badr had witnessed the apprehension of the Ḫazrağ at the tumbling of the spears! They would invoke God's name, beaming joyfully, and would then say: O Yazîd, may you not be paralyzed! We have killed the chief of their overlords and made it equivalent and even with Badr. I would not be of the Ḫandaf if I did not take revenge on the offspring of Aḥmad for what was done."

I have examined the text of Zaynab's response in five authors: Ibn Abî Ṭâhir Ṭayfûr, who died in 280/893, in his *Balâġât al-nisâ'*, al-Ṭabarsî, two-and-a-half centuries later in his *Kitâb al-iḥtiğâğ ʿalâ ahl al-liğâğ*, his contemporary, the Sunnî Ḥanafî scholar al-Ḫawârizmî in his *Maqtal al-Ḥusayn*, Ibn Ṭâ'ûs, writing a century later in his *Kitâb al-luhûf fî qatlâ al-ṭufûf*, and Ibn Namâ al-Ḥillî, almost contemporaneous with Ibn Ṭâ'ûs, in his *Muṯîr al-aḥzân*. Both al-Ṭabarsî and Ibn Ṭâ'ûs are transmitted by al-Mağlisî.[211] Ibn Abî Ṭâhir Ṭayfûr is the least developed of the five, at times offering nothing but a skeleton of the protest; al-Ṭabarsî is substantially longer and more developed than the other four.

Al-Ṭabarsî takes up the account of Zaynab's reaction to Yazîd's poem and mistreatment of al-Ḥusayn's head:

> When Zaynab saw that, she grasped the collar of her robe and tore it, and then cried out with a sad voice that censured hearts: "O my Ḥusayn! O beloved of the Messenger of God! O son of Mecca and Minâ! O son of Fâṭima al-Zahrâ', mistress of

---

[210] Ibn Katîr., *al-Bidâya wa-l-nihâya*, vol. VIII: 192.

[211] Ibn Abî Ṭâhir Ṭayfûr., *Balâġât al-nisâ'*: 35–36, al-Ṭabarsî., *Kitâb al-iḥtiğâğ ʿalâ ahl al-liğâğ*, vol. II: 308–309 (with its transmission in al-Mağlisî., *Biḥâr al-anwâr*, vol. XLV, bb. 39: 157–160), al-Ḫawârizmî., *Maqtal al-Ḥusayn*, bk. 2, bb. *fî maqtal al-Ḥusayn*: 71–4, Ibn Ṭâ'ûs., *Kitâb al-luhûf fî qatlâ al-ṭufûf*: 105–108 (with its transmission in al-Mağlisî., *Biḥâr al-anwâr*, vol. XLV, bb. 39: 133–135) and Ibn Namâ al-Ḥillî., *Muṯîr al-aḥzân wa munîr subul al-ashğân*, Part 3: 101–102.

the women! O son of Muḥammad a-Muṣṭafâ!"[212] By God, all who were present wept, while Yazîd remained silent. Then she got to her feet, and looking down at the gathering, commenced the sermon, an exposition of the perfections of Muḥammad, God bless him and his family, and a declaration that, with neither fear nor dismay, we be patient for the satisfaction of God. Then Zaynab, daughter of ʿAlî, and whose mother was Fâṭima daughter of the Messenger of God, went before Yazîd and said:

"Praise be to God, Lord of the worlds,[213] and blessings upon my grandfather, leader of those sent. God, far above is He (*subḥâna-hu*), spoke the truth when He said: "*Then evil was the consequence to those who dealt in evil, because they denied the revelations of Allah and made a mock of them*".[214] Did you suppose, Yazîd, having cut us off from the regions of the earth and besieged us to the horizons of the sky, so that we have ended up in chains for you, herded before you, goaded in a train, that you have power over us, and that for us there is ignominy from God, while for you there is nobility and favour from Him? Or that this is on account of the greatness of your importance and the loftiness of your power? You were arrogant and conceited,[215] behaving insolently,[216] rejoicing, threatening vainly,[217] exuberant, when

---

212 Cf. Ibn Ṭâʾûs., *Kitâb al-luhûf fî qatlâ al-ṭufûf*: 104.

213 Q. 1: 2.

214 Q. 30: 10.

215 Lit. 'you looked at your sides' (cf. LANE E.W., *An Arabic-English Lexicon*, vol. V, 1968: 2080).

216 Lit. 'you came beating [with your hands] your two sides' (cf. LANE E.W., *An Arabic-English Lexicon*, vol. IV, 1968: 1662). The sense is that of being empty-handed, not have accomplished the object of one's desire, or of extreme arrogance or insolence.

217 Lit. 'you came shaking the two extremities' or 'the two uppermost parts of the buttocks' (cf. LANE E.W., *An Arabic-English Lexicon*, vol. III, 1968: 965). The phrase is applied to someone who is behaving threateningly or arrogantly or vainly, or to those who have not accomplished what they sought to do.

you saw the earth become possible[218] for you and matters well-ordered for you, and when our rule became untroubling for you and our authority belonged to you. But slowly! Slowly! Do not strike impetuously! Have you forgotten the words of God, mighty and lofty: "*And let not those who disbelieve imagine that the rein We give them bodeth good unto their souls. We only give them rein that they may grow in sinfulness. And theirs will be a shameful doom*"?[219] Is it just, son of the freedmen,[220] your keeping your noble women and slaves in seclusion and your herding the daughters of the Messenger of God as captives? You ripped apart their veils and displayed their faces! The enemies moved them from place to place, the (people of the)[221] braziers raising their eyes to them and conspicuous to the people of the watering places;[222] those near and far, the concealed and the one

---

218 Al-Ḫawârizmî and al-Ṭabarsî read 'to become possible' (*mustawsiq*), while Ibn Ṭâ'ûs narrates 'to be made certain, made sure, secured' (*mustawṯiq*). Although he is following Ibn Ṭâ'ûs, al-Mağlisî deviates from him, preserving 'to become possible'. While some who transmit the text follow al-Mufîd, al-Ṭabarsî and al-Mağlisî (cf. for example KAḤÂLA ʿU., *Aʿlâm al-nisâ' fi ʿâlamî al-ʿarab wa-l-islâm*, Mu'assat al-Risâla, Beirut 1984: 97 and al-ḤASANÎ N., *Sabâyâ âl Muḥammad, al-ʿAtba al-Ḥusayniyya al-Muqaddasa*, Karbalâ' 2012: 221), Ibn Ṭâ'ûs' rendering seems more likely (cf. for e.g. ʿABD AL-RAḤMÂN ʿÂ., *Tarâğim sayyidât bayt a-nubûwa*, Dar al-Diyan lil-Turath, Beirut 1988: 774. This authoress – known as Bint al-Shâṭi' – transmitted the same word in her book *Sayyida Zaynab*). It should be noted that the transmission of Zaynab's words in *Aʿlâm al-nisâ' fi ʿâlamî al-ʿarab wa-l-islâm* contains substantial differences and omissions. Ibn Namâ's text offers both possibilities.

219 Q. 3: 178.

220 Wehr defines *al-ṭulaqâ'* as the name for those Meccans who remained heathen until the surrender of Mecca. The editor of al-Mağlisî notes the words of Muḥammad to Yazîd's grandfather Abû Sufyân: "You are free". Cf. WEHR H., *A Dictionary of Modern Written Arabic*, 1980: 663.

221 These words, present in other texts, are missing in transcript of al-Ṭabarsî.

222 The phrases 'people of the braziers' and 'people of the watering places' refer to the nomadic tent dwellers or country people.

who bears testimony, the eminent and the humble, the lowly and the lofty, scrutinizing their faces? None of their men is with them as guardian and none of their patrons as protection. Insolence from you towards God, disavowal of the Messenger of God, driving off what comes with him from God; this is hardly surprising, coming from you, and there is no wondering at your deed! How could you[223] hope for control from one whose mouth spat out the livers of the martyrs[224] and who nourished his flesh with the blood of the auspicious[225] and declared war on the chief of the prophets, gathered the troops, declared the wars, and brandished the swords in the face of the Messenger of God! The most vehement of the Arabs in disavowal, the most reprehensible of them to him as prophet, the most manifest of them to him as enemy, the most insolent of them towards the Lord in disbelief and tyranny; is this not due to the characteristics of disbelief and the pouring forth that roars in the breast for those killed on the day of Badr? He is not found slow in detesting us, the people of the house, one whose view of us was loathing and hatred and grudges, his disbelief in the Messenger of God manifest and spoken clearly with his tongue, for he spoke joyfully in the killing of his children and the taking captive of his offspring. Without refraining from sin or from arrogance, his elders acclaim him: 'they would invoke God's name, beaming joyfully, and would then say: O Yazîd, may you not be paralyzed!'

Leaning on the teeth of Abû ʿAbd Allâh, where the Messenger of God, God bless him and his family, used to kiss, striking them with his staff, his face shining with pleasure! By my life, you have reopened the wound and exterminated the root, in your shedding the blood of the leader of the youths of the

---

223 The text reads *tartaǧî* (second person singular, 'you hope'): in others transmissions, *yartaǧî* (third person singular, 'he/one hopes').

224 Here, *al-shuhadâ'*, as opposed to al-Maǧlisî's 'the blameless' and Ibn Ṭâ'ûs' 'the intelligent'.

225 Here, *al-suʿadâ'*, as opposed to al-Maǧlisî's and Ibn Ṭâ'ûs' 'the martyrs'.

people of paradise, the son of the chief of the religion of the Arabs and the sun of the family of ʿAbd al-Muṭṭalib. You applauded your elders and by his blood sought to gain favour with the obstinate infidels among your forebears. Thereupon, you called out your appeal, and by my life, you summoned them as if they could see you! Well, imminently you will see them, but they will not bear witness to you. Then how you will wish that your right hand, as you alleged, was paralyzed for you from its elbow, and cut off; you would prefer that your mother had not carried you and had never given birth to you, when you come to the anger of God Most High and your adversary is the Messenger of God, God bless him and his family.

O God, obtain what is our right and take revenge on our oppressor! Discharge Your anger against the one who shed our blood and broke with our honour and killed our patrons and tore apart our veils.

You have done your deed, and you have split nothing but your own skin, cut off nothing but your own flesh, and you will come to the Messenger of God, God bless him and his family, with all that you bear of the blood of his offspring, and have desecrated of his sanctity, and have shed of the blood of his family and his flesh – when God reunites them, puts their affairs in order, takes revenge on their oppressors and obtains for them what is their right from their enemies. Do not let their killing incite you to happiness. "*Think not of those, who are slain in the way of Allah, as dead. Nay, they are living. With their Lord they have provision. Jubilant (are they) because of that which Allah hath bestowed upon them of His bounty*".[226]

God is sufficient for you as guardian and judge, and the Messenger of God, God bless him and his family, as adversary, and Ǧibraʾîl as (his) supporter.[227] He will know who associated

[226] Q. 3: 169 and the first phrase of 170.

[227] Ibn Ṭâʾûs reads 'Ǧibraʾîl', al-Ṭabarsî, 'Ǧibrâʾîl' and al-Maǧlisî 'Ǧibrîl' – throughout the Shîʿî and Sunnî Islamic corpora of *aḥâdîṯ*, the name that we are accustomed to translate as 'Gabriel' is written in a varie-

with you[228] and gave you power over the necks of the Muslims: "*calamitous is the exchange for evil-doers*"[229] and you are "*worse in position*"[230] and "*further from the road*".[231]

Neither my deeming as paltry your power nor my thinking your chiding significant makes delusional the resorting to a public address to you, after you left the eyes of the Muslims tearful and their breasts burning upon remembrance of him. Those merciless hearts and tyrannical souls and bodies are filled with the anger of God and the curse of the Messenger. Satan has nested and hatched in them, and one like you he does not outgrow.

The surprise of all surprises, the killing of the devout and the grandsons of the prophets, the descendant of the trustees, at the hands of the freedmen, the filth (*ḫabîṯa*) and the progeny of the immoral fornicatress. Their hands drip with our blood and and their mouths run with our flesh. The wolves beset those pure bodies on the surrounding earth, and mothers of the wild beasts cover them with dust. Even if you took us as booty, you would find us an imminent loss, when you do not find anything but what you have perpetrated. And God "*is not at all a tyrant to His slaves*".[232] Before God is the complaint and the reliance, and before him the refuge and the hope. So, plot your ruse and attempt your endeavour, but by God, who honoured us with Revelation and the Book and the Prophethood and the

---

ty of ways: sometimes 'Ǧibrîl', at other times 'Ǧibra'îl' and occasional 'Ǧibrâ'îl'.

228 Al-Maǧlisî reads, almost certainly incorrectly, 'to equalize, level, straighten' (*sawwâ*) while Ibn Ṭâ'ûs transmits as 'to talk someone into', 'to entice or seduce' (*sawwala*). I have followed the latter.

229 Q. 18: 50.

230 Cf. Q. 19: 75.

231 Cf. Q. 17: 72.

232 A slightly misquoted Q. 3: 182 or Q. 8: 51, in the sense that it is not written exactly as it occurs in the Qur'ân (where the negation is *laysa*, not *mâ*). Cf. also Q. 22: 10, Q. 41: 46 and Q. 50: 29 for an almost identical rendering.

> Selection, you will neither overtake our span of time, nor exhaust our purpose, nor efface our memory, nor wash from yourself its blemish. Is your opinion anything but error in judgment, your days anything but numbered, your community anything but dispersed, on the day when the caller will cry; now God curses the oppressor and the enemy? Praise be to God, who has awarded His holy ones with happiness, and sealed His sincere friends with martyrdom and attainment of the will, and brought them to mercy, compassion, delight and pardon. None is split from them other than you and none is afflicted because of them apart from you. We ask Him to complete for them the recompense and to give them openhandedly the reward and the laid-up treasure and we ask of Him the excellence of succession and the beauty of delegation. Truly, he is "*merciful, Loving.*"[233]

Noting in his *Biḥâr al-anwâr* that he transmits the narrative more than once because of many differences, al-Mağlisî reads:

> Zaynab, daughter of ʿAlî b. Abî Ṭâlib, stood up and said: Praise be to God, Lord of the worlds. God bless His prophet and all of his family. God[234] spoke the truth when He spoke thus: "*Then evil was the consequence to those who dealt in evil, because they denied the revelations of Allah and made a mock of them*".[235] Did you imagine, Yazîd, having cut us off from the regions of the earth and the horizons of the sky, so that we have become herded, as captives are herded, that with us there is ignominy from God, while with you there is nobility? And that this is on account of the greatness of your significance with Him? You were arrogant, and looked on in your disdain, exuberant and delighted, since you saw the earth secured for you and matters in good order, and since our rule and our authority have became untroubling for you. Slowly! Slowly! Have you forgotten the words of God the Most High: "*And let not those who disbelieve imagine that the rein We give them bodeth good unto their souls. We only*

[233] Q. 11: 90.
[234] Ibn Ṭâ'ûs adds 'Glorified is He'.
[235] Q. 30: 10.

give them rein that they may grow in sinfulness. And theirs will be a shameful doom".[236]

Is it just, son of the freedmen, your keeping your noble women and slaves in seclusion and your herding the daughters of the Messenger of God as captives, having ripped apart their veils and displayed their faces, the enemies moving them from place to place, the people of the watering places and the people of the braziers raising their glances to them, and those near and far, the lowly and the eminent, scrutinizing their faces? None of their men is with them as guardian and none of their patrons as protection. But how could one hope for control from one whose mouth spat out the livers of the blameless[237] and who nourished his flesh with the blood of the martyrs? How could he be slow in detesting us, the people of the house,[238] the one who looks at us with loathing and hatred, with deep rooted odium and malice? Furthermore, without restraint or regard, you say:

Cheering and raising their voices joyfully, they would then say: Yazîd! May you never be paralyzed!

How would you not say that, leaning on the teeth of Abû ʿAbd Allâh, leader of the youths of the people of Paradise, striking them with your staff? You have already reopened the wound and extirpated the root, in your shedding the blood of the offspring of Muḥammad and the stars of the earth from the family of ʿAbd al-Muṭṭalib. You call upon your elders, alleging that you invoke them; but certainly, you will arrive imminently at their place of destination and certainly, you will wish that you had been paralyzed and had held your tongue – that you had not said what you have said or done what you have done!

---

[236] Q. 3: 178.

[237] Al-Mağlisî reads 'the blameless' (*al-azkiyâʾ*) and Ibn Ṭâʾûs 'the intelligent' (*al-ankiyâʾ*). I have followed al-Mağlisî in this instance.

[238] In a small discrepancy, al-Mağlisî reads 'the detestation of us, the people of the house' and Ibn Ṭâʾûs, 'the detestation of the people of the house'.

O God, obtain what is our right and take revenge on our oppressor![239] Discharge Your anger against the one who shed our blood and killed our patrons.

For by God, you have split nothing but your own skin, cut[240] off nothing but your own flesh, and certainly, you will come to the Messenger of God with all that you bear in the shedding of the blood of his offspring and your desecrating his sanctity in his family and his kinship, when God reunites them, puts their affairs in order and obtains what is their right. "*Think not of those, who are slain in the way of Allah, as dead. Nay, they are living. With their Lord they have provision*".[241] God is sufficient for you as judge, and Muḥammad as adversary, and Ğibra'îl as (his) supporter. He will know who seduced[242] you into evil and gave you power over the necks of the Muslims – "*calamitous is the exchange for evil-doers*"[243] – and which of you "*is worse in position*» and «*weaker as an army*".[244]

Even if your public speech has brought down calamity upon me, I make light of your power, I find your scolding astonishing,[245] and I deem your censure excessive.[246] But eyes are tear-

---

[239] Al-Mağlisî reads 'our oppressor' (*ẓâlim*) and Ibn Ṭâ'ûs 'our oppression' (*ẓulm*). In the context, the former seems more likely, although the latter is transmitted by a number of authors.

[240] Al-Mağlisî, in what may be nothing more than an error by the editors, reads 'to clip off' (*ğazza*) and Ibn Ṭâ'ûs 'to cut' (*ḥazza*). I have followed the latter.

[241] Q. 3: 169.

[242] Al-Mağlisî reads, almost certainly incorrectly, 'to equalize, level, straighten' (*sawwiya*) (سوى) while Ibn Ṭâ'ûs transmits as 'to talk someone into', 'to entice or seduce' (*sawwala*). I have followed the latter.

[243] Q. 18: 50.

[244] Cf. Q. 19: 75.

[245] Cf. STEINGASS F., *Learner's Arabic English Dictionary*, 1993: 706.

[246] Al-Mağlisî reads 'to deem great or important' (*istakbara*) and Ibn Ṭâ'ûs 'to deem too much, excessive' (*istakṯara*). I have followed the latter. However, cf. LANE E W., *An Arabic-English Lexicon*, vol. VII, 1968: 2585,

ful and chests are burning; is not the killing of the noble party of God by the party of Satan, the freedmen, the surprise of all surprises? These hands drip with our blood and mouths run with our flesh. The wolves[247] beset those most righteous and blameless corpses, and the mothers of the wild beasts[248] efface[249] them. Even if you took us as booty, you would find us an imminent loss, when you do not find anything but what you have perpetrated.[250] "*And thy Lord is not at all a tyrant to His slaves*".[251] To God the complaint, and the reliance is on Him. So, plot your ruse and attempt your endeavour and make an open show of your attempt, but by God you will not efface our memory, nor put to death our revelation, nor reach our span of time, nor wash from yourself its blemish. Is your opinion anything but error in judgment, your days anything but numbered, your community anything but dispersed, on the day when the caller will cry: "*Now the curse of Allah is upon wrongdoers*"?[252]

Praise be to God,[253] who sealed the first of us with happiness[254] and the last of us with martyrdom and mercy! We ask God to complete for them the reward and grant them the superabundance (the utmost, maximum), and to ameliorate for

---

where he suggests that the word as rendered by al-Mağlisî could carry the sense of 'to disdain'.

247 Wolves or jackels (*al-ʿawâsil*). Cf. LANE E W., *An Arabic-English Lexicon*, vol. V, 1968: 2046.

248 The word *al-farâʿil* refers to young hyenas. IBN MANẒÛR., *Lisân al-ʿarab*, vol. X: 241.

249 Ibn Ṭâʾûs reads 'to begrime, to cover with dust' (*ʿafara*) and al-Mağlisî 'to efface, obliterate' (*ʿafâ*).

250 Ibn Ṭâʾûs reads 'what your hands have perpetrated'.

251 Q. 41: 46.

252 Q. 11: 18.

253 Ibn Ṭâʾûs adds 'Lord of the worlds' (*rabb al-ʿâlamîn*).

254 Ibn Ṭâʾûs adds 'forgiveness' (*al-mağfira*) after 'happiness' (*al-saʿâda*).

> us the succession. He is "*Merciful, Loving.*[255] *Allah is Sufficient for us! Most Excellent is He in Whom we trust*".[256]

Yazîd's laconic response, ("O cry, extolled among cries, how easy death is among professional mourners")[257] belies the fact that Zaynab's address is a crushing indictment of his morality, his politics, his religious faith and his leadership. Sentence after sentence demolishes his integrity, his political dexterity, his ethical principles and his administrative abilities. He is, in Zaynab's view, entirely irreligious, a man devoid of humanity and decency, whose distance from the field of Karbalâʾ in no way diminishes his guilt.

It is at this moment that public role of indomitable Zaynab comes to an end; she has, in a few short days, been her brother's chief apologist and defender, his theologian and spokeswoman, preserving by her words and dauntless gestures not only the integrity of Shîʿî teaching, but also its line of Imâms and what is surely the paramount juncture of its history. In spite of all she has suffered, and even in the face of the murder of most of her family, she completes her task on a note of utter trust in the excellence and the sufficiency of God. She will live out the rest of her life in the shadows of history, dying around seventeen months after Karbalâʾ, in 62/682.

---

[255] Q. 11: 90.

[256] Q. 3: 173.

[257] Put by Sibṭ al-Ğawzî in a different context, when al-Ḥusayn's women and Ziyâd's women lament together. Cf. Sibṭ al-Ğawzî., *Taḏkirat ḫawâṣṣ al-umma bi-ḏikr ḫaṣâʾiṣ al-aʾimma*: 222. However, cf. also al-ʿÂmilî., *Aʿyân al-Shîʿa*, vol. VII: 140.

THREE ADDENDA

1. THE CHILDREN OF ZAYNAB

While historians such as al-Balâḏurî and al-ʿAsqalânî note merely that Zaynab 'bore children' for her husband, but provide neither names nor number,[1] according to tradition Zaynab was the mother of four sons and a daughter: ʿAlî, known as ʿAlî al-Zaynabî,[2] ʿAwn al-Akbar, ostensibly killed at Karbalâʾ, ʿAbbâs, about whom there is little information, Muḥammad, also supposedly a martyr at Karbalâʾ, and Umm Kulṯûm.[3] However, the names and number of sons that she (as opposed to another wife) bore for ʿAbd Allâh b. Ǧaʿfar remain a matter of debate. While the majority of texts which report four sons and one daughter[4] name the girl as Umm Kulṯûm, the boys are variously and unaccountably named as ʿAlî, ʿAwn (al-Akbar), ʿAbbâs, Ǧaʿfar or Muḥammad.[5] Consequently, the texts

---

[1] al-Balâḏurî., *Kitâb ansâb al-ashrâf*, vol. III: 393, al-ʿAsqalânî., *al-Iṣâba fî tamyîz al-ṣaḥâba*, vol. IV, n. 510: 314–315.

[2] Cf. for e.g. al-ʿÂmilî., *Aʿyân al-Shîʿa*, vol. VII: 137.

[3] QUTBUDDIN B.T., "Zaynab bint Ali" in Lindsay Jones (ed.), *Encyclopedia of Religion*, 2nd edn., 2005: 9937. Cf. Ibn al-Aṯîr., *Usd al-ġâba fî maʿrifat al-ṣaḥâba*, vol. VI, bb. 6961 (*Zaynab bt. ʿAlî b. Abî Ṭâlib*): 136–137, al-ʿÂmilî., *Aʿyân al-Shîʿa*, vol. VII: 137, quoting from Sibṭ al-Ǧawzî.

[4] Cf. for e.g. Ibn al-Aṯîr., *Usd al-ġâba fî maʿrifat al-ṣaḥâba*, vol. VI, bb. 6961 (*Zaynab bt. ʿAlî b. Abî Ṭâlib*): 136–137 (mentioning her marriage to ʿAbd Allâh b. Ǧaʿfar and that she gave birth to ʿAlî, ʿAwn al-Akbar, ʿAbbâs, Muḥammad and Umm Kulṯûm) and Ibn Saʿd., *Kitâb al-ṭabaqât al-kabîr*, vol. XII, n. 5464 (*Zaynab*): 431.

[5] Cf. for e.g. al-Suyûṭî., *al-ʿAǧâba al-zarnabiyya fi-l-sulâlat al-zaynabiyya*: 2, AL-TÛNǦÎ M., *Muʿǧam aʿlâm al-nisâʾ*, Muʾassasat al-Rayyân, Beirut 2000. Al-Mûsawî notes that Zaynab bore three sons for ʿAbd Allâh b.

about Zaynab's marriage and specifically about the number of children she bore are contradictory and unclear.

Among the classical Sunnî scholars, al-Ṭabarî narrates two traditions: one holds that she bore two children, named ʿAlî and ʿAwn, while a second strand names her children as ʿAlî, Ğaʿfar, ʿAbbâs, ʿAwn and Umm Kulṯûm, all from her husband ʿAbd Allâh b. Ğaʿfar.[6] Ibn Saʿd notes that ʿAbd Allâh b. Ğaʿfar also married one Layla bt. Masʿûd, and that both she and Zaynab lived as his wives, but mentions no children from Layla.[7] Writing some years later, al-Balâḏurî transmits that Zaynab bore children for her husband, with no mention of names or number;[8] three hundred years after him, Ibn al-Ğawzî names just two sons, ʿAbd Allâh and ʿAwn.[9] His near contemporary Ibn al-Aṯîr transmits that she brought forth children for ʿAbd Allâh b. Ğaʿfar b. Abî Ṭâlib, without naming them; in a second strand, having confirmed that she was indeed the daughter of Fâṭima and ʿAlî and that she had married ʿAbd Allâh b. Ğaʿfar b. Abî Ṭâlib, staying with him for life, Ibn al-Aṯîr names two children: ʿAlî b. ʿAbd Allâh and ʿAwn. In a third strand, that number devolves into five, with the addition of ʿAbbâs, Muḥammad and Umm Kulṯûm.[10] A little over half-a-century before, his fellow historian Ibn ʿAsâkir had named two sons, ʿAlî b. ʿAbd Allâh and ʿAwn in one report, and four, ʿAlî, ʿAwn al-Akbar, ʿAbbâs, Muḥammad in another. Ibn ʿAsâkir also noted the name of Layla bt. Masʿûd, a second wife .[11] Three centuries later, al-Suyûṭî will name five children for Zaynab and her hus-

---

Ğaʿfar, naming them ʿAlî, Ğaʿfar and ʿAwn al-Akbar. Cf. AL-MÛSAWÎ M., *al-Kawṯar fî aḥwâl Fâṭima bt. al-nabî al-aṭhar*, vol. VII, ch. 17, n. 7/3864: 100.

[6] al-Ṭabarî., *Ḏaḫâʾir al-ʿuqbâ*: 285–6. He notes in his text that al-Dâraquṭnî names the children as ʿAlî, ʿAwn and Ruqayya.

[7] Ibn Saʿd., *Kitâb al-ṭabaqât al-kabîr*, vol. XII, n. 5464 (*Zaynab*): 431–432.

[8] al-Balâḏurî., *Kitâb ansâb al-ashrâf*, vol. II: 411.

[9] Ibn al-Ğawzî., *Ṣifat al-ṣafwa*, vol. II, bb. *Fâṭima bt. Rasûl Allâh*: 2.

[10] Ibn al-Aṯîr., *al-Kâmil fî al-târîḫ*, vol. II: 443.

[11] Ibn ʿAsâkir., *Târîḫ madînat Dimashq*, vol. LXIX, bb. 9353 (*Zaynab al-Kubrâ bt. ʿAlî b. Abî Ṭâlib*): 175–176.

band, as did Ibn al-Aṯîr before him: ʿAlî, ʿAwn al-Akbar, Abbâs, Muḥammad and Umm Kulṯûm.[12]

Whatever the number of sons and their names, two of those frequently specified, ʿAwn and Muḥammad, are of particular interest, because ostensibly, they accompanied Zaynab to Karbalâʾ, and both died on the field.[13] A substantial number of texts name them among the dead, although they are almost always referred to as the two sons of ʿAbd Allâh b. Ğaʿfar, without any mention of Zaynab as their mother.

Al-Balâḏurî, for example, records the death of ʿAwn and Muḥammad, sons of ʿAbd Allâh b. Ğaʿfar, as does Ibn Kaṯîr in two places, where he records specifically the names of six deceased sons of ʿAlî', two of al-Ḥusayn and three of al-Ḥasan, besides the two deceased sons of ʿAbd Allâh b. Ğaʿfar. The Shîʿî transmitter al-Mufîd records their names as ʿAwn and Muḥammad, sons of ʿAbd Allâh b. Ğaʿfar, both killed at Karbalâʾ while another Shîʿî scholar, Ibn Namâ, records the death of ʿAwn ʿAbd Allâh b. Ğaʿfar b. Abî Ṭâlib, but curiously, makes no mention that he is the son of Zaynab, who otherwise features prominently in his work.[14]

Three *maqâtil* works are worth noting: al-Iṣbahânî in his *Maqâtil* and ʿAbd al-Razzâq al-Muqarram (d. 1370/1951) in his *Maqtal*, when recording the death of ʿAwn, name Zaynab as his mother, while his brother Muḥammad b. ʿAbd Allâh b. Ğaʿfar, killed after him, is named as the son of al-Ḫawsâ.[15] In the course of

---

[12] al-Suyûṭî., *al-ʿAǧâǧa al-zarnabiyya fî-l-sulâlat al-zaynabiyya*: 2.

[13] HUSAIN A.A.T., (trans.), *House of Sorrows*, Islamic Publishing House, Ontario 2010: 182, al-ʿÂmilî., *Aʿyân al-Shîʿa*, vol. VII: 137, who notes that they were killed 'before her eyes', although this is not a detail emphasized in the classical texts.

[14] al-Balâḏurî., *Kitâb ansâb al-ashrâf*, vol III: 422, Ibn Kaṯîr., *al-Bidâya wa-l-nihâya*: vol. II: 545, 551, al-Mufîd., *al-Irshâd fî maʿrifat ḥuǧaǧ Allâh ʿalâ al-ʿibâd*, vol. II: 107, 125, Ibn Namâ al-Ḥillî., *Muṯîr al-aḥzân wa munîr subul al-ashǧân*, Part 2: 67.

[15] Cf. al-Iṣbahânî., *Maqâtil al-ṭâlibîyyîn*: 91, AL-JIBOURI Y.T., (trans.), *Maqtal al-Ḥusain*, CreateSpace Independent Publishing Platform, 2014: 213. This is a translation of ʿAbd al-Razzâq al-Muqarram's *maqtal*; one of its chief weaknesses is that he is one of a group of scholars who

his narrative, al-Iṣfahânî also draws our attention to the fact that there are two men named ʿAwn ʿAbd Allâh b. Ǧaʿfar: al-Akbar, who was killed at Karbalâʾ, and al-Aṣġar, son of Ǧumâna bt. Musayb.[16] Al-Ḫawârizmî, in his *Maqtal*, narrates that the first member of the *ahl al-bayt* to emerge and be killed was ʿAbd Allâh b. Muslim b. ʿAqîl, followed by Ǧaʿfar b. ʿAqîl b. Abî Ṭâlib, followed by his brother ʿAbd al-Raḥmân b. ʿAqîl. Immediately after these deaths, al-Ḫawârizmî records the death of Muḥammad b. ʿAbd Allâh b. Ǧaʿfar b. Abî Ṭâlib followed by ʿAwn b. ʿAbd Allâh b. Ǧaʿfar b. Abî Ṭâlib. He does not mention that these are the two sons of Zaynab, although in other cases (such as that of Abû Bakr b. ʿAlî, ʿUṯmân b. ʿAlî and the other brothers of al-Ḥusayn) he does mention the name of the deceased's mother.[17]

Writing in his *al-Kâmil fî al-târîḫ*, Ibn al-Aṯîr, in his Karbalâʾ martyrology, regularly mentions the names of the mothers of the deceased (even if it is just *umm walad*, that is, 'a slave girl'), but fails to name Zaynab as the mother of ʿAwn and Muḥammad. So, for example, among those killed with al-Ḥusayn he records ʿAbd Allâh b. al-Ḥusayn b. ʿAlî, son of al-Ḥusayn by his wife Rubâb and ʿAlî b. al-Ḥusayn b. ʿAlî son of al-Ḥusayn by his wife Laylâ bt. Abî Murra b. ʿArwa al-Ṯaqafî. He then lists as killed ʿAwn b. Abî Ǧaʿfar b. Abî Ṭâlib, recording his mother not as Zaynab, but as one Ǧumâna bt. al-Musayb b. Naǧiyya al-Fazârî as well as Muḥammad ʿAbd Allâh b. Ǧaʿfar, recording his mother not as Zaynab, but as one al-Ḫawṣâʾ bt. Ḫaṣfa b. Taym Allâh b. Ṯaʿlaba. It is not entirely certain that these are indeed the two sons of ʿAbd Allâh b. Ǧaʿfar, but it seems remarkably coincidental.[18] There is no other ʿAwn in Ibn al-

---

believe that Zaynab and Umm Kulṯûm were the same person, i.e. that there was no other daughter of ʿAlî and Fâṭima named Umm Kulṯûm. This argument has been clearly refuted by Jaffer Ladak (LADAK J., *The Hidden Treasure. Lady Umm Kulthum, Daughter of Imam Ali and Lady Fatima*, 2011), especially since it contradicts most of the classical sources.

[16] al-Iṣfahânî., *Maqâtil al-ṭâlibîyyîn*: 124.

[17] al-Ḫawârizmî., *Maqtal al-Ḥusayn*, bk. 2, bb. *fî maqtal al-Ḥusayn*: 30–32.

[18] Ibn al-Aṯîr., *al-Kâmil fî al-târîḫ*, vol. II: 443.

Aṯîr's martyrology,[19] and the other Muḥammad is clearly someone different. It seems inexplicable that Ibn al-Aṯîr should have omitted the sons of ʿAlî's daughter.[20]

Ibn al-Aṯîr's contemporary Sibṭ al-Ğawzî is equally unclear, in spite of his Shîʿî sympathies (as alleged by Ibn Saʿd and al-Ḏahabî); he names among the dead of Karbalâʾ ʿAwn b. ʿAbd Allâh b. Ğaʿfar b. Abî Ṭâlib, whose mother he names as Ğumâna bt. al-Musayb, and Muḥammad ʿAbd Allâh b. Ğaʿfar b. Abî Ṭâlib, whose mother he records as al-Ḥawṭ bt. Ḥafṣa Tamîmî. He then notes that Ğaʿfar had a second son called ʿAwn, whose mother was Asmâʾ bt. ʿUmays. There is no mention of Zaynab.[21]

Ibn Kaṯîr too records the names of some of those killed, specifically six of ʿAlî's sons, two sons of al-Ḥusayn and three sons of al-Ḥasan. He also names two the deceased sons of ʿAbd Allâh b. Ğaʿfar, ʿAwn and Muḥammad, but without mentioning Zaynab as their mother.[22] Al-Ḏahabî notes the death of Muḥammad and

---

[19] There are, however, two in al-Balâḏurî's list, one of them being a son of ʿAqîl (cf. al-Balâḏurî., *Kitâb ansâb al-ashrâf*, vol III: 422).

[20] Ibn al-Aṯîr., *al-Kâmil fî al-târîḫ*: vol. II: 429, 443.

[21] Sibṭ al-Ğawzî., *Taḏkirat ḫawâṣṣ al-umma bi-ḏikr ḫaṣâʾiṣ al-aʾimma*: 229. The editor of Abû Miḫnaf quotes al-Ṭabarî, naming ʿAwn's mother as Ğumâna bt. Musayb b. Nağâba al-Ġazari, but notes that al-Iṣfahânî in his *Maqâtil* names ʿAwn's mother as Zaynab. Abû Miḫnaf's editor names Muḥammad's mother as Ḫawṣâʾ bt. Ḫaṣafa b. Ṯaqîf and notes that al-Iṣfahânî agrees (cf. HOWARD I.K.A., (trans.), *The History of al-Ṭabarî*, vol. XIX, 1990: 180, al-Iṣfahânî., *Maqâtil al-ṭâlibîyyîn*: 91), but that Sibṭ al-Ğawzî in *Taḏkirat* names her as al-Ḥawṭ bt. Ḥafṣa Tamîmî (Sibṭ al-Ğawzî., *Taḏkirat ḫawâṣṣ al-umma bi-ḏikr ḫaṣâʾiṣ al-aʾimma*: 229). Cf. LIMBA M., (trans.), *The Event of Taff, the Earliest Historical Account of the Tragedy of Karbala*, 2012: n.n. It is of note that Sibṭ al-Ğawzî, besides noting that ʿAbd Allâh b. Ğaʿfar had two sons called ʿAwn and one called Muḥammad, and naming women other than Zaynab as their mothers, also devotes a paragraph to the children of ʿAbd Allâh b. Ğaʿfar in which he names Zaynab as the mother of four of his children; ʿAwn al-Akbar, Muḥammad, ʿAbbâs and Umm Kulṯûm (Sibṭ al-Ğawzî., *Taḏkirat ḫawâṣṣ al-umma bi-ḏikr ḫaṣâʾiṣ al-aʾimma*: 175).

[22] Ibn Kaṯîr., *al-Bidâya wa-l-nihâya*: vol. II: 551.

ʿAwn, sons of ʿAbd Allâh b. Ǧaʿfar b. Abî Ṭâlib, but makes no mention of Zaynab; in fact, she features rarely in his brief Karbalâʾ accounts.[23] Curiously too, an early writer, al-Dînawarî, in his *Kitâb al-aḫbâr al-ṭiwâl*, names, in his Karbalâʾ martyrology, one ʿAdwa b. ʿAbd Allâh b. Ǧaʿfar b. al-Ṭayyâr; since the name of the father is correct, one must presume that he has made a mistake and means ʿAwn. There is no other ʿAwn (or Muḥammad b. ʿAbd Allâh b. Ǧaʿfar) in his list.[24] To add to the mix, Ibn Shahrâshûb names three sons of ʿAbd Allâh b. Ǧaʿfar killed on the field of Karbala': Muḥammad b. ʿAbd Allâh b. Ǧaʿfar, ʿAwn al-Akbar b. ʿAbd Allâh and ʿAbd Allâh b. ʿAbd Allâh (Ibn Shahrâshûb names ʿAwn and Muḥammad, sons of ʿAqîl as well as Muḥammad and ʿAwn al-Akbar, sons of ʿAbd Allâh b. Ǧaʿfar).[25] In fact, al-Maǧlisî in *Biḥâr al-anwâr* notes the discrepancies in the number of members of the *ahl al-bayt* killed, and gives lists from Ibn Shahrâshûb, Muḥammad b. Abî Ṭâlib Ḥâ'irî, al-Iṣfahânî and Ibn Nâma'.

Who, then, are more regularly understood as Zaynab's sons?

Karbâssî says she bore seven children for ʿAbd Allâh b. Ǧaʿfar, five sons and two daughters: Ǧaʿfar al-Akbar, born in 21/642, ʿAlî al-Aṣġar, born around 23/644, ʿAwn al-Akbar, born in 25/646 and died in 61/681, al-ʿAbbas, born around 26/647, Umm Kulṯûm, born around 40/660 and died in 61/681, Ibrâhîm, dates unknown and Umm ʿAbd Allâh, dates unknown. He tells us that ʿAwn al-Akbar was ascribed that title in respect of his brother, ʿAwn al-Aṣġar, from his father but by a different mother (despite the thin evidence for the existence of such a brother); the same applies to Ǧaʿfar al-Akbar. However, Karbâssî does not take these names and dates directly from primary sources, but from secondary texts. Intriguingly, he only names one son as killed at Karbalâʾ. This, he posits, is as much as can be stated about the children sired by Zaynab. There is one Muḥammad b. ʿAbd Allâh al-Ṭayyâr, martyred at Karbalâʾ and attributed to Zaynab (as, he notes, in *Usd al-*

---

[23] al-Ḏahabî., *Siyar aʿlâm al-nubalâʾ*, vol. III, bb. 48: 320–321.

[24] al-Dînawarî., *Kitâb al-aḫbâr al-ṭiwâl*: 268.

[25] Ibn Shahrâshûb., *Manâqib âl Abî Ṭâlib*, vol. IV, bb. *fî maqtali-hi*: 112.

ġâba), but verification leads us to see that his mother was al-Ḫawṣâʾ.[26]

Equally problematic is that there are no texts describing any reaction on Zaynab's part when ʿAwn and Muḥammad are killed on the battlefield. In at least two other well-transmitted instances, the deaths of her nephews al-Ḥusayn b. ʿAlî, upon whose lifeless corpse she throws herself, and ʿAbd Allâh b. al-Ḥasan, whom she tries to dissuade from the field, Zaynab emerges, grief-stricken, from her tent. It is more than puzzling, then, to find no recorded reaction of Zaynab to the deaths of her own two sons. Popular piety might well believe that this suggests her enormous reverence for the sons of her brothers, to whom she gives preference, but this is hardly a satisfactory explanation. Zaynab's biographer Shahin writes that when her son ʿAwn was killed, she received his body and offered it to God, but the author neither provides references for this, nor does he mention the death of her other son, Muḥammad.[27]

If her sons ʿAwn and Muḥammad were killed at Karbalâʾ, one must ask what happened to her other sons, supposedly ʿAlî and al-ʿAbbâs? According to one of her biographers, her husband ʿAbd Allâh b. Ǧaʿfar had been too ill to travel to Kûfa (and thus Karbalâʾ) and had sent two of the sons with her, the other two remaining at home with their father.[28] Shahin records a story, not well-attested in the classical sources, that Zaynab's husband mourned more deeply for al-Ḥusayn than for his own sons, insisting that the Imâm was more favoured to him than his own boys; he gives thanks to God that even though he could not support al-Ḥusayn, his two sons could. The story seems to form part of the hagiographical writings around al-Ḥusayn, as do the stories that Zaynab put the children of her brother before her own, but remains of little help in explaining her behaviour on the field.[29]

---

[26] KARBÂSSÎ M.S. *Muʿǧam anṣâr al-Ḥusayn – al-nisâʾ*, 2009: 353.

[27] SHAHIN B., *Lady Zaynab*, 2002: 79.

[28] BILGRAMI M.H., *The Victory of Truth: The Life of Zaynab bint ʾAli*, 1986: 7. Cf. al-Maǧlisî., *Biḥâr al-anwâr*, vol. XLIV, bb. 37: 366.

[29] SHAHIN B., *Lady Zaynab*, 2002: 73.

A possible solution to the dilemma is to conclude that ʿAwn and Muḥammad, sons of ʿAbd Allâh b. Ǧaʿfar and killed at Karbalâʾ, were the stepsons rather than the sons of Zaynab. Her own children by ʿAbd Allâh b. Ǧaʿfar would have been younger, and these stayed at home with their ailing father. This is underscored by the fact that there is no recorded reaction from Zaynab at the death of these two boys, even though she does emerge from her battlefield tent at other deaths, especially those of her nephews; and further, that in the causality lists not only is she not named as their mother, even though other mothers are named, but also that at least one transmitter names other women as the mother of ʿAwn and Muḥammad.

Henri Lammens, in his polemical *Fāṭima et les filles de Mahomet*, is as disparaging of Zaynab as he is of her mother Fâṭima. She 'was said', he notes, to be exceptionally intelligent, referring the reader to Ibn al-Aṯîr's *Usd al-ġâba*, but questions her presence at Karbalâʾ where, he remarks, she showed a certain decisiveness and served as a cushion for her brother's lamentable collapse. The only reason she could be there, concludes Lammens, referring the reader to al-Balâḏurî's *Kitâb ansâb al-ashrâf*, is because she was divorced (*bânat min-hu*) from her husband Ibn Ǧaʿfar, who was extremely hostile to the 'pitiful adventure' of Karbalâʾ. Almost certainly, Lammens has misread al-Balâḏurî; as Wehr, Lane and Kazimirsky note, the verb *bâna-yabînu* could indeed denote divorce, when qualified by the crucial *bi-l-ṭalâq* or the preposition *ʿan*. But as it stands in *Kitâb ansâb al-ashrâf*, with its preposition '*min*', and no other qualification, its most basic meaning is to 'separate from', 'to part from' (as in Wehr, who does not mention divorce). Lane notes that it can refer to the separation of a girl from her parental home when she marries, or to be separated by a journey, by moving to a far-off distance. Lane also notes that it can mean to 'become distinct', as though separate from the others, an easily understandable description of Zaynab's view of Karbalâʾ compared to that of her husband. Kazimirsky too notes the concept of being separated from someone by a distance. While the verb may indeed carry the sense of divorce, its usage by al-Balâḏurî with the preposition '*min*', as well as the absence of reports of Zaynab's divorce in other texts, suggests that Lammens has been over-zealous in his reading of al-Balâḏurî. Zaynab did indeed part from her husand and go a distance from him; she to the field of Karbalâʾ, accompanied by the two sons he had sent, while he remained at home.[30]

Ultimately, there is no really satisfactory answer to this puzzle. It remains persistently enigmatic that Zaynab should emerge from her tent to mourn the deaths of some (although not all) of her nephews but not of her own sons. The pious opinion that she had greater devotion to the children of her brother's than to her own, or that she did not wish to further distress al-Ḥusayn, fails to satisfy. If some of her children are in fact her step-children, we must ask why the step-children are sent with her to Karbalâʾ and her own children remain behind with their ailing father, a man who had, ostensibly, attempted to dissuade his wife from going.[31] If, as Karbâssî claims, he was only a teenager when he married Zaynab, one has to ask if she was, in fact, his first wife, or if he was already married.[32] If, on the other hand, his sons came from a later marriage, the children she bore him would have been older; why then would the younger sons be sent to Karbalâʾ and the older sons remain at home? There is the possibility that all the children were in fact Zaynab's, leading us to question the discrepancies in the

---

[30] "Cette attitude de prudente réserve fut adoptée envers la descendance des filles de Fāṭima, les sœurs des «deux Ḥasan». En bonne règle, elles pouvaient invoquer au même titre le privilège de perpétuer la famille de Mahomet. L'aînée Zainab fut, dit-on, remarquablement intelligente. Cette réputation, elle la doit à son attitude pendant l'équipée de Karbalā, où seule elle aurait montré de la décision. On s'expliquerait mal comment s'y trouva mêlée cette éspouse d'Ibn Ǧaʿfar, si nous ne la savions divorcée d'avec son mari, très hostile à cette pitoyable aventure. Nos auteurs ont tenu à l'y faire figurer pour atténuer le lamentable effondrement de son frère Ḥosain." Cf. LAMMENS H., *Fāṭima et les filles de Mahomet*, Sumptibus Pontificii Istituti Biblici, Rome 1912: 128–129, WEHR H., *A Dictionary of Modern Written Arabic*, 1980: 105–106, LANE E.W., *An Arabic-English Lexicon*, vol. I, 1968: 285–286, KAZIMIRSKI A., *Dictionnaire Arabe-Français*, vol. I, 1860: 186.

[31] Cf. for e.g. HOWARD I.K.A., (trans.), *The History of al-Ṭabarî*, vol. XIX, 1990: 73.

[32] KARBÂSSÎ M.S., *Muʿǧam anṣâr al-Ḥusayn – al-nisâʾ*, 2009: 340–341.

sources, and ask why she is not mentioned as their mother in the very sources which mention the mothers of other Karbalâʾ martyrs.

2. THE CHILDREN OF AL-ḤUSAYN

A number of factors raise uncertainties about ʿAlî b. al-Ḥusayn, whose life would be saved by Zaynab's intervention after Karbalâʾ. In the first place, it is difficult to establish his age with any precision; doubt is cast by the use of terms like *ġulâm* to describe him,[33] as well as by texts that put the oldest son at eighteen or nineteen and finally by Ibn Ziyâd's curious order that ʿAlî b. al-Ḥusayn's manhood be physically verified.[34] Zaynab's extremely protective

[33] While Wehr renders the meaning of *ġulâm* somewhat indefinably as 'boy', 'youth' or 'lad', Lane suggests 'young man', 'youth' or 'boy, 'one whose mustache is growing forth'. He notes that some determine this as the period from birth until age seventeen, or from the time of birth until the time one reaches what is termed *shabâb*. This concept *shabâb* is in itself hard to define, delineated by some as ages sixteen to thirty-two, or thirty to forty, or even seventeen until fifty-one. Cf. LANE E.W., *An Arabic-English Lexicon*, vol. V, 1968: 2287–2288, vol. IV: 1493–1494. The texts insist that his inability to fight was due to illness, and not to his age.

[34] I tend to believe that this invasive investigation of the young Imâm, which was both verbal and physical, whatever form the latter took, was primarily a form of mockery and scorn by the unstable Ibn Ziyâd, rather than a genuine perplexity about the young man's chronological age. It comes at a moment when the governor has already had a bruising verbal clash with Zaynab, and has had to back off and be calmed by one of his attendants. The key issue, therefore, seems not to be an actual doubt about the boy's age as much as a heaping of scorn upon the 'boy' Imâm and son of al-Ḥusayn. There are texts in which Imâm Abû Ǧaʿfar Muḥammad b. ʿAlî al-Bâqir (born around 56/676), son of ʿAlî b. al-Ḥusayn, claims to have been present as a very young child (al-Fattâl al-Nîsâbûrî., *Rawḍat al-wâʿiẓîn wa-tabṣirat al-muttaʿiẓîn*, vol. I: 190); and although it seems infeasible that Ibn Ziyâd should not know the name of al-Ḥusayn's son, there is little evidence to show that he would also have known who al-Bâqir was. The presence of his own young son in itself suggests that the fourth Imâm was quite patently no longer a child.

instincts also cause us to ponder his age, as do one or two textual statements found in other authors.

Secondly, it is not always easy to determine which of al-Ḥusayn's sons the young Imâm is. Hussein notes that al-Ḥusayn named all three of his sons ʿAlî,[35] ostensibly as a response to Muʿâwiya's constant denigration of the husband of Fâṭima; but Hussein seems to be presuming that al-Ḥusayn only had three sons. He goes on to note the lack of concord between Shîʿî scholars as to which of al-Ḥusayn's sons survived the battle and succeeded his father as the fourth Imâm. It would be as well to make a brief attempt at establishing the number of al-Ḥusayn's sons in an effort to determine the names and the ages of those killed and of the surviving fourth Imâm.

Al-Ṭabarsî[36] lists six children:

1. ʿAlî al-Akbar Zayn al-ʿÂbidîn
2. ʿAlî al-Aṣġar, killed with his father at Karbalâʾ
3. Ǧaʿfar, who died in his father's lifetime
4. ʿAbd Allâh, killed with his father at Karbalâʾ
5. Sukayna
6. Fâṭima

According to Ibn Shahrâshûb in his *Manâqib*,[37] al-Ḥusayn's children were nine:

---

[35] HUSSEIN A.J., *A Developmental Analysis of Depictions of the Events of Karbalāʾ in Early Islamic History*, PhD diss., University of Chicago, 2001, n. 52: 102.

[36] al-Ṭabarsî., *Iʿlâm al-warâ bi-aʿlâm al-hudâ*: 255.

[37] Ibn Shahrâshûb., *Manâqib âl Abî Ṭâlib*, vol. IV, bb. *fî tawârîḫi-hi wa-l-qâbi-hi*: 77. Noting that six among the children of al-Ḥusayn were killed, Ibn Shahrâshûb also mentions that opinions differ concerning them. He provides a list: ʿAlî al-Akbar, Ibrâhîm, ʿAbd Allâh, Muḥammad, Ḥamza, ʿAlî, Ǧaʿfar, ʿUmar, Zayd, and ʿAbd Allâh (killed 'in his confinement'). He then refers to al-Ḥasan b. al-Ḥasan, captured, and who had his hand cut off (but this is almost certainly not a son of al-Ḥusayn – Sibṭ al-Ǧawzî tells us that this boy, together with ʿUmar b. al-Ḥasan, were both deemed

1. ʿAlî al-Akbar, killed with his father at Karbalâʾ

2. ʿAlî al-Awsaṭ, the fourth Imâm, sick in bed on the day of Karbalâʾ, and forbidden by his father to fight because of his illness[38]

3. ʿAlî al-Aṣġar

4. Muḥammad, about whom he provides no details

5. ʿAbd Allâh, killed with his father at Karbalâʾ

6. Ǧaʿfar (he refers us to al-Mufîd's *al-Irshâd*)

7. Sukayna

8. Fâṭima

9. Zaynab

Ibn Shahrâshûb refers to the infant son as ʿAlî al-Aṣġar; Ibn Ṭâʾûs in his *Kitâb al-iqbâl bi-l-aʿmâl al-ḥasana* does the same (in al-Ḥusayn's *ziyâra* on the day of ʿÂshûrâ). However, those who name the infant as ʿAbd Allâh, whose mother was al-Rubâb, include al-Mufîd in his *al-Iḫtiṣâṣ* and al-Iṣfahânî in his *Maqâtil*.[39]

Writing more than three hundred years before Ibn Shahrâshûb, al-Ṭabarî in his *Dalâʾil al-imâma* confirms that there were three sons named ʿAlî, and lists al-Ḥusayn's children as nine in number: [40]

1. ʿAlî al-Akbar, killed with his father at Karbalâʾ

---

too small to be killed and thus survived the battle; cf. Sibṭ al-Ǧawzî., *Taḏkirat ḫawâṣṣ al-umma bi-ḏikr ḫaṣâʾiṣ al-aʾimma*: 229), before returning to Zayn al-ʿÂbidîn, not killed because he was sick in bed and failed to obtain his father's permission to fight. Ibn Shahrâshûb remarks that some say Muḥammad b. al-Aṣġar b. ʿAlî b. Abî Ṭâlib (again, clearly not a son of al-Ḥusayn) was another not killed because of his illness, and that others say that he was indeed killed by a man from the Banû Dârim. Cf. Ibn Shahrâshûb., *Manâqib âl Abî Ṭâlib*, vol. IV, bb. *fî maqtali-hi*: 113.

38 Ibn Shahrâshûb., *Manâqib âl Abî Ṭâlib*, vol. IV, bb. *fî maqtali-hi*: 113.

39 al-Iṣfahânî., *Maqâtil al-ṭâlibîyyîn*: 89–90, al-Mufîd., *al-Iḫtiṣâṣ*: 83.

40 al-Ṭabarî., *Dalâʾil al-imâma*, n. 26/95: 181.

2. ʿAlî Zayn al-ʿÂbidîn, who would be the fourth Imâm
3. ʿAlî al-Aṣġar
4. Muḥammad
5. ʿAbd Allâh (al-Shahîd, killed with his father at Karbalâʾ)
6. Ǧaʿfar
7. Zaynab
8. Sakîna
9. Fâṭima

For his part, al-Balâḏurî names only four children: ʿAlî al-Akbar, killed with his father at Karbalâʾ, ʿAlî al-Aṣġar, who succeeded his father, Fâṭima and Sukayna.[41] Less than one hundred years after al-Balâḏurî, al-Ḫaṣîbî proposes a different enumeration of al-Ḥusayn's children in his *al-Hidâya*: ʿAlî Sayyid al-ʿÂbidîn al-Akbar (the fourth Imâm), ʿAlî al-Aṣġar, martyred with his father, the baby ʿAbd Allâh who was also martyred, pierced by arrows, Muḥammad, Ǧaʿfar, Zaynab, Sukayna and Fâṭima.[42]

In his *al-Irshâd*, al-Mufîd names six children for al-Ḥusayn, but almost certainly gets the order wrong: [43]

---

[41] al-Balâḏurî., *Kitâb ansâb al-ashrâf*, vol III: 1332/406, 1287–1288/361–362. His list is somewhat expanded by Sibṭ al-Ǧawzî, writing four centuries later; ʿAlî al-Akbar, killed with his father at Karbalâʾ, ʿAlî al-Aṣġar, who succeeded his father, Ǧaʿfar, ʿAbd Allâh, killed with his father at Karbalâʾ, Fâṭima, Sukayna and Muḥammad, killed with his father at Karbalâʾ. Cf. Sibṭ al-Ǧawzî., *Taḏkirat ḫawâṣṣ al-umma bi-ḏikr ḫaṣâʾiṣ al-aʾimma*: 249. Disconcertingly, Sibṭ al-Ǧawzî has a second, a slightly different list of names of al-Ḥusayn's sons killed with him: ʿAlî al-Akbar, ʿAbd Allâh and Abû Bakr. He informs us that ʿAlî b. al-Husayn was not killed 'because he was deemed too small' but fails to mention his illness. Later, he underscores al-Ḥusayn's martyred sons as two named ʿAlî and one named ʿAbd Allâh. Cf. Sibṭ al-Ǧawzî., *Taḏkirat ḫawâṣṣ al-umma bi-ḏikr ḫaṣâʾiṣ al-aʾimma*: 229.

[42] al-Ḫaṣîbî., *al-Hidâya (al-Kubrâ)*, bb. 5: 202.

[43] al-Mufîd., *Kitâb al-Irshâd*, vol. II, bb. *ḏikr wuld al-Ḥusayn b. ʿAlî*: 137.

1. ʿAlî b. al-Ḥusayn al-Akbar, the future Imâm, who is aged twenty-three

2. ʿAlî b. al-Ḥusayn al-Aṣġar, killed at Karbalâʾ at the age of nineteen[44]

3. Ǧaʿfar b. al-Ḥusayn, who died in his father's lifetime

4. ʿAbd Allâh b. al-Ḥusayn, killed as an infant at Karbalâʾ

5. Sukayna

6. Fâṭima

In his *Kashf al-ġumma*, al-Irbilî enumerates four lists of children for al-Ḥusayn. The first, which al-Irbilî claims is taken from al-Ṣadûq's *Ikmâl (kamâl) al-dîn*,[45] names six boys and three girls:

1. ʿAlî al-Akbar, who was martyred with his father

2. ʿAlî al-Awsaṭ, who as the next Imâm would be known as Zayn al-ʿÂbidîn

3. ʿAlî al-Aṣġar, who was martyred with his father

4. Muḥammad

5. ʿAbd Allâh

6. Ǧaʿfar

7. Zaynab

8. Sakîna

9. Fâṭima

A second list, transmitted from Ibn al-Ḫashshâb, repeats the first one. A third, diverse list is transmitted from al-Ḥâfiẓ ʿAbd al-ʿAzîz

---

[44] Op. cit., vol. II, bb. *wâqiʿ Karbalâʾ wa baṭûla Imâm al-Ḥusayn wa aṣḥâbi-hi*: 106.

[45] al-Ṣadûq's text claims nine children for al-Ḥusayn, but without providing a definitive list of names. Cf. al-Ṣadûq., *Ikmâl (kamâl) al-dîn wa-itmâm (tamâm) al-niʿma fî iṯbât al-ġayba wa-kashf al-ḥayra*, vol. II, bb. 47, n. 1: 527.

al-Aḫḍar al-Ǧanâbiḏî, which enumerates ʿAlî al-Akbar, who was martyred with his father, ʿAlî al-Aṣġar, Ǧaʿfar, ʿAbd Allâh, Sakîna and Fâṭima. His fourth list is from al-Mufîd.[46]

According to some contemporary scholars like Ahmed,[47] there were far fewer children: Sukayna, Fâṭima, Ǧaʿfar, and ʿAlî al-Akbar. The names and numbers of his daughters are no less difficult to determine, although a number delineate Fâṭima as the eldest and many maintain three daughters (at least two of whom were Karbalâʾ): Sukayna, Fâṭima, Zaynab,[48] or Zaynab, Sakîna, Fâṭima,[49] or Fâṭima and Sukayna[50] or Sakîna and Fâṭima.[51] Numerous works make references to his daughters individually: Fâṭima,[52] Sakîna,[53]

---

[46] al-Irbilî., *Kashf al-ġumma fî maʿrifat al-aʾimma*, vol. II: 38–39. Cf. al-Mufîd., *Kitâb al-Irshâd*, vol. II, bb. *ḏikr wuld al-Ḥusayn b. ʿAlî*: 137, al-Maǧlisî., *Biḥâr al-anwâr*, vol. XLV, bb. 48, n. 1: 329.

[47] AHMED A.Q., *The Religious Elite of the Early Islamic Hijaz*, Unit for Prospographical Research, Oxford 2011: 168.

[48] Ibn Shahrâshûb., *Manâqib âl Abî Ṭâlib*, vol. IV, bb. *fî tawârîḫi-hi wa-l-qâbi-hi*: 77, Ibn ʿAsâkir., *Târîḫ madînat Dimashq*, vol. XIV, bb. 1566 (*al-Ḥusayn b. ʿAlî b. Abî Ṭâlib*): 111, 122, vol. LXIX, bb. 9349 (*Zaynab bt. al-Ḥusayn b. ʿAlî b. Abî Ṭâlib*): 168, al-Ḫaṣîbî., *al-Hidâya* (*al-Kubrâ*), b. 5: 202.

[49] al-Ṭabarî., *Dalâʾil al-imâma*, n. 26/95: 181, al-Irbilî., *Kashf al-ġumma fî maʿrifat al-aʾimma*, vol. II: 38–39. Sukayna and Sakîna seem to be interchangeable.

[50] al-Balâḏurî., *Kitâb ansâb al-ashrâf*, vol III: 1332/406, 1287–1288/361–362, al-Ṭabarsî., *Iʿlâm al-warâ bi-aʿlâm al-hudâ*: 255, Sibṭ al-Ǧawzî., *Taḏkirat ḫawâṣṣ al-umma bi-ḏikr ḫaṣâʾiṣ al-aʾimma*: 233, al-Mufîd., *Kitâb al-Irshâd*, vol. II, bb. *ḏikr wuld al-Ḥusayn b. ʿAlî*: 137.

[51] al-Irbilî., *Kashf al-ġumma fî maʿrifat al-aʾimma*, vol. II: 38–39.

[52] al-Kûfî., *Tafsîr Furât b. Ibrâhîm*: 392, 544, al-Kulaynî., *al-Kâfî fî ʿilm al-dîn*, vol. I, n. 6: 291, n. 1: 303, vol. II, bb. 64, n. 5/763: 18, bb. 68, n. 1/785: 53, al-Mufîd., *al-Irshâd fî maʿrifat ḥuǧaǧ Allâh ʿalâ al-ʿibâd*, vol. II: 26, 121, 135, 140, 174, 209, al-Fattâl al-Nîsâbûrî., *Rawḍat al-wâʿiẓîn wa-tabṣirat al-muttaʿiẓîn*, vol. I: 191, vol. II: 494, al-Ṭabarsî., *Iʿlâm al-warâ bi-aʿlâm al-hudâ*: 254, 246, 291, al-Ṭabarsî., *Kitâb al-iḥtiǧâǧ ʿalâ ahl al-liǧâǧ*, vol. II, 230, Ibn Namâ al-Ḥillî., *Muṯîr al-aḥzân wa munîr subul al-ashǧân*: 99, 100, 111, Ibn Ṭâʾûs., *Kitâb al-luhûf fî qutlâ al-ṭufûf*: 187, al-Irbilî., *Kashf al-ġumma fî maʿrifat al-aʾimma*, vol. I: 580, vol. II: 39, 84, 120, 161, 180, al-Ḥurr al-ʿÂmilî., *Iṯbât al-hudât bi-l-nuṣûṣ wa-l-muʿǧizât*, vol. II: 14, vol. IV: 58 (Fâṭima described as

Sukayna,[54] and occasionally Umm Kultûm (possibly the *kunya* for Ruqayya said to have died in childhood).[55] In his *Târîḫ madînat Dimashq*, Ibn ʿAsâkir records that two daughters, Fâṭima and Sukayna, all transmitted about their father al-Ḥusayn;[56] he also notes that Sukayna was otherwise known as Amîma, or Amîna, or Âmna.[57]

The fourth Imâm, says al-Ṭabarî, was born in the year 38/658 (and thus making him around twenty-three years on the day of Karbalâʾ). Ibn Saʿd also gives Zayn al-ʿÂbidîn's age as twenty-three on that day, as does Sibṭ al-Ğawzî.[58] In general agreement with al-Ṭabarî, al-Mufîd (although he seems to be mistaken in identifying which son is the Imâm)[59] and others, Ibn ʿAsâkir notes that some say Zayn al-ʿÂbidîn was twenty-three, and others twenty-five.[60] Ibn

---

the eldest), al-Baḥrânî., *al-Burhân fî tafsîr al-qurʾân*, vol. II: 335 (Fâṭima described as the eldest), al-Mağlisî., *Biḥâr al-anwâr*, vol. XXIII, bb. 13: 242.

53 al-Irbilî., *Kashf al-ğumma fî maʿrifat al-aʾimma*, vol. II: 38. This might be Sukayna.

54 al-Ṣadûq., *Kitâb al-amâlî fî-l-aḥâdîṯ wa-l-aḫbâr*, *mağlis* 31, n. 3: 166, 167, al-Ṭabarsî., *Iʿlâm al-warâ bi-aʿlâm al-hudâ*: 214, al-Mufîd., *al-Irshâd fî maʿrifat ḥuğağ Allâh ʿalâ al-ʿibâd*, vol. II: 135, al-Fattâl al-Nîsâbûrî., *Rawḍat al-wâʿiẓîn wa-tabṣirat al-muttaʿiẓîn*, vol. I: 191, al-Irbilî., *Kashf al-ğumma fî maʿrifat al-aʾimma*, vol. II: 39, al-Mağlisî., *Biḥâr al-anwâr*, vol. XLV, bb. 39: 128.

55 al-Ṣadûq., *Kitâb al-amâlî fî-l-aḥâdîṯ wa-l-aḫbâr*, *mağlis* 30: 163–164, al-Fattâl al-Nîsâbûrî., *Rawḍat al-wâʿiẓîn wa-tabṣirat al-muttaʿiẓîn*, vol. I: 188–190, al-Mağlisî., *Biḥâr al-anwâr*, vol. XLIV, bb. 37: 322.

56 Ibn ʿAsâkir., *Târîḫ madînat Dimashq*, vol. XIV, bb. 1566 (*al-Ḥusayn b. ʿAlî b. Abî Ṭâlib*): 111, 122.

57 Op. cit., vol. LXIX, nn. 9349, (*Zaynab bt. al-Ḥusayn b. ʿAlî b. Abî Ṭâlib*): 168, bb. 9361 (*Sakîna*): 204.

58 Ibn Saʿd., *Kitâb al-ṭabaqât al-kabîr*, vol. V: 156, Sibṭ al-Ğawzî., *Taḏkirat ḫawâṣṣ al-umma bi-ḏikr ḫaṣâʾiṣ al-aʾimma*: 273–274. It is of note that in the same text, Sibṭ al-Ğawzî tells us that the boy survived the battle because the enemy 'deemed him too small' (*istaṣġar*) to kill him. Cf. Sibṭ al-Ğawzî., *Taḏkirat ḫawâṣṣ al-umma bi-ḏikr ḫaṣâʾiṣ al-aʾimma*: 215.

59 al-Mufîd., *Kitâb al-Irshâd*, vol. II, bb. *ḏikr wuld al-Ḥusayn b. ʿAlî*: 137.

60 Ibn ʿAsâkir., *Târîḫ madînat Dimashq*, vol. XLI, bb. 4875 (*ʿAlî b. al-Husayn b. ʿAlî b. Abî Ṭâlib b. Hâshim b. ʿAbd al-Manâf*): 366–367.

al-Ǧawzî gives his age on that day as twenty-three, insisting, contrary to al-Mufîd for example, that this is ʿAlî al-Aṣġar, as opposed to his brother ʿAlî al-Akbar, who was killed with al-Ḥusayn, and adding that he was sick in bed on the day, and it was this that prevented him fighting.[61] Al-Dînawarî in his *Kitâb al-aḫbâr al-ṭiwâl*,[62] raises a divergent note, that after the battle, none of al-Ḥusayn's companions or sons (or the sons of his brother) remained except for ʿAlî al-Aṣġar; he was 'near puberty' or 'a teenager' (*râhiq*),[63] without long life, but had already attained four years.[64]

In his *Qiṣaṣ al-anbiyâʾ* (written in 709/1310) al-Rabġûzî, like al-Dînawarî, raises a discordant note, maintaining the age of the surviving boy as seven, while his brother, ʿAlî al-Akbar, who fought and died, as ten.[65] Al-Ḏahabî names only ʿAlî al-Akbar, killed at Karbalâʾ, and ʿAlî Zayn al-ʿÂbidîn,[66] while al-ʿAsqalânî merely refers to the latter as a boy (*ġulâm*) who was sick.[67]

In his *Biḥâr al-anwâr*, al-Mağlisî describes the emergence onto the field of Karbalâʾ of ʿAlî b. al-Ḥusayn, immediately after the deaths of most of al-Ḥusayn's brothers (except for al-ʿAbbâs, who would die later). Al-Mağlisî notes that while some transmitters, such as al-Iṣfahânî in his *Maqâtil*, put the boy at eighteen, others like Ibn Shahrâshûb in his *Manâqib* put him at either eighteen or

---

[61] Ibn al-Ǧawzî., *Ṣifat al-ṣafwa*, vol. II, bb. *ʿAlî b. al-Ḥusayn b. ʿAlî b. Abî Ṭâlib*: 52. Ibn al-Ǧawzî recalls many of the boy's virtues but gives no details of the battle.

[62] al-Dînawarî., *Kitâb al-aḫbâr al-ṭiwâl*: 270.

[63] According to Lane, this means ten or eleven years old; near to attaining puberty. Cf. LANE E W., *An Arabic-English Lexicon*, 1968, vol. III: 1170–1.

[64] (و قد كان راهق و الا عمر و قد كان بلغ اربغ سنين)

[65] Cf. BOESCHOTEN H.E. & O'KANE J., (eds.), *Al-Rabghūzī. The Stories of the Prophets*, vol. II, Brill, Leiden 2015: 630. Al-Ḫawârizmî puts ʿAlî al-Akbar at eighteen years (cf. al-Ḫawârizmî., *Maqtal al-Ḥusayn*, bk. 2, bb. *fî maqtal al-Ḥusayn*: 34).

[66] al-Ḏahabî., *Siyar aʿlâm al-nubalâʾ*, vol. III, bb. 48: 320–321.

[67] al-ʿAsqalânî., *Tahḏîb al-tahḏîb*, vol II, (*Ḥusayn b. ʿAlî b. Abî Ṭâlib*): 323.

twenty-five.[68] A few passages later, al-Mağlisî, transmitting from *Maqâtil*, notes that this ʿAlî is the first martyr from the children of Abû Ṭâlib, and that he is ʿAlî al-Akbar.[69] Narrating again from al-Iṣfahânî in his *Maqâtil*, al-Mağlisî notes the problem; that while some, imagining ʿAlî al-Aṣġar to be the future Imâm Zayn al-ʿÂbidîn, note that he was not killed because of his illness, others imagine al-Aṣġar to have been shot and killed, i.e. the infant ʿAlî.[70] Al-Mağlisî transmits a claim by Ibn Shahrâshûb in his *Manâqib* that ʿAlî Akbar b. al-Ḥusayn was about thirty at Karbalâʾ and survived as the next Imâm, while ʿAlî al-Aṣġar, the smaller of the two, was aged about twelve and was killed.[71] However, as we have noted, Ibn Shahrâshûb transmits another strand, claiming that al-Ḥusayn had nine children, including ʿAlî al-Akbar, who was killed with his father, ʿAlî al-Awsaṭ, the surviving son who would be known as Zayn al-ʿAbidîn and the next Imâm, and ʿAlî al-Aṣġar.

It seems most likely that al-Ḥusayn had six sons, three of whom were named ʿAlî:

1. The first is ʿAlî al-Akbar, the eldest, killed at Karbalâʾ with his father; many put him at around eighteen at Karbalâʾ, but he must have been in his late twenties, born around 33/654.

2. The second is ʿAlî al-Awsaṭ, the fourth Imâm (Zayn al-ʿÂbidîn), born around 38/658, thus putting him around twenty-three years at Karbalâʾ (while the dates suggested in the texts for his birth range between the years 31/651 and 38/658, it seems certain that he was in his early twenties on the day his father was killed).

3. The third is Ğaʿfar, who died before the Karbalâʾ events.

4. The fourth is the infant, ʿAbd Allâh, known as ʿAlî al-Aṣġar, born around 60/680 and killed in his father's arms at Karbalâʾ.

5. The fifth is Muḥammad, martyred at Karbalâʾ, but about whom we have little information.

---

68 Ibn Shahrâshûb., *Manâqib âl Abî Ṭâlib*, vol. IV, bb. *fî maqtali-hi*: 109.

69 al-Mağlisî., *Biḥâr al-anwâr*, vol. XLV, bb. 37, n. 2: 43, 45.

70 al-Mağlisî., *Biḥâr al-anwâr*, vol. XLV, bb. 37, n. 2: 62–63.

71 Op. cit., vol. XLV, bb. 48, n. 2: 329.

6. The sixth is al-Muḥsin, whose unnamed mother was among the captives after Karbalâ' and who miscarried.

In theory then, ʿAlî al-Akbar, killed at Karbalâ' with his father, was destined to be the next Imâm. Like the son of Ǧaʿfar al-Ṣâdiq, he dies in his father's lifetime, so that the Imamate passes to his younger brother, ʿAlî al-Awsaṭ. Furthermore, the narrative of al-Ḫawârizmî, in which the younger brother comes out to fight and is resolutely sent back to his sick bed by his father, may well serve as the moment of delegation.[72] If ʿAlî al-Akbar, killed with his father, is indeed the eldest son, it seems unlikely that he should be only eighteen, when his father was near sixty. If the texts cannot agree even on the age of al-Ḥusayn at Karbalâ', easily calculable by the date of his birth and the date of the battle, it seems unlikely that they will find concordance on the names and number of his offspring.

3. THE CONSOLATION OF ZAYNAB

A third and final addendum concerns an instant when ʿAlî b. al-Ḥusayn is remembering back to the Karbalâ' event and is overcome with remorse at the deportation of the survivors to Kûfa while the bodies of his family and comrades lay about unburied. Although we have already noted that by the time the survivors left Karbalâ' the bodies had already been buried, Zaynab's long discourse is nonetheless worth narrating. It is an attempt by this daughter of ʿAlî and Fâṭima to console and hearten her traumatised nephew, of whose grief she has taken account, a grief which will eventually become one of the chief hallmarks of his life. Although found in fragments in various other texts, (as for example, the *ḥadîṯ* recounted by Umm Ayman and which Zaynab asks her father to retell on his deathbed), as it stands the narration is transmitted only by al-Qummî and al-Maǧlisî from him.[73] Addressing her nephew as

[72] al-Ḫawârizmî., *Maqtal al-Ḥusayn*, bk. 2, bb. *fî maqtal al-Ḥusayn*: 36. Al-Ḫawârizmî seems not to get the ages right.

[73] al-Qummî., *Kâmil al-ziyârât*: 260–266, al-Maǧlisî., *Biḥâr al-anwâr*, vol. XXVII, bb. 6, n. 23: 57–61, vol. XLV, bb. 30, n. 30: 179–183. In fact,

'all that remains of my grandfather, and my father and my brothers', Zaynab says to him: "Why do I see you giving up your spirit?" ʿAlî b. al-Ḥusayn, who is the narrator of the incident, replies:

> "How could I not be sad and in despair when I have seen my master, my brothers, my uncles, my cousins and my people smeared with their blood, soiled, in the open air, plundered, neither shrouded nor buried! Not a single one inclines towards them, and not a person approaches them, as though they were people of the house of al-Daylam[74] and al-Ḫazar!"[75] Zaynab replied: "What you see must not make you sad, because by God, it is due to an injunction from the Messenger of God to your grandfather and your father and your uncle. For God has made a covenant with a people of this nation – not known by the pharoahs[76] of this earth but known among the people of the heavens – that they will gather these scattered limbs and bury them, and these stained bodies too, and erect in this al-

---

the narration is not part of al-Qummî's *Kâmil al-ziyârât*, but was added later by one of his students, Ḥusayn b. Aḥmad b. Muġîra. The chain of transmission (*isnâd*) is ʿUbayd Allâh b. al-Faḍl b. Muḥammad b. Hilâl, on the authority of Saʿîd b. Muḥammad, on the authority of Muḥammad b. Sallâm al-Kûfî, on the authority of Aḥmad b. Muḥammad al-Wâsiṭî, on the authority of ʿÎsâ b. Abî Shayba al-Qâḍî, on the authority of Nûḥ b. Darrâǧ, on the authority of Qudâma b. Zâʾida, on the authority of his father, transmitting from ʿAlî b. al-Ḥusayn.

[74] The tribe inhabitating the highlands of Gîlân (Iran), uncertain in origin, who opposed the Arab invasions, but whose defeat is recorded by al-Ṭabarî, al-Balâḏurî and others. They practiced a form of paganism, and perhaps some Zoroastrianism and Christianity. Cf. MINORSKY V., "Daylam" in C E Bosworth et al., (eds.), *The Encyclopaedia of Islam*, vol. II, Brill, Leiden 1991: 189–194.

[75] In the final analysis, the reference to al-Daylam and al-Ḫazar (a nomadic tribe which flourished in the early Islamic period) is a reference to those groups held in least esteem by the Arabs. Cf. BARTHOLD W. and GOLDEN P. B., "Khazar" in C E Bosworth et al., (eds.), *The Encyclopaedia of Islam*, vol. IV, 1991: 1172–1181.

[76] Representing any tyrant who uses power or authority to commit injustice.

> Ṭaff a standard for the tomb of your father, leader of the martyrs, the vestige of which will never be blotted out and whose inscription will never be effaced with the succession of nights and days. Should the leaders of misbelief[77] and the adherents[78] of error try hard to obliterate and destroy it, its vestige will do nothing but increase in splendour and in height."

ʿAlî b. al-Ḥusayn then asks for clarification about the injunction and for more information about it, and Zaynab replies:

> "Umm Ayman reported to me that one day the Messenger of God visited the house of Fâṭima, and she made *ḥarîra* (a traditional soup) for him, while ʿAlî brought him a plate of dates. Then Umm Ayman said: I brought them a large vessel containing milk and cream. The Messenger of God, ʿAlî, Fâṭima, al-Ḥasan and al-Ḥusayn ate some of this *ḥarîra* and the Messenger of God drank and they all drank the milk. Then he ate and they all ate some of the dates with the cream. The Messenger of God washed his hands and ʿAlî poured the water for him, and when he had finished washing his hands, he wiped his face. Then he looked intently at ʿAlî, Fâṭima, al-Ḥasan and al-Ḥusayn, and we noted the joy on his face. He looked with his eyes towards heaven for a while and then turned his face towards the *qibla* and spread out his hands in prayer. He then fell into a prostration, sobbing with a prolonged weeping; his lamentation ascended and his tears streamed. Then he lifted his head and bowed deeply to the ground, and his tears flowed as though they were torrential rain. Fâṭima, ʿAlî, al-Ḥasan and al-Ḥusayn grieved, and I (Umm Ayman) grieved with them when we saw the Messenger of God, but it frightened us to ask him

---

[77] The concept of *kufr* and its derivatives has a wide range of meaning, running from the idea of veiling, hiding or concealing something, through ingratitude, the refusal to be thankful for a favour, to falling short of one's duty with respect to the law. Bearing in mind the difference between disbelief and misbelief, I have chosen to render it as the latter, with its adherents as 'misbelievers'. Cf. LANE E.W., *An Arabic-English Lexicon*, 1997, vol. VII: 2620.

[78] In the text, the word is *ashyâʿ*, the plural of *shîʿa*.

while this was so prolonged. Then ʿAlî and Fâṭima said to him: What is making you cry, O Messenger of God? May God not cause your eyes to weep! Our hearts have been wounded, seeing the state you are in! He replied: O my brother, I was happy for you all!

Muzâḥim b. ʿAbd al-Wâriṯ said in his *ḥadîṯ* concerning us that Muḥammad said: O my dear ones, I was so very happy for you all – I have never been so happy – and looking at you I praised God for His favour towards me in you, when Ǧabra'îl came down to me and said: O Muḥammad, God the Blessed, the Most High is acquainted with what is in your spirit and knows the happiness you feel for your brother and your daughter and your grandsons, and he completes the favour for you and delights you with a gift, in that He places them and their offspring and those who love them and their Shîʿa with you in the Garden. There is no difference between you and them; they live as you live and receive as you receive until you are satisfied and above satisfaction, in spite of the many afflictions they received in the world and the adversities incurred by them at the hands of a people professing your creed and pretending that they are of your nation, devoid of God and of you, struck and killed, their killing in different places, their tombs remote, chosen by God for them and for you. Praise God, Majestic and Glorious, for His choice and be satisfied with His provision! So I praised God and was satisfied with His provision concerning what He had chosen for you all. Then Ǧabra'îl said: O Muḥammad, your brother will be persecuted after you, vanquished by your nation, worn out by your enemies and then killed after you, killed by the evillest of mankind and of creation, the most wretched of creation, like the slaughtering of the camel[79] in the land to which which he will migrate, the place of

---

79 God sent the prophet Ṣâliḥ to the materialistic and unspiritual people of Ṯamûd, and from whom they demanded a sign or miracle; the sign given by God was a special camel, which the people (led by nine particularly wicked men) promptly hamstrung and killed, suffering severe

planting for his Shîʿa and the Shîʿa of his children and in which, in every situation, their afflictions will increase and their sufferings become greater. This grandson of yours (he indicated al-Ḥusayn with his hand) will be killed in a group of your offspring the people of your house and the best of your nation, on the bank of the Euphrates in the land called Karbalâʾ, because of which, sufferings and afflictions will increase on account of your enemies and the enemies of your offspring on that day, the suffering of which will never come to an end and the grief of which will never cease. That land is the purest of the areas of the earth and the greatest in terms of sanctity, and truly it is part of the plain (*al-baṭḥâʾ*)[80] of the Garden. When that day comes, on which your grandson and his people will be killed, surrounded by battalions of misbelievers and the cursed, the earth will shake violently from its horizons, the mountains will tremble, so great their agitation, the waves of the oceans will be in tumult, the inhabitants of the heavens will heave, angry for you, O Muḥammad, and for your offspring, and regarding as significant all that has been violated of your sanctity and for the evil that is equal to it in your offspring and your family.

Nothing will remain but to ask permission of God, Majestic and Glorious in support of your oppressed and tyrannized people, who are the proof of God (*ḥuǧǧat Allâh*) for His creation after you. For God reveals to the heavens and the earth, to the mountains and the seas and all that they contain; in truth, I am God, the King, the All Powerful, whom no fugitive can elude and whom no resister can cause to fail. I am more

---

consequences for their action. Cf. Q. 7: 73–78, Q. 27: 45–51, Q. 11: 64–65.

[80] "Mecca," notes The Encyclopaedia of Islam, "lies in a kind of corridor between two ranges of bare steep hills, with an area in the centre rather lower than the rest. The whole corridor is the *wādī* or the *baṭn Makka*, 'the hollow of Mecca', and the lower part is al-Baṭḥāʾ, which was doubtless the original settlement and where the Kaʿba stands." Cf. WATT W.M., "Makka" in C E Bosworth et al., (eds.), *The Encyclopaedia of Islam*, vol. VI, 1991: 144.

powerful in victory and retribution. By my Majesty and Glory, I will most certainly castigate those who harmed My Messenger, My Choice One, and violated his sanctity, and killed his family and spurned his injunction and tyrannized his people, "*with a punishment wherewith I have not punished any of (My) creatures*".[81] With that, everything in the heavens and the lands[82] will raise a shout, cursing whoever tyrannized your family and usurped your sanctity. When that group comes out to their resting places, God, Majestic and Glorious will take charge of seizing their souls with His hand. Angels will come down to earth from the seventh heaven bearing vessels of ruby and emerald, filled with the water of life, and garments and perfumes of the garments and perfumes of the Garden. They will wash their corpses with that water, clothe them with the garments and embalm them with those perfumes. Then row by row the angels will make *ṣalât* over them. God will then call forth a people from your nation, whom the misbelievers do not know, and who did not participate in that blood-shedding by word or deed or intention. They will bury their bodies and raise a distinguishing mark for the tomb of the leader of the martyrs in that *al-baṭḥâ'*, which will be a sign for the people of the truth and a rope for the believers for success. One hundred thousand angels from every heaven will surround it day and night; they will ask blessings upon him and will glorify God near him and ask of God forgiveness for his pilgrims and write the names of those from your nation who come to him as a pilgrim, drawing near to God, and thus to you, and the names of their fathers and their clans and their countries, and will brand their faces with a mark of light from the throne of God: 'This is a pilgrim to the tomb of the best of the martyrs and the son of the best of the prophets'. On the Day of Resurrection, a light will shine on their faces from the vestige of that mark; perceptions will be veiled by it, indicating them and by which they will be known. It is as if I am with you, O Muḥammad,

---

[81] Q. 5: 115.

[82] The word in the text occurs in the genitive plural (*fî-l-araḍîn*). I have chosen to translate it here as 'lands' rather the clumsier 'earths'.

(with you) between me and Mîkâ'îl,[83] and ʿAlî in front of us, and with us, angels of God, their number impossible to count. We will gather those who have the mark on their faces from among all the creatures, so that God will rescue them from the terror of that day and its adversities. For that is the judgment of God, and His gift to the one who visits your tomb, O Muḥammad, or the tomb of your brother, or the tomb of your grandsons, desiring by it nothing but God, Majestic and Glorious. A people, who deserve the curse and the anger of God, will try hard to obliterate the standard of that tomb and efface its vestige, but God the Blessed, the Most High will make it impossible for them to do so'.

Then the Messenger of God said: 'It is this that made me weep and grieve'." Zaynab said: "When Ibn Mulǧam, may God curse him, struck my father, and I saw the traces of death in him, I said to him: 'My father! Umm Ayman recounted to me this and this, but I would have loved to hear it from you!' He replied: 'My daughter, the *ḥadîṯ* was as Umm Ayman recounted it to you. It was as though I was with you and the daughters of your people, captives in that country, ignominious, reduced to submission, "*in fear lest men should extirpate you*",[84] but be patient, be patient, for by the One who split the grain[85] and created the breath of life, on that Day God will not have on the earth a *walî* better than you (pl), better than those who love you (pl) and better than your Shîʿa. For when he was informing us of these things, the Messenger of God said to us: On that day, Iblîs[86] will fly gleefully and will roam the whole of the earth

---

[83] The angel named in Q. 2: 98. By tradition, he has never laughed since the creation of Hell, and weeps for pity over sinners, imploring God's mercy for them. Cf. WENSINCK A.J., "Mīkāl" in *SEI*, H.A.R Gibb et al. (eds.), E.J. Brill, Leiden 1995: 378–379.

[84] Q. 8: 26.

[85] Q. 6: 95.

[86] One of the Islamic titles denoting Satan. Before the fall of Âdam, Iblîs appears to be his personal name, of disputed etymology. Some scholars suggest that it might be from the Greek 'diabolos': others that it de-

among his satans and his demons, saying: O company of satans, among the offspring of Adam we have reached the desire and arrived, in their annihilation, at the objective, and have bequeathed them to the Fire, except for those who adhere to this group. Make it your concern to cause the people to doubt concerning them, prompt them to hostility to them, and the enticement of them and their friends, until the error and misbelief of mankind becomes strong and not a survivor among them will be rescued. Iblîs has spoken the truth about them, although he is a liar, that a good work will not avail hand in hand with hostility to you, nor a sin, except the major ones, do harm hand in hand with love for you and your patrons."[87]

---

rives from the Arabic root *b-l-s*, in the sense that Satan has nothing to expect – *ublisa* – from God (*'balas'* is a person of desperate character). The fourth form of the verb (*ablasa*) means 'to be overcome with grief', 'to be desperate', 'to be struck with despair'. Then again, it finds a possible derivation from the Hebrew for 'adversary'. Cf. PENRICE J., *A Dictionary and Glossary of the Kor-an*, Asian Educational Services, New Delhi 1995: 19. Satan has a number of designations in the Qur'ân, but none of these can be considered as proper names. 'Shayṭân' appears in the singular form in the period of Medina (622–632), replacing Iblîs.

[87] The distinction between 'grave' (*kabâ'ir*) and 'lesser' (*ṣaġâ'ir*) sins found in the Qur'ân (cf. for e.g. Q. 42: 37, Q. 53: 32), which God may pardon immediately or may punish for a specific period, according to His will, (cf. Q. 2: 284 and Q. 3: 129, "*He will forgive whom He will and he will punish whom He will*") and the corpus of *aḥâdîṯ*, while developed at great length by various theologians and legal schools (*maḏâhib*), remains inconsistent in its definition. The generally accepted idea of moral lapse or sin was one of disobedience to the *sharî'a*, so that 'disobedience' often became a synonym for 'sin'. It was thought that the seriousness of the sin lay in the hardening of the heart and persistence in evildoing, as expressed by Ibn 'Abbâs: "Everything forbidden by God, once persisted in, becomes a grave sin." In this sense, persistence in lesser sins makes them grave. Cf. LAGARDE M., "Sin, Repentance and Forgiveness in the Qur'an and Tradition" in *Encounter*, n. 107 (July-August 1984): 1–10, WENSINCK A.J., "Khaṭî'a" in H A R Gibb et al (eds.), *SEI*, E.J. Brill, Leiden 1995: 251.

AFTERWORD

By the time the Twelfth Imâm, Abû al-Qâsim Muḥammad b. al-Ḥasan al-Mahdî, went into concealment in the 'greater Occultation' (*al-ġayba al-kubrâ*) in 327/940,[1] the theology of the Shîʿa had moved far beyond the aspirations and tendencies, some of them extremist, of its beginnings. Unarguably, an acute component of the ethos of those various groupings that would come to be called the Shîʿa was the abiding realization that they would never attain to the power they maintained was their due but that had been usurped by others, and concomitantly, their turning increasingly to a supernatural, other-worldly power. This would intensely colour and shape their conception of what would come to be regarded as the principal foundational moments in the Shîʿî story – the Karbalâʾ event in particular would be a growing trauma – and of the members of the *ahl al-bayt*, the 'holy family', who perpetuated the bloodline of Muḥammad. From about the 4th/10th century, with the rise of a number of Shîʿî or pro-Shîʿî dynasties (the Fâṭimid of Egypt[2] and the Bûyid of Persia[3]), the image of Zaynab's mother Fâṭima would

[1] Preceded by the 'lesser Occultation' (*al-ġayba al-ṣuġrâ*) from 257/872 until 327/940 when the Imâm was present but not seen and dealt with people through deputies and agents (*nuwwâb*). With the greater Occultation, he is entirely concealed, and there is no longer access to him, nor does he work any longer through agents. This event would give significant impetus to the development of theology and the codification of *aḥâdîṯ* among the early Shîʿî scholars.

[2] 297/909 – 567/1171. Cf. BOSWORTH C.E., *Islamic Surveys 5. The Islamic Dynasties*, Edinburgh University Press, Edinburgh 1967: 46.

[3] 320/932 – 454/1062. Cf. BOSWORTH C.E., *Islamic Surveys 5. The Islamic Dynasties*, 1967: 94.

change substantially. The Fâṭimids would claim descent from her, and by the mid-4th/10th century, the Bûyids would initiate public commemorations of Karbalâʾ. By the time of the Ṣafavid dynasty in the 10th/16th century, Fâṭima had become increasingly more flawless and ever less a woman with ordinary human traits, an image that would remain moderately unchanged until the writings of scholars like ʿAli Shariati (d. 1977).

The development of Zaynab's character would follow similar lines, although it would be less clearly articulated in the texts; it would be the contemporary hagiographers, both those of a pietistic strain who emphasized the more numinous aspects of her upbringing (embodied in her knowledge, her piety and her modesty), as well as those who attempted to shape Zaynab into a contemporary model for the ideal Islamic women, who would build a theology around ʿAlî's eldest daughter.

When 'Zaynab the liar' mounted her donkey and declared herself to be a trickster, she was at that very instant the antithesis of Zaynab, daughter of ʿAlî and Fâṭima, who is called *al-Ṣiddîqa*, and who, at the level of popular theology, won the day not just because she was tenacious, but primarily because she told the truth. For her devotees, Zaynab did not cause Ibn Ziyâd to back down, or reduce Yazîd to chastened silence because she was strong, but chiefly because, in spite of the burden of weakness and sorrow she carried, she had truth and right on her side.

Whether recognized or not, for a few days crucial days, all of that impulse that would later develop into Shîʿî Islam in its major branches, was articulated, defended, and perhaps even guaranteed by a woman, the granddaughter of Muḥammad, sister of al-Ḥusayn. Some might indeed be tempted to nominate her the 'saviour' of Shîʿî Islam, since by her protecting the life of ʿAlî b. al-Ḥusayn, she saved the line of Imâms, without whom, some Shîʿî theology holds, neither Islam, as understood by those who would later be called the Shîʿa, nor even the world could go on. The theology of the Imamate, understood as a consequence of God's kindness (*lutf*) as well as of rational divine justice, and believed, at least by the Ismaʿîlî and the *iṯnâ ʿasharî* Shîʿa to be indispensable for a proper interpretation of the revelation, went through a vigorous development long after Karbalâʾ and Zaynab, and resulted in major disagreements between the main Shîʿî branches, the Zaydî, the Ismaʿîlî and the *iṯnâ ʿasharî*. These disagreements included issues of designation, recognition and the Imâm's political authority. At the very least, the Isma^cîlî and the *iṯnâ* ʿ*asharî* hold at a theological level that an Imâm is necessary at all times for a correct interpretation of the revelation.

This being said, it seems unlikely that Zaynab, in saving the life of her nephew, would have clearly grasped the theological consequences of her action. Nonetheless, there is a strand, found in the Sunnî al-Ḫawârizmî, and examined earlier in this work, in which, in the midst of the battle, Zayn al-ʿÂbidîn emerges from his tent, undeterred by his father's strict prohibition. He would be the one, says al-Ḫawârizmî, who would continue the family of Muḥammad, but at this stage he was not strong enough even to carry his sword. From behind him, his aunt, not Zaynab but her sister Umm Kulṯûm, attempts to order him back, to which he replies: "Let me fight in front of the son of the Messenger of God!" Al-Ḥusayn intervenes, telling Umm Kulṯûm to seize the boy and return him to his tent, since the earth could not continue devoid of the progeny of the family of Muḥammad, that is, without the members of the *ahl al-bayt*. In his hagiography, Shahin notes that in bidding his final farewell to the women, al-Ḥusayn had ordered Zaynab to prevent ʿAlî b. al-Ḥusayn from fighting, and that she does this quite forcefully, but gives no references to any classical text and does not repeat the story told by al-Ḫawârizmî.[4]

It could be proposed that Zaynab took on in those Karbalâʾ days some of the tasks and qualities that later Shîʿî scholars would define as pertaining to the Imâm even if, technically, she herself could never be called by that title, making herself worthy of imitation even if, technically, she herself could never be called a *marǧa*ʿ.[5]

---

[4] SHAHIN B., *Lady Zaynab*, 2002: 184.

[5] This was a concept that arose within the Uṣûlî School, those who adhere to certain principles (*uṣûl*) of jurisprudence, between the 12th/18th and 14th/20th centuries although, as Haider notes, some scholars attempted to read the concept back into Shîʿî history in order to fit much earlier personalities (HAIDER N., *Shi'i Islam: An Introduction*, 2014: 162). The *marǧa*ʿ would be the most learned jurist of each age, who as such would be the chief representative in the world of the Imâm, now in Occultation. His position would be determined by a number of factors, including learn-

Ibn Ziyâd picks her out instantly from the crowd and addresses Zaynab as though he accedes to her authority; both she and her nephew are immediately recognized by both Ibn Ziyâd and Yazîd as the leaders of the group.

Even if it cannot be said that Zaynab was, albeit for a few days, the 'leader' of the Shî^ca, it might be justifiably construed that she was the prototype and forerunner of those four agents or deputies (*nuwwâb*) who would arise to represent the Twelfth and final Imâm, who, after succeeding his father, was present but not seen in the 'lesser Occultation' from 257/872 until 327/940. Admittedly, the situation of ʿAlî b. al-Ḥusayn was somewhat different; nonetheless, in those critical post-Karbalâʾ days he was, because of illness, present but not seen, so that Zaynab could be said to be his spokesperson and agent. This is underscored by a number of texts which we have examined, and in which she steps into the background soon after her challenge to Yazîd, ceding the place to her nephew. Al-Mağlisî records more than one moment in which either ʿAlî b. al-Ḥusayn invites her to remain silent so that he can speak, or, unbidden, she cedes the place to him. I believe that such texts comprise the symbolic moment of the new Imâm taking his rightful place as Zaynab, her specific task heroically completed, steps back from the center. This is noteworthy, for example in Ibn al-Aṯîr, who records the instant when Yazîd tells Zaynab to speak and she defers to ʿAlî b. al-Ḥusayn, saying: "He is the speaker."[6]

Numerous corollaries, for those with an eye to comparative theology, can be drawn, for example, between al-Ḥusayn and the New Testament figure of Jesus; aside from the claims their respective adherents make about them, both are charismatic figures who take a stand for integrity and truth, and suffer severe consequences, submitting to a martyrdom that has healing and redemptive qualities. Likewise, there are strong parallels between Fâṭima, mother of al-Ḥusayn and Mary, mother of Jesus, in the theology constructed around their lives by Shîʿî Islam in the case of Fâṭima and Catholic

---

ing and seniority, and in times of disagreement, there may be more than one *marğaʿ*.

[6] Cf. for example Ibn al-Aṯîr., *al-Kâmil fî al-târîḫ*, vol. II: 439, al-Mağlisî., *Biḥâr al-anwâr*, vol. XLV, bb. 39, n. 22: 175.

Christianity in the case of Mary. Both are virgin[7] mothers and women of untold sorrow and grief; both have martyr sons whose deaths have a cosmic impact. Both are given extraordinarily powerful intercessory prerogatives by God. Although there is always the temptation to overstretch an analogy, such juxtapositions may be regarded as authentic without necessarily being absolute or incontrovertible.

In the case of Zaynab, two feasible parallels come immediately to mind. The first concerns the 2nd century BC Seleucid king Antiochus IV Epiphanes, whose story is narrated in the Second Book of Maccabees[8] and who, Yazîd-like, imposed a rigorous and, in their eyes, entirely ungodly regime upon the Jewish people, forbidding worship in the temple, outlawing the Sabbath and holy day observance and disallowing obedience to the precepts of the Torah, including the crucial and foundational rite of circumcision. The capital punishment that he imposed for those who would not submit to this Hellenization resulted in a legion of martyrs, among whom one particular individual is pertinent to the Zaynab model. It is the story of a widow and her seven sons, narrated in the texts in II Maccabees 7: 1–42. Arrested and ill-treated in an attempt to force them to submit to the de-Judaizing initiatives of the king, the first six sons refuse and are killed in the presence of their mother, who persistently encourages her sons to die nobly rather than fail the precepts of divine law. The texts do not fail to remark upon her example:

> The mother was especially admirable and worthy of honorable memory. Although she saw her seven sons perish within a single day, she bore it with good courage because of her hope in the Lord. She encouraged each of them in the language of their ancestors. Filled with a noble spirit, she reinforced her woman's reasoning with a man's courage (II Maccabees 7: 20–21)

---

[7] As noted in the first chapter, there is a substantial difference between what Catholic Christians understand by the virginity of Mary and what Shî'î Muslims understand by that same phenomenon in the life of Fâṭima.

[8] II Maccabees 6: 7 – 7: 42.

Even when the king urges her to persuade her last remaining son with reason, the mother, using a language that the king cannot understand, urges the boy not to give way, and is eventually martyred with him. While some of the differences are palpable – Zaynab, for example, directly addresses Ibn Ziyâd and Yazîd, while the Maccabees widow talks only to her sons, and always in a language the king cannot understand – both incidents are clear examples of human emotion being subdued by a determined and judicious adherence to the Law, or at the very least to justice. Both women, who might in ordinary circumstances be deemed powerless, especially since they are left in a situation without a male to protect them, show themselves able to draw upon superhuman courage and strength in a situation of crisis. They reveal that real strength is found is faithfulness to the commandments of God, rather than in the paradigm put forward by intolerant rulers. However, while the Maccabees widow is praised for being like a man, the Zaynab paradigm is understood differently; she is a woman who clearly illustrates that traits once regarded as being proper to the domain of males, belong equally to women. Both Zaynab and the Maccabees mother are archetypal women, whose tenacity and daring, emboldened by a profound conviction and fidelity to the faith that they profess.

A second correspondence is equally compelling; in the New Testament accounts of the Resurrection, for a brief but undetermined period, the whole content of New Testament Christianity rests entirely upon the shoulders of a woman named Mary Magdalene. According to the Christian scriptures, she is the first witness to the Resurrection and the first to relay news of the event to the other members of the nascent Church. In this, for a brief period of time she carries the whole of that that message which is called *kerygma* – the proclamation of the Resurrection upon which the New Testament Church and its theology is built. The early Church's first evangelist and eyewitness to the person of Jesus is a woman, as six centuries later Zaynab would, for a brief period, be al-Ḥusayn's chief defender, apologist and advocate.

This monograph aimed at a number of things; it was an attempt to construct the beginnings of a biography for ʿAlî's daughter that would be based primarily on the classical texts of Sunnî and Shîʿî Islam. At the very least, those texts offer fragments of a life, some of which would later be used by the pietists and hagiographers who, in works with little academic value but which tapped into the vein of popular religion, recounted the numinous events in Zaynab's childhood and upbringing, proposing these as model events for faithful Islamic women.

Centuries later, a new generation of hagiographers sought to present an alternate version of Zaynab, one that would capture popular imagination; this would be the Zaynab shaped by a specific politico-social discourse. If the Zaynab of earlier pieties was known for her reserve and her modesty, this was a Zaynab who expressed her *taqwâ* (piety)[9] by plunging herself more deeply into society and its needs, the fighter for justice and defender of the Islamic way, an altruistic and courageous woman upon whom every contemporary Muslim woman could model herself.

One of the objectives of this work was, therefore, an attempt to hear again the Zaynabian voice as she articulates her grief, her *apologia*, her theological defense of al-Ḥusayn's struggle at the level of the classical texts. Even if her picture there is fragmentary, she speaks nonetheless in a voice that could help to shape a genuine Zaynabian theology and praxis, and which is the antithesis of the inhabitants of Kûfa, who remained silent or looked the other way in the face of oppression and injustice. A solid Zaynabian praxis renders her archetypal, placing her beyond the boundaries of nation and religion, situating her within the grasp of all people as one who can be emulated; as wife and mother, as defender of her brother and the continuation of his voice, as a woman wrapped in sorrow, Zaynab's struggle is no less pertinent even to people whose struggles may be nothing more than a little private sorrow, but who nonetheless need the same courage with which to negotiate daily life as she needed to confront and Ibn Ziyâd-Yazîd tyranny.

It would be germane to conclude this search for the voice of Zaynab by listening to the voices of her devotees, using examples of the prayers of blessing and salutation offered her by all who

---

[9] The word *taqwâ* in its various forms occurs over two hundred times in the Qur'ân, and is often translated as 'piety', although this may be a weak rendering; I use it here of Zaynab because as a concept, it aptly articulates that moral grounding or conscience that renders human beings aware of their responsibilities to God and society.

make the pilgrimage visit (*ziyâra*) to her tomb. Like the 'theological titles' listed by Karbâssî, these 'litanies of approach' (*ziyârât*) are not found in the classical sources, but are drawn from works of popular spirituality. Their lines epitomize Zaynab in her lineage, in her titles of honor and in her manifold sufferings, and look to her intercessory powers to win forgiveness, fulfilment and relief in this life; even after death, Zaynab continues to speak a word for all who cry out in need. There are a number of 'litanies of approach' for the tomb of Zaynab, those reproduced below being only two examples. The first example is concise and concentrates on Zaynab' titles and virtues:

زيارة السيدة زينب الكبرى (سلام الله عليها (بنت الامام علي) عليه السلام)
بسم الله الرحمن الرحيم

The visit to the tomb of the mistress Zaynab al-Kubrâ, daughter of Imâm ʿAlî.
In the name of God, the perfect mercy, the enduring mercy:

السلام عليك يا بنت سلطان الانبياء، السلام عليك يا بنت صاحب الحوض واللواء، السلام عليك يا بنت فاطمة الزهراء، السلام عليك يا بنت خديجة الكبرى، السلام عليك يا بنت سيد الاوصياء وركن الاولياء أمير المؤمنين، السلام عليك يا بنت ولي الله، السلام عليك يا ام المصائب يا زينب بنت علي ورحمة الله وبركاته

Peace be upon you, daughter of the ruler of the prophets.
Peace be upon you, daughter of the one entrusted with the Pond[10] *and the Standard.*
Peace be upon you, daughter of Fâṭima al-Zahrâʾ.
Peace be upon you, daughter of Ḫadîǧa al-Kubrâ.
Peace be upon you, daughter of the master of the trustees and support of the holy ones of God, the Commander of the Faithful.

---

[10] In Shîʿî eschatology, the 'Pond' or 'Basin' (*al-ḥawḍ*) is the pool of *al-Kawṯar*, the great symbol of the authority of Muḥammad and his descendants over all creation. On the Day of Resurrection, the 'day of great thirst', ʿAlî will be given authority over this Pond, to give its life-giving waters to his adherents and supporters, and to send his enemies away thirsty. Cf. AYOUB M., *Redemptive Suffering in Islam. A Study of the Devotional Aspects of ʿAshura in Twelver Shiʿism*, 1978: 198, 200–201.

Peace be upon you, daughter of God's holy one.
Peace be upon you, mother of afflictions, Zaynab daughter of ʿAlî, and the mercy of God and His blessings.

السلام عليك أيتها الفاضلة الرشيدة، السلام عليك أيتها العاملة الكاملة، السلام عليك أيتها الجليلة الجميلة، السلام عليك أيتها التقية النقية، السلام عليك أيتها المظلومة المقهورة، السلام عليك أيتها الرضية المرضية، السلام عليك يا تالية المعصوم

Peace be upon you, the Virtuous, the Rightly Guided.
Peace be upon you, the Active, the Perfect.
Peace be upon you, the Lofty, the Beautiful.
Peace be upon you, the Pious, the Immaculate.
Peace be upon you, the Tyrannized, the Humiliated.
Peace be upon you, the Satisfied, the One who Satisfies God.
Peace be upon you, Follower of the Immaculate Ones.

السلام عليك يا ممتحنة في تحمل المصائب بالحسين المظلوم، السلام عليك أيتها البعيدة عن الآفاق، السلام عليك أيتها الاسيرة في البلدان، السلام على من شهد بفضلها الثقلان، السلام عليك أيتها المتحيرة في وقوفك في القتلى وناديت جدك رسول الله بهذا النداء: صلى عليك مليك السماء هذا حسين بالعراء مسلوب العمامة والرداء مقطع الاعضاء وبناتك سبايا

Peace be upon you, tested in the bearing of afflictions with the tyrannized al-Ḥusayn.
Peace be upon you, distant from the regions.[11]
Peace be upon you, prisoner in the countries.
Peace be upon the one to whose excellence humans and ğinn bore testimony.
Peace be upon you, dismayed at the killing, and who cried out to your grandfather with the appeal: May the Sovereign of heaven bless you! This is Ḥusayn in the open, stripped of turban and gown, limbs dismembered, your daughters, captives.

السلام على روحك الطيبة وجسدك الطاهر، السلام عليك يا مولاتي وابنة مولاي وسيدتي وابنة سيدتي ورحمة الله وبركاته

[11] Possibly a reference words used by Zaynab in her protest against Yazîd: "Did you suppose, Yazîd, having cut us off from the regions of the earth…"

أشهد أنك قد أقمت الصلاة وآتيت الزكاة وأمرت بالمعروف ونهيت عن المنكر وأطعت الله ورسوله وصبرت على الاذي في جنب الله حتى أتاك اليقين

Peace be upon your kind spirit and your pure body.
Peace be upon you, my protector and daughter of my protector, my mistress and daughter of my mistress, and the mercy of God and His blessings.
I bear witness that you performed the prayer,[12] *and have given the legal charity,*[13] *and have enjoined what is good and forbidden was is evil,*[14] *and obeyed God and His Messenger, and exercised patience in injury, on the side of God until He gave you certainty.*

فلعن الله من جحدك ولعن الله من ظلمك ولعن الله من لم يعرف حقك ولعن الله أعداء آل محمد من الجن والانس من الاولين والآخرين وضاعف عليهم العذاب الاليم

The curse of God upon whoever disavowed you.
The curse of God upon whoever ill-treated you.
The curse of God upon whoever did not recognize your due.
The curse of God upon the enemies of the family of Muḥammad, from among the ǧinn and humanity, from first to last, and double torment for them in the utmost degree.[15]

أتيتك يا مولاتي وابنة مولاي قاصدا وافدا عارفا بحقك فكوني شفيعا إلى الله في غفران ذنوبي، وقضاء حوائجي، واعطاء سؤلي وكشف ضري، وأن لك ولابيك وأجدادك الطاهرين جاها عظيما وشفاعة مقبولة، السلام عليك وعلى آبائك الطاهرين المطهرين وعلى الملائكة المقيمين في حرمكِ الشريف المبارك

---

12 That is, the ritual prayer of Islam (*ṣalât*).

13 The *zakât*.

14 One of the specific duties incumbent upon a Shîʿî Muslim is the Muʿtazilî principle of enjoining others to do good (*amr bi-l-maʿrûf*) and forbidding others from doing evil (*naḥî ʿan al-munkar*); the theology expressed is of a God desires the establishment of a just social and political order who thus requires Muslims to intervene in the affairs of community. This principle is patently seen in Zaynab's stand against oppression and tyranny.

15 Cf. Q. 33: 30.

Protector and daughter of my protector, I come to you directly, an envoy, recognizing your due. Be an intercessor before God for the forgiveness of my sins and the fulfilment of my needs and the granting of my request and the lifting of my injury.
To you and to your father and to your pure grandparents great standing and accepted intercession!
Peace be upon you and upon your pure and immaculate fathers, and upon the angels who reside in your noble and blessed sanctuary.

The second example is longer and more theological; like many of these litany prayers, as is the case in other religious traditions, it is catechetical, mixing a didactic motive with spirituality as, as many prayers are wont to do, it attempts to instruct the devotee in various tenets of faith. More than that, it has a certain mystical bent, with its use of terminology such as *fanâʾ* ('absorption' or 'annihilation') and its designation of a pre-existence (*nûr muḥammadî*) to Muḥammad.[16]

اَلسَّلامُ عَلَيْكِ يا بِنْتَ سَيِّدِ الأَنْبِياءِ
اَلسَّلامُ عَلَيْكِ يا بِنْتَ صاحِبِ الْحَوْضِ وَاللِّواءِ
اَلسَّلامُ عَلَيْكِ يا بِنْتَ مَنْ عُرِجَ بِهِ إِلَى السَّماءِ وَوَصَلَ إِلَى مَقامِ قابَ قَوْسَيْنِ أَوْ أَدْنى
اَلسَّلامُ عَلَيْكِ يا بِنْتَ نَبِيِّ الْهُدى وَسَيِّدِ الْوَرى وَمُنْقِذِ الْعِبادِ مِنَ الرَّدى
اَلسَّلامُ عَلَيْكَ يا بِنْتَ صاحِبِ الْخُلُقِ الْعَظِيمِ وَالشَّرَفِ الْعَمِيمِ وَالآياتِ وَالذِّكْرِ الْحَكِيمِ
اَلسَّلامُ عَلَيْكِ يا بِنْتَ صاحِبِ الْمَقامِ الْمَحْمُودِ وَالْحَوْضِ الْمَوْرُودِ وَاللِّواءِ الْمَشْهُودِ
اَلسَّلامُ عَلَيْكِ يا بِنْتَ مَنْهَجِ دِينِ الإِسْلامِ وَصاحِبِ الْقِبْلَةِ وَالْقُرْآنِ وَعَلَمِ الصِّدْقِ وَالْحَقِّ وَالإِحْسانِ
اَلسَّلامُ عَلَيْكِ يا بِنْتَ صَفْوَةِ الأَنْبِياءِ وَعَلَمِ الأَتْقِياءِ وَمَشْهُورِ الذِّكْرِ فِي السَّماءِ وَرَحْمَةُ اللهِ وَبَرَكاتُهُ

Peace be upon you, daughter of the master of the prophets.[17]

---

[16] For a brief outline of the *nûr muḥammadî*, cf. CLOHESSY C., *Fatima, Daughter of Muhammad*, 2009: 74–76.

[17] The word 'daughter' (*bint*) is used here and later in the litany in terms of lineage, since it is Muḥammad, and not ʿAlî, who is master of the prophets and, as will be noted later, none of Muḥammad's daughters was present at Karbalâʾ. That being said, it does seem at times that this litany confuses (perhaps deliberately so) two Zaynabs; one, the daughter of

Peace be upon you, daughter of the one entrusted with the Pond and the Banner.
Peace be upon you, daughter of the one who was made to ascend[18] *to heaven and arrived at a station "two bows' length or nearer".*[19]
Peace be upon you, daughter of the prophet of guidance, the master of humankind, the deliverer of humanity from ruin.
Peace be upon you, daughter of the one entrusted with "a tremendous nature",[20] *great distinction and "a revelation and a wise reminder".*[21]
Peace be upon you, daughter of the one entrusted with the praised estate,[22] *the Pond of Destiny and the Notable Banner.*

Muḥammad, married to Abû al-ʿÂṣ b. Rabîʿ and who died around the age of twenty-nine in Medina, and the other his granddaughter. Nonetheless, the litany is reproduced as it stands.

[18] For a brief outline of Muḥammad's 'night journey' (*isrâʾ*) and 'ascension' (*miʿrâǧ*) and how these are understood in Sunnî and Shîʿî Islam, cf. CLOHESSY C., *Fatima, Daughter of Muhammad*, 2009: 16–20.

[19] Q. 53: 9.

[20] Q. 68: 4.

[21] Q. 3: 58.

[22] The specific reference to Muḥammad's station in the afterlife is found in Q. 17: 70 ("*It may be that thy Lord will raise thee to a praised estate*"). A number of the texts of Sunnî *aḥâdîṯ*, such as al-Buḫârî and Muslim, link this 'praised estate' with Muḥammad's intercessory prerogatives. Cf. for e.g. al-Buḫârî., *Ṣaḥîḥ*, vol. II, bk. 24 (*Kitâb al-zakât*), bb. 51, n. 553: 321–322, Muslim., *Ṣaḥîḥ*, vol. I, Book 1 (*Kitâb al-îmân*), bb. 84, n. 320: 179–180. Transmissions in al-Buḫârî, al-Nasâʾî, Ibn Mâǧa and al-Tirmiḏî for example, seem to underscore that according to Muḥammad himself, it is indeed intercession that is meant by his 'praised estate' (Q. 17: 79). Cf. al-Buḫârî., *Ṣaḥîḥ*, *Kitâb al-zakât*, ch. 52, n. 1475: 323, *Kitâb al-tafsîr*, ch. 11, n. 4718: 193, *Kitâb al-tawḥîd*, ch. 19, n. 7440: 325–8, al-Nasâʾî., *Sunan*, *Kitâb al-adhân*, ch. 38, n. 681: 400–1, Ibn Mâǧa., *Sunan*, *Abwâb al-adhân*, ch. 4, n. 722: 477. This remains a highly debated question in Islam; the Sunnî scholars are divided over the issue, although the weight of Islamic teaching seems to fall on the side of intercession rather than against it (cf. FITZGERALD M.L., "Mediation in Islam" in *Studia Missionalia*, vol. XXI, 1972: 196). The Shîʿa generally, within their theological tradition and piety, have no reservations about intercession, and uphold not merely the possibility but also the reality of the intercession of the prophets and the Imâms on behalf of

Peace be upon you, daughter of the manifest way of the religion of Islam, the one entrusted with the qibla and the Qurʾân and the distinguishing mark of sincerity, truth and beneficence.

Peace be upon you, daughter of the best of the prophets, the distinguishing mark of the God-fearing, the celebrated of reputation in heaven, and the mercy of God and His blessing.

اَلسَّلَامُ عَلَيْكِ يَا بِنْتَ خَيْرِ خَلْقِ اللهِ وَسَيِّدِ خَلْقِهِ وَأَوَّلِ الْعَدَدِ قَبْلَ إِيجَادِ أَرْضِهِ وَسَماواتِهِ وَآخِرِ الْأَبَدِ بَعْدَ فَنَاءِ الدُّنْيَا وَأَهْلُهُ الَّذِي رُوحُهُ نُسْخَةُ اللَّاهُوتِ وَصُورَتُهُ نُسْخَةُ الْمُلْكِ وَالْمَلَكُوتِ وَقَلْبُهُ خَزَانَةُ الْحَيِّ الَّذِي لَا يَمُوتُ وَرَحْمَةُ اللهِ وَبَرَكَاتُهُ.

اَلسَّلَامُ عَلَيْكِ يَا بِنْتَ الْمُظَلَّلِ بِالْغَمامِ سَيِّدِ الْكَوْنَيْنِ وَمَوْلَى الثَّقَلَيْنِ وَشَفِيعِ الْأُمَّةِ يَوْمَ الْمَحْشَرِ وَرَحْمَةُ اللهِ وَبَرَكَاتُهُ

اَلسَّلَامُ عَلَيْكِ يَا بِنْتَ سَيِّدِ الْأَوْصِيَاءِ

اَلسَّلَامُ عَلَيْكِ يَا بِنْتَ إِمَامِ الْأَتْقِيَاءِ

اَلسَّلَامُ عَلَيْكِ يَا بِنْتَ رُكْنِ الْأَوْلِيَاءِ

اَلسَّلَامُ عَلَيْكِ يَا بِنْتَ عِمَادِ الْأَصْفِيَاءِ

اَلسَّلَامُ عَلَيْكِ يَا بِنْتَ يَعْسُوبِ الدِّينِ

Peace be upon you, daughter of the best of God's creation and the master of His creation, the first of the numbered before the foundation of His earth and His heavens and the last enduring after the annihilation[23] *of his world and its*

---

their communities. Cf. CLOHESSY C., "A Heart Attuned to Mercy: the Intercession of Mary and of Fatima" in *Encounter*, vol. 41/1 (2016), Pontificio Istituto di Studi Arabi e d'Islamistica, Rome: 5–39.

[23] The word *fanâʾ* has a certain resonance: traditionally (although disputed by some scholars), the emergence within Islamic mysticism (*taṣawwuf*) of this concept, which is read to mean 'annihilation' or 'absorption', (the substitution of human attributes with divine ones), is accredited to Bâyazîd al-Bisṭâmî (d. 261/874), a man whose ecstatic utterances caused great discomfiture and disturbance in 'orthodox' circles in the middle of the 3rd/9th century. Others endorse Abû Saʿîd al-Ḥarrâz (d. 286/899), contemporary al-Tustarî, as the first to speak of *fanâʾ* in Baghdad. The general idea is that humankind is essentially dependent upon God, and inexorably perishable (*fanâʾ*). Only God is permanent (*baqâʾ*), as noted in Q. 55: 26–27: "*Everyone that is thereon will pass away; there remaineth but the Countenance of thy Lord of Might and Glory*". Al-Bisṭâmî's mystical ascent (*miʿrâǧ*) denotes an ascent into God through the process of *fanâʾ* and

people,[24] *whose spirit is a copy of His divinity and whose image is a copy of the sovereignity and the kingdom, and whose heart is a container of the Life*[25] *which does not die, and the mercy of God and His blessing.*
Peace be upon you, daughter of the one shaded by cloud,[26] *master of the two existences,*[27] *lord of the two weighty things,*[28] *intercessor for the community on the Day of the Place of Congregation, and the mercy of God and His blessing.*

---

baqâ'. Cf. for e.g. BALDICK J., *Mystical Islam. In Introduction to Sufism*, Tauris Parke, London 2000: 40–42.

24 This is a mistake in the text and should read *ahli-hâ*.

25 *al-Ḥayy*, one of the ninety-nine names of God.

26 Traditionally, it is Mûsâ and his people who are shaded by clouds (cf. Q. 2: 57, Q. 7: 16), but for a tradition concerning the same favour for Muḥammad, cf. al-Tirmiḏî., *Sunan*, vol. VI, bk. 46 (*Kitâb al-manâqib*), bb. 3, n. 3620: 318–319. It is in the context of the meeting of the young Muḥammad with a monk called Baḥîrâ.

27 That is, those existences termed *al-dunyâ* (the world) and *al-âḫira* (the hereafter).

28 The *ḥadîṯ al-ṯaqalayn* (the 'two weighty things') is crucial to the Shîʿa, not least of all because it has been transmitted in *ṣaḥîḥ* narrations by a substantial number of Sunnî transmitters. The setting is usually at ʿArafât during Muḥammad's 'Farewell Pilgrimage', or at a watering place between Mecca and Medina (Ġadîr Ḫumm) on the way back from that Pilgrimage. Sometimes, the setting changes to the mosque at Medina or Muḥammad's bedroom during his last illness (Shîʿî scholars recognize four occasions, all pertaining to Muḥammad's last days, on which he publicly proclaimed the *ḥadîṯ al-ṯaqalayn*): "I have left among you two things, one of them greater than the other; the Book of God, may He be exalted, and my family. Watch how you follow me concerning them! They will not be separated until they return to me at the Pond." Cf. Muslim., *Ṣaḥîḥ*, vol. IV, bk. 44 (*Kitâb faḍâ'il al-ṣaḥâba*), bb. 4 (*Faḍâ'il ʿAlî b. Abî Ṭâlib*), n. 36: 1873 (with a careful qualification that includes all Muḥammad's wives), Ibn Ḥanbal., *Musnad*, vol. IV, *Musnad Abî Saʿîd al-Ḫudarî*, n. 11104: 30, n. 11131: 26–27, n. 11212: 54, vol. V*, Ḥadîṯ Zayd b. Arqam*, n. 19285: 75, al-Tirmiḏî., *Sunan*, vol. IX, bk. 46 (*Kitâb al-manâqib*), *Manâqib ahl bayt al-nabî*, bb. 77, n. 3788: 340–341, n. 7390: 342, al-Nasâ'î., *al-Sunan al-kubrâ*, bk. 76 (*Kitâb al-manâqib)*, bb. 4 (*Faḍâ'il ʿAlî*), n. 8148, al-Ḥâkim al-Nîsâbûrî., *Kitâb (Talḫîs) al-mustadrak ʿalâ al-ṣaḥîḥayn*, vol. III, Part 3, bk. 31 (*Kitâb maʿrifat al-ṣaḥâba*), *Manâqib ahl bayt rasûl Allâh*, n. 4774: 173–174, vol. III, Part 3, bk.

Peace be upon you, daughter of the master of those mandated.
Peace be upon you, daughter of the Imam of the God-fearing.
Peace be upon you, daughter of the support of the friends of God.
Peace be upon you, daughter of the buttress of the sincere friends.
Peace be upon you, daughter of the chief of the religion.

اَلسَّلامُ عَلَيْكِ يا بِنْتَ أَمِيرِ الْمُؤْمِنِينِ
اَلسَّلامُ عَلَيْكِ يا بِنْتَ سَيِّدِ الْوَصِيِّينَ
اَلسَّلامُ عَلَيْكِ يا بِنْتَ قائِدِ الْبَرَرَةِ
اَلسَّلامُ عَلَيْكِ يا بِنْتَ قامِعِ الْكَفَرَةِ وَالْفَجَرَةِ
اَلسَّلامُ عَلَيْكِ يا بِنْتَ وارِثِ النَّبِيِّينَ
اَلسَّلامُ عَلَيْكِ يا بِنْتَ خَلِيفَةَ سَيِّدِ الْمُرْسِلِينَ
اَلسَّلامُ عَلَيْكِ يا بِنْتَ ضِياءِ الدِّين
اَلسَّلامُ عَلَيْكِ يا بِنْتَ النَّبَأِ الْعَظِيمِ عَلَى الْيَقِينِ
اَلسَّلامُ عَلَيْكِ يا بِنْتَ مَنْ حِسابُ النَّاسِ عَلَيْهِ وَالْكَوْثَرُ فِي يَدَيْهِ وَالْنَصُّ يَوْمُ الْغَدِير عَلَيْهِ وَرَحْمَةُ اللهِ وَبَرَكاتُهُ.

Peace be upon you, daughter of the Commander of the Faithful.
Peace be upon you, daughter of those enjoined.
Peace be upon you, daughter of the leader of the reverent.
Peace be upon you, daughter of the surpressor of the disbelievers and the immoral.
Peace be upon you, daughter of the heir of the prophets.
Peace be upon you, daughter of the successor of the master of those sent.

---

31 (*Kitâb maʿrifat al-ṣaḥâba*), *Manâqib amîr al-muʾminîn ʿAlî b. Abî Ṭâlib*, n. 4641: 126–127, al-Baġdâdî., *Târîḫ Baġdâd*, vol. VIII, n. 4551: 442, Ibn ʿIyâḍ., *Ikmâl al-muʿlim sharḥ ṣaḥîḥ Muslim*, vol. VII, bk. 44 (*Kitâb faḍâʾil al-ṣaḥâba*), bb. 4 (*Min faḍâʾil ʿAlî b. Abî Ṭâlib*), nn. 36–37: 416–418, al-Ḫawârizmî., *Maqtal al-Ḥusayn*, Part I, ch. 6, *Faḍâʾil al-Ḥasan wa-l-Ḥusayn*, no. 47: 156, Ibn Taymiyya., *Minhâǧ al-sunna al-nabawiyya fî naqḍ kalâm al-shîʿa wa-l-qadariyya*, vol. IV: 85; al-Tibrîzî., *Mishkât al-maṣâbîḥ*, vol. III, bk. 30 (*Kitâb al-manâqib*), bb. 10 (*Manâqib ʿAlî b Abî Ṭâlib*), n. 6131: 1732, al-Mizzî., *Tahḏîb al-kamâl fî asmâʾ al-riǧâl*, vol. X, n. 2098: 50–51, Ibn Kaṯîr., *al-Bidâya wa-l-nihâya*, vol. V: 209; al-Hayṯamî., *Maǧmaʿ al-zawâʾid wa-manbaʿ al-fawâʾid*, vol. IX, Part 9, bb. *fî faḍl ahl al-bayt*: 162–163, al-ʿIṣâmî., *Simṭ al-nuǧûm al-ʿawâlî*, vol. II, bb. 7, Part 3: 503, al-Ṣabbân., *Isʿâf al-râġibîn* in the margins of *Nûr al-abṣâr fî manâqib âl bayt al-nabî al-muḫtâr*: 143.

Peace be upon you, daughter of the light of the religion.
Peace be upon you, daughter of the great tidings concerning certitude.
Peace be upon you, daughter of the one upon whom is the reckoning of the people, in whose hands is al-Kawṯar, upon whom is the delegation on the day of Ġadîr,[29] *and the mercy of God and His blessings.*

اَلسَّلامُ عَلَيْكِ يا بِنْتَ مَنْ قادَ زِمامَ ناقَتِها جِبْرائِيلُ وَشارَكَها فِي مُصابِها إِسْرافِيلُ
وَغَضِبَ بِسَبَبِها الرَّبُّ الْجَلِيلُ وَبَكى لِمُصابِها إِبْراهِيمُ الْخَلِيلُ وَنُوحٌ وَمُوسَى الْكَلِيمُ فِي
كَرْبَلاءِ الْحُسَيْنِ الشَّهِيدِ الْغَرِيبِ
اَلسَّلامُ عَلَيْكِ يا بِنْتَ الْبُدُورِ السَّواطِعِ
اَلسَّلامُ عَلَيْكِ يا بِنْتَ الشُّمُوسِ الطَّوالِعِ وَرَحْمَةُ اللهِ وَبَرَكاتُهُ

Peace be upon you, daughter, the halter of whose she-camel Ğibrâ'îl[30] *guided, and whose partner in her afflictions was Isrâfîl,*[31] *and for whose cause the Lord, the Majestic*[32] *grew angry,*[33] *and over whose afflictions wept Ibrâhîm al-*

---

[29] Together with Karbalâ', one of the historical narratives shared by all the main branches of Shî'i Islam. The sermon of Ġadîr Ḫumm, set during Muḥammad's 'Farewell Pilgrimage' (*ḥağğat al-wadâ'*) in the last year of his life, was an event during which, the Shî'a claim, Muḥammad unambiguously and confirmed 'Alî as his successor.

[30] Ğibrâ'îl's importance in Islam is described in the first chapter of this work.

[31] The angel who sounds the last trumpet. Cf. WENSINCK A.J., "Isrāfīl" in H.A.R Gibb et al. (eds.), *EI*^{2}, 1995: 184.

[32] *al-Ğalîl*, one of the ninety-nine names of God.

[33] This sounds very familiar to an infrequently transmitted *ḥadîṯ* that reads: "Fâṭima, verily God is angry when you are angry." Cf. al-Ḥâkim al-Nîsâbûrî., *Kitâb (Talḫîs) al-mustadrak 'alâ al-ṣaḥîḥayn*, vol. III, bk. 31 (*Kitâb ma'rifat al-ṣaḥâba*), *Manâqib Fâṭima bt. rasûl Allâh*, n. 4793: 181, al-Ḫawârizmî., *Maqtal al-Ḥusayn*, Part 1, bb. *Faḍâ'il Fâṭima al-Zahrâ' bt. rasûl Allâh*, n. 2: 90, Ibn al-Aṯîr., *Usd al-ġâba fî ma'rifat al-ṣaḥâba*, vol. V, bb. *ḥarf al-fâ'*: 522, al-Ḏahabî., *Mîzân al-i'tidâl fî tarâğim al-riğâl*, vol. II, n. 4560: 492, Ibn Ḥağar al-'Asqalânî., *al-Iṣâba fî tamyîz al-ṣaḥâba*, vol. IV, bb. *ḥarf al-fâ'*, n. 830: 366–367, *Tahḏîb al-tahḏîb*, vol. XII, *Kitâb al-nisâ'*, n. 4434: 441, al-Muttaqî al-Hindî., *Muntaḫab kanz al-'ummâl* in the margins of *Musnad Ibn Ḥanbal*, vol. V: 97.

ḫalîl and Nûḥ and Mûsâ al-kalîm,[34] *regarding the Karbalâʾ of al-Ḥusayn the martyr, the stranger.*[35]
Peace be upon you, daughter of the luminous full moons.
Peace be upon you, daughter of the rising suns, and the mercy of God and His blessings.

اَلسَّلامُ عَلَيْكِ يا بِنْتَ زَمْزَمَ وَصَفا
اَلسَّلامُ عَلَيْكِ يا بِنْتَ مَكَّةَ وَمُنى
اَلسَّلامُ عَلَيْكِ يا بِنْتَ مَنْ حُمِلَ عَلَى الْبُراقِ فِي الْهَوآءِ
اَلسَّلامُ عَلَيْكِ يا بِنْتَ مَنْ أُسْرِيَ بِهِ مِنَ الْمَسْجِدِ الْحَرامِ إِلَى الْمَسْجِدِ الأَقْصى
اَلسَّلامُ عَلَيْكِ يا بِنْتَ مَنْ ضَرَبَ بِالسَّيْفَيْنِ
اَلسَّلامُ عَلَيْكِ يا بِنْتَ مَنْ صَلَّى الْقِبْلَتَيْنِ
اَلسَّلامُ عَلَيْكِ يا بِنْتَ الْمُصْطَفى
اَلسَّلامُ عَلَيْكِ يا بِنْتَ عَلِيٍّ الْمُرْتَضى
اَلسَّلامُ عَلَيْكِ يا بِنْتَ فاطِمَةَ الزَّهْراءِ
اَلسَّلامُ عَلَيْكِ يا بِنْتَ خَدِيجَةَ الْكُبْرى
اَلسَّلامُ عَلَيْكِ وَعَلى جَدِّكِ مُحَمَّدٍ الْمُخْتارِ
اَلسَّلامُ عَلَيْكِ وَعَلى أَبِيكِ حَيْدَرِ الْكَرّارِ
اَلسَّلامُ عَلَيْكِ وَعَلَى السّاداتِ الأَطْهارِ الأَخْيارِ وَهُمْ حُجَجُ اللهِ عَلَى الأَقْطارِ ساداتُ الأَرْضِ وَالسَّماءِ مِنْ أَخِيكَ الْحُسَيْنِ الشَّهِيدِ الْعَطْشانِ الظَّمآنِ وَهُوَ أَبُو التِّسْعَةِ الأَطْهارِ وَهُمْ حُجَجُ اللهِ فِي الشَّرْقِ وَالْغَرْبِ وَالأَرْضِ وَالسَّماءِ الَّذِينَ حُبُّهُمْ فَرْضٌ عَلَى أَعْناقِ كُلِّ الْخَلائِقِ الْمَخْلُوقِينَ لِخالِقِ الْقادِرِ السُّبْحانِ

Peace be upon you, daughter of Zamzam[36] *and Ṣafâ.*
Peace be upon you, daughter of Mecca and Minâ.
Peace be upon you, daughter of the one who was carried through the air on al-Burâq.[37]

---

[34] While Ibrâhîm is nominated 'friend of God' (*ḫalîl Allâh*; cf. Q. 4: 125), Mûsâ's title is 'the one who spoke to God' (*kalîm Allâh*).

[35] The evening, starting at sunset, of ʿÂshûrâ (10th Muḥarram) is referred to in Farsi literature and poetry as 'the evening of strangers', meaning the strangers who are in a foreign land, separated from their supporters and helpers and home.

[36] The sacred well in Mecca.

[37] A reference to the camel involved in Muḥammad's 'night journey' (*isrâʾ*) and 'ascension' (*miʿrâǧ*).

Peace be upon you, daughter of the one who was made to journey by night from the sacred mosque (al-masğid al-ḥarâm) to the furthest mosque (al-masğid al-aqṣâ).
Peace be upon you, daughter of the one who struck with two swords.[38]
Peace be upon you, daughter of the one who prayed towards the two directions of prayer.[39]
Peace be upon you, daughter of the Chosen One.
Peace be upon you, daughter of ʿAlî the Approved One.
Peace be upon you, daughter of Fâṭima the Radiant.
Peace be upon you, daughter of the greater Ḫadîğa.
Peace be upon you, and upon your grandfather, Muḥammad the Chosen One.
Peace be upon you, and upon your father, the courageous lion.[40]
Peace be upon you, and upon the masters, the virtuous, the excellent, who are the proofs of God over the regions of the earth, masters of the earth and of heaven, from your brother al-Ḥusayn the martyr, the thirsty, the parched, who is the father of the nine virtuous ones, who are the proofs of God in the east and the west, the earth and heaven, love for whom is encumbent upon the necks of all created creatures by the Creator, the all-Capable,[41] *the One Far Beyond (al-subḥân).*

اَلسَّلامُ عَلَيْكِ يا بِنْتَ وَلِيِّ اللهِ الأَعْظَمِ

---

[38] Since popular tradition holds that Muḥammad had up to nine swords or more, possibly a reference to the famous *ḏû al-fiqâr*, one of Muḥammad's swords that had two points which he gave to ʿAlî. It could also refer to two swords given to Muḥammad by ʿAlî (or possible vice versa), named in popular tradition as *al-rasûb* and *al-miḫdam.*

[39] In Medina stands the 'mosque of the two qiblas' (*masğid al-qiblatayn*) marking the place where, in Islamic tradition, Muḥammad received the command to change the direction of prayer (*qibla*) from Jerusalem to Mecca. For a while, it housed two niches indicating the two prayer directions. Cf. Q. 2: 144 for the command to change the direction of prayer.

[40] The Arabic *karrâr* is an antonym for *farrâr*, which means 'deserter' or 'defector'. By tradition, ʿAlî is thus designated by Muḥammad during the Ḫaybar battle. Equally by tradition, it was ʿAlî's mother who named him *Ḥaydar* (حيدر).

[41] *al-Qâdir*, one of the ninety-nine names of God.

اَلسَّلامُ عَلَيْكِ يا بِنْتَ وَلِيِّ اللهِ الْمُعَظَّمِ
اَلسَّلامُ عَلَيْكِ يا عَمَّةَ وَلِيِّ اللهِ الْمُكَرَّمِ
اَلسَّلامُ عَلَيْكِ يا أُمَّ الْمَصائِبِ يا زَيْنَبُ وَرَحْمَةُ اللهِ وَبَرَكاتُهُ.
اَلسَّلامُ عَلَيْكِ أَيَّتُهَا الصِّدّيقَةُ الْمَرْضِيَّةُ
اَلسَّلامُ عَلَيْكِ أَيَّتُهَا الْفاضِلَةُ الرَّشِيدَةُ
اَلسَّلامُ عَلَيْكِ أَيَّتُهَا التَّقِيَّةِ النَّقِيَّةِ
اَلسَّلامُ عَلَيْكِ يا مَنْ ظَهَرَتْ مَحَبَّتُهَا لِلْحُسَيْنِ الْمَظْلُومِ فِي مِوارِدَ عَدِيدَةٍ وَتَحْمِلُ الْمَصائِبَ الْمُحْرِقَةِ لِلْقُلُوبِ مَعَ تَحَمُّلاتٍ شَدِيدَةٍ
اَلسَّلامُ عَلَيْكِ يا مَنْ حَفِظْتِ الْإِمامَ فِي يَوْمِ عاشُوراءِ فِي قَتْلَه وَبَذَلَتْ نَفْسِها فِي نَجاةِ زَيْنِ الْعابِدِينِ عليه السَّلام فِي مَجْلِسِ أَشْقَى الْأَشْقِياءِ وَنَطَقَتْ كَنُطْقِ عَلِيٍّ عَلَيْهِ السَّلامُ فِي سِكَكِ الْكُوفَةِ وَحَوْلَها كَثِيرٌ مِنَ الْأَعْداءِ
اَلسَّلامُ عَلَيْكِ يا مَنْ نَطَحَتْ جَبِينُها بِمُقَدَّمِ الْمَحْمِلِ إِذْ رَأَتْ رَأْسَ الشُّهَداءِ وَيَخْرُجُ الدَّمُ مِنْ تَحْتِ قِناعِها وَمِنْ مَحْمِلِها بِحَيْثُ يَرى مِنْ حَوْلِهَا الْأَعْداءُ
اَلسَّلامُ عَلَيْكِ يا تَالِيَ الْمَعْصُومِ
اَلسَّلامُ عَلَيْكِ يا مُمْتَحَنَةُ فِي تَحَمُّلاتِ الْمَصائِبِ كَالْحُسَينِ المظْلُومِ وَرَحْمَةُ اللهِ وَبَرَكاتُهُ.

Peace be upon you, daughter of God's greater holy one.
Peace be upon you, daughter of God's revered holy one.
Peace be upon you, aunt of God's venerated holy one.
Peace be upon you, mother of afflictions, Zaynab, and the mercy of God and His blessings.
Peace be upon you, O the truthful, the one who satisfies God.
Peace be upon you, O the virtuous, the rightly-guided.
Peace be upon you, O the pious, the pure.
Peace be upon you, whose love for al-Ḥusayn the tyrannized, was manifested at many watering places and bearing with immense forbearance, afflictions that scorched hearts.
Peace be upon you, who defended the Imâm in his being killed on the day of ʿÂshûrâ and offered herself in the deliverance of Zayn al-ʿÂbidîn, peace be upon him, in the council of the most wretched of criminals and spoke as with the speech of ʿAlî, peace be upon him, in the lanes of Kûfa, surrounded by many enemies.

Peace be upon you, who thrust her brow against the front of the carriage when you saw the chief[42] *of the martyrs, so that the blood ran from under her veil and from her carriage, to the point that it was seen by the enemies surrounding her.*
Peace be upon you, following after the infallible ones.
Peace be upon you, the tested in the bearing of afflictions like al-Ḥusayn the tyrannized, and the mercy of God and His blessings.

اَلسَّلامُ عَلَيْكِ أَيَّتُهَا الْبَعِيدَةُ الْمُتَحَيِّرَةُ فِي خَرابَةِ الشّامِ
اَلسَّلامُ عَلَيْكِ أَيَّتُهَا الْمُتَحَيِّرَةُ فِي وُقُوفِكِ عَلَى جَسَدِ سَيِّدِ الشُّهَداءِ وَخاطَبْتِ جَدَّكِ رَسُولِ اللهِ بِهذَا النِّداءِ صَلَّى عَلَيْكَ مَلِيكُ السَّماءِ هذا حُسَيْنٌ بِالْعَراءِ مَسْلُوبُ الْعِمامَةِ وَالرِّداءِ مُقَطَّعُ ٱلأَعْضاءِ وَبَناتُكَ سَبايا وَإِلَى اللهِ الْمُشْتَكي وَقالَتْ يا مُحَمَّدُ صلّى الله عليه وآله وسلَّم هذا حُسَيْنٌ تُسْفِي عَلَيْهِ رِيحُ الصَّبا مَجْذُوذُ الرَّأْسِ مِنَ الْقَفى قَتِيلُ أَوْلادِ الْبَغايا وا حُزْناهُ عَلَيْكَ يا أَبا عَبْدِ اللهِ
اَلسَّلامُ عَلَى مَنْ تَهَيَّجَ قَلْبُها لِلْحُسَيْنِ الْمَظْلُومِ الْعُرْيانِ الْمَطْرُوحِ عَلَى الثَّرى وَقالَتْ بِصَوْتٍ حَزِينٍ بِأَبِي مَنْ نَفْسِي لَهُ الْفِداءِ بِأَبِي الْمَهْمُومِ حَتّى قَضى بِأَبِي الْعَطْشانِ حَتّى مَضى بِأَبِي مَنْ شَيْبَتُهُ تَقْطُرُ بِالدِّماءِ
اَلسَّلامُ عَلَى مَنْ بَكَتْ عَلَى جَسَدِ أَخِيها بَيْنَ الْقَتْلى حَتّى بَكَى لِبُكائِهَا كُلُّ عَدُوٍّ وَصَدِيقٍ وَرَأَى النّاسُ دُمُوعَ الْخَيْلِ تَنْحَدِرُ عَلَى حَوافِرِها عَلَى التَّحْقِيقِ
اَلسَّلامُ عَلَى مَنْ تَكَلَّفَتْ وَاجْتَمَعَتْ فِي عَصْرِ عاشُوراءَ بَناتِ رَسُولِ اللهِ وَأَطْفالِ الْحُسَيْنِ وَقامَتْ لَهَا الْقِيامَةُ فِي شَهادَةِ الطِّفْلَيْنِ الْغَرِيبَيْنِ الْمَظْلُومَيْنِ
اَلسَّلامُ عَلَى مَنْ لَمْ تَنَمْ عَيْنُها لأَجْلِ حَراسَةِ آل اللهِ فِي طَفِّ نَيْنَوى وَسارَتْ أَسِيراً ذَلِيلاً بِيَدِ الأَعْداءِ
اَلسَّلامُ عَلَى مَنْ رَكِبَتْ بَعِيراً غَيْرَ وَطاءٍ وَنادَتْ أَخِيها أَبا الْفَضْلِ بِهذَا النِّداءِ أَخِي أَبَا الْفَضْلُ أَنْتَ الَّذِي رَكَّبْتَنِي إِذا أَرَدْتُ الْخُرُوجَ مِنَ الْمَدِينَةِ
اَلسَّلامُ عَلَى مَنْ خَطَبَتْ فِي مَيْدانِ الْكُوفَةِ بُخُطْبَةٍ نافِعَةٍ حَتّى سَكَنَتِ ٱلأَصْواتُ مِنْ كُلِّ ناحِيَةٍ
اَلسَّلامُ عَلَى مَنِ احْتَجَّتْ فِي مَجْلِسِ ابْنِ زِيادٍ بِاحْتِجاجات وَاضِحَةٍ وَقالَتْ فِي جَوابِهِ بِبَيِّناتٍ صادِقَةٍ إِذْ قالَ ابْنُ زيادِ لِزَيْنَبِ سَلامُ اللهِ عَلَيْها كَيْفَ رَأَيْتِ صُنْعَ اللهِ بِأَخِيكِ الْحُسَيْنِ قالَتْ ما رَأَيْتُ إِلاَّ جَمِيلاً
اَلسَّلامُ عَلَيْكِ يا أَسِيراً بِيَدِي ٱلأَعْداءِ فِي الْفَلَواتِ وَرَأَيْتِ أَهْلَ الشَّامِ فِي حالَةِ الْعَيْشِ وَالسُّرُورِ وَنَشْرِ الرّاياتِ

---

[42] The word *ra'as* (رَأس) could be read to mean 'head' or 'chief'. The theme of the martyrs' heads is prevelant in texts such as these; nonetheless, because in this sentence 'head' is in the singular and 'martyrs' in the pural, I have chosen to read it as 'chief'.

Peace be upon you, banished, isolated in the ignominy of Syria.
Peace be upon you, O dismayed in your halting by the body of the master of the martyrs, and adressing your grandfather the Messenger of God with this cry: "The sovereign of heaven bless you! Here is Ḥusayn in the open, turban and gown plundered, dismembered of limbs, your daughters captives. To God, this complaint!" And she said: "Muḥammad, God bless and save him and his family, this is Ḥusayn in the open air, the wind covering him with sand, head cut off at the nape, killed by the children of prostitutes. And O, our deep grief is upon you, Abû ʿAbd Allâh."
Peace be upon the one whose heart was agitated for al-Ḥusayn the tyrannized, stripped naked, cast down on the ground, and who said with a sad voice: "I swear by my father, for whom I would ransom myself! I swear by my father! Distressed until he was spent. I swear by my father! Thirsty until he departed. I swear by my father! His beard dripped with blood."
Peace be upon the one who wept over the body of her brother amidst the dead, until every enemy and friend wept for her weeping and, upon investigation, the people saw the tears of the horses flowing onto their hooves.
Peace be upon the one who took upon herself and gathered together on the afternoon of ʿÂshûrâ the daughters of the Messenger of God and the children of al-Ḥusayn and was greatly distressed by the martyrdom of the two tyrannized children, the strangers.
Peace be upon the one whose eyes did not sleep for watching over the family of God in Ṭaff,[43] *Nineveh, and who traveled as a humilated captive in the hands of the enemy.*
Peace be upon the one who mounted a caravan without any covering and called out to her brother Abû al-Faḍl with this cry: "My brother Abû al-Faḍl, you are the one who placed me on my mount when I wanted to depart from Medina!"
Peace be upon the one who preached a profitable address in the square of Kûfa, to the point that voices were stilled on every side.
Peace be upon the one who remonstrated in the council of Ibn Ziyâd with lucid protests and who replied with truthful statements in answer to him when Ibn Ziyâd said to Zaynab, the peace of God be upon her: "How do you see what God has done to your brother al-Ḥusayn?" and she replied: 'I see nothing but beauty!"

---

[43] Karbalâʾ.

Peace be upon you, captive in the hands of the enemy in the open country, and who beheld the people of Syria in the state of life and gladness and the unfolding of the banners.

BIBLIOGRAPHY

1. BOOKS

ABU-ZAHRA N., *The Pure and Powerful: Studies in Contemporary Muslim Society*, Garnet & Ithaca Press, Reading 1997.

AGHAIE K.S., *The Martyrs of Karbala: Shiʿi Symbols and Rituals in Modern Iran*, University of Washington Press, Seattle 2004.

AGHAIE K.S., (ed.), *The Women of Karbala*, University of Texas Press, Austin 2005.

ALI A., *Husain: The Saviour of Islam*, Baldwin, New York: Anjumane Aza Khana-Az-Zahra, n.d.

AYOUB M., *Redemptive Suffering in Islam. A Study of the Devotional Aspects of ʿAshura in Twelver Shiʿism*, Mouton Publishers, The Hague 1978.

BERNHEIMER T., *The ʾAlids: The First Family of Islam, 750–122*, Edinburgh University Press, Edinburgh 2014.

BILGRAMI M.H., *The Victory of Truth: The Life of Zaynab bint ʾAli*, Zahra Publications, Pakistan 1986.

BOESCHOTEN H.E. & O'KANE J., (eds.), *Al-Rabghūzī. The Stories of the Prophets*, vol. II, Brill, Leiden 2015.

CHELKOWSKI P., (ed.), *Taʾziyeh: Ritual and Drama in Iran*, New York University Press, New York 1979.

CHELKOWSKI P., (ed.), *Eternal Performance. Taʾziyeh and Other Shiite Rituals*, Seagull Books, Calcutta 2010.

CLOHESSY C., *Fatima, Daughter of Muhammad*, Gorgias Press, Piscataway 2009.

DEEB L., *An Enchanted Modern. Gender and Public Piety in Shiʾi Lebanon*, Princeton University Press, Princeton 2006.

D'SOUZA D., *Partners of Zaynab. Gendered Perspective of Shia Muslim Faith*, University of South Carolina Press, Columbia 2014.

FISCHER M., *Iran: From Religious Dispute to Revolution*, Harvard University Press, Cambridge, MA 1980.

HALAWI M., *A Lebanon Defied: Musa al-Sadr and the Shia Community*, Westview Press, Boulder, Colorado 1992.

AL-ḤASANÎ N., *Sabâyâ âl Muḥammad*, al-ʿAtba al-Ḥusayniyya al-Muqaddasa, Karbalâʾ 2012.

HOWARD I.K.A., (trans.), *Kitāb al-Irshād. The Book of Guidance by Shaykh al-Mufid*, Balagha Books, West Sussex 1981.

HOWARD I.K.A., (trans.), *The History of al-Ṭabarî*, vol. XIX, State University of New York Press, Albany 1990.

HOWARD I.K.A., (trans.), *The Rising of al-Husayn. Its Impact on the Consciousness of Muslim Society*, The Muhammadi Trust, London 1985.

HUSAIN A.A.T., (trans.), *House of Sorrows*, Islamic Publishing House, Ontario 2010.

HYDER S.A., *Reliving Karbala. Martyrdom in South Asian Memory*, Oxford University Press, Oxford 2006.

AL-JIBOURI Y.T., (trans.), *Maqtal al-Ḥusain*, CreateSpace Independent Publishing Platform 2014.

KARBÂSSÎ M.S., *Muʿǧam anṣâr al-Ḥusayn – al-nisâʾ*, Hussaini Charitable Trust, London 2009.

KAḤÂLA ʿU., *Aʿlâm al-nisâʾ fî ʿâlamî al-ʿarab wa-l-islâm*, Muʾassat al-Risâla, Beirut 1984.

AL-KÂSHÂNÎ A., 250 *Karâma li-l-sayyida Zaynab wa sayyidât bayt al-nubuwwa*, Dâr al-Ǧawâdayn li-l-Ṭibâʿa wa-l-Nashr wa-al-Tawzîʿ, Beirut 2008.

KEDDIE N., (ed.), *Religion and Politics in Iran: Shiʾism from Quietism to Revolution*, Yale University Press, New Haven 1983.

LADAK J., *The Hidden Treasure. Lady Umm Kulthum, Daughter of Imam Ali and Lady Fatima*, Sun Behind the Cloud Publications, Birmingham 2011.

LIMBA M., (trans.), *The Event of Taff, the earliest Historical Account of the Tragedy of Karbala*, Ahlul Bayt Digital Islamic Library Project, 2012.

MODARRESSI H., *Crisis and Consolidation in the Formative Period of Shiʿite Islam*, Darwin Press, Princeton, NJ: 1993.

MODARRESSI H., *Tradition and Survival. A Bibliographical Survey of Early Shīʾite Literature*, vol. 1, Oneworld, Oxford 2003.

MOTTAHEDEH R., *The Mantle of the Prophet*, Simon and Schuster, New York 1985.

AL-MÛSAWÎ M., *al-Kawṯar fî aḥwâl Fâṭima bt. al-nabî al-aṭhar*, 7 vols., Qum 2000.

PEDERSEN M.H., *Iraqi women in Denmark. Ritual performance and Belonging in Everyday Life*, Manchester University Press, Manchester 2013.

PIERCE M., *Twelve Infallible Men. The Imams and the Making of Shiʿism*, Harvard University Press, Cambridge 2016.

PINAULT D., *The Shiites: Ritual and Popular Piety in a Muslim Community*, St. Martin's Press, New York 1992.

PINAULT D., *Horse of Karbala*, St. Martin's Press, New York 2000.

RUFFLE K.G., *Gender, Sainthood, and Everyday Practice in South Asian Shiʾism*, University of North Carolina Press, Chapel Hill 2011.

SCHUBEL V.J., *Religious Performance in Contemporary Islam: Shia Devotional Rituals in South Asia*, University of South Carolina Press, Columbia 1993.

SHAHIN B., *Lady Zainab*, Ansariyan Publications, Qum 2002.

SHOSHAN B., *Poetics of Islamic Historiography: Deconstruction of Tabari's History*, Brill, Leiden 2004.

AL-TÛNĞÎ M., *Muʿǧam aʿlâm al-nisâʾ*, Muʾassasat al-Rayyân, Beirut 2000.

2. Articles

AGHAIE K.S., "The Karbala Narrative in Shii Political Discourse in Modern Iran in the 1960s–1970s" in *The Journal of Islamic Studies* 12(2) 2001:151– 176.

AGHAIE K.S., 1994. "Reinventing Karbala: Revisionist interpretations of the Karbala Paradigm" in *Jusur: The UCLA Journal of Middle Eastern Studies* 10, 1994:1–30.

AGHAIE K.S., "The Passion of Ashura in Shiite Islam" in *Voices of Islam*, vol. II, Praeger, Westport, Connecticut: 2007: 110–124.

AKHTAR S.V., "Karbala, an Enduring Paradigm of Islamic Revivalism" in *Al-Tawhid* 13 (1996): 113–25.

AL-ADEEB D., "Migratory Sacred Spaces. (Re)creating 'Ashura" in Nadje al-Ali, Deborah al-Najjar (eds.), *We Are Iraqis. Aesthetics and Politics in a Time of War*, Syracuse University Press, New York 2013: 127–143.

AMORETTI B.S., "How to Place Women in History. Some Remarks on the Recent Shiite Interest in Women's Shrines" in *Oriente Moderno*, Nuova serie, Anno 89, Nr. 1 (2009): 1–12.

ASANI A., "Marthiya: Imam Husayn's Conversation with God" in J Renard (ed.), *Windows on the House of Islam: Muslim Sources on Spirituality and Religious Life*, University of California Press, Berkeley: 1998.

CALMARD J., "Shii Rituals and Power. The Consolidation of Safavid Shiism: Folklore and Popular Religion" in C Melville (ed.), *Safavid Persia*, I. B. Tauris, London 1996: 139–190

CHITTICK W., "Rumi's View of the Imam Husain" in *al-Ṣerat* 12, Muhammadi Trust of Great Britain and Northern Ireland, London 1986: 4.

CLARKE L., "Some Examples of Elegy on Imam Husayn" in *al-Ṣerat* 12, Muhammadi Trust of Great Britain and Northern Ireland, London 1986: 13–28.

CLOHESSY C., "The Face of Islam Flushed: The Karbalā' Event" in *Encounter*, n. 285 (June 2002), Pontificio Istituto di Studi Arabi e d'Islamistica, Rome.

CLOHESSY C., "Mary and Fāṭima in the Catholic and Shī'ī Traditions" in A. Mahony et al. (eds.), *Catholics and Shi'a in Dialogue*, Melisende, London 2004.

CLOHESSY C., "Notes on Fatima, Daughter of Muhammad" in *Encounter*, N. 314 (April 2005), Pontificio Istituto di Studi Arabi e d'Islamistica, Rome.

CLOHESSY C., "Weeping Mothers. Tears and Power in Fāṭima and Mary" in *Islamochristiana* 36 (2010), Pontificio Istituto di Studi Arabi e d'Islamistica, Rome: 101–115.

CLOHESSY C., "A Heart Attuned to Mercy: the Intercession of Mary and of Fatima" in *Encounter*, vol. 41/1 (2016), Pontificio Istituto di Studi Arabi e d'Islamistica, Rome.

CLOHESSY C., "Some Notes on mağlis and taʿziya" in *Encounter*, vol. 41/1 (2016), Pontificio Istituto di Studi Arabi e d'Islamistica, Rome.

DEEB L., "Living Ashura in Lebanon: Mourning Transformed to Sacrifice" in *Comparative Studies of South Asia, Africa and the Middle East*, vol. 25, n. 1, 2005: 122–137.

DEEB L., "Doing Good, Like Sayyida Zaynab: Lebanese Shiʿi Women's Participation in the Public Sphere" in A Salvatore and M LeVine (eds.), *Religion, Social Practice, and Contested Hegemonies: Reconstructing the Public Sphere in Muslim Majority Societies*, Palgrave Macmillan, New York 2005: 85–107.

DEEB L., "Emulating and/or Embodying the Ideal: The Gendering of Temporal Frameworks and Islamic Role Models in Shi'i Lebanon" in *American Ethnologist*, vol. 36, n. 2 (May, 2009): 242–257.

D'SOUZA D., "The Figure of Zaynab in Shîʿî Devotional Life" in *The Bulletin of The Henry Martyn Institute*, Volume 17/1, January-June 1998.

D'SOUZA D., "In the Presence of the Martyrs. The ʿAlam in Popular Shiʿi Piety" in *The Muslim World*, vol. LXXXV111, Number 1, January 1998: 67–80.

FRIEDL E., "Ideal Womanhood in Postrevolutionary Iran" in J Brink and J Mencher (eds.), *Mixed blessings: Gender and Religious Fundamentalism Cross Culturally*, Routledge, New York 1997: 143–157.

HAMBLY G., "Zaynab Bint Ali and the Place of the Women of the Households of the First Imams in Shiite Devotional Literature" in G Hambly (ed.), *Women in the Medieval Islamic World*, St. Martin's Press, New York: 69–98.

HAMDAR A., "Jihad of Words: Gender and Contemporary Karbala Narratives" in *The Yearbook of English Studies*, Vol. 39, No. 1/2, Literature and Religion (2009), Modern Humanities Research Association, Cambridge: 84–100.

HEGLAND M.E., "Two Images of Husain: Accommodation and Revolution in an Iranian Village" in N R Keddie (ed.), *Religion and Politics in Iran: Shi'ism from Quietism to Revolution*, ed. Yale University Press, New Haven 1983: 218–236.

HEGLAND M.E., "Shi'a Women of Northwest Pakistan and Agency through Practice: Ritual, Resistance, Resilience" in *Political and Legal Anthropology Review*, vol. 18, no. 2, Regroupings (November 1995): 65–79.

HEGLAND M.E., "Popular Piety During Muharram" in *The Bulletin of The Henry Martyn Institute*, Volume 17/1, January-June 1998: 76–88.

HEGLAND M.E., "Flagellation and Fundamentalism: (Trans)Forming Meaning, Identity, and Gender Through Pakistani Women's Rituals of Mourning" in *American Ethnologist*, vol. 25, no. 2 (May 1998): 240–266.

HEGLAND M.E., "Shi'a Women's Rituals in Northwest Pakistan: The Shortcomings and Significance of Resistance" in *Anthropological Quarterly*, vol. 76, no. 3 (Summer, 2003): 411–442.

HJORTSHOJ K.G., *Kerbala in Context: A Study of Muharram in Lucknow*, Ph.D. diss., Cornell University, 1977.

HUSSAIN A.J., "The Mourning of History and the History of Mourning: the Evolution of Ritual Commemoration of the Battle of Karbala" in *Comparative Studies of South Asia, Africa and the Middle East*, vol. 25, n. 1, 2005: 78–88.

HUSSEIN A.J., *A Developmental Analysis of Depictions of the Events of Karbalā᾽ in Early Islamic History*, PhD diss., University of Chicago, 2001.

KIPPENBERG H.G., "How Dualistic Beliefs Are Performed by Shiis: The Stages of Kerbala" in H G Kippenberg (ed.), *Struggles of Gods*, Mouton, Berlin 1984: 125– 142.

NAKASH Y., "An Attempt to Trace the Origin of the Rituals of Āshūrā" in *Die Welt des Islams* 33 (2) 1993: 161–181.

PANDYA S., "Women's Shiʿi Ma᾽atim in Bahrain" in *Journal of Middle East Women's Studies*, vol. 6, no. 2 (Spring 2010): 31–58.

PIERCE M., "Remembering Fatimah: New Means of Legitimizing Female Authority in Contemporary Shi'i Discourse" in M Bano and H Kalmbach (eds.), *Women, Leadership, and Mosques. Changes in Contemporary Islamic Authority*, Brill, Leiden 2012: 345–362.

PINTO P.G., "Pilgrimage, Commodities, and Religious Objectification: The Making of Transnational Shiism between Iran and

Syria" in *Comparative Studies of South Asia, Africa and the Middle East* 27 (2007): 109–25.

QARA'I A. Q., "Husayn ibn Ali the Saviour of Islam" in *Al-Tawhid*, vol. 1, n. 1, Muḥarram 1404: 39–44.

QUTBUDDIN B.T., "Zaynab bint ʿAlī" in Lindsay Jones (ed.), *Encyclopedia of Religion*, 2nd edn., vol. XIV, Macmillan Reference USA, Detroit 2005.

ROWE R.E., *Lady of the Women of the Worlds. Exploring Shi'i Piety and Identity through a Consideration of Fatima al-Zahra'*, MA Thesis, University of Arizona 2008.

ROSINY S., "The Tragedy of Fāṭima al-Zahrā' in the Debate of Two Shiite Theologians in Lebanon" in R Brunner and W Ende (eds.), *The Twelver Shia in Modern Times*, Brill, Leiden 2001: 207–219.

SCHAEFFER K., "Suffering with Al-Husayn" in *The Bulletin of The Henry Martyn Institute*, v. 12/1–2, January-June 1993, 74–84.

SCHIMMEL A., "Karbala and Husain in Literature" in *al-Ṣerat* 12, Muhammadi Trust of Great Britain and Northern Ireland, London 1986: 31–32.

SCHUBEL V.J., "The Muharram Majlis: The Role of Ritual in the Preservation of Shiʿa Identity" in E H Waugh, et al, (eds.), *Muslim Families in North America*, University of Alberta Press, Edmonton 1991: 186–203.

SINDAWI K., "The Zaynabiyya Ḥawza in Damascus and its Role in Shī'ite Religious Instruction" in *Middle Eastern Studies*, vol. 45, no. 6 (November 2009): 859–879.

SINDAWI K., "Fiḍḍa l-Nūbiyya: The Woman and her Role in Early Shiʿite History" in *al-Masāq. Journal of the Medieval Mediterranean*, v. 21. 2009: 269–287.

SPELLBERG D., "The Politics of Praise: Depictions of Khadija, Fatima, and 'A'isha in Ninth-Century Muslim Sources" in *Literature East and West* 26, 1990: 130–148.

SZANTO E., "Sayyida Zaynab in the State of Exception: Shii Sainthood as 'Qualified Life' in Contemporary Syria" in *International Journal of Middle East Studies* 44 (2), 2012: 285–299.

SZANTO E., "Beyond the Karbala Paradigm: Rethinking Revolution and Redemption in Twelver Shi'a Mourning Rituals" in *Journal of Shi'a Islamic Studies*, Winter 2013, vol. VI, n. 1: 75–91.

THAISS G., "Religious Symbolism and Social Change: The Drama of Husain" in Nikki R. Keddie (ed.), *Scholars, Saints and Sufis: Muslim Religious Institutions since 1500*, University of California Press, Berkeley 1972: 349–366.

WAUGH E.H., "Muharram Rites: Community Death and Rebirth" in E H Waugh (ed.), *Religious Encounters with Death: Insights from the History and Anthropology of Religions*, Pennsylvania State University Press, University Park 1977: 200–213.

ZAIDI N., "Karbala as Metaphor in the Poetry of Agha Shahid Ali" in *Indian Literature*, vol. 51, n. 1 (237) (January-February 2007: 154–167.

ZIMNEY M., "History in the Making: The Sayyida Zaynab Shrine in Damascus" in *ARAM* 19 (2007): 695–703.

INDEX OF PROPER NAMES

A

ʿAbbâsid dynasty: 7
ʿAbd al-Raḥmân, ʿÂʾisha (Bint al-Shatiʾ): 212nt.
Abû Bakr, ʿAbd Allâh (Caliph): 16, 62, 64–66, 72, 120nt.
Âdam (Adam): 47nt., 245nt.
al-Aḥmarî, Marwân: 187
Ahmed, A.Q: 235
al-ʿÂʾiḏî, Muḥaffiz b. Ṯaʿlaba: 190, 192, 202
ʿÂʾisha, bt. Abî Bakr (wife of Muḥammad): 5nt., 40, 72–74
ʿAlawiyya: 31
ʿAlid: 132nt., 181
al-ʿÂmilî, Ǧaʿfar: 16
al-ʿÂmilî, Muḥsin: xviii, 44nt., 56nt., 81, 95nt., 105, 114, 148–149, 186
al-ʿÂmilî, Zayn al-ʿÂbidîn: xvii, 33
Âmina bt. Wahb (Muḥammad's mother): 73nt.
al-ʿÂmirî, ʿAbd Allâh: 109
al-Anṣârî, ʿAbd al-Raḥmân: 83
al-Anṣârî, Ǧâbir b. ʿAbd Allâh: 153nt.
al-Anṣârî, Maslama: 83
al-Anṣârî, al-Nuʿmân b. Bashîr: 100, 206
Antiochus IV Epiphanes, king: 251
ʿArafât: 260nt.
al-Asadî, Bashîr: 159nt.
al-Asadî, Ḥadîm: 159nt., 160nt.
al-Aṣbaḥî, Ḫawalî b. Yazîd: 104, 145, 156, 173, 174nt.
al-Aṣfahânî, Ibn Manda: 42
al-Ashdaq, ʿAmr b. Saʿîd: 82, 100
ʿÂshûrâ: 6nt., 9, 86, 119nt., 122nt., 173, 263nt.
al-ʿAskarî, Abû Muḥammad (Eleventh Imâm): 71, 128nt.
Asmâʾ, bt. ʿAqîl: 205
Asmâʾ, bt. ʿUmays: 67–68, 225
al-ʿAsqalânî, Ibn Ḥaǧar: xvii, 33, 45, 70, 94, 197, 205, 221, 237
Ayoub, M: 12, 101
al-Azdî, Ḥumayd b. Muslim: 104, 133–135, 143, 145–147, 151, 154, 174nt., 184
al-Azhar: 29, 83

B

Badr, battle of: 40, 42, 209nt.
Baghdad: 259nt.
al-Baǧdâdî, al-Ḫaṭib: xiv, 28
Baḥîrâ: 260nt.
Bahrain: 18
al-Baḥrânî, ʿAbd Allâh: xviii, 32, 91, 93, 107
al-Baḥrânî, Hâshim b. Sulaymân: xvii, 33, 71, 107
al-Balâdurî, Abû al-ʿAbbâs: xi, 28, 34, 70, 113–114, 117, 122, 134, 137, 144, 148,

149nt., 150nt., 155, 184, 191, 193, 206, 221–223, 225nt., 228, 233, 240nt.
Banû Asad: 105, 148
Banû Hâshim: 55, 64, 80, 82, 137
Baqîʿ (cemetery): 68, 81
al-Bâqir, Abû Ǧaʿfar (Fifth Imâm): 180, 230nt.
al-Baraġânî, Muḥammad: 94
al-Bâriqî, ʿAbd Allâh b. ʿAmmâr: 144
al-Barqî, Aḥmad: 80nt.
Baṣra: 28
Beirut: 96
Bilgrami, M.H: 34, 39, 57, 82
al-Bisṭâmî, Bâyazîd: 259nt.
Brockelmann C: xiiint., xvint., xvii, 32, 43, 74nt., 96nt., 97nt., 107nt.
al-Buḫârî, Abû ʿAbd Allâh: xi, 5nt., 53nt., 97nt., 258nt.
Bûyid dynasty: 247–248

C

Cairo: 84
Camel, battle of: 72
Catholic Church: 36, 250, 251nt.
Christianity: 36, 119nt., 183, 240nt., 252

D

Dabashi, H: 6nt., 15
Damascus: 6nt., 7–9, 14, 29, 81nt., 82, 84, 176, 189–191, 203
al-Dâraquṭnî, Abû al-Ḥasan: 222
al-Daylam: 240nt.
al-Daylamî, Ḥasan: xvii, 32, 64
Deeb, L: 17, 20–22
al-Dînawarî., Abû Ḥanîfa: xi, 27–28, 191, 206, 226, 237

Ḏ

al-Ḏahabî, Abû ʿAbd Allâh: xvi, 29, 31nt., 186nt. 193, 225, 237

E

Egypt: 57, 82-84

F

Fadak: 57, 64–65, 120nt.
Faḍlallâh, Muḥammad: 16
al-Fârsî, Salmân: 60–61
Fâṭima, bt. ʿAlî: 190, 196, 199nt., 201, 203, 207
Fâṭima, bt. al-Ḥusayn: 4, 86, 146, 148, 194–196, 198, 199nt., 200, 203, 207, 231–236
Fâṭima, bt. Muḥammad: ix, 4, 10, 15–19, 24nt., 34, 36–45, 48–49, 51, 53–58, 61–69, 74–75, 88–89, 91, 93, 96, 110, 111nt., 112, 120, 122, 126, 128nt., 134, 136, 153, 169, 175–176, 178, 198nt., 200, 222, 231, 239, 247–248, 250, 251nt.
Fâṭimid dynasty: 247–248
al-Fattâl al-Nîsâbûrî, ʿAlî Muḥammad: xiv, 32, 103, 107, 110, 112–113, 127, 139, 156–157, 177nt., 179–180, 182, 197nt., 198, 209, 230nt.
Fiḍḍa: 63, 67

G

Golan Heights: 84nt.
Goldziher I: 128nt.

Ǧ

al-Ǧâmadî, ʿAbd Allâh: 180nt.
al-Ǧanâbiḏî, al-Ḥâfiẓ: 234

Ǧawn (Ǧuwayn, Ḥuwayy): 114–116, 123–124
al-Ǧazâʾirî, Niʿmat Allâh: 32, 107
Ǧibrîl: 24nt., 46–48, 59, 61–62, 79, 214nt., 215nt., 262nt.
Ǧîlân (Iran): 240nt.
Ǧinn: 106–108, 205
Ǧumâna, bt. al-Musayb: 224–225

Ġ

Ġadîr Ḫumm: 260nt., 262nt.
al-Ġifârî, Abû Ḏarr: 60nt., 115, 127

H

al-Hâdî, Abû al-Ḥasan (Tenth Imâm): 38
Haider, N: 35nt., 99nt., 249nt.
al-Hamdânî, al-Muǧâlid: 183, 185
Hamdar, A: 17, 20–21
Hârûn (prophet): 48
al-Hâshimî, Aḥmad: 97
al-Hayṯamî, Ibn Ḥaǧar: 33
al-Hayṯamî, Nûr al-Dîn: xvii, 33, 108, 148, 193, 195, 203
al-Hilâlî, Ibn Qays: 128nt.
Howard, I.K.A: 118, 131nt., 133nt., 150nt., 181nt., 197
Hussein, A.J: 28, 31nt., 189, 231
Hyder, S.A: 176

Ḥ

al-Ḥaḍramî, Hânî b. Ṯubayt: 141
Ḥafṣa, bt. ʿUmar (wife of Muḥammad): 72–74
Ḥâʾirî, Muḥammad b. Abî Ṭâlib: 226
al-Ḥâkim al-Nîsâbûrî,: xiii, 24nt., 32, 96nt., 107
Ḥanafî School: 5nt., 30, 210,
Ḥanbalî School: 5nt., 33
Ḥawṭ bt. Ḥafṣa: 225
Ḥawwâʾ (Eve): 47nt.
al-Ḥillî al-ʿAllâma, Ǧamâl al-Dîn: xvi
al-Ḥurr al-ʿÂmilî, Muḥammad: xvii, 32

Ḫ

Ḫadîǧa, bt. Ḫuwaylid: 4, 88
al-Ḫarrâz, Abû Saʿîd: 259nt.
al-Ḫaṣîbî, Abû ʿAbd Allâh: xii, 31, 45, 64nt., 68, 233
al-Ḫawârizmî, Abû al-Muʾayyad: xiv, 24nt., 28, 30, 31nt., 78nt., 79, 105, 106nt., 107, 111–115, 118, 124–126, 134–135, 139–143, 145, 148, 149nt., 150–151, 153, 156, 159nt., 160nt., 161nt., 163nt., 164nt., 165nt., 166nt., 167–168, 169nt., 170nt., 174, 179, 182, 187, 197, 198nt., 210, 212nt., 224, 237nt., 239, 249
Ḫawâriǧ: 72
Ḫawla bt. Azwar: 5nt.
al-Ḫawṣâʾ, bt. Ḫaṣfa (Ḫaṣafa): 224–225, 227
al-Ḫawwâṣ, ʿAlî: 83
al-Ḫazar: 240nt.
Ḫaybar: 64, 264nt.
al-Ḫuḍrî, Saʿd b. Mâlik (Abu Saʿîd): 64, 153nt.
al-Ḫunn: 149nt.
al-Ḫuzaymiyya: 26, 103, 105–109, 150

I

Iblîs: 128nt., 246nt.
Ibn ʿAbbâs, ʿAbd Allâh: 55, 57, 100, 105
Ibn ʿAbd Allâh, Muḥammad: 4, 5nt., 6nt., 13–17, 24nt., 26,

34nt., 37–38, 39nt., 40, 45–49, 53nt., 57–62, 63nt., 64–66, 68, 69nt., 72, 73nt., 79, 80nt., 83, 88–91, 93, 96, 98nt., 100, 111, 115nt., 119nt., 120, 122–123, 126, 128nt., 132nt., 136, 140, 152nt., 153, 169nt., 175, 178, 190, 207, 212nt., 247–249, 254nt., 257, 258nt., 260nt., 262nt., 263nt., 264nt.
Ibn ʿAbd Allâh b. Ǧaʿfar, ʿAbbâs: 70, 221–223, 225–227
Ibn ʿAbd Allâh b. Ǧaʿfar, ʿAbd Allâh: 226
Ibn ʿAbd Allâh b. Ǧaʿfar, ʿAlî: 70, 221–223, 227
Ibn ʿAbd Allâh b. Ǧaʿfar, ʿAwn: 70, 106, 142, 221–228
Ibn ʿAbd Allâh b. Ǧaʿfar, Ǧaʿfar: 221–222, 226
Ibn ʿAbd Allâh b. Ǧaʿfar, Ibrâhîm: 226
Ibn ʿAbd Allâh b. Ǧaʿfar, Muḥammad: 70, 106, 142, 221–228
Ibn ʿAbd al-Barr, Abû ʿUmar: xiv, 33, 41
Ibn ʿAbd al-Muṭṭalib, ʿAbd Allâh b. Ǧaʿfar: 43nt., 55, 68–69, 72, 75, 78nt., 81nt., 105–106, 221–228
Ibn ʿAbd al-Muṭṭalib, Ḥamza: 138, 153
Ibn Abî Rashîd, Sulaymân: 184
Ibn Abî Shayba, ʿÎsâ: 240nt.
Ibn Abî Sufyân, Muʿâwiya: 23, 55, 72, 79–81, 120, 128nt., 231
Ibn Abî Ṭâlib, ʿAlî: ix, 16, 34, 37–38, 40–48, 52–54, 56–57, 60–62, 64–72, 74–79, 81nt., 83, 84nt., 86, 89–91, 93nt., 96, 101, 111nt., 112, 120, 122, 125–126, 128nt., 131nt., 134, 138, 152nt., 153, 160nt., 169nt., 172, 175–176, 178, 180nt., 187, 198nt., 200, 207, 222–223, 225, 239, 248, 252, 254nt., 257nt., 262nt., 264nt.
Ibn Abî Ṭâlib, Ǧaʿfar: 61, 68
Ibn Abî al-Waqqâṣ, Saʿd: 144nt.
Ibn Abî al-Waqqâṣ, ʿUmar: 26, 103–104, 128nt., 131, 133, 144–147, 155–156
Ibn ʿAffân, ʿUṯmân (Caliph): 55
Ibn ʿAlî b. Abî Ṭâlib, al-ʿAbbâs: 103, 137, 142–143, 237
Ibn ʿAlî b. Abî Ṭâlib, Abû Bakr: 142, 224
Ibn ʿAlî b. Abî Ṭâlib, ʿAqîl: 225
Ibn ʿAlî b. Abî Ṭâlib, al-Ḥasan: 40–44, 46–48, 52–54, 57, 59, 61, 66–68, 73nt., 75, 78–80, 89, 91, 93nt., 95, 101, 110, 111nt., 112, 120, 122–123, 126, 138, 169nt., 178, 223, 225
Ibn ʿAlî b. Abî Ṭâlib, al-Ḥusayn: ix, 1–4, 5nt., 6nt., 7–8, 10, 13–14, 19, 23, 24nt., 25–31, 35, 39–44, 46–48, 52–55, 57–59, 61, 66–68, 72, 73nt., 75, 78nt., 79, 80nt., 81–83, 86, 89, 91, 92nt., 93nt., 95–96, 101nt., 103, 105–112, 114, 116, 119nt. 120, 122–126, 128nt., 131–135, 137–153, 155, 157–158, 165nt., 169–171, 173–175, 178, 181, 188, 191–194, 197, 199–200, 202, 204–206, 208–210, 220nt., 223–225, 227, 229, 230nt., 231–234, 236–239, 248, 250, 252–253

Ibn ʿAlî b. Abî Ṭâlib, ʿUṯmân: 142
Ibn Anas, Sinân: 104, 143, 145, 153, 155–156
Ibn al-Anbârî, Abû Bakr: 204
Ibn ʿAqîl b. Abî Ṭâlib, ʿAbd Allâh b. Muslim: 224
Ibn ʿAqîl b. Abî Ṭâlib, ʿAbd al-Raḥmân: 224
Ibn ʿAqîl b. Abî Ṭâlib, Ǧaʿfar: 224
Ibn Arqam, Zayd: 175, 180nt.
Ibn ʿAsâkir, Abû al-Qâsim: xiv, 29, 57, 108, 134, 156, 201–202, 204, 206, 222, 236
Ibn al-Aṯîr, Abû al-Ḥasan: xv, 28–29, 45, 57, 110, 111nt., 112–113, 137–138, 145–148, 149nt., 150nt., 156, 179, 181nt., 182, 189, 191nt., 192nt., 193–194, 199, 201, 203–204, 206, 222–225, 228, 250
Ibn Baʿîṯ, Hânî: 141
Ibn Bakkâr al-Zubayrî, al-Zubayr: 134nt.
Ibn Bashîr, Ḥaḏlam: 159nt.
Ibn al-Biṭrîq, Abû al-Ḥasan: 45
Ibn Darrâǧ, Nûḥ: 240nt.
Ibn Ḏî al-Ǧawshan, Shimr: 104, 131–133, 143, 145, 147, 156, 191–192
Ibn Furât al-Kûfî, Furât: 49nt.
Ibn al-Ǧawzî, Abû al-Faḍâʾil: xv, 28, 33, 197, 199nt., 222, 237
Ibn Ǧubayr, Abû al-Ḥusayn: 84nt.
Ibn al-Ḥadîd, ʿIzz al-Dîn: xv, xvint., 42, 45, 63
Ibn Ḥaḏlam, Bashîr: 159nt.
Ibn Ḥanbal, Aḥmad: xi, 5nt., 24nt., 69nt., 111nt.
Ibn Ḥarb, Abû Sufyân: 212nt.
Ibn al-Ḥasan, ʿAbd Allâh: 137–138, 140, 142–143, 227
Ibn al-Ḥasan, al-Ḥasan: 231nt.
Ibn al-Ḥasan, al-Qâsim: 135, 139–143
Ibn al-Ḥasan, ʿUmar: 231nt.
Ibn Hilâl, ʿUbayd Allâh: 240nt.
Ibn Hishâm, Abû Muḥammad: xi
Ibn Hishâm, ʿAmr (Abû Ǧahl): 53nt., 128nt.
Ibn al-Ḥusayn, ʿAbd Allâh: 26, 104, 142, 224, 231–235, 238
Ibn al-Ḥusayn, Abû Bakr: 233nt.
Ibn al-Ḥusayn, ʿAlî al-Akbar: 26, 104, 134, 139–140, 189, 224, 231–235, 237–239
Ibn al-Ḥusayn, ʿAlî (Fourth Imâm): ix, 6nt., 14, 26, 35, 80nt., 82, 89, 94, 103–104, 114–118, 125, 127, 132–134, 140–141, 146–148, 150, 171–172, 183–195, 199nt., 201, 203–207, 209, 227, 230–241, 248–250
Ibn al-Ḥusayn, Ǧaʿfar: 231–235, 238
Ibn al-Ḥusayn, Ḥamza: 231nt.
Ibn al-Ḥusayn, Ibrâhîm: 231nt.
Ibn al-Ḥusayn, al-Muḥsin: 239
Ibn al-Ḥusayn, Muḥammad: 231nt., 232–234, 238
Ibn al-Ḥusayn, ʿUmar: 231nt.
Ibn al-Ḥusayn, Zayd: 231nt.
Ibn al-Ḫaṭṭâb, ʿUmar (Caliph): 62–63
Ibn ʿInaba, Ǧamâl al-Dîn: 54, 95
Ibn Kâhil, Ḥarmala: 138, 142
Ibn Kaʿb, Abǧar: 138
Ibn Kaṯîr, Abû al-Fiḍâʾ: xvi, 29, 62, 110, 112–114, 116nt., 118, 123, 135, 145, 147–148,

149nt., 150nt., 156, 175nt., 179, 182–183, 185–186, 193, 197, 204, 206, 210, 223, 225
Ibn Mâǧa, Abû ʿAbd Allâh: xi, 5nt., 13, 258nt.
Ibn Manẓûr, Ǧamâl al-Dîn: 121
Ibn Marwân, ʿAbd al-Malik: 81nt.
Ibn Miḫnaf, Lûṭ b. Yaḥyâ (Abû Miḫnaf): 26–28, 30, 34, 36nt., 109, 114–115, 117, 132–134, 137, 147–148, 149nt., 174, 181–184, 195–197, 199nt., 206–207, 225nt.
Ibn Muġîra, Ḥusayn b. Aḥmad: 240nt.
Ibn Muʿâwiya, Yazîd: 2–4, 6nt., 7–8, 14, 18–21, 23, 26–27, 71, 82, 108–109, 117, 128nt., 131nt., 150, 157, 174, 176, 180nt., 188–195, 197–209, 212nt., 220, 248, 250–253, 255nt.
Ibn Mulǧam, ʿAbd al-Raḥmân: 72, 74nt., 78–79, 120, 128nt.
Ibn Muslim, Ḥumayd: 104
Ibn al-Nabbâḥ, ʿÂmir: 76
Ibn al-Nadîm, Muḥammad: 128nt.
Ibn Namâ al-Ḥillî: xvi, 31, 107–108, 113–115, 127, 134–135, 138–140, 142, 146, 149, 153, 159nt., 160nt., 161nt., 163nt., 166nt., 167–168, 169nt., 170, 176, 177nt., 179, 182, 186, 192nt., 198nt., 200, 210, 212nt., 223
Ibn Qays, Zaḥr: 191
Ibn Qudâma, Aḥmad b. Muḥammad: 5nt.
Ibn Qutayba, Abû Muḥammad: 41
Ibn Rabîʿ, Abû al-ʿÂṣ: 258nt.
Ibn Saʿd, Muḥammad al-Wâqidî: xi, 28, 34, 57, 65, 148, 181, 195, 222, 225
Ibn Satîr, Ḥaḏlam: 55nt., 159-160
Ibn Shahrâshûb, Abû Ǧaʿfar: xv, 10, 32, 37, 41, 43, 105, 107, 113, 127, 149nt., 153-154, 156, 161nt., 164nt., 166nt., 167–168, 170, 226, 231, 237–238
Ibn Tamîm, al-Ḥusayn: 181
Ibn Ṭâʾûs, Raḍî al-Dîn: xvi, 29, 30, 31nt., 85, 105, 110–115, 123–125, 127, 134, 138–142, 144–145, 149, 151–154, 159nt., 160nt., 161nt., 162, 163nt., 164nt., 166nt., 167–168, 169nt., 170nt., 173–174, 176, 179, 182, 187–188, 199–201, 208nt., 210, 212nt., 213nt., 214nt., 215nt., 216nt., 217nt., 218nt., 219nt.
Ibn ʿUbayd Allâh, Baḥr b. Kaʿb: 104, 138
Ibn Yazîd b. Muʿâwiya, Ḫâlid: 193
Ibn Zâʾida, Qudâma: 240nt.
Ibn Zibaʿrî, ʿAbd Allâh: 208
Ibn Ziyâd, ʿUbayd Allâh: 6nt., 14, 18–19, 27, 103–104, 108–109, 117, 128nt., 131, 132nt., 133–134, 145, 148, 150, 153, 156–157, 171–184, 185nt., 186–193, 195, 201–202, 206, 220nt., 230, 248, 250, 252–253
Ibn Yûsuf, al-Ḥaǧǧâǧ: 128nt.
Ibn al-Zubayr, ʿAbd Allâh: 105
Ibrâhîm (prophet): 263nt.
Iran: 17–18

al-Irbilî, Bahâʾ al-Dîn: xvi, 30, 41–42, 175, 177nt., 179, 182, 186, 234
ʿÎsâ b. Maryam: 42nt.
Ismâʿîlî Shîʿa: 1nt., 35nt., 248–249
al-Iṣâmî, ʿAbd al-Malik: xvii, 29, 40, 144–145, 182, 185
al-Iṣbahânî, Abû Nuʿaym: xiii
al-Iṣfahânî, Abû al-Farâğ: xiii, 31, 57, 113–114, 116nt., 117nt., 125, 127, 134, 137–139, 157, 180, 189, 201, 224, 225nt., 226, 237–238
Iṣfahânî, Muḥammad: 95nt.
iṯnâ ʿasharî Shîʿa: 1, 6nt., 24nt., 34, 99nt., 248–249

J

Jeffery, A: 149nt.
Jerusalem: 264nt.
Jesus, son of Mary: 3, 183, 193, 250, 252

K

Karbalâʾ: ix, 1–4, 5nt., 6nt., 7–10, 13–15, 17–22, 25–30, 34–35, 36nt., 55nt., 59, 61, 70–71, 77nt., 81, 82, 84nt., 85, 92nt., 96, 102–103, 105–109, 114–115, 119nt., 128nt., 129, 131–133, 137, 141, 143–144, 146–147, 149, 151, 154, 157–159, 165nt., 172–173, 174nt., 178, 180–181, 190, 202, 220–221, 223–226, 228–230, 235–239, 247–250, 257nt., 262nt., 267nt.
al-Karâğakî, Abû al-Fatḥ: 96nt.
Karbâssî, M.S: 34, 39, 44–45, 54–55, 59–61, 66, 68–69, 71–77, 79–80, 82, 84–85, 88–91, 92nt., 93, 96–97, 100–101, 226, 254
al-Kâshânî, A: 39, 43, 45, 53–54, 59, 66, 90, 93–95, 96nt., 97
Kâshânî, M: 66nt.
al-Kawṯar: 254nt.
Kazimirsky, A: 228
Kohlberg, E: 128nt.
Kûfa: 6nt., 8, 14, 19, 25, 27, 55nt., 70–72, 85, 89, 101nt., 105, 120, 131nt., 137, 145–147, 151, 155, 159, 167, 171, 181, 188, 239, 253
al-Kulaynî, Muḥammad: xii, 10, 31, 63nt., 80nt., 127

L

Ladak, J: 45, 73–76, 101, 224nt.
Lammens H: 228
Lane, W: 41, 53nt., 55nt., 72nt., 73nt., 86nt., 120, 166nt., 228, 230nt., 237nt.
Layla bt. Abî Murra: 4, 132, 224
Layla bt. Masʿûd: 222
Lebanon: 18
Leiden: 43
Levi Della Vida, G: 121
al-Lubnânî, ʿUmar: 96

M

al-Madâʾinî, Abû Muḥammad: xvint.
Maccabees, Second Book of: 251
al-Mağlisî, Muḥammad Bâqir: xviii, 32, 37, 42–43, 49–50, 53, 63, 66–67, 74, 77, 79nt., 80nt., 105, 107, 112–114, 118, 121–122, 134, 138, 149nt., 153–154, 159nt., 163nt., 164nt., 165nt., 166nt., 167–168, 169nt., 170nt., 171–172, 179, 192nt., 210, 212nt., 213nt.,

214nt., 215nt., 216, 217nt., 218nt., 219nt., 226, 237–239, 250
al-Mahdî, Abû al-Qâsim (Twelfth Imâm): 247
al-Maḥallî, Ğalâl al-Dîn: 161nt.
al-Maḫzûmî, ʿAmr b. Ḥurayṯ: 27, 181–182
al-Maḫzûmî, Ibn Hubayra: 76
Mâlikî School: 33
Mary, Mother of Jesus: 36, 250–251
Maryam bt. ʿImrân: 36, 42nt., 52, 98nt., 120
Mary Magdalene, St.: 252
al-Masʿûdî, Abû al-Ḥasan: xii, 28–29
al-Maydânî, Abû al-Faḍl: 121
Maymûna, bt. al-Ḥâriṯ (wife of Muḥammad): 107nt.
al-Mâzanî, Yaḥyâ b. Salîm: 92
McKenzie, A: 1nt.
Mecca: 23, 25, 29, 88, 105, 200, 260nt., 263nt., 264nt.
Medina: 8, 23, 27, 38–40, 65, 71, 80–82, 203, 205–206, 212nt., 258nt., 260nt., 264nt.
Mîna: 200
Modarressi H: xiiint., xvnt., 60nt., 115nt., 128nt.
Momen, M: 24nt.
Mottahedeh, N: 6–7nt.
al-Mufîd, *Shayḫ*: xiv, 28, 31–32, 56, 64, 74–76, 78–79, 101, 105, 111, 113–114, 118, 127, 131nt., 134–135, 138–141, 145, 159, 160nt., 162, 163nt., 165nt., 166nt., 167–168, 169nt., 170nt., 171nt., 175, 177nt., 178nt., 179, 181nt., 182, 186, 192nt., 197, 199nt., 212nt., 223, 233, 235–237
Muhammad, M: 57
Muḥarram: 6nt., 7, 26, 81nt., 103–105, 110–111, 114, 131, 145–149, 151, 263nt.
Muḥassin (Muḥsin), b. ʿAlî: 39nt., 41, 43, 44nt., 45
Muʿtazila: xvint., 256nt.
al-Muqarram, ʿAbd al-Razzâq: 108, 223
Murâd (Yuḥâbir) tribe: 121
Mûsâ (prophet): 48, 260nt., 263nt.
al-Mûsawî, M: 64nt., 221nt
Muslim, Abû al-Ḥusayn: xi, 258nt.
al-Mustawfî, ʿAbbâs: 95nt.
al-Mutawakkil, Caliph: 37-38

N

Nağaf: 84nt.
Nahrawân, battle of: 72
al-Nasâʾî, Abû ʿAbd al-Raḥmân: xii, 258nt.
Nizârî Shîʿa: 35nt.
al-Nucmân, al-Qâḍî: 107

P

Pahlavî dynasty: 17
Pandya, S: 17, 22
Persia: 94nt.
Pickthall, M.M: ix, 162nt., 194nt.
Pilate, Pontius: 183, 193

Q

Qanâṭir al-sibâʿ (Egypt): 83
Qajar dynasty: 94nt.
Qum: 31
al-Qummî, ʿAlî b. Ibrâhîm: 128nt.
al-Qummî, Ibn Qûlûyû: xiii, 31, 106–107, 239–240
al-Qummî, ʿAlî b. Muḥammad: xiii

Quraysh: 37, 88
Qutbuddin, B.T: 39, 68

R

al-Rabġûzî, Naṣîr al-Dîn: 237
Ramaḍân: 75, 101
Ramla, bt. ʿAqîl: 205
al-Rawandî, Quṭb al-Dîn: xv, 37, 95nt., 209
Râwiyya (Syria): 84nt.
al-Râzî, Faḫr al-Dîn: 161nt.
al-Riḍâ, Abû al-Ḥasan (Eighth Imâm): 128nt.
Rizvi, A.A: 39
Rosiny, S: 15
Rubâb, bt. Imrâʾ al-Qays (wife of al-Ḥusayn): 142, 224
al-Rubayyiʿ, bt. Muʿawwiḏ: 5nt.
Ruffle, K.G: 17–18
Ruqayya, bt. al-Ḥusayn: 4, 236

S

al-Saraḫsî, Muḥammad: 5nt.
Sarwar, M: 152nt.
Satan (Shayṭân): 120, 245nt., 246nt.
Saudi Arabia: 5nt., 149nt.
Sayyida Zaynab (Syria): 84nt.
Sezgin F: 33nt., 96nt.
Sibṭ al-Ğawzî, Shams al-Dîn: xv, 33, 119nt., 143nt., 149nt., 150nt., 178nt., 180nt., 198, 220nt., 221nt., 225, 233nt., 236
al-Siğistânî, Abû Dâwûd: xi
Sindawi, K: 84
Steingass, F: 53nt.
Sukayna (Sakîna), bt. al-Ḥusayn: 4, 67, 91nt., 122, 124nt., 148, 194–195, 203–204, 209, 231–236
al-Suyûṭî, Abû al-Faḍl: 43, 64, 95, 108, 161nt., 222,
Syria: 37, 72, 81nt., 82, 85
Szanto, E: 84nt.

SH

Shabbar (son of Hârûn): 48
Shabbîr (son of Hârûn): 48
al-Shablanğî, Muʾmin: xviii, 83, 163nt., 164nt., 165nt., 166nt., 167–168, 169nt., 170nt., 204
Shahin, B: 34, 39, 45–46, 81–83, 85nt., 141, 155, 227
al-Shaʿrânî, Abû al-Mawâhib: 83
Shâfiʿî School: 83nt.
al-Shahrastânî, Muḥammad: 28, 54–55
Shariati, ʿAlî: 17–19, 21, 92nt., 248–249
Sharîf al-Raḍî, Abû al-Ḥasan: 76
Shoshan, B: 28nt.

Ṣ

al-Ṣabbân, ʿAbd al-ʿIrfân: xviii
al-Ṣâdiq, Abû ʿAbd Allâh (Sixth Imâm): 80nt., 81nt., 239
al-Ṣadûq, *Shayḫ*: xiii, 10, 31, 49–50, 53, 80nt., 107nt., 125, 127, 131nt., 156–158, 164nt., 175, 177, 179–180, 182, 197, 209, 234
Ṣafavid dynasty: 248
al-Ṣaffâr, Muḥammad: 128nt.
Ṣâliḥ (prophet): 242nt.
Ṣiffîn, battle of: 72, 131nt.
Ṣûfî (mysticism): 83

T

al-Tamîmî, al-Ḥurr b. Yazîd: 131
al-Tamîmî, Qurra b. Qays: 147, 149, 153–154
al-Tirmiḏî, Abû ʿÎsâ: xi, 100nt., 258nt.
Turabi, Rashid: 176

al-Tustarî, Sahl: 259nt.

Ṭ

al-Ṭabarî, Abû Ğaʿfar: xii, 26–28, 33nt., 34–35, 36nt., 40, 57, 62–63, 68, 85, 92nt., 103, 105, 109–111, 113, 117, 121, 127nt., 131–132, 137–138, 140–141, 143, 145, 148–149, 150nt., 151, 154–156, 159, 161nt., 165nt., 173–175, 179, 181–182, 184–187, 189, 191–193, 195, 197, 199nt., 201–202, 206–207, 222, 225nt., 236, 240nt.
al-Ṭabarî, Ğarîr b. Rustam: xii, 33nt., 34, 45
al-Ṭabarî, Muḥib al-Dîn: xv, 24nt., 33, 57
al-Ṭabarsî, al-Ḥâğğ Mîrzâ: xviii, 32
al-Ṭabarsî, Raḍî al-Dîn: xiv, 33, 45, 64, 89, 112, 114, 127nt., 138, 159nt., 160nt., 161nt., 163nt., 164nt., 165nt., 166nt., 167–168, 169nt., 170–171, 175, 177nt., 178nt., 179, 182, 186, 192nt., 208–210, 212nt., 214nt., 231
Ṭaff (Karbalâʾ): 54–55
Ṭayfur, Ibn Abî Ṭâhir: xii, 34, 97, 160, 210
al-Ṭûsî, *Shayḫ*: xiv, 32, 107, 161nt., 162, 168

Ṯ

al-Ṯaʿlabî, Abû Isḥâq: xiii
Ṯamûd: 242nt.

U

Uḥud, battle of: 40, 41, 209
Umâma, bt. Abî al-ʿÂṣ: 67
Umayyad dynasty: 22, 28, 45, 82–83, 100, 128nt., 132nt.
Umm ʿAbd Allâh, bt. ʿAbd Allâh b. Ğaʿfar: 226
Umm ʿAṭiyya, al-Anṣâriyya: 5nt.
Umm Ayman: 23nt., 73, 94, 239
Umm al-Faḍl, bt. al-Ḥâriṯ: 23nt.
Umm Hâniʾ, bt. ʿAqîl: 205
Umm Kulṯûm, bt. ʿAbd Allâh b. Ğaʿfar: 70, 221–223, 225
Umm Kulṯûm, bt. ʿAlî: 4, 26, 39, 41–45, 52–56, 67–68, 74–79, 84nt., 97, 101, 124–125, 140, 160nt., 224nt., 249
Umm Luqmân, bt. ʿAqîl: 205
Umm Kulṯûm, bt. al-Ḥusayn: 4, 157–158, 180
Umm Kulṯûm, bt. Muḥammad: 40
Umm Salama (wife of Muḥammad): 23nt., 73, 106–108, 111nt., 112nt., 153nt. 202
Umm Wahb, bt. ʿAbd: 5nt.
Uṣûlî School: 249nt.

W

al-Wâlibî, al-Ḥâriṯ b. Kaʿb: 196, 199nt.
al-Wâsiṭî, Aḥmad: 240nt.
Wehr, H: 55nt., 212nt., 228, 230nt.,
Witkam, J.J: 43

Y

Yabrîn (oasis): 149
al-Yaʿqûbî, Aḥmad: xii, 28nt., 29, 113, 122, 127nt.

Z

al-Zamaḫasharî, Abû al-Qâsim: 30
Zaynab, bt. ʿAqîl: 204

Zaynab, bt. Ǧaḥsh (wife of Muḥammad). 74nt.
Zaynab, bt. al-Ḥusayn: 134, 232–233, 235
Zaynab, bt. Muḥammad: 67
Zaydi Shīʿa: 1nt., 34nt., 248
Zoroastrianism: 240nt.